Atlanta Restaurant Guide

Atlanta Restaurant Guide

Christiane Lauterbach

PELICAN PUBLISHING COMPANY
Gretna 1996

Copyright © 1982 by Harold V. Shumacher
Copyright © 1988 by Bill Cutler and Christiane Lauterbach

Copyright © 1996
By Christiane Lauterbach
All rights reserved

First edition, October 1982
Second edition, July 1988
Third edition, June 1996

Some of the information in this guidebook appeared originally in a different form in *Knife & Fork* and/or *Atlanta Magazine*.

Library of Congress Cataloging-in-Publication Data

Lauterbach, Christiane.
   Atlanta restaurant guide / Christiane Lauterbach. — 3rd ed.
     p.   cm.
   Rev. ed. of: Atlanta restaurant guide / Bill Cutler. 1988.
   Includes indexes.
   ISBN 1-56554-031-X (pbk. : alk. paper)
   1. Restaurants—Georgia—Atlanta—Guidebooks. 2. Atlanta (Ga.)—Guidebooks. I. Cutler, Bill. Atlanta restaurant guide. II. Title.
TX907.3.G42A8554 1996
647.95758'231—dc20   95-39910
                                                             CIP

Maps by Frank Drago

Manufactured in the United States of America

Published by Pelican Publishing Company, Inc.
1101 Monroe Street, Gretna, Louisiana 70053

In loving memory of Bill Cutler, who wrote many of the original reviews now revised and expanded by his partner and friend, Christiane Lauterbach, who still feels his guidance and abides by his rigorous, humorous standards

Contents

Acknowledgments 11
Introduction 15
How to Use This Guide 33
Hotel Dining 35
For Nostalgia-Seekers Only 37
Restaurant Reviews Listed Alphabetically 39
Beyond Atlanta 332
Indexes 335
  Type of Cuisine
    American 335
    Chinese 336
    Continental 336
    French 337
    Indian 337
    Italian 337
    Japanese 337
    Korean 338
    Mexican 338
    Middle Eastern 338

- Pizza 338
- Sandwiches and Light Food 338
- Seafood 339
- Soul Food 339
- Southern 339
- Southwestern 339
- Steaks 339
- Thai 340
- Vegetarian 340
- Miscellaneous Ethnic 340

Top-Rated Restaurants 340
Full Meals Under $15 341
Open on Sunday 342
Open Late at Night 345
Breakfast 346
Brunch 346
Outdoor Seating 347
Recommended for Children 348
Proximity to MARTA Station 349
Knife & Fork Order Form 351

List of Maps

Map A	Downtown	23
Map B	Buckhead	24
Map C	Intown/Midtown	25
Map D	Northeast Atlanta/Chamblee/Doraville	26
Map E	Decatur/Emory/Little Five Points	27
Map F	Southside/Airport	28
Map G	Northwest Atlanta/Marietta/Smyrna	29
Map H	Sandy Springs/Roswell/Dunwoody	30
Map I	Tucker/Stone Mountain/Gwinnett	31

Acknowledgments

I WISH TO THANK my two daughters, Hillary and Pauline, who have developed a fine appreciation of food and have helped me in innumerable ways, whether by their presence at my side or their participation in reading and sometimes improving copy. I am profoundly grateful to my friend Helen Sebba, who for years has helped convince the world that I, although French by birth, have a flawless command of the English language. Thank you to my friend, colleague, and *Knife & Fork* collaborator Terrell Vermont, who has gone with me to hundreds, perhaps thousands, of restaurants, to my friend and colleague Cliff Bostock, with whom I have laughed through countless meals, to Lee Walburn, editor of *Atlanta Magazine,* who has supported me unfailingly, to my editors at the magazine, Susan Percy and Emma Edmunds, both of whom I admire and respect, and to the many friends who have put up and helped with my life as a galloping gourmet.

Atlanta Restaurant Guide

Information in this guidebook is based on authoritative data available at the time of printing. Hours of operation and other information concerning businesses listed are subject to change without notice. Readers are asked to take this into account when consulting this guide. For the most recent updates and commentaries on the dining scene, subscribe to Knife & Fork: The Insider's Guide to Atlanta Restaurants, *published locally as a monthly newsletter. An order form is provided at the end of this book.*

Introduction

NEW YORK HAS MORE RESTAURANTS and Los Angeles crazier ones. New Orleans takes good eating for granted. Atlanta, however, isn't crying her pretty eyes out. The great Southern belle has awakened from her gastronomic torpor, smiles coyly at her big sisters, and drawls, "Look what I can do."

Thirty years ago, you needed local connections if you wanted to eat anything interesting at all. People took their meals at home or at the club. Period. Atlanta had only a handful of reputable restaurants, and these provided the same kind of fare the traveler could find in a number of other major cities. But over the course of the past decades, the demographic profile has changed radically, and the food craze has swept over the South.

Atlanta's young, dynamic population forms a good support base for restaurateurs, though the quest for new places, discovering them, "making" them, isn't quite as passionate as in New York or L.A. Many Atlantans are new residents or transients. They are frequently single and have a considerable amount of disposable income, which they willingly spend exploring the gastronomic resources of this city to the fullest. And there is much to choose from: nouvelle hotel cuisine at its poshest, fancy regional fare, serious kitchens run by devoted chef-owners, places featuring California-style exuberant creativity, old-fashioned establishments with European flair, cute delis, and hundreds of ethnic holes-in-the-wall.

The city's first big-budget Continental restaurant, The Midnight Sun, opened in Peachtree Center downtown in 1968. (It closed in 1985.) The success of that Danish enterprise (inspired by Atlanta's honorary Danish consul, architect

John Portman) sparked numerous ambitious ventures at hotels and small independent establishments. Over the next five years, Atlanta developed the lodging, meeting, and food resources needed to attract the major convention business it now enjoys. This new industry, in turn, brought into the city a different type of restaurant client, one accustomed to exotic foods and a more sophisticated approach to eating than the region had been used to.

In order to staff their new Atlanta operations, hotel managers went on raiding expeditions to the Bahamas and other international resort areas. Budding chefs and ambitious apprentices from the famous hotel schools of Switzerland, France, and Germany left Denmark, Canada, the Caribbean, the Ozarks, and Disney World because they saw Atlanta as a great new market open to their creativity. After establishing themselves in hotel kitchens and discovering that they liked living in Atlanta, many of these chefs and maître d's went on to open their own restaurants here.

While all of this was going on in the hotel industry, Atlanta was being introduced to a different type of sophisticated dinner theater (not the kind where customers eat bland food while watching a weak performance of Camelot). Until The Pleasant Peasant opened in a tiny space on Peachtree Street on February 12, 1973, Atlanta didn't know that eating out could be fun. The two young founders of the business, Steve Nygren and Dick Dailey, had worked as hard to establish a desired tone and environment as to develop an intriguing Continental menu. The suave formula worked because customers believed they were being individually catered to and entertained by waiters performing like a chorus line and introducing each course like a new act in a play.

As restaurants grew increasingly sophisticated and diverse, Atlantans found themselves falling in love with more daring combinations of foods. The excesses of nouvelle cuisine never made it to the Deep South. We haven't seen art-for-art's-sake creativity misspent on stuff like rutabagas and trash fish. But we have seen a breaking of traditional forms. The distinction between European and American cuisine is no longer very sharp.

New pride in things American has also been expressed in

local restaurants in such dishes as a cold soup made with tart Granny Smith apples and rhubarb, sun-dried sweet potato ravioli, croquettes of cheddar cheese on a bed of mustard greens, baby rabbit with basil sauce, fried chicken salad with sweet onions, beignets of red snapper, and Florida pompano with hazelnut butter. The garnishes can be black-eyed peas, corn crêpes, or small pattypan squashes. For dessert, fresh fruit compotes, lovely small scoops of sherbets such as pear, raspberry, and melon, and new cheesecakes lighter than air have been replacing heavy layer cakes.

In an era when the tricks of mass food production are increasingly demeaning the quality of dishes in expensive restaurants and when the quest for novelty threatens to trivialize the experience of eating out, it is heartening to note the large number of establishments that insist on using only first-rate ingredients—and in sensible ways. The biggest single influence in improving local restaurants has been the availability of foodstuffs scarcely even dreamed of a decade ago.

Serious gastronomes should not miss a visit to the area farmers' markets—Harry's Market in Alpharetta and Gwinnett and Your DeKalb Farmers Market in Decatur. Restaurant owners come here to buy in bulk Chinese cabbages, Caribbean tubers, Malaysian mollusks, and peppers of many sizes, colors, and degrees of fieriness. Here visitors will find not only a bewildering assortment of exotic produce and seafood from all over the world, but evidence that Atlanta really has become the "international city" trumpeted by promoters and local officials. In the absence of clearly demarcated ethnic neighborhoods—the Little Havanas and Little Italys and Chinatowns of other cities—the markets provide a rare opportunity to observe how much the population of Georgia's capital has been diversified by new arrivals from Asia, Africa, South America, Europe, the Caribbean—indeed, every corner of the globe.

Atlanta's food wholesalers have also contributed significantly to the improvement in fresh marine as well as agricultural products in local restaurants. Twenty-five years ago, eating fish in a fine establishment meant either stuffed flounder (yawn) or Dover sole given a royal interment under a shroud of rich sauce. Now, innovations in freezing and shipping techniques have made it possible for seafood distributors to provide this land-locked city with fish from all the world's oceans.

In addition, multiple restaurant ownership has played a role in providing new exotic foodstuffs for public larders. It used to be a commonplace of restaurant criticism that an owner had to be on the premises of his one and only establishment in order to ensure top-quality cooking and service. In Atlanta, however, a number of the most glamorous and successful eating places benefit from being part of a group of comparable restaurants. Most notably, the team of Pano Karatassos and Paul Albrecht can afford to bring rare, choice produce into Atlanta from California in containers, then parcel out the goods among their establishments.

Like any convention city, Atlanta has an inner core of places maintained for and populated by the credulous plastic-badge crowd. There's no need to get trapped by stereotyped luxury and glorified TV dinners, or, just as bad, synthetic Southern hospitality that promotes chemical mint juleps, greasy chicken, and prefab biscuits. Rule of thumb: if you have to pay more than $6 for one meat and two vegetables, it's not the South, or at least not the Old South. Regional pride has slowly blossomed in the last few years, finally giving Atlantans the kind of New South restaurants they had been waiting for.

These days, the real flavor of the Old South is hard to catch inside the city. The tearoom is a dying genre, Southern cafeterias often resemble geriatric wards, and only obscure kitchens in out-of-the way neighborhoods dish out authentic soul food. The diner madness that obsessed America in the late eighties, however, brought back into prominence the authentic foods beloved by previous generations of Georgians.

American cuisine has progressed by leaps and bounds, although, when Atlantans want to eat fancy, they are still likely to go to an Italian restaurant. French cuisine has muscled its way back to the top with several distinguished French restaurants opening in the last couple of years. Mediterranean cuisine, rightfully perceived as healthy and tasty, is an important current trend. Bistro cuisine, with its unpretentious and comfortable fare, gives Atlantans a feeling that they had been missing, and vegetarianism has become increasingly more sophisticated.

Coffeehouses, from hard-core espresso bars such as Aurora to delightful small cafés such as Virginia's and competing national chains, have exploded on the market. Bakeries, most of them relying on a bit of light cuisine to make ends meet, are suddenly everywhere.

Another gastronomic phenomenon is the rage for Cajun, Southwestern, and Thai cuisine that has burned its way through America's heart. While Atlanta has yet to be fully convinced that good old Georgia cooking is quite fit for company, the city relates easily to the loud, joyous food of Louisiana, the hearty simplicity of Texas, the vibrant colors of New Mexico, and the vigor of Thailand. Blackened fish of various sorts still appear on countless menus hereabouts, Southwestern cafés are a big hit, and jalapeño and other chili peppers flavor all sorts of dishes, not always to good purpose. Yuppie theme places are exploiting the trends, of course, but the cheerful news is that truly dedicated and caring cooks are mastering some of the old techniques, to the gourmet's great benefit. In today's free-form approach to cooking, kitchen work reinvents the classics and pares them down to the essential.

Light eating, or "grazing," has become a lasting trend to which clever operators have been catering as fast as they can. On some menus, the list of appetizers is expanding and that of entrées shrinking, both in size and ambition. It is not uncommon to see people sharing a selection of fun first courses and salads instead of ordering a serious meal. Atlantans nibble on warm onion and wild mushroom tarts, red potatoes stuffed with Brie and escargots, smoked goose breast with mustard fruit, and linguine salad with prosciutto. Fitness cuisine was never more appealing: terrines of young vegetables, frittatas of veal with orange pekoe, grilled halibut with watercress sauce.

On the whole, though, Atlantans remain faithful to places that heap plates with mountains of food. They like sweet sauces and resist bitter ingredients like Belgian endive. Restaurateurs continue to complain that the local public will not order dishes that challenge their imaginations because of unfamiliar seasonings or unaccustomed methods of preparation.

Fortunately, however, the public is now diverse enough to support adventuresome eating places that could never have survived here when the population was more homogeneous. The proliferation of first-rate ethnic establishments, especially Thai and Chinese, has been the most astonishing evidence of Atlanta's gastronomic maturity. Twenty-five years ago, Oriental food fanciers had to be satisfied with a few places offering Cantonese dishes of the chop suey-chow mein variety. The first Mandarin kitchen, Peking, did not open in Atlanta until September 1973. Now, preparations from all of China's major culinary districts are represented here, most prominently the distinguished seafood cooking of Canton. Dozens of Thai restaurants have also opened all over the metropolitan area.

Sushi has taken Atlanta by storm, and the suburbs are now dotted with sushi bars appealing to young American jet-setters and to the Japanese businessmen who are increasingly evident in the city. Distinctive regional dishes from Vietnam, Korea, India, Morocco, Turkey, and Mexico may be enjoyed in a variety of establishments.

Much as they like tracking down unusual food in obscure surroundings, people in Atlanta really want to live it up when they go out to dinner. They like to be dazzled, amused, pampered. When a local takes a visitor to a favorite restaurant, he doesn't want to be embarrassed by decor that cries "small town" or an inadequate serving staff trying its best to intimidate a patron who has seen the world and knows a thing or two about true sophistication.

The design of Atlanta restaurants took a new turn in 1978 when the team of Pano Karatassos and Paul Albrecht hired residential designer Penny Goldwasser to create a sensuous environment for Pano's & Paul's. Goldwasser's skill at taking the threat out of large public spaces was put to increasingly imaginative uses in a succession of interiors. She spent a great deal of her considerable budget on artists' labor: faux marbre, gilding, polychrome work, custom lamp shades. She used sumptuous draperies, not only lined but interlined, and gorgeous antiques. World-famous designers such as Patrick Kuleto and Adam Tihany have made their mark in Atlanta. Bill Johnson of Johnson Studio Design and Peter Zakas of Zakaspace are in extraordinary demand on the local scene.

The negative side of so great an emphasis on elaborate decorative details is that modest establishments serving excellent food in subdued surroundings sometimes have difficulty surviving in Atlanta. The city's requirement to be entertained in novel ways seems insatiable, often putting impossible demands on solid restaurants that would be content to go on providing good food in an unchanged environment if they didn't have to compete with their ever-swankier neighbors.

The restaurant industry in Atlanta may be no more volatile than elsewhere in the country, but it is not markedly less so. Do not be surprised, therefore, if information included in this guidebook as accurate early in 1996 proves no longer to hold true by year's end and beyond. Chefs will have moved on; thriving establishments will have folded or been sold. If a review names a particular chef or owner whose presence has been a guarantee of distinction in the past, it would be a good idea to verify the continuing involvement of that individual when calling to make reservations.

As restaurants have been growing prettier and glitzier, they have made tremendous progress in wine service. Many lists are now computerized, not carved in stone, and updated weekly to provide correct vintage information. While fewer than a dozen restaurants can afford a sommelier, the number of places where the staff is well informed about wine has increased significantly. Bruce Galphin, wine journalist and local historian, sees "fewer and fewer wine lists turned over to a single wholesaler, but more and more lists thoughtfully prepared on the premises and showing different sources." The widespread use of Cruvinet machines (a system that pumps inert gas into an open bottle to prevent oxidation of the contents) now enables even modest restaurants to offer numerous fine wines by the glass.

Fine wining and dining have, indeed, come a long way in

Atlanta. The city has developed a palate and an eye for quality. The process is irreversible. Whatever food trends sweep the nation, Atlanta will be watching and picking what she wants.

MAP A

MAP B

MAP C

MAP D

MAP E

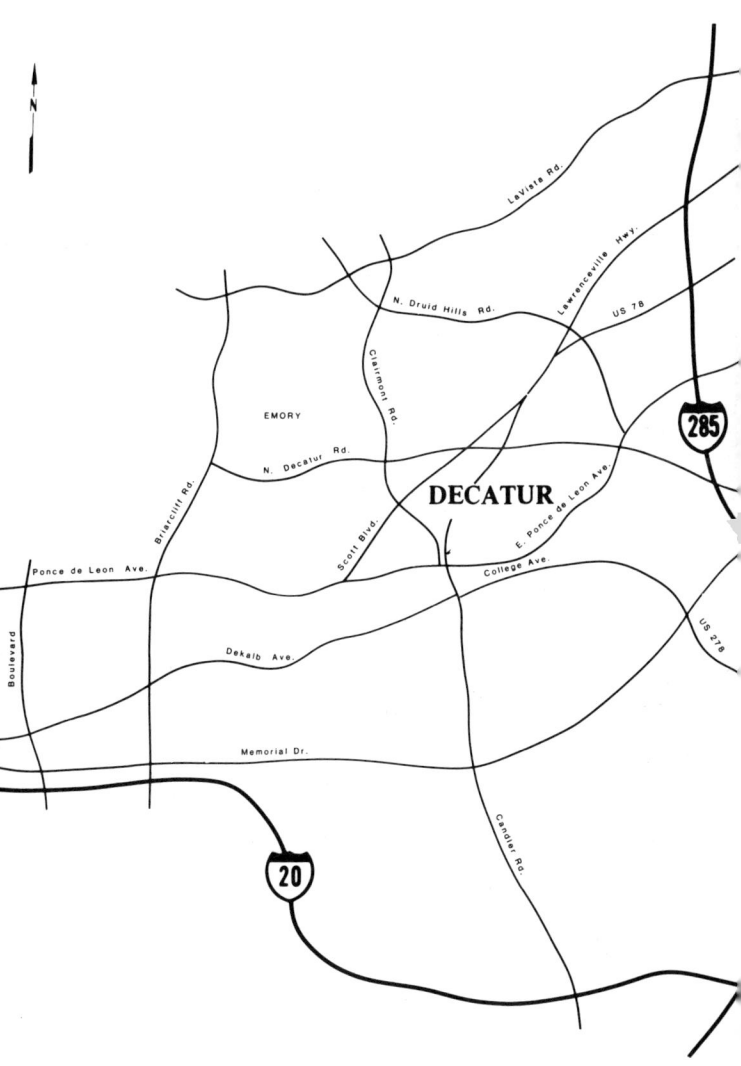

MAP F

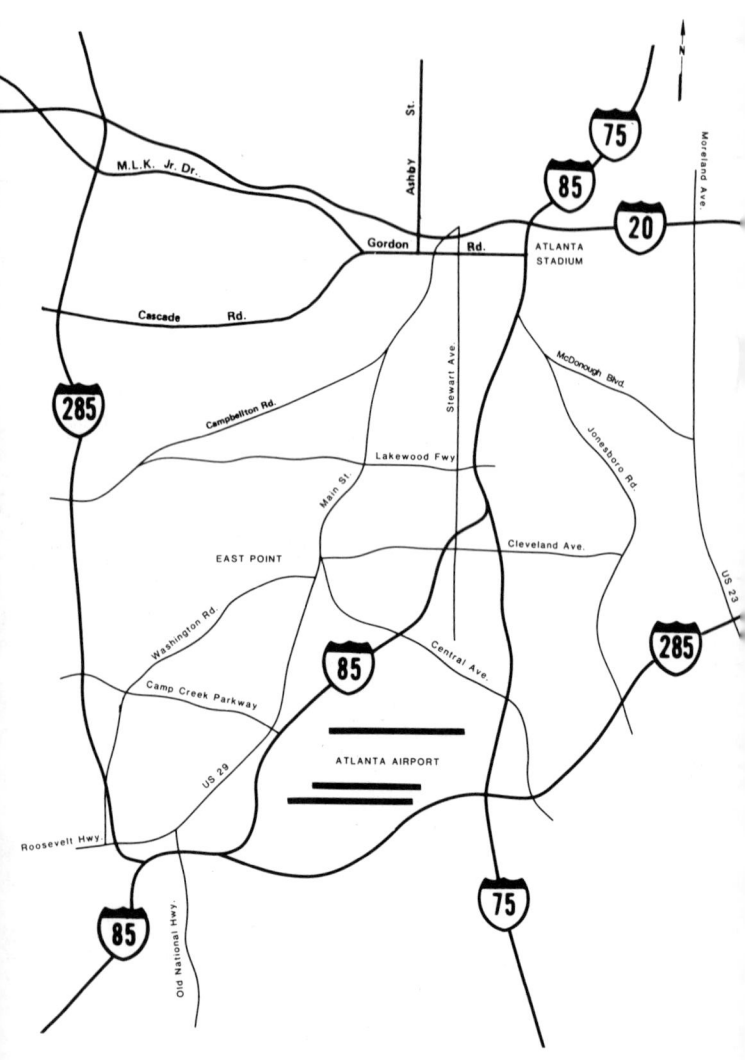

MAP G 29

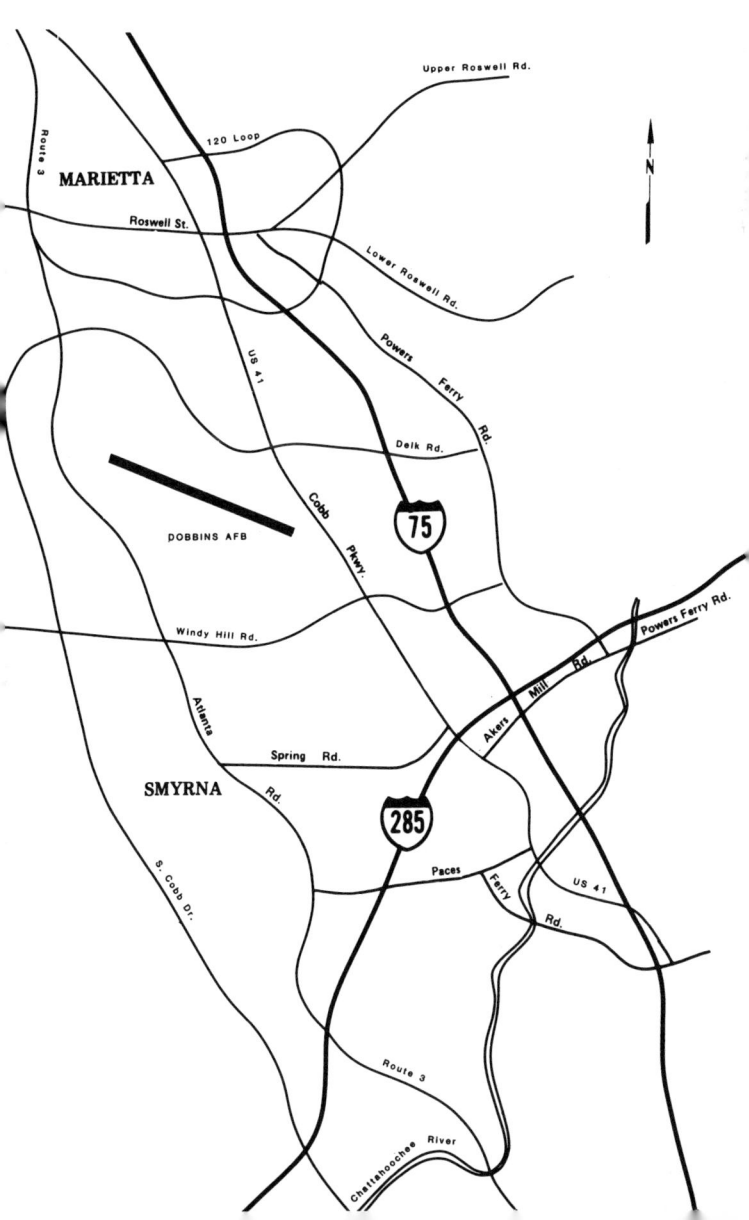

MAP H

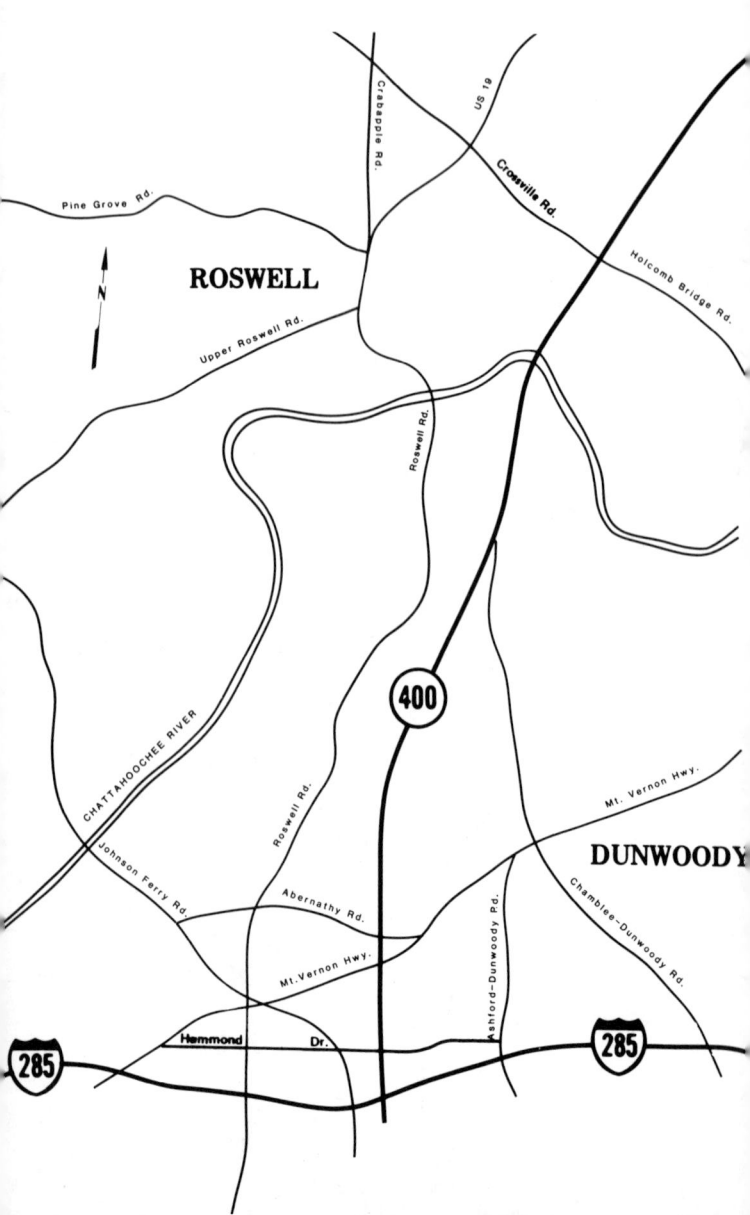

MAP I

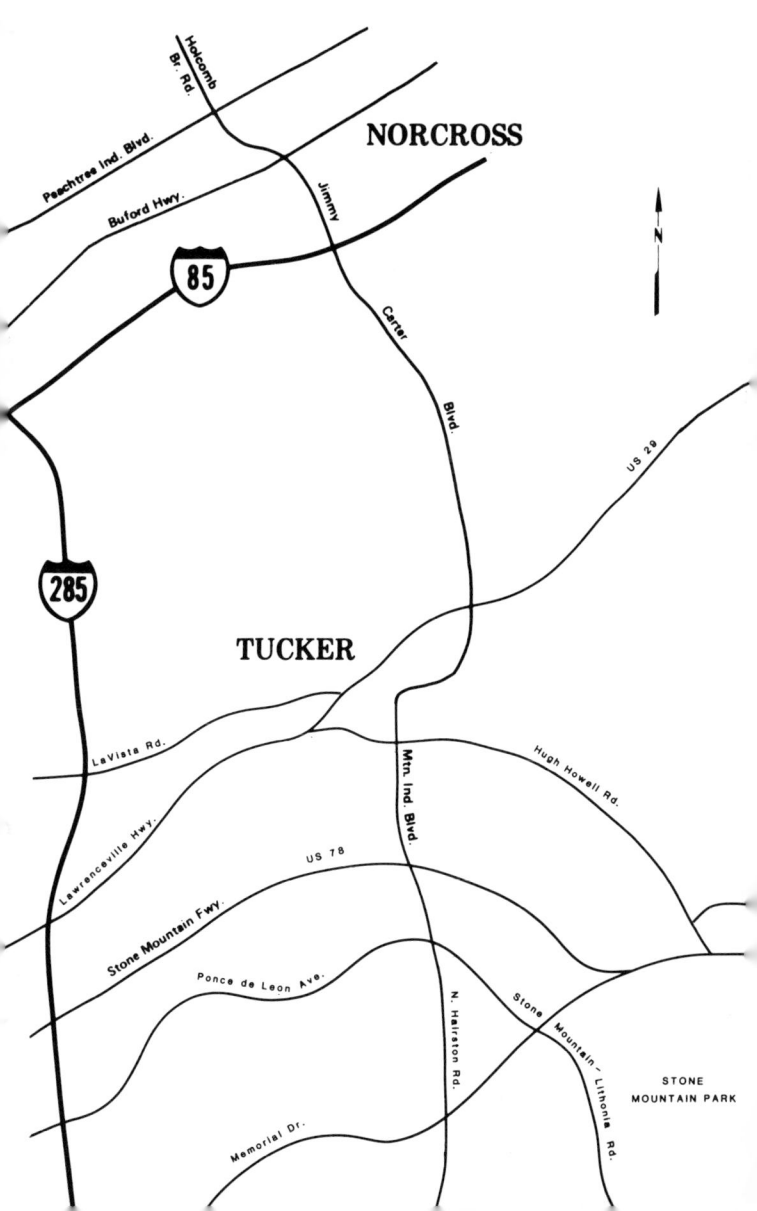

How to Use This Guide

THE RESTAURANTS INCLUDED in this guide are listed alphabetically, with a separate "Beyond Atlanta" section reviewing several restaurants within a two-hour drive of the city. A series of indexes is provided at the end of the book for quick reference to the restaurants' special features.

Each restaurant's address is followed by a letter (A to I) that refers to one of the nine maps. Also included is information about hours, reservation policies, credit cards accepted (V stands for Visa, MC for Mastercard, AE for American Express, DC for Diner's Club, and Dis for Discovery), and parking.

Restaurants are rated in three categories: food quality, atmosphere, and price.

Food ratings range from four stars to "Acceptable":

★★★★	
★★★	Recommended
★★	
★	
☆	Acceptable

Stars indicate the author's evaluation of an establishment's excellence. Patrons visiting any recommended restaurant may expect to find at least some dishes prepared with special care and meals that represent good food value. The greater the number of solid stars, the higher the likelihood of consistent superiority across the board. Average restaurant food is rated "Acceptable."

Atmosphere is rated from one to four knife and fork symbols. The more of these symbols, the higher the level of comfort to be expected.

These ratings take into consideration the quality and professionalism of a restaurant's serving staff as well as the appeal of its decor. An absence of knife and fork symbols indicates that the establishment offers no special atmospheric pleasures.

Cost is rated by dollar signs, from one to four. These ratings are computed on the basis of three-course meals including wine and reasonable tip.

$ $ $ $	Over $45 per person
$ $ $	30 to $45 per person
$ $	15 to $30 per person
$	Less than $15 per person

Hotel Dining

Two types of restaurants are sparsely represented in this book—and for opposite reasons. Chain operations like Olive Garden, TGI Friday's, and Bennigan's have been omitted because, wherever they are found—in Kansas City, Denver, Wilmington, as well as Atlanta—the corporation's basic formula is rigidly adhered to and no surprises may be expected from the decor, atmosphere, or food preparation. A few exceptions, places that are either upscale or too much fun to ignore, have been included where unusually sound values may be counted on.

By contrast, most hotel restaurants have been omitted because there is no way of predicting what the consumer will find in such establishments from one year to the next. Hotel managers continually tinker with their formulas, and kitchen personnel move about within a corporation's properties with dizzying rapidity.

Indeed, value for the food dollar is remarkably low at most hotel dining rooms. It is now common practice for hotels to charge $25 and more for a single entrée—and what do you get? Something you could get anywhere in the nation in a comparable hotel. Dull and dutiful cuisine at one end of the scale, overwrought and self-indulgent at the other end, the offense is widespread, not limited to any particular section of town. The captive audience that forms the core of most hotels' business finds nearly identical food everywhere.

The dubious distinction of having the largest number of mediocre restaurants goes to the Marriott Marquis downtown. Winner in the contest for Most Promising Restaurants that Never Realize Their Potential is the Omni International downtown. The Omni's big-deal French Restaurant tried every gimmick in the book before folding, and the hotel's Italian operation, Bugatti, has become near invisible.

On the bright side, the opening of two Ritz-Carltons in Atlanta during the mid-1980s brought a new level of luxury to hotel residency hereabouts. Although lunch and dinner in both the Buckhead and downtown Cafés achieve no special preeminence, the pampering bestowed at breakfast in both establishments is guaranteed to put patrons in a cheerful mood to start off the day. And dinner in The Dining Room of the Ritz Buckhead is not only the city's ultimate restaurant experience, but one of the highest eating pleasures to be found anywhere in the United States.

For Nostalgia-Seekers Only

Food lovers who last ate publicly in Atlanta twenty years ago will not recognize the city today. Such restaurant landmarks in the central business district as The Midnight Sun, Emile's, The Diplomat, and Herren's were swept away during the 1980s. The Patio By the River and Aunt Fanny's Cabin are gone, too. S & W Seafood Company packed its fish nets and Bernard's its French knickknacks. A few familiar places from the previous decade remain downtown, such as Nikolai's Roof and Pittypat's Porch, but, overall, change rather than stability characterizes the local restaurant scene. In that respect, the food industry reflects the general tenor of public life here. After all, the Georgia capital likes to picture itself as a phoenix, rising from the ashes of General Sherman's March to the Sea and recreating its destiny out of rubble. The old and venerated appeal little to the imagination of Atlantans, the majority of whom moved here recently from other cities or other countries.

Nonetheless, tourists interested in knowing how local residents ate a decade and more ago can find a number of establishments that have changed little over the years. These places are not reviewed in detail in this book because they are essentially irrelevant to the reader's quest for authoritative, innovative restaurant food. Nostalgia-seekers may find some pleasure in searching out these old-timers, however, especially since several of the interiors are amusing or distinctive or both. Listed here are the most prominent of Atlanta's restaurant hangers-on.

Those curious to see what French food was like in Atlanta a decade or two ago might want to check out one of the following. **South of France** (2345 Cheshire Bridge Rd. at

LaVista; 404-325-6963), conveniently located and cozy, also with a charming fireplace, can hardly hide the fact that this is a low-ceilinged shopping-center space with walls of industrial-style brick. **Petite Auberge** (in the Toco Hill Shopping Center) still serves as the area's fanciest dining room and gets considerable mileage out of its French identity, despite the fact that the owners are German and that a mural of the old city of Munich decorates its dining room.

Seafood dishes in Atlanta used to taste more of the freezer than of the sea. Despite remarkable improvements in the handling of fish and marine products, older Southsiders remain loyal to **The Captain's Roost** (2873 Main St. in East Point; 404-761-9468), a net-draped, fluorescent-lit box serving nice fresh raw oysters as well as reliable broiled and fried seafood. There's no telling whom you'll see sitting at **Jim White's Half Shell** (2349 Peachtree Rd. in Peachtree Battle shopping center; 404-237-9924), still a haunt for moneyed Atlanta and a place to eat scamp whenever fancy strikes, no matter how obsolescent the decor and service.

Genteel ladies' lunchrooms are another throwback to America's days of gustatory innocence. To experience the Atlanta Historical Society's notion of elegance, stop in at **Swan Coach House** (3130 Slaton Dr. in Buckhead; 404-261-0636), where the gossip flies over grilled Monte Cristo sandwiches topped with powdered sugar and timbales of chicken salad served with cheese straws. A similar clientele takes time off from shopping at Neiman-Marcus in Lenox Square to nibble on quiche and salad (and wolf down high-calorie desserts) at **Zodiac Room** (3393 Peachtree Rd.; 404-266-8200).

Restaurant Reviews

Listed Alphabetically

★ ★ The Abbey $$$$ ⊗⊗⊗

163 Ponce de Leon Ave. (at Piedmont Ave.). Map A. (404) 876-8532. Dinner only, nightly 6 to 10:45. Reservations and all major credit cards accepted. Valet parking.

Dining in a church, attended by monks in knee-length frocks, and listening to a harpist plucking away above the flower-decked altar as though preparing for a first-class interment could be a grotesque experience. But it's not. Once you get over the usual awkwardness (including fear of ridicule and a bit of an attitude about finding yourself among a fair number of conventioneers), you open up to truer feelings. The Abbey is beautiful. There is nothing funny about the architecture, the great soaring windows, the harpist playing in the choir loft, or any of the religious and secular displays, which include spectacular old copper basins. Oh, all right . . . the waiters' costumes still make you chuckle, but you get used to them and the service is excellent.

The biggest relief, however, is to find chef Richard Lindamood with a solid grip on the kitchen and an attractive new menu. A Maine lobster crème brûlée in ginger crust with a mango-vanilla sauce and lobster roe and a napoleon of house-smoked salmon and crisp potatoes with Mascarpone cheese, sturgeon caviar, and chive oil are both show-offish and excellent introductions to the contemporary continental menu created by an experienced hands-on chef. Rosemary-roasted free-range chicken with mashed potatoes, napa cabbage, and a flageolet bean stew is a delicious heartwise selection approved by the American Heart Association.

An herb-crusted rack of lamb with fresh goat-cheese pasta

and a cake of Japanese eggplant and artichoke comes on a considerable amount of rich demiglace but the diminutive chops and garnishes are flavorful and compatible. If words such as citrus emulsion, lobster potato hash, saffron aioli, and corn risotto in tomato essence (all with separate dishes) read like poetry to you, you can rest assured. Even though you may not have been to The Abbey in eons, the restaurant is no disgrace to Atlanta's gastronomic reputation. A light dessert, perhaps a Key lime mousse napoleon, is a good way to end a substantial but by no means killing dinner.

The Abbey has always had a big cellar, but the wine list used to be as unmanageable as some medieval opus. Now it is a model of clarity and a very useful tool. It contains not only all the relevant data a consumer can use, but also maps of the major wine districts and a clear, sensible, attractive ordering of the vast inventory. The restaurant willingly dispenses small tastes of its wines by the glass to help you make a meaningful selection and the staff is both enthusiastic and knowledgeable about the wine. The Abbey stays remarkably busy and reservations are a good idea.

★★ Abruzzi Ristorante $$$$ ⊗⊗⊗

2355 Peachtree Rd. (in Peachtree Battle shopping center, at Peachtree Battle Ave.). Map B. (404) 261-8186.

Lunch Monday to Friday 11:30 A.M. to 2:30 P.M. Dinner Monday to Thursday 5:30 to 10 P.M., Friday and Saturday 5:30 to 11 P.M. Reservations recommended. All major credit cards. Crowded parking lot.

When Nico Petrucci left Il Valetto on 61st Street in New York, he took more with him than some key staff and a great deal of experience. Abruzzi, an elegant replacement for the once-believed-to-be-eternal Brass Key, feels like a Manhattan power restaurant. The charm can be turned on or off depending on the perceived importance of a particular customer. This, of course, makes the restaurant especially attractive to the corporate heavies and other big egos who favor the place.

If you make a modest impression, you may well slip through the cracks in Abruzzi's polish. Not for you the fresh wheel of Parmesan stabbed into chunks as a complimentary nibble at the beginning of the meal. You'll watch little flatteries being lavished around you while you worry in a corner that perhaps, yes, you should have been wearing your power suit.

Abruzzi won't feel warm and fuzzy to you, but the dining room, wallpapered in discreet stripes, fitted with large mirrors and opalescent sconces, seems like the epitome of good taste. An elegant small bar has been created at the end near the entrance. The private dining rooms receive heavy use. There are some grand old waiters with a touch of the eccentric and, a rarity in Atlanta, some genuine Italian staff members.

The menu is classy and restrained: smoked salmon with red onions and capers, prosciutto with fresh melon, angel-hair pasta alla Nico (a Bolognese sauce touched with cream), plump and delicious quails on a bed of polenta, and classic risotto with wild mushrooms.

The cuisine never feels particularly sexy, but you never go wrong here with fresh seafood or pasta (especially the rustic pappardelle or the fun orecchiette). The kitchen has a good track record with seasonal specialties (including game) and don't dream of skipping the homemade desserts (profiteroles to tiramisú). The restaurant is well worth cultivating and those who are serious about wine will find excellent selections from all over Italy.

★ Aleck's Barbecue Heaven $

783 Martin Luther King Jr. Dr. (east of Ashby St.). Map F. (404) 525-2062.

Monday to Thursday 11 A.M. to 10 P.M. Friday and Saturday 11 A.M. to 1 A.M. Sunday 1 to 8 P.M. No reservations or credit cards. Difficult street parking exclusively.

A worn counter, a few stools, a couple of booths behind a short row of noisy video-game machines: the thickly painted door has just let you into a not too carefully preserved piece of Atlanta's past. Started in 1942 by Ernest Alexander, Aleck's is one of the city's oldest barbecue places, on a block that was a center of Atlanta's black commercial enterprise in the days of segregation. A few doors away, down what used to be known as Hunter Street, is the famous Paschal's Motor Lodge.

People wander in and out, rattling change in their pants pockets or wrestling with giant rib sandwiches that ooze dark sauce out of waxed paper wrappers. A frantic young man is standing between the massive stone wall pierced with an open pit of medieval proportions and an ancient butcher block cratered by years of heavy use. Thud, thud—he chops a deliciously charred hunk of pork. He whacks the short end from an impressive slab of ribs, slaps some sauce on it from a banged-up old pan, and runs to the cash register, all the while keeping up a steady banter with the customers.

Prepare yourself for the shock. This is black barbecue, violently seasoned and vinegary, not some piggy-wiggy with a bit of ketchup. The meat must be pried from the bones with strong teeth. The sauce is harsh, complex, and spine-tinglingly hot. Now operated by the original owner's youngest daughter, Aleck's serves, wraps, and caters some of the most aggressive barbecue you'll ever eat. To soothe your rattled taste buds, buy a phenomenal sweet potato pie, an old-fashioned beauty in a six-inch tin pan.

★★ Alon's $ ⓧ

1394 N. Highland Ave. Map C. (404) 872-6000. 659 Peachtree St. (in the Georgian Terrace). Map A. (404) 724-0444.

Highland location Monday to Friday 7 A.M. to 7 P.M. Saturday and Sunday 8 A.M. to 7 P.M. Georgian Terrace location Monday.to Thursday 7:30 A.M. to 11 P.M. Friday and Saturday 7:30 A.M. to midnight. No reservations. V, MC. Small parking lot for the bakery, validated parking in the Georgian Terrace for the café.

Alon Balshan, formerly head baker for Murphy's More Than a Delicatessen, grabbed the opportunity that presented itself when a short row of undistinguished warehouses became a development project in Morningside. Zoning regulations still prevent his charming bakery from expanding into a sit-down place but the new location in the Georgian Terrace is a sophisticated intown café. Alon's bread is light and delicious, a terrific vehicle for his excellent made-to-order sandwiches. Two thick slices of freshly sliced country French with half a chicken breast, a noble amount of pesto mayonnaise, some leaf lettuce, and ripe tomato make an unbeatable sandwich combination. There are also roasted lamb, turkey breast (also with pesto mayonnaise), rare roast beef, Mediterranean vegetables, and a delicious Niçoise tuna with ripe olives and fresh lemon juice.

Balshan bakes extraordinarily good croissants: perfectly shaped, light and buttery, plain or filled. Beautiful Danishes come in several traditional variations. From rugulach to lemon poppy-seed cake, apple walnut cake, and sophisticated pound cakes baked in small bundt forms, the full range of goodies is more than attractive.

The café recently opened in the Georgian Terrace takes the concept one step farther, offering salad platters as well as sandwiches, pastries, and coffees. Classy nibbles are easy to come by. Consider a pretty eggplant terrine with strips of roasted red peppers and layers of herbed goat cheese and chopped olives with a light pesto dressing. The quiche of the day (choices include sweet Vidalia onion and fresh spinach) is a cute and light individual shell. Bruschetta offers the taste of ripe tomatoes, basil, and olive oil on toasted country French bread. Wine and beer are available.

Validated parking in the building (up to an hour) makes it easy to treat Alon's as a destination for an unusually delicious lunch or a light supper on the town. The advantage is obvious if you attend a performance across the street or nearby.

★★ Amusé $$$ ⊗⊗

2140 Peachtree Rd. (in Brookwood Square). Map B. (404) 352-3770. Lunch Tuesday to Friday 11:30 A.M. to 2:30 P.M. Dinner nightly 5:30 to 10:30 (Friday and Saturday till 11:30). Reservations and all major credit cards accepted. Adequate parking.

The decor, a stifling continental room including a semi-open kitchen behind a wall of stuccoed brick suitable for a pizzeria, is a poor match to the vision of a young chef who trained at such prestige restaurants as Daniel Boulud's Daniel's in New York before attempting his own version of a chic fusion café.

Each meal at Amusé starts with a tiny, usually Oriental style freebie: a little bit of smoked salmon with cucumber crème fraîche, a Thai-style marinated beef salad with crushed peanuts, or a small mushroom with cilantro and shredded carrots.

Dangerously complicated at first, the culinary style is improving and chef Si Huynh makes the most of his Asian background and classical French training. An Asian crawfish risotto with sweet corn, pencil asparagus, wild mushrooms, and a warm orange-tangerine jus is a delicious and substantial starter. Sake-steamed mussels with black beans, baby corn, and tomato come in a shallow bowl with tender vegetable wontons. Crispy "cigarettes" rolled around a combination of boursin and ricotta cheese are stacked prettily around a pool of mango chutney with caramelized Vidalia onions. The new section of fresh Vietnamese-style spring rolls with julienne vegetables, aromatic herbs, and fillings such as cracked-pepper chicken with chili-ginger sauce or shrimp and pork with spicy roasted peanut sauce is outstanding. Vegetarians will appreciate the tofu, bean sprout, and rice vermicelli rolls with tamarind sauce.

Entrées include a pretty bacon-wrapped halibut over red mashed potatoes and spinach with a roasted garlic, ginger jus; a pan-roasted duck breast buried in a zillion dark saucy things; and, listed under pasta, a delicious and affordable Vietnamese-style beef stir-fry over rice vermicelli, cucumbers, shredded cabbage, and Thai basil, with a cruet of nuoc man sauce on the side.

The desserts are delicious, and far simpler. Hurrah for the warm chocolate gâteau with a walnut crust served over a warm creamy peanut sauce. The new version of Asian pear (poached in white wine, served over a salsa of tropical fruit) is pure heaven. Ditto the fresh peach and walnut strudel, but the terrine of white and dark chocolate doesn't have much going for it beyond the mere visual effect.

The dining room, frequently near empty, has no energy of

its own. The staff can hover anxiously. The kitchen crew, with the exception of chef Si Huynh, tends to stare at the diners for long periods of time. Dinner is maddeningly expensive. Lunch prices are reasonable, however, and most of the noon specialties are sensible Vietnamese dishes.

★★ Anis $ ⊗⊗

2974 Grandview Ave. (at Pharr Rd.). Map B. (404) 233-9889.
  Lunch Tuesday to Saturday 11:30 A.M. to 2:30 P.M. Dinner Tuesday to Thursday 6 to 10 P.M., Friday and Saturday 6 to 11 P.M., Sunday 6 to 10:30 P.M. Brunch Sunday 11:30 A.M. to 3 P.M. No reservations. V, MC, AE. Steep and awkward parking lot.

Take two very young men from the south of France. Pair them with a third countryman, an experienced chef and part-time father-figure for the youngsters. Fire them up with entrepreneurial spirit and let them happen upon a tiny house in Buckhead. The three friends loved the charming terrace and the little rooms that gave them the feeling of being on familiar ground. What you have now is a typical Provençal restaurant complete with a small café-bar, a comfortable main dining room with light-hearted murals, and the true-French terrace with pretty plantings.

At the beginning, proprietors and customers were amazed by each other. The first had no idea that they would attract respectable Buckheadites of the kind that had patronized the previous incarnations of their restaurant. The second could hardly believe in a blackboard listing something like "gratinéed lentil soup $2.75."

A classic, well-dressed salade Niçoise with black olives, hard-boiled eggs, ripe tomatoes, green beans, anchovies, and tuna marinated in extravirgin olive oil tastes particularly good with a ray of sun and a fresh breeze on the terrace. The salade maison with goat cheese and tapenade (black olive purée) tartines is delicious as well, as are the warm focaccio (*sic*) toasts loaded with sliced tomatoes, mozzarella, fresh basil, and olive oil. The carpaccio, made of small, fairly thick slices of grainy beef, would, however, gag a tiger at the zoo.

The house signature dish, shrimp à l'anis sautéed in olive oil with fresh tomatoes, bell peppers, and onions, has been modified several times in view of the clientele's lack of enthusiasm for the licorice taste of anise. The dish has also been adjusted to feature rice instead of the original mound of green pasta. The grilled lamb chops Corsican style (with fresh ground thyme) have been right from the start. Simple ravioli served Niçoise style with tomato and basil coulis are filling and inexpensive. You can also trust the specials: wonderful roasted chicken with wild mushrooms, garnished with golden potatoes and herbed zucchini; tender pork stewed with green olives served over pasta; authentically fragrant and complex soupe de poisson enriched with fresh pasta; bouillabaisse and cassoulet alternating with the seasons.

Casse-croûtes (a French term for a typical snack of bread and cheese or charcuterie) are served all day. Sunday brunch is a relaxed affair, with Provençal-style open-face omelets.

★★★ Annie's Thai Castle $$ ⊗⊗

3195 Roswell Rd. (just north of Peachtree). Map B. (404) 264-9546. Lunch Monday to Friday 11:30 A.M. to 2:30 P.M. Dinner nightly 5:30 to 11 (Friday and Saturday till midnight). V, MC, AE. Small parking lot.

Why does a restaurant succeed where its predecessor failed with a nearly identical concept? In the case of this upscale Thai restaurant following the short-lived Tamarind in an attractive free-standing building, one would have to say through a better understanding of the local market.

The eponymous proprietor of Annie's Thai Castle operated the famous Thai Restaurant of Norcross for several years before moving up in the world and enjoying the perks of her new neighborhood. The restaurant, originally a hardware store, has a great deal of charm. The design is comfortably American, down to the cozy separate bar and the small patio. Peacock feathers inserted into clay urns are strategically placed in the dining room, adding quality exotica to the peaceful surroundings. A large golden panel with a sequined elephant guards the doorway to the kitchen. The staff, including the owner, possesses excellent English skills.

Annie's Thai Castle uses better, fresher ingredients than the average ethnic competition. The size of the shrimp, the quality of the mussels, and the generosity of the servings are amazing. Annie's cuisine is fresh and complex. The traditional preparations include beautifully made soups pungent with lemon grass, Thai noodles with sprouts and shrimp, rich green curries with coconut milk, larb (a minced-meat salad with toasted rice and chile peppers), and squid marinated with lime juice, mint and crushed garlic.

The restaurant does a terrific job with Thai-style catfish combined with firm-fleshed eggplant and colorful peppers. Nontraditional dishes such as Spicy Spaghetti and soft rice-paper rolls stuffed with avocado and cream cheese are as delicious as the more classic basil rolls or glass noodles with shrimp and pork. Annie's follows the seasons closely and always serves delicious, fragrant rice.

★ Anthonys $$$$ ⊗⊗⊗

3109 Piedmont Rd. (south of Peachtree). Map B. (404) 237-5988.
Dinner only, Monday to Saturday 6 to 11 P.M. Reservations and all major credit cards accepted. Valet parking.

Take a spacious old plantation home built with slave labor in Washington, Georgia, in 1797. Number its every stone and board. Disassemble and truck it to Atlanta, rebuild it on a wooded lot—and voilà! You have a piece of the Old South smack in the middle of entertainment-minded Buckhead. Anthonys has been a tourist attraction since the mid-seventies. But unless you are a visitor to Atlanta or an occasional party planner in search of a hosting facility, you are probably barely aware of this old-timer hiding its gracious Southern structure behind a blind wall.

If you have been badly burned at Anthonys, whether as a host or guest, chances are you have never been back. You don't know that the management has changed and that the concept has evolved.

Behind the big gates remains an exceptionally pretty house. Anthonys, if not crowded, is at least relatively cheerful, with people dining on the upstairs porch and in the private dining rooms. The rooms are well kept. Many of them, such as the downstairs and the wine cellars, would be interesting for a gathering. The servers are older than the Atlanta average and although they wait on tables adequately one senses a certain "I'm here whether you are or not" weariness.

The regional focus of the new menu is admirable but some of the dishes look like final exams for culinary school. The kitchen shows off with deadly things like a sautéed filet of red snapper on artichoke ravioli with black-olive purée and basil oil (a lot of basil oil) topped with crispy shaved onion. An applewood-smoked pork loin with a walnut, apple, dried cherry, and Gouda strudel in a Merlot sauce earned the chef a first place in a national pork competition, but may not be suitable to anchor a real menu. A purée of corn and jalapeño soup is buttery and rich but garnished with a rubbery miniature crab cake.

For appetizers the chicken and morel terrine on black-eyed pea purée with scallion cornbread sticks is pretty, delicate even, but almost lifeless. The grilled Gulf shrimp with gazpacho vinaigrette on a delicious Tuscan bean salad is much closer to a real dish. Anthonys still offers the "Roasts Carved from our Silver Chariot" of the olden days. The wine list hasn't been modernized to the same extent as the menu, but the selections (supervised by a sommelier) are credible.

★★★ Arturo's $ ⊗

5486 Chamblee-Dunwoody Rd. (in the Shops of Dunwoody). Map H. (770) 396-0335.

> Monday to Thursday 11 A.M. to 10 P.M. Friday and Saturday 11 A.M. to 11 P.M. Sunday 5 to 10 P.M. No reservations. V, MC. Large parking lot.

Proudly sizzling above the door of this new Dunwoody eatery, the neon patronym advertises to the world the fact that Danny Arturo, formerly the chef at Broadway Danny's, has become his own boss.

If he were still living in the Big Apple, Arturo would probably be running a pocket-size operation. But this is Atlanta, better yet, suburban Atlanta, and there is space aplenty. The dining room fits into one large open space. The pizza makers work behind a long counter that does triple duty as bar, pick-up station for phoned orders, and cashier's desk. The only colors are black, white, and red. Everything is reflected in a wall of mirrors. Booths and tables set on a checkerboard floor have plenty of elbow room. The artwork (a mural of the Brooklyn Bridge, a few exceptionally large and unpleasant oils) isn't enough to ruin the positive impression.

The pies are still huge and thin. The crusts come in several exotic flavors (including black pepper, sourdough, spinach, and sweet red bell pepper). Arturo's hits good flavor notes with combinations such as white pizza with pesto or sun-dried tomatoes and eggplant, but the focus is no longer pizza. What is truly delicious at Arturo's is the kind of old-fashioned food one hardly expects a young chef to appreciate, let alone deliver. Stuffed sole, for example, looks incredibly strange: two tightly rolled filets revealing nothing about their contents. But the first forkful explodes with flavor. The fish melts in your mouth, the crab stuffing is fluffy and assertive, and the wine sauce is just acidic enough to bring everything to life.

Chicken sautéed in wine sauce over fettuccine is another great taste experience. Zuppa di Pesce (a combination of fresh red snapper, clams, mussels, calamari, and shrimp) has been transformed into a topping for linguine. Linguine with white clam sauce (big, sliced clams), eggplant lasagne, splendid fried calamari, and equally perfect fried zucchini all pass with flying colors. The marinara sauce is as bright as can be; the pasta always has a firm bite. Add a simple minestrone and a couple of well-made desserts and you are out of Arturo's with a feeling of things being done right and flowing from solid traditions.

★★ Asiana Garden $$ ⊗

5150 Buford Hwy. (in Asian Square, just north of Peachtree-Dunwoody Rd., Doraville). Map D. (770) 452-1677.

Daily noon to 2 A.M. Reservations accepted. V, MC, Dis. Large parking lot.

If you rated restaurants according to the level of anxiety you experience, authentic Korean establishments would be right at the top of your list. You are almost invariably told by your servers that you won't like what you order. And even when you manage to get your point across ("we'll eat anything"), you aren't always comfortable with the results. You forget to pour the broth on the cold noodles. Or you don't know that you are supposed to wrap the rice with the meat in lettuce leaves or toss all the ingredients of a dish together and add sauce.

Asiana Garden is only borderline hospitable to the culinary naive but the restaurant is physically appealing and easy to understand. The tables are arranged in several long rows, offering a great view of who's eating what. A posh sushi bar stretches on one side of the room. Tables equipped for hibachi cooking seat six comfortably. Most surfaces are wood, clean, and uncluttered.

If you opt to cook your own dinner, thinly sliced prime beef is about the best thing you can throw on the grill. Marinated butterflied shrimp are excellent as well but have to be watched closely for signs of overcooking. Tripe marinated with hot sauce must steam on the grill for quite a while before becoming enjoyably tender.

Complimentary with any entrée, tiny pickled goodies extend the meal. Dried whitebait, raw oysters in hot pepper paste, daikon in various incarnations, kimchee (fermented cabbage), the pickled stems of some vegetable, marinated cucumber, agar-agar jelly with hot topping, and more remain on the table throughout dinner, providing interesting diversion and unusual tastes.

If you want an appetizer, pan-sautéed gyoza (Japanese-style dumplings) are served with big leaves of an obnoxious-tasting herb meant as a wrap. The sushi rolls are fresh and appealing, if a little soft. Among the entrées, squid in red pepper sauce is fiercely hot and delicious. B-bim-bop (rice with wonderful leafy vegetables, meat, and a soft egg) stands out as an extraordinarily tasty option. Cold buckwheat noodles with crisp daikon chunks and hard-boiled egg make a particularly refreshing summer dish. Asiana Garden serves dinner until 2 A.M. and occupies a special place in the community.

★★★ Asuka $$ ⓧ

3567 Chamblee-Dunwoody Rd. (one block east of Peachtree Industrial). Map D. (770) 455-1163.

Lunch Tuesday to Saturday noon to 3 P.M. Dinner Tuesday to Sunday 6 to 10:30 P.M. No reservations. V, MC, AE. Adequate parking.

Great things come in small packages. With an enormous number of Japanese restaurants to choose from, overlooking this modest newcomer would be easy. The concept of serving authentic, seasonal cuisine to a largely Oriental clientele without excluding the rest of the world isn't extraordinary per se, but there is something special about Asuka's utter lack of pretension and the management's eagerly welcoming attitude toward Westerners.

You won't feel like an intruder when you enter the small detached building just big enough for a square dining room, easy to encompass at a glance, and a sushi counter, set as a separate area defined by sharply peaking dark wooden beams. The chef is willing to educate without shaming, materializing in the dining room to retrieve a beautiful thick sheet of what looks like homemade paper with gold flecks after you have casually bunched it up on the table. "No, no," he says with a smile. "In Japan you keep the sashimi covered to keep it moist." He delicately pulls the paper over an exquisite plate of sliced seafood and folds it back to expose just a few bites of translucent squid.

The chopped-yellowtail roll with scallions is impeccable and the rainbow roll (eel, salmon, crab, cucumber) spectacularly beautiful. The chef's special "no name roll" is a mosaic wrapped in thin cucumber. Even the salmon roe passes the test: the skin is supposed to disappear in your mouth.

The hot appetizer menu is chock-full of unusual things: fried squid dumplings resembling little envelopes with fresh squid as the message, pungent steamed gyoza dumplings filled with natto (a fermented soy product), flash-fried tofu squares bristling with bonito flakes, a grilled radish steak braised in sauce, wonderful pickles (eggplant and daikon). Beyond the appetizers everything is organized logically: fried foods, grilled foods, chilled seafood with grated yam, vinegared dishes, noodle dishes, rice bowls with green tea.

The following are of particular interest: grilled yellowtail neck, salt grilled mackerel, nabeyakiudon (a stew of chicken, vegetables, fish cakes, and fat white noodles topped with shrimp tempura), wonderfully slurpy soba noodles. Offered on the lunch menu but available at dinner with a bit of persuasion are two memorable dishes: a Korean-influenced rice hot pot with assorted seafood and vegetables tossed tableside like a b-bim-bop and an unusual tonkatsu called "sutamina [Japanese for stamina] tonkatsu" consisting of slivers of pork and chopped scallions in a crisp batter. Complimentary dessert is a sweet but refreshing grapefruit granita. The staff maintains a consistently pleasant attitude.

★ Atkins Park $$ ⊗

794 N. Highland Ave. (between Ponce de Leon and Virginia). Map C. (404) 876-7249.
   Daily 11 A.M. to 4 A.M. (Saturday till 3 A.M.). No reservations. V, MC, AE. Difficult parking on congested streets.

Gentrification came in two phases for the oldest continuously licensed bar in the city of Atlanta, open since February 1922. In 1980 the dark, dank drinking area lost most of its sense of mystery when walls were knocked down, a spiffy glass and wood facade erected, and a handsome dining room opened featuring exposed bricks, historical photographs, and a fern-bar menu. The old customers were still free to cluster in the funky booths and along the magnificent ancient bar, leaving the other parts of the restaurant to the up-and-coming Virginia-Highlanders, most of whom had never heard the term "Atkins Park" applied to the residential community north of the intersection of Ponce de Leon and Highland avenues.

Then the people who operate Buckhead's popular singles bar, Aunt Charley's, took over, bringing in their own brand of rambunctiousness. The old barroom hasn't lost its pungent charm, but the age of the clientele has dropped sharply. Crowds carry on late into the night. A bar menu is available long after the dining room has closed. Hamburgers dripping with meat juices boost many a failing spirit. Strong, hot coffee keeps the dead alive.

The food served in the main dining room is indistinguishable from fare at hundreds of other fern bars. Sunday brunch is a popular event, more as an opportunity for neighborhood camaraderie than for gourmandizing. In clement weather, seating spills over into an adjacent alleyway so narrow you can almost touch both sides with your outstretched arms.

★★★ Atlanta Fish Market $$$ ⊗⊗

265 Pharr Rd. Map B. (404) 262-3165.
Lunch Monday to Friday 11:30 A.M. to 2:30 P.M. Dinner Monday to Thursday 5:30 to 11. Friday and Saturday 5:30 to midnight. Sunday 4:30 to 10. Reservations and all major credit cards accepted. Valet parking.

Built to replicate some locales from owner Pano Karatassos's Savannah childhood, Atlanta Fish Market creates the illusion that you are in the vital center of some imaginary town where brick, clapboard, mosaic, glass, a panoramic mural, railroad ties, and even oyster shells have formed a varied landscape over many decades. The main room has immensely high ceilings from which descend massive globes custom designed to look like astral representations of the world.

The menu, a crowded large-format sheet printed on a daily basis, is wonderfully dense. Take your time to read everything on each visit. You wouldn't want to miss the tastiest, largest stone-crab claws available outside of Miami's famous Joe's Stonecrab and featuring the same remoulade sauce, or the latest West Coast oysters served on the half-shell with mignonette and traditional cocktail sauce, horseradish on the side. The side dishes are to be taken every bit as seriously as the appetizers. Don't fill up on fried Maine calamari with aioli and slightly hot marinara or on candied rock shrimp on fried rice noodles or you may feel too full to explore the choice of mashed potatoes (scallion aioli or creamed veggie), the white corn grits with garlic butter, and the creamed spinach, all of which are available à la carte.

A half-order of linguine with tiny clams and Pen Cove mussels in white-wine sauce is a far better way to get yourself started than any number of fried starters, but what you really don't want to miss are the sautéed halibut cheeks over a bowl of grits or the home-smoked peppered salmon served thinly sliced with capers and onions.

The fish come in two genres: plain (e.g., charbroiled) and fancy (incorporated into a special recipe). In the latter category, you will go wild for the potato-crusted cod on garlic- and scallion-mashed potatoes and the thickly sliced grouper on ratatouille in a ring of lobster-sweet-pepper sauce. The swordfish with roasted cashews and cracked pepper crust is meaty and spicy over white-corn cheese grits. Striped bass, often presented in spectacular gourmet contexts, seems regal simply grilled over mashed potatoes.

The homemade desserts aren't to be missed. A gourmet market and a separate barroom with its own appetizer station complete the facility.

★★ August Moon $$ ⊗

5715 Buford Hwy. (one-quarter mile outside I-285, Doraville). Map D. (770) 455-3464.
> *Lunch Monday to Friday 11:30 A.M. to 2 P.M. Dinner Monday to Saturday 5:30 to 10:30 P.M. Reservations and all major credit cards accepted. Adequate parking.*

Ethnic restaurants intimidate many people. What to order, how much to order, how to deal with a foreign staff—questions like these can strike terror in otherwise stout hearts. August Moon won't make you feel this way. The personnel are very young—full of cheer that energizes a clientele belonging roughly to the same generation. The sushi bar, hibachi room, and conventional dining room have a convivial Occidental feel far removed from soul-freezing austerity.

Sushi is most fun at the bar, where you can watch the molding, rolling, twisting, and bantering by the chefs. Fish eggs inside the rice, fish eggs outside, seaweed in, seaweed out, tuna slivers proudly astride, salmon demurely hidden under the avocado. Be sure to request something with quail egg. First, it's delicious. Second, watch the exquisite motion of two big hands cracking a tiny speckled shell, letting the white run between fingers and slipping the diminutive yolk into a cone of seaweed.

Just because August Moon is a fun sort of place doesn't mean it doesn't do traditional dishes well or that it doesn't have esoteric stuff. The appetizer menu lists scallop butter, beef sashimi, broiled whole Japanese sardine "with fish in its body," and natto ("Japanese authentic fermented soybeans"). Also offered is grated raw fish, layered with microscopic silvery whitebait complete with eyes the size of a pin prick.

Japanese tofu is a revelation to anyone familiar only with the stronger, cheesier Chinese stuff. The bean curd is strained through silk, a process that removes some of the nutrients, but gives it a quivering, creamy texture. The yu dofu (boiled bean curd and vegetables) is painfully beautiful in its severe plainness. Age dofu (deep-fried bean curd in special sauce) is more ordinary. The gyoza (meat dumplings) and chicken negima (tender breast meat rolled around melted cheese and scallions) are easy to like by any standard. So is the splendid broiled eel served over rice in a lacquered box. The outlandish nuta preparations (raw tuna, octopus, or giant clam in a thick, sweet rice vinegar dressing) are somewhat of a challenge.

★★★ Aurora $

992 N. Highland Ave. Map C. (404) 892-7158.
  Monday to Thursday 6:30 A.M. to 10 P.M. Friday 6:30 A.M. to midnight. Saturday 7 A.M. to midnight. Sunday 8 A.M. to 10 P.M. No reservations or credit cards. Small parking lot, street parking. Other locations (downtown in Peachtree Center, in Little Five Points, and right across from Ansley Mall) with varying hours.

Aurora, goddess of the dawn in Roman mythology, doesn't waste much time rubbing the sleep out of her eyes in this hardcore espresso bar that is a combination retail shop and freshbrew center with a definite culture of its own. Owner Booth Buckley, a recent transplant from Seattle, has had trouble grasping a city without a coffeehouse on every street corner, but in his own quiet way has done more for coffee awareness than you can begin to imagine. Aurora sells, grinds, and brews uniformly dark and beautiful coffee beans roasted West Coast style and with sensitivity. Costa Rica, Guatemala, Colombia, Yemen, Kenya, Ethiopia, and Indonesia are the ports of call on your coffee tour of the world. None of the coffees are flavored but a few are decaffeinated.

The store is stark and modern by intown standards, almost Milanese in its commitment to clean design. Excellent graphics give a sense of quality. A clever little newsletter, good T-shirts, and house mugs all highlight coffee culture. You can even learn to speak coffee lingo at Aurora. The basic vocabulary includes: tall, short, bald (no milk), skinny (low-fat milk), decaf, iced, single, double. Aurora serves remarkably good caffé latte with one or two shots of espresso and excellent macchiato (a shot of espresso with milk froth floating on top). For the summer there is a delicate cold-brewed iced coffee ("cool Joe") with no harsh aftertaste.

Aurora serves biscotti, scones, and a few little sweet cakes. If you want to spend money on coffee-brewing/keeping paraphernalia, you can do it in style.

★★ Azalea $$$ ⊗⊗

3167 Peachtree Rd. (two blocks south of Piedmont Rd.). Map B. (404) 237-9939.

Dinner only, Sunday to Thursday 5 to 11 P.M., Friday and Saturday 5 P.M. to midnight. No reservations. V, MC, AE. Valet parking.

The cool, cutting-edge glamor of the room designed by Hero Isogai is a good background for the East-meets-West cuisine of this chic fusion restaurant. Strong industrial materials project an image of low-maintenance honesty. Galvanized steel coats many of the surfaces with a silvery, nonreflective sheen. Under an asymmetrical dropped ceiling the kitchen is fully open, a powerful environment of icy metal, shiny tiles, and fiery activities. Kitchen and dining room look at one another without any visual obstacles. Noise comes with the territory in a room that is nothing but hard surfaces.

Whereas advanced cuisine is usually delivered in minuscule installments appreciated only by the wasp-waisted dandy set, Azalea made the decision to put plenty on the plate. The biggest show-stopper is a sizzling catfish Chinese style with fermented black beans. Hot smoked salmon in a fine crust of shredded potatoes is a delicious signature dish.

Each day the kitchen features a different carpaccio, such as peppered tuna with Japanese horseradish, regular tuna, scallops, or lamb with a centerpiece of warm ratatouille. Spicy stir-fries, abundant pasta dishes (with linguine rolled like a tidal wave), and a wealth of pedigreed dishes are the order of the day. Over the years, Azalea has offered scallops dipped in spicy almond-sesame batter; lobster in a soft taco with Texas salsa; sliced lamb with goat cheese and white-bean couscous; herb-seared striped bass with tomato-olive relish; and grilled breast of chicken with rice cooked in black-bean broth, served with tomato goat cheese.

Desserts have their own menu: almond-sesame lace basket filled with Heath-bar-crunch ice cream and Tahitian vanilla sauce, trio of crèmes brûlées in sake cups, ginger bread pudding, and other extravagant sweets are a must. Celebrities and restaurateurs abound among the clientele, and with the no-reservations policy waits can be trying. A new patio and greatly expanded dining room have eased the problem.

★ Azio $$ ⓧ

220 Pharr Rd. (at Buckhead Ave.). Map B. (404) 233-7626. Other location downtown.

Sunday to Wednesday 11 A.M. to 11 P.M. Thursday 11 A.M. to 11:30 P.M. Friday and Saturday 11 A.M. to midnight. No reservations. All major credit cards. Valet parking.

No longer the haunt solely of frantic singles with their dating rituals, this casual Buckhead restaurant has become more and more useful for a variety of reasons. Hardly the place on which to focus an entire evening, Azio has the fast pace and the handsome decor of a grazing bistro. The original Tuscan Italian menu has lightened up and is now in synch with the realities of the kitchen.

The pizza list has grown to include such experiments as blue-corn pizza topped with black beans and Cuban pizza with red beans and sausage. There are more classic pies as well, on a thin cracker crust flavored with rosemary. The Margharita with fresh tomatoes, basil and mozzarella is particularly elegant. A cheeseless vegetarian pizza has a clean, tasty appeal. Some of the better pastas (i.e., angel hair marinara) look absolutely awful until you begin tossing them and mixing the flavors yourself.

The grilled-vegetable salad is big enough to make an attractive full meal. Robust wedges of peppers, delicious potatoes, portobello mushrooms, sweet fresh baby beets, corn on the cob, radicchio, and crumbled gorgonzola come lightly dressed with extravirgin olive oil and lemon. Add a glass of wine and a few triangles of cracker bread (planted decoratively among the vegetables) and you have an excellent late-night meal that won't give you acid indigestion. The calamari have fallen on hard times, however. Formerly crisp and light and full flavored, they seem to have turned into spiced fried rubber bands.

The bar scene is frisky. The lamp shades (red silk with black fringes) remind you of naughty lingerie. The proportions of the room (an upscale airplane hangar filled with noise) are exciting. A new location downtown is more classically elegant and better suited to the needs of the business community.

★★ Azteca Grill $ ⊗

1140 Morrow Industrial Blvd. (at Southlake Mall). Map F. (770) 968-0907.

Monday to Thursday 11 A.M. to 10 P.M. Friday 11 A.M. to 11 P.M. Saturday noon to 11 P.M. No reservations. All major credit cards. Adequate parking.

People flock from Jonesboro, Riverdale, Macon, and even Birmingham to this bustling operation a stone's throw from Southlake Mall. There is nothing at first to distinguish Azteca from a blur of other good-time cantinas. The same folks drink big margaritas dispensed frozen from a large machine or mixed by hand if so specified. The chips and salsa are good but hardly special, at least until you figure out how to order the alternative salsas (verde, ranchero, asada, fresca) at the back of the menu.

The signs are there, however, that there is more to Azteca than meets you at the door. When was the last time you saw the word *posole* written on a slate? In Houston? In Mexico? There is green chili as well, offered on special, and carne guisada. Azteca Grill, owned by the same team as Sundown Café, is more casual, but just as fun as its illustrious offspring.

Posole, a magnificent one-pot meal based on hominy (hulled, dried corn) cooked with pork and ancho chile, first appeared on the menu around Christmastime one year. Back by popular demand, it has been delighting the connoisseurs, who plunge their spoons below the surface filmed with ancho oil in order to retrieve the swollen golden kernels of corn and the oinky morsels of meat.

Green chili, a comfort soup based on Anaheim peppers and smoked pork, slides creakily down your gullet. "Eddie's Special Turnip Greens" perked up with vinegar and hot peppers qualify more as a soup than a vegetable. Speaking of peppers, Eddie's chili features seven different ones, and the chile relleno is made with a mild poblano or, as a separate listing, an even milder Anaheim.

The menu encourages you to order the specials. Carne guisada (small, tender chunks of beef stewed with onions, black pepper, and chile peppers), for example, carries a great deal of authority. The first entrée on the menu, pollo loco, is every bit as encouraging, with two grilled chicken-breast cutlets resting, plump and juicy, on a bed of blanched tomatoes, diced banana peppers, and poblanos. The plate is further garnished with a chicken enchilada in lemon cream sauce and fresh yellow rice. Spicy charro beans and warm flour tortillas come on the side.

Chicken flautitas, chimichangas, and enchiladas do not disgrace the restaurant, but none of them will give you special access to the chef's mind. Sweet nachos, a dessert, have a trashy, trailer-park quality, topped with whipped cream and strawberries. Bread pudding numbs the tongue with its heat, and your taste buds won't recover in time to pick up an actual taste.

The restless floor plan, a gridlock of small gazebos, is canvassed by efficient waiters. So much is happening overhead (flaps of fabric, piñatas, and more) that you could get dizzy. Concentrate on the food.

★★ Azuni Grill $$ ⓧⓧ

4279 Roswell Rd. (in Chastain Square). Map H. (404) 255-5501.
Monday to Thursday 11 A.M. to 10 P.M. Friday 11 A.M. to 11 P.M. Saturday 5 to 11 P.M. No reservations. All major credit cards. Ample parking.

Instead of simply cloning their restaurants, the partners behind Azteca Grill, Sundown Café, and now Azuni Grill build interesting variations on the concept in order to suit the community in which they operate. More adventurous and gourmet oriented than Azteca, Azuni is a simplified as well as glamorized Sundown appealing to a different market in a larger facility.

The core dishes are the same at Azuni, with no difference in flavor or quality. Eddie's turnip greens are made according to the original recipe. The Waco chili, poblano corn chowder, and rancheros beans are all deliciously familiar. Azuni offers daily specials on a par with those of Sundown: shrimp cakes on chipotle cream sauce, bronzed salmon tostada with vegetables, a delicate seasonal New Mexican chile done relleno style with Colby and Monterey Jack and a crust of blue cornmeal, vegetable enchiladas trio.

The Southwestern meatloaf with ancho mashed potatoes on special at Sundown, easily one of the spiciest and best in the city, has made it onto the regular menu at Azuni. Ditto the chile en nogada, a *Like Water for Chocolate* inspired poblano stuffed with a light picadillo and served in a walnut cream sauce. The tortilla soup garnished with avocado is picture pretty and intensely flavorful.

From a fish taco with jalapeño tartar sauce and tilapia with citrus salsa over rice to chocolate chimichanga and creamy, cool nantilla topped with a dollop of caramel, a meal at Azuni is no letdown. One major shortcut, though, is in the salsa department. Instead of a choice of ten to twelve deliciously individual salsas on any given day like at Sundown, one (red and delightful) is offered to the Azuni clientele, as well as tricolor tortilla chips instead of the expected basket of blue and yellow corn tortillas.

On the other hand, the restaurant looks a hundred times better than Sundown. The language is clearly Southwestern. Not only can you enjoy a cleverly landscaped and lit patio with a poetic tin roof and a cactus garden, but the inside of the restaurant itself feels like the outdoors. Tender natural wood freshly stripped of its bark spans the large open space. The floor is natural Mexican tile. Clay pots hanging from ropes have been pressed into service as lampshades. Ristras of red chile peppers have been fastened on big wooden pegs protruding from walls of rough white stucco. There are beautiful shadows and no art whatsoever on the walls. The overall feel is dynamic and serene in equal proportions.

Azuni serves authentic little tacos and its full dinner menu at lunch, and the service remains upbeat.

★★ Babette's Café $$ ⓧⓧ

471 N. Highland Ave. (two blocks south of Ponce de Leon). Map C. (404) 523-9121.

Dinner Tuesday to Thursday and Sunday 6 to 10 P.M. Friday and Saturday 6 to 11 P.M. Brunch Sunday 11:30 A.M. to 4 P.M. No reservations. All major credit cards. Small, steep parking lot.

As far south on North Highland Avenue as you can go without crossing an invisible but significant border, restaurants have slowly displaced other commercial operations in a tiny strip serviced by its own barely adequate parking lot. Babette's Café is making the most of a charming intown renovation. It has the same kind of beautiful wooden floors, warm brick nicked by time, and clean and elegant look based on genuine materials as many of the surrounding Inman Park homes. A poetic idea was to hang old windows and weathered shutters on the walls instead of budget artwork. All are different but charmingly compatible down to their hints of window sills. White tablecloths and a staff in traditional café aprons add a touch of classicism to the simple scheme.

Chef-owner Marla Adams knows a thing or two about café operation and real cuisine. A veteran of the former Trio and Buckhead Diner, she chose something simple and personal for her first restaurant. Not all her ideas work well, but those that do are true charmers. Her bouillabaisse isn't orthodox. Her cassoulet lacks some of the grand complexity one would hope to find in a French cassoulet. Both dishes, however, taste remarkably good, much better, in fact, than the frequent anemic versions peddled in froufrou restaurants.

You will love the artichoke and black-olive ravioli in a Tuscan wine sauce and the cocktail-party-pretty fried oyster on a fresh small dill biscuit with spicy pepper jelly. Steamed mussels with a strawberry serrano sauce are daring and delicious. Comforting soups and pretty salads vary with the seasons.

Rustic tastes prevail as in a sensible navarin of lamb with baby vegetables, a grilled chicken with shoestring potatoes, or a stuffed pork chop smothered with sweet onion sauce. Vegetarians can look forward to risotto with artichokes and grilled vegetables. Everyone who loves dessert will be charmed by the elegant Mascarpone-filled crêpe with a simple brown-sugar glaze or the simpler strawberry shortcake and double chocolate cake. Babette's serves a few nice wines by the glass and the small wine list has been selected with care. The restaurant organizes quarterly feasts with a culinary theme.

★★★ Bacchanalia $$$ ⓧⓧ

3125 Piedmont Rd. (at Martina Dr.). Map B. (404) 365-0410.
Dinner only, Tuesday to Saturday 6 to 10. Reservations recommended. All major credit cards. Street parking.

The name evokes wild partying and immoderate drinking. But instead of flute-playing satyrs, it's cherubs you will see everywhere in this charming restaurant. If you lived in northern California, you would happen upon this kind of decor and cuisine in the most unexpected places. Some would be inns deep in the wine valleys, others restaurants worth a detour in the countryside.

Bacchanalia is a delicious eccentricity, a Victorian cottage that seems to have migrated from Inman Park to Buckhead. Some of the decorating has been done on a budget: gold-painted twigs and black velvet bows are used to hang inexpensive swags of muslin in the windows; many of the pictures on the walls are of sentimental little angels; there is a basket of apples on the front porch. Anne Quatrano and Clifford Harrison, both graduates of the California Culinary Academy in San Francisco, have also used some beautiful family antiques: Anne's grandmother's sofa made into a banquette; a pretty sideboard; old gilt-edged bone china.

The menu is a delight. The decisions are remarkably fresh. The formula, two prix-fixe menus, gives everyone a chance to taste a big range of flavors.

From one week to the next, the dishes change significantly. The salmon offered Mediterranean style over couscous has become lighter and, if possible, purer, seasoned with fresh cucumber juice and a julienne of cucumbers. Braised oxtail in red wine sauce has replaced Moroccan lamb shanks with dried fruit. The roasted monkfish with fried leeks has turned into an appetizer. Gone are the grilled oysters in pancetta but Texas white prawns are on the menu with salsa verde and grilled red onions. Hallelujah, the warm potato and Georgia goat-cheese terrine with mesclun greens is here to be tried again!

What you can count on is creativity: pear vinaigrette, porcini syrup, wheatberry salad, barley, and white bean purée assert their wonderful presence in unexpected dishes. A preappetizer bite may be a perfect shrimp over aioli or a sliver of rare seared tuna with a dollop of seasoned mustard. Fresh country bread meted out one slice at a time comes with a big pat of sweet butter.

The first course can be a risotto with sun-dried tomatoes, a salad with Stilton and pear, or a small plate of sweetbreads with shiitake mushrooms. You can go light with the entrées or wallow in wonderfully rustic tastes such as rabbit loin with parsley and trumpet mushrooms or oxtail in red wine over perciatelli (fresh macaroni).

Desserts are wonderful. There is usually a cheese on the list and you may elect it as an extra course, thus meeting a perfect Stilton with walnuts and mission figs or a warm Brie with honey and strawberries before sinking your fork into the desserts.

Pristine sorbets (blackberry, white pear, tangerine, to name a few) will refresh your palate but you may want the comfort of an old-fashioned but unusually light strawberry-rhubarb cobbler, a lemon chess pie with candied zest, or a warm banana betty with Chantilly cream. Spiced green-apple soup or warm date tart with shaved reggiano Parmesan will be next on your list of "must try."

The restaurant is serious about its wines: many of the bottles come from unusual California boutique wineries; delicious dessert wines have a menu of their own.

★ Baker's Café $ ⊗

1126 Euclid Ave. (in Little Five Points). Map E. (404) 223-5039.
Lunch Tuesday to Friday 11 A.M. to 2:30 P.M. Dinner Tuesday to Thursday 5:30 to 9 P.M., Friday and Saturday 5:30 to 10 P.M. Breakfast/brunch Saturday and Sunday 9 A.M. to 2:30 P.M. No reservations. V, MC. Street parking or lots nearby.

Moving a restaurant a few doors down the street isn't usually an especially big deal from the consumer's point of view but in the case of Baker's Café, there is an obvious difference between being one of many storefronts in a row and occupying a snug little building of one's own. Cheerful eccentricity has taken over the former Roger's, where blue-collar cuisine and baseball cards coexisted with religious proselytism. Baker's Café (formerly Baker's Deli), known for years for its jazzy New Orleans brunch, its sandwiches, and its sprinkling of Cajun style, has held on to the best of its predecessor: traditional breakfasts with biscuits and gravy, now served weekends only.

Everything seems to taste better under the garlands of lights burning against a black ceiling like stars in a pretty night. Someone went through the brightest paint chips to select half a dozen colors to repaint the wooden chairs. Old creaky banquettes hide under fresh and funky vinyl. The building itself has been repainted an outrageous shade of purple. The menus are in artist-built boxes with glued-on Mardi Gras beads and assorted trashy knickknacks. Instead of service by people who look as though they slept in a coffin, pony-tailed dudes move

★ Basil's $$ ⊗

2985 Grandview Ave. (at Pharr Rd.). Map B. (404) 233-9755.
Lunch Monday to Saturday 11:30 A.M. to 2:30 P.M. Dinner Monday to Thursday 6 to 10 P.M., Friday and Saturday 6 to 11 P.M. Reservations and all major credit cards accepted. Small awkward parking lot.

Long on charm and sometimes short on authenticity, Basil's is an informal Buckhead hangout. Transformed with muted pinks and rich teals, cheerful trompe l'oeil windows, and faux landscapes to open up the space, the converted little house has become a credible Mediterranean café. In fair weather, the long and skinny wooden deck seats a good crowd of sun worshippers. The music is Middle Eastern and sexy.

Particularly marvelous are the Lebanese appetizers: hummus, baba ghannoug, tabbouleh, stuffed grape leaves served with wedges of pita bread. The Mediterranean tuna salad with lemon, olive oil, and fresh cilantro and the falafel sandwich are also winners.

The entrées have improved greatly and, although they still seem expensive in comparison with the appetizers, one can appreciate the efforts of the kitchen. Pretty sauces are drizzled on and around items such as grilled sea bass or a Mediterranean mixed grill presented over couscous. The garnishes keep up with new trends (big pearls of couscous instead of the regular small-grained semolina, grilled Italian eggplant, caramelized shallots) and the plates feel substantial. The fish is still too firm; a fancy veal dish chewy enough to be unpleasant. The desserts are good: light, crisp baklava with pistachios and honeyed pastries filled with walnuts end the meal on a strong authentic note.

The owners are suave and well connected to the restaurant community. Basil's clientele, older and more polished than that of the surrounding Buckhead bars, appreciates the atmosphere as much as the food.

★ Beautiful $

397 Auburn Ave. (at Jackson St., opposite Ebenezer Baptist Church). Map A. 223-0080. Other locations.
   Daily 7 A.M. to 8:30 P.M. No reservations or credit cards. Small parking lot.

Beautiful is a misnomer. This chain of soul-food cafeterias operated by the modestly named Perfect Church serves good biscuits, Southern-style vegetables stewed with fatback, lean and tasty oxtails, various versions of chicken, and garish cakes, all in a strictly functional environment. Service is restricted to a cafeteria line, and the manner of the servers is reserved, correct, impassive.

The menu changes daily, but you can often count on finding ribs, baked chicken with dressing, and six or so vegetable choices, including some of the best collard greens in town, their naturally bitter flavor a faint undertaste in the tender, sweet leaves. The corn muffins are well flavored and textured. The biscuits are tight and crusty, with a pleasant taste of darkly baked flour. Sweet potato pie and cakes, including red velvet and various chocolate and cream confections, aren't as dependable as the banana pudding under an abundance of vanilla wafers. For any meal here, come early for the best flavors, before food dries out.

☆ Bertolini's $$ ⓧ

3500 Peachtree Rd. (in Phipps Plaza). Map B. (404) 233-2333.
   Monday to Thursday 11:30 A.M. to 10 P.M. Friday and Saturday 11:30 A.M. to midnight. Sunday 11 A.M. to 10 P.M. Reservations and all major credit cards accepted. Valet parking available.

The amazing thing about Bertolini's is how little time it took to turn a beautiful, elegant room (the former Caffe Donatello) into something far more trivial. It was just enough time to dismantle the pretty food counter, roll out a grey carpet over a beautiful if noisy floor, and substitute a cartoonish mural for the formerly distinguished scene hanging upon the back wall. Columns have a new striped look. Granita machines with plastic covers churn their contents near the bar. The waiters write their names in crayon on white paper stretched over tables.

Though far from memorable, both the carpaccio of beef with capers and shaved Parmesan and the angel-hair pasta with tomato, basil, and garlic could be useful in the context of Phipps Plaza if one desired a light collation with a glass of good Chianti. But who wants pasta drowning in cream and Caesar salad drenched in thick dressing? Taglioni al limone con pollo features strips of grilled chicken breast in a mess of ribbon pasta trapped in cream sauce flavored by lemon zest. Cream is again the guilty party in a fazzoletto con funghi described as a handkerchief of fresh pasta with spinach, ricotta cheese, and wild mushrooms that don't taste wild. It is even more inexcusable in a heavy-handed version of spaghetti carbonara with pancetta, green peas, and fresh tomatoes.

The dressing seems to have been applied with a trowel to the spears of fresh romaine in a mediocre Caesar but the fresh insalata mista with aged balsamic vinegar and olive oil is a pleasure. If one could get better fried calamari on top of a delicious chilled tomato caper dipping sauce or order a pizzetta that didn't taste of acrid garlic and salty Parmesan, one would feel better about this newcomer out of Las Vegas. The servers are very friendly even when the management shows signs of stress.

★★★ Bien Thuy $

5095 Buford Hwy. (2 miles south of I-285 in Northwood Plaza). Map D. (770) 454-9046.

Sunday to Thursday 10 A.M. to 10 P.M. Friday and Saturday 10 A.M. to 1 A.M. No reservations or credit cards. Parking lot in front.

This is a prototypical hole-in-the-wall that transcends its decor and serves some of the best ethnic food in the city. A first glance conjures up little to suggest fine dining in this poorly lit, hazy-with-smoke Vietnamese café at the end of a strip shopping center. An almost exclusively Asian crowd occupies the basic utilitarian furniture, booths as well as tables and chairs. A bamboo awning and a constant string of Vietnamese music supply the exotic feel.

Bien Thuy is widely acknowledged as the city's best authentic Vietnamese restaurant, with a menu full of endless delights. The cha gio, Vietnamese spring rolls served with a platter of lettuce leaves and fresh herbs, are the best you can dunk in a clear bowl of nuoc man (a fermented fish sauce with an unusually delicate taste).

Once you have dipped your spoon into one of the soups, you will be hooked on the gentle, wholesome flavors of Vietnamese cuisine. Soups are served in large bowls and may contain an amazing number of ingredients from pâté to quail egg, crisped bits of pork, sliced meat, and fresh vegetables. Purple basil, mint, and bean sprouts are provided on the side to enhance further the fresh taste of the broth. The Hu Thieu soup, a typical Saigon offering, is particularly good, rich in glass noodles and attractive tidbits.

Crisp Vietnamese pancakes filled with sprouts, jellyfish salad with pork and shrimp, grilled marinated pork chops on rice, lemon grass and chile chicken, and the milder ginger chicken on rice are all delicious. The bun dishes, marinated grilled items over long and tender noodles, are spectacularly good.

The owner, a busy, friendly woman who came to the U.S. as a war bride, is good at establishing communication. Regular customers become privy to wonderful specials such as a platter of fabulous scallops or a Vietnamese beef fondue based on coconut soda and served in several courses.

Bien Thuy is a good spot for lunch. If you are in the mood for unusual sandwiches, the French-style combinations of sliced meats (including pig ears) in buttered French rolls are wonderful.

★★ Bistango $$$ ✘✘

1100 Peachtree St. (at 11th St.). Map C. (404) 724-0901.
 Lunch Monday to Friday 11:30 A.M. to 2:30 P.M. Dinner Monday to Saturday 5:30 to 10 P.M. Reservations and all major credit cards accepted. Valet parking.

If there is one thing chef Thomas Coohill knows how to do it is pick good names for his restaurants. Ciboulette and now Bistango (French slang for bistro) sound immediately appealing. How does one live up to a name like Bistango? Redecorated rather than remodeled, Bistango is warmer than its predecessor, the staunchly unlovable Bice.

Gone is the atrocious plaid carpet, replaced by something suitably neutral. A long row of colorful new Tiffany-style chandeliers transforms the narrow corridor between bar and dining room into a visually exciting pathway. A gigantic version of the same light fixtures dangles ominously from the central cupola, a feature that both draws attention to and compensates for what has always been the dining room's main architectural flaw.

If you are looking for glamor, go no farther than the bar. With its handsome proportions, satiny glow of precious wood, and posh furniture, Bistango's front room is one of the most sophisticated cocktail lounges in town. The dining room, on the other hand, feels dull and dutiful. The tables grouped at the center of the restaurant are particularly poorly lit, so that anyone seated there takes on a desolate complexion.

Bistango has an unstable culinary identity. You can eat some wonderful things: a warm vegetable terrine with a light gloss of olive oil and an entrancing flavor of freshly grilled Mediterranean vegetables; a pretty seared beef carpaccio with a garlic-scented wild mushroom salad; a roasted eggplant and yellow tomato soup; a lively citrus fettuccine with coins of fresh scallops; a terrific grilled pork chop stuffed with oven-dried tomatoes, spinach, and Spanish cheese; a bistro-style roasted codfish on soft polenta garnished with fresh tomato compote.

But there are many flaws as well. Chilled may not be the ideal temperature for a salad of grilled vegetables with lumpy couscous and muscular may not be the appropriate texture for an otherwise tasty lamb ossobucco with polenta. The ceviche of scallops and sea bass is an unpleasant affair more along the line of a tartar with a slimy mouth-feel. Parma ham served with an arugula salad loses some of its elegance in the slicing. Paella, meant as signature dish for the kitchen, is a major disappointment, with wet rice and no taste of olive oil or saffron.

The pastry chef is marvelous. The macadamia-nut tart with buttermilk ice cream, honey sauce, and fresh berries is prizewinning material. An ephemeral napoleon, triangles of impossibly crisp dough, cassis crème fraîche, berries poached in their own juice, is among the prettiest things you'll ever see. Fresh cannelloni filled with raspberry mousse, beautifully burnished orange crème brûlée, exquisite homemade ice cream (buttermilk lemon or burnt honey tops) and fruit sorbets are all in a day's work. The dining-room crew goes about its duties in a lively, friendly manner, the beginners paired with more experienced colleagues, servicing a clientele that suggests more business than romance.

★★★ The Bistro at Andrews Square $$ ⊗⊗

56 E. Andrews Square. Map B. (404) 231-5733.
Dinner only, Tuesday to Saturday 6 to 10 P.M. Reservations and all major credit cards accepted. Large parking lot.

Where did this frequently overlooked Gallic bistro come from? Chef-owner Jim Brown lived (and cooked) for ten years in Paris. His partner, Gary Siegler, owns Buckhead Fine Wines. You don't have to dress and you don't have to fear. The marriage of good food and fine wines takes place in a relaxed atmosphere. The decor is timeless: pleasant warm neutrals, white tablecloths, a sophisticated bar visible from both ends of the *L*-shaped dining room. The staff knows its trade but no one will bore you with details or invade your comfort zone. There are no big French words on the menu. The expensive wines are worth their small mark-up and you will find some reasonable bargains as well, especially if you know your French reds.

The menu fits neatly on one side of a sheet of paper: six appetizers, eight entrées, two salads, and a few desserts. Carpaccio of beef with shavings of aged Parmesan weighs next to nothing but makes a big impression. Carpaccio of salmon garnished with smoked salmon is even lighter and smoother. You will have a near-sushi experience with pearly scallops sautéed with fresh herbs. Mussels in a Sicilian tomato broth couldn't be cleaner, nicer, or more delicious. Oyster stew with tiny cubes of celery and green onions is the kind of mild, milky, and fresh dish one associates with the holidays. Lightly sautéed foie gras imbibes a warm vinaigrette mixed with a deep reduction of raspberries.

A salad of mixed curly endive and tender lettuce with Roquefort, walnuts, and crisp tiny lardons (matchsticks of smoked bacon) is ineffably French. Snow-white sea bass balanced on asparagus spears or, on other evenings, equally delicious halibut are the picture of simplicity. Grilled lamb chops are exceptionally large and tender and you'll swear they are still hissing from their encounter with the grill. A massive veal chop submitted to the same treatment cuts like a charm, each silky slice ready to be swirled in an intense red-wine sauce. Two small salmon steaks are like apostrophes framing a perfect béarnaise.

Warm chocolate-mousse cake baked in an individual round mold is a thing of beauty: lightly crusted over, meltingly tender, and hiding a delicious cache of vanilla ice cream. Thin strips of apple tart are classic French treats. The tarte Tatin, much thicker and cakier and with thick slices of apple embedded in its dough, is vastly different but equally authentic.

★★★ Blue Ridge Grill $$$ ✕✕✕

1261 W. Paces Ferry Rd. (at Northside Pkwy.). Map B. (404) 233-5030.

Lunch daily 11:30 A.M. to 3 P.M. Dinner nightly 5:30 to 11. Brunch Saturday and Sunday 11:30 A.M. to 3 P.M. Limited reservations. All major credit cards. Valet parking.

Bone's meets Kudzu Café in a posh mountain resort. Such is the corporate vision for this substantial new restaurant, a well-researched, well-built, ruggedly handsome addition to the family of Susan DeRose and Richard Lewis, who have grown increasingly serious about showing their Southern roots.

The inner architecture is particularly impressive. One walks into a spacious, rambling mountain lodge, a place of beautiful timber and mortared stone pillars with sharply peaked ceilings.

An enclosed sun porch catches the overflow of the bar. There are roomy booths and all sorts of comfortable furniture, including some beautiful antiques.

The muted leopard-print carpeting, the heavy horse blankets suspended from overhead beams, the canoes under the eaves, the imposing fireplace above which hangs the oil portrait of a gentleman rabbit depicted as a hunter with a gun convey a Ralph Lauren feeling of wealth and gentility. The staff, partially culled from Bone's and Kudzu, wear their names embroidered on the pocket of their old-fashioned burgundy smocks.

Entrées typically come with a couple of fresh vegetables served the old-fashioned family way in rustic bowls meant for passing around, and a homemade spicy peach chutney. You can expect a great deal of sophistication, though: chiffonade of Brussels sprouts with smoked almond butter, corn pudding with okra and lime sauce, hominy au gratin, collards with honey-roasted pecan butter. The vegetables come à la carte as well.

The skillful blending of old traditions and new ideas is impressive. Spicy BBQ fried oysters come with a suave wild-mushroom bread pudding. Pretty little sweet potato and crabmeat fritters have their own Asian dipping sauce. A delicate wood-grilled quail stuffed with pecan-apple spoon bread seems to have landed, crackling and brown, on a thicket of greens. Vegetarians and light eaters concur that the skewered grilled vegetables over wild-mushroom barley are one of the most decorative and best dishes on the menu.

Other things to like include fried calamari with Vidalia-onion tartar sauce, chicken and sweet potato dumplings, pan-seared sea bass in a girdle of tasty ham, and smoked-trout crab cakes over creamed leeks. More mainstream eaters or people with a yen for some specialties closer to Bone's will trust the steaks (strip, filet mignon, or aged ribeye served with onion rings) and the salmon steak with corn relish.

The desserts carry the same weight as the rest of the menu. Most are spectacular in a gentle, old-fashioned way. The buttermilk lemon pie, blackberry crisp à la mode, caramel-pear bread pudding, and big sassafras float with homemade molasses cookies are too good to miss. There is a serious wine list and serious drinks.

★★★ Bone's $$$$ ⓧⓧ

3130 Piedmont Rd. (south of Peachtree). Map B. (404) 237-2663.
Lunch Monday to Friday 11:30 A.M. to 2:30 P.M. Dinner nightly 6 to 10:45 (Saturday till 11:45). Reservations recommended. All major credit cards. Valet parking.

Top-of-the-line chain steak operations out of Chicago and New Orleans have moved into Atlanta but they haven't displaced Richard Lewis's and Susan DeRose's homegrown version of a classic steakhouse as the local favorite. Bone's is a place for big spenders: advertisement dictators who shape our buying habits, entertainers and the media persons who make them known to us, people who make a million a year selling Cadillacs or real estate. If you think you are a personality, or want to be one or see one, you go to Bone's. If you are timid or romantic, you go someplace else.

Bone's is basically an upstairs and a downstairs, with tables and chairs and aisles—nothing ostentatious. The floors are bare, the walls covered with black-and-white photos of Atlanta street scenes and caricatures of local personalities. Compared to other rich men's haunts, Bone's is intensely comfortable. There has never been a dress code. As long as you bring the money, you can wear blue jeans without shame.

The waiters wear short buff jackets and move about the crowded dining rooms like skilled foremen in a model factory. There is no unnecessary chitchat, no calling attention to themselves, none of that maddening "I'm uncorking your wine now" routine.

If you're going to pay a lot for a T-bone (priced according to size—and who would order a tiny one?), it better be good. And it is. The formidable steak knife cuts smoothly through the well-seared surface of the meat. Little rivulets of blood spring from the fresh cut. The New York strip and the filet are juicy red, too. If requested medium-rare, the veal chop (two and a half inches thick) comes with a promising lightly charred outside and a blushing pink core, moist and buttery. The appetizers, soups, salads, vegetable side dishes (*everything* must be ordered à la carte), desserts, and other dispensable items are ruinously expensive.

Bone's has grown deep roots into Atlanta. Chef Greg Gamage has refined the menu and added many regional Southern touches such as grits fritters and an elegant black-eyed pea soup with a relish of fresh peppers. There are some good desserts on the menu. A perfectly balanced pecan pie (not too sweet, not too gooey, not too caramelized) is served plain or à la mode. The chiffon cheesecake (lime zest and a bed of mandarin-orange coulis) is definitely Southern in its lightness and sweetness.

The new wine gallery is an ideal spot for the wine hobbyists and those in need of privacy. There is an enormous inventory (ten or eleven thousand bottles) and the staff is educated about the selections.

★★★ Brasserie Le Coze $$$ ⓧⓧⓧ

3393 Peachtree Rd. (in Lenox Square near Neiman-Marcus). Map B. (404) 266-1440.
 Monday to Friday 11:30 A.M. to 10:30 P.M. Saturday 11:30 A.M. to 11 P.M. Reservations and all major credit cards accepted. Valet parking available.

Grafting, a horticultural trick that forces a host plant to accept and nurture the full genetic material of another one, seems to be the only way a miracle like Brasserie Le Coze could have happened in Atlanta. There isn't—there has never been—anything more authentically French than this impeccable new restaurant.

Inspired by such traditional turn-of-the-century establishments as the famous Brasserie Lipp in Paris, Brasserie Le Coze is good taste incarnate. It is also related to the immensely famous Le Bernardin in New York, operated by the formidably charming Maguy Le Coze.

Brasserie Le Coze is an exceedingly pretty restaurant without a trace of ostentation. The dining room, with beautiful hand-painted tiles and mirrors on the walls, comes right out of Paris. The posh banquettes, the sconces, the staff in traditional vests and aprons, the rigorously symmetrical ferns—all fit the same perfect picture. The lighting underlines the classicism of the scenery.

The food is as classic and impeccable as the decor. For appetizers you can't go wrong with the following: suave mussels marinière in a creamy wine broth with fresh parsley; unctuous duck rillettes on toast with cornichons; puréed white-bean soup fragrant with white truffle oil; salade gourmande with baby greens, foie gras mousse, and sliced smoked duck breast. A special features a variation on the salade gourmande with tiny slices of poached skate fanned out over a mixture of baby greens.

Skate in brown butter is the kind of simple dish that will tolerate no mistake whatsoever. Brasserie Le Coze's is absolutely perfect, served in a state of total relaxation with plain poached potatoes. A pavé of cod with leeks and beurre rouge and a rosefish served bouillabaisse style are two other signature dishes for the restaurant. Only God, the chef, and Mademoiselle Le Coze know how much excellent red wine goes into the coq au vin and how long it takes to reduce it to the ultimate state of intensity. You only know that this is the best coq au vin you can remember ever having eaten, baby onions, small potatoes, tender fowl, sauce, and all.

The season for choucroute is probably short in the muggy South, but any cool spell supplies the perfect excuse for a glorious plate of golden, long-stranded sauerkraut cooked in wine, topped with an assortment of proud sausages (one of them white and veal) and smoked pork served with a crock of strong mustard.

The desserts by Frederic Monti are flawless as well: warm chocolate soufflé cake with a secret core of melted dark chocolate; sugar-glazed wafers balanced on ice cream; classic crème brûlée; mille feuille built of immaterial layers; richly caramelized apple tarte Tatin; and the show-stopper, a charming vacherin with walls of angelic meringue, filled with ice cream to the brim, set on a gentle sauce of tropical fruit.

Brasserie Le Coze has a lunch menu where traditional baguette sandwiches and hachis Parmentier (a French version of shepherd's pie) join most of the dinner specialties. One can also snack at the bar with pommes frites, cheese allumettes, or tiny warm profiteroles filled with a cheese béchamel. The small café corner with a view of the mall's high and low life serves a limited menu including most of the lunch specialties and all the marvelous desserts. Twenty or so wines by the glass are available. The Brasserie has a direct entrance from the parking lot and a pretty terrace open in fair weather.

★★ Break Away Café $ ⊗

6405 Peachtree Industrial Blvd. (at Jimmy Carter Blvd., Norcross). Map I. (770) 242-5817.
Monday to Thursday 7 A.M. to 3 P.M. Friday 7 A.M. to 9 P.M. Saturday 8 A.M. to 9 P.M. Sunday 8 A.M. to 3 P.M. No reservations. All major credit cards. Adequate parking.

You, the customer, are the one getting all the breaks in this nontraditional café halfway between a diner and a deli, with a touch of espresso bar. Breaking away from all stereotypes, the business explores interesting alleys. Egg creams and phosphates fizz from an old-fashioned fountain but the kitchen, which cooks its own corned beef, also offers one of the greatest veggie burgers available in the city. All pasta is made daily on premises.

Although the architecture of the building is ordinary in a short row of stores, the room is funny, original, and terrifically bright. The soda counter is marble and twice the usual width. From the stools (bigger and plumper than most) to the glassware and all the equipment (the best espresso machine in the business), everything shows an unusual commitment to good, functional design.

Break Away Café feels modest yet exuberant and definitely up-to-date. The kitchen is fashionably on display. Your first impulse will probably be to order fresh pasta and one bubbling sauce or another. The options are limited: homemade lasagna, radiatori with pesto sauce, spicy shrimp marinara over linguine, an excellent meat sauce served on fettuccine. Vegetables may extend the pesto sauce. The staff offers freshly grated Parmesan just like in the expensive restaurants. The flavor of the pesto is questionably musty and the pasta isn't always well cooked but more often than not the experience is comforting.

Other plain good dishes include baked-potato soup with bacon; flavorful hamburger in an onion roll; home-style corned beef sandwich with tangy, thick slices snugly fitted between good rye bread; and an excellent veggie burger that will remind you of meatloaf in tomato sauce. Break Away Café bakes its own plain and fancy croissants. The ice cream (Greenwood's fanciest grade) is a wonderful treat. Straight-arrow folks will do extremely well with the light, sweet cheesecakes or a fresh, crumbly apple spice cake with light caramel sauce.

★ The Brickery $ ⊗

6125 Roswell Rd. Map H. (404) 843-8002.
Monday to Thursday 11:15 A.M. to 9:30 P.M. Friday and Saturday 11:15 A.M. to 11 P.M. Sunday noon to 9:30 P.M. Reservations not accepted. V, MC, AE. Adequate parking lot.

The scene is suburbia, a skip and a jump from the fancy Northside neighborhoods. The design has the soothing quality found in resorts coast to coast. Massive old beams, weathered paneling, rough floors, and breezy peppermint-striped curtains give an air of charming respectability to the dining room. Heavily mortared, stacked into free-standing walls, bricks are everywhere. Clever accents involve the use of blinds to create the illusion of windows, wooden gateways separating one dining room from its nonsmoking counterpart, and a bright mosaic of ceramic tiles used as a bar top.

The menu is a compendium of foods America likes. There are chicken wings, chips with salsa, chicken tenders, hamburgers, big fresh salads, a decent steak, fresh fish grilled or blackened, prime rib served as a dinner or a sandwich, and many other easy options.

An excellent fresh hamburger stuffed in a tender bun and a lavish Ashford Salad (thickly sliced fresh mushrooms, artichoke hearts, alfalfa sprouts, big rings of bell pepper, homemade croutons, and a bit of grated cheddar scattered on fresh greens in a deep white plate) are truly outstanding in their simplicity. The dilled shrimp (an appetizer), chargrilled salmon (an excellent value), and prime-rib sandwich give honest answers to the "what's good to eat?" question.

Broccoli casserole, often a textureless staple, is a winner among the side dishes, made with big chunks of broccoli tossed in a mushroom and sour-cream sauce. The coleslaw is fresh and crisp with a hint of sweetness and no mayonnaise. French fries vary considerably but you don't have to accept a stale batch. Luchen kugel, a hearty, sweet noodle casserole with raisins, is an excellent filler on its own or as part of a brisket platter.

Be sure to avoid the chicken wings (gunked with sauce) and baby-back ribs. Once you get used to the soft texture of the apple streusel (made with excellent Granny Smiths) you will become addicted to it.

★ Bridgetown Grill $ ⊗

1156 Euclid Ave. (at Moreland Ave.). Map E. (404) 653-0110. Other locations in Midtown and Sandy Springs.
    Sunday to Thursday 11:30 A.M. to 10:30 P.M. Friday and Saturday 11 A.M. to 11:30 P.M. No reservations. V, MC, AE. Difficult parking in crowded lot or surrounding streets.

Reggae lulls you into a hypnotic stance while the surrounding colors aggressively demand that you stay awake. Thin metal cut-outs, many of them fish, float on tropical-hued bricks. Bright white plank booths establish a perpendicular pattern in the narrow space. Like the light at the end of the tunnel, a hotly painted patio pulsates in the distance.

More of a good-time restaurant than an ethnic gem, Bridgetown's concept revolves around island cuisine: jerk pork, jerk chicken, jerk seafood with a few patties and skewers for good measure, and hot chicken wings for fun. Rubbed and/or marinated with a blend of hot spices, most food finds its way to the grill. Everything is served on big plates lavishly garnished with rice, beans, and spicy cucumber salad. There is a little dish of dipping sauce as well, usually a thinned-out fruit glaze such as raspberry-tamarind or passion fruit and pineapple.

Eating a basket of jerk chicken wings may be a socially embarrassing performance (grease up to your elbows, bits of charred skin between your teeth), but you'll atone later. Pull the darn things apart, put fingerprints all over your bottle of Jamaican beer, and enjoy the yummy fun. If you need an appetizer or a light entrée, patties are the ticket. Flaky yellowish turnovers come in two varieties: all-vegetable filling (mostly thinly sliced cabbage) and ground meat. Both are spicy and can be combined with rice, beans, and salad.

The concept, bought from the original creators, is expanding. Locations have opened in Midtown and Sandy Springs. Quality has been somewhat shaky but the atmosphere is a big draw.

★★ The Brooklyn Café $$ ⊗⊗

220 Sandy Springs Cir. (off Hammond Dr., 1 mile outside I-285, Sandy Springs). Map H. (404) 843-8377.
 Lunch Monday to Friday 11:30 A.M. to 2:30 P.M. Dinner Sunday to Thursday 5:30 to 10:30 P.M., Friday and Saturday 5:30 to 11 P.M. Brunch Sunday 11:30 A.M. to 3 P.M. No reservations. All major credit cards. Large parking lot.

Nothing in Atlanta can quite match the Brooklyn experience. The strong Italian presence, the ethnic diversity, the funky chic of being in sight of Manhattan, the culture that binds, all are alien to Sandy Springs. Where a weaker restaurant might not have gotten its point across, Brooklyn Café forwards the cause of individuality. The restaurant is oddly shaped with two branches of unequal length meeting at a centrally located bar built as an extension of the open kitchen.

A thin and misty mural of the Brooklyn Bridge spans the entire back wall. Lights from the parking lot intrude into the dining room but even they make you feel connected to a city. The atmosphere is that of a busy intown café: bare checkerboard floor, a total absence of pretension in the details, a happy brouhaha spreading from table to table.

It's wise to adopt a relaxed grazing policy. Order as many small samples as possible (half-orders of pasta, sides of vegetables requested without their entrées, big salads to pass around, lots of country Italian bread to dip in olive oil mixed with freshly grated Parmesan and coarse pepper). Choose from the following with confidence: an enormous portobello mushroom sautéed with roasted garlic, fresh rosemary, and balsamic vinegar; Caesar salad served in a Parmesan-cheese basket; homemade mozzarella rolled with salami, mortadella, and roasted red pepper and served in thin slices over an abundance of baby lettuces; calamari fried or sautéed with artichokes, lemon, and oregano.

Buccatini (macaroni thickness, no hole) with pancetta, chile peppers, and tomatoes may well be the ultimate sensible pasta in the restaurant. Also good are a simple dish of penne (quill shaped) aglio e olio, a fabulous linguine with white-pepper cilantro clam sauce, and firm gnocchi with chive and natural tomato jus. Shrimp sautéed with portobello mushrooms, prosciutto, and port wine, a little heavy compared to the preceding dishes, mix deliciously with linguine and shoestring vegetables. Entrées and pasta look splendid in oversize, deep plates with broad rims.

Desserts have improved steadily and lunch is an excellent value. With several Chiantis by the glass, all of them frisky and delicious, and cups of strong coffee, you can still manage to spend a very reasonable amount of money for food you could recommend to any of your friends.

★★★ Buckhead Diner $$ ⊗⊗⊗

3073 Piedmont Rd. (at E. Paces Ferry Rd.). Map B. (404) 262-3336. Monday to Saturday 11 A.M. to midnight. Sunday 10 A.M. to 10 P.M. No reservations. All major credit cards. Valet parking.

A million-dollar restaurant combining glamor, star appeal, and marvelous food at an affordable price, Buckhead Diner is the Buckhead Life Restaurant Group's greatest triumph to date. The rooms of this fantasy interior by Patrick Kuleto (creator of the Fog City Diner in San Francisco) are all shaped like luxurious railroad dining cars, with curved ceilings and plump, wide banquettes.

Impeccable waiters tread on opulent carpet. Heavy silverplate gleams on the tables. Sconces shaped like fancy tail lights and ceiling fixtures that resemble Art Deco brooches cast a sensual glow reflected by panels of ribbed, frosted glass between the dining booths. Bird's-eye maple, cherry, mahogany, and some delicate ebony inlays are used in oversize booths that recall the Orient Express. The neon stripes around the shiny facade are custom colored. The massive chrome doors cost a king's ransom.

The luxurious environment invites expectations that culinary refinements will be part of the package. You will not be disappointed with a fun, contemporary menu that starts with great little snacks (shrimp wontons in lobster ginger sauce, homemade potato chips with Maytag blue cheese, steamed Louisiana oysters with leek fondue, crispy calamari hotly flavored with jalapeño pepper) and moves right on to more serious items.

Two thick smoked pork chops, grilled and garnished with Swiss chard, polenta, and cranberry chutney, make a splendid, filling meal. The veal meatloaf with celery mashed potatoes is a cult item. You'll love the warm goat cheese salad with pencil asparagus and roasted pine nut dressing and the crisped softshell crabs over mixed greens. The open-face grilled salmon B.L.T. with tarragon mayonnaise is the best sandwich.

Among desserts, homemade ice cream, tarte Tatin, and a banana cream pie made with sliced bananas and curls of white chocolate are pure heaven. More wines are available by the glass than in the other restaurants under the same management. A flute of champagne would be appropriate to toast the gorgeous decor. Celebrities are an everyday happening in a place that remains on everyone's "must" list.

★★ Buford Tea House $ ⊗

5150 Buford Hwy. (1 mile inside I-285 in Asian Square). Map D. (770) 458-1818.
 Tuesday to Thursday 11 A.M. to 9 P.M. Friday to Sunday 11 A.M. to 10 P.M. No reservations. V, MC, AE. Ample parking.

Amy Tan would be right at home in this very special Asian teahouse. The famous author of *The Joy Luck Club* and *The*

Kitchen God's Wife would certainly cause a sensation, but she could quickly find her place among the bright and talented women who gather at the new Buford Tea House to talk about life, their music studies, their yoga lessons, and their writings.

You will be charmed by the atmosphere, entranced by the music (regular performances on Friday, Saturday, and Sunday; impromptu playing on weeknights), and may even learn to drink unstrained chrysanthemum tea. Buford Tea House has a wonderfully unusual menu: special teas (some of them medicinal) served in covered mugs, refined little snacks, and a growing list of specialties from various regions of Asia.

Don't be surprised if your waitress goes up on stage to play the pipa (a Chinese lute) or if a very dignified customer turns out to be one of the evening's stars, coaxing eerie and melodious sounds from a one-stringed instrument played with a bow. The owner of the restaurant trades her sporty clothes for a beautiful yellow silk gown and sits at the zi'n, a long horizontal string instrument played with little metal spikes taped to her slender fingers. At once ethereal and decisive, she is clearly worshipped by the audience.

★★ Burton's Grill $

1029 Edgewood Ave. (at Hurt St. opposite Inman Park MARTA station). Map E. (404) 658-9452.

> *Monday to Friday 7 A.M. to 4 P.M. No reservations or credit cards. Street parking only, sometimes difficult.*

Deacon Burton, the affable chef and owner of this soul-food institution open since the early sixties, defined the standards for fried chicken. Mr. Burton's passing away is a sore loss for the city but while the surrounding neighborhood gets glossier and flossier all the time, Burton's retains a no-frills, no-nonsense authenticity.

At lunch, three-piece-suited lawyers wait patiently beside uniformed sanitation workers in the cafeteria line that snakes among the tables, proving that the search for superb food value knows no class or income limitation. Generous platters of a meat, two vegetables, and dessert for lunch, or two eggs, grits, a meat, and biscuits for breakfast are priced lower than low. Good, natural, sweet iced tea and decent coffee are also bargains, with unlimited refills.

The food is as uncompromising in its ethnic assertiveness as the decor is spare. Patrons afraid to try the salt-encrusted fried fatback served as bacon or the thick and fatty sausage links should spring for Deacon Burton's classic fried chicken, available at breakfast as well as lunch. The secret of the latter is frying the bird in a cast-iron skillet on top of the stove, not in some industrial vat. The skin gets crisp, not greasy, while the meat stays moist and tender.

At lunch, chicken and dumplings, stew meat, or more exotic cuts and innards may also be offered. Don't miss the ham if given the choice—lean, succulent, not overly salty. For vegetables, stick to sound soul-food staples like collard greens rather than such items as creamed corn, likely to be canned. Biscuits, cornbread, pound cake, and cobblers are all honest and direct.

★★ The Cabin $$ ⊗⊗

2678 Buford Hwy. (near N. Druid Hills Rd.). Map D. (404) 315-7676.

Lunch Monday to Friday 11:30 A.M. to 2:30 P.M. Dinner Monday to Thursday 5:30 to 10 P.M., Friday and Saturday 5:30 to 11 P.M. Reservations and all major credit cards accepted. Valet parking.

This true cabin, a secret landmark on Buford Highway with a well-documented history, would be the perfect location for a sports outfitters store. Back in circulation as a restaurant, The Cabin is suddenly a scene with fancy cars and valet parking.

Owners Barry Lennon and Michael Cofer are both suave and well connected. Popular at Chops and Atlanta Fish Market, where they held managerial positions, they now greet their old clientele on their own newly found turf.

The Cabin is appropriately woodsy and intimate. Animal trophies (mostly the head and forepaws) are used in strategic locations. Lodge furniture, quilts, and manly accessories have been arranged in various tableaux, including the Ralph Lauren inspired loft in the foyer.

One of the charms of The Cabin is its cramped and dark setting. The side porch is a bit claustrophobic, the wine-red main dining room far cozier, but the truly wonderful space is in the basement. Put up with the bar and the smokers. You will love to slide into one of the comfortable booths between big walls of rugged brick and a wonderfully creative row of painted old doors original to the upstairs.

The prices seem high for both the location and the level of skill. At least things are improving. The Sea Island BBQ shrimp come with intolerable chunks of greasy bread improperly billed as bruschetta, but their size, texture and sauce are good. The Louisiana-style scallops are plump and sweet on mashed potatoes. You will like the old-fashioned corn and crab chowder a whole lot better than the pricy, terribly stodgy Charleston crab cake, which seems to contain sugar and comes on a viscous creamy mustard sauce.

In the seafood department, the puny and flat horseradish-crusted grouper has absolutely no taste of horseradish. The Savannah steam pot is put together wrong (the shrimp, clam, and mussels hide at the bottom, while the potatoes and corn have been put right on top) but the dish is fun and delicious. The steaks are quite good, with an aged and rich flavor. The vegetables and the Southern-Style Casserole of the Day (macaroni and cheese or squash and zucchini, e.g.) seem perfectly mundane.

There are some good desserts, including cream-cheese brownies with Cherry Garcia ice cream and a buttercrunch pie with vanilla whipped cream. The cobblers are fair; the microwave-hot Maker's Mark pecan pie is a lot of gunk. The Cabin has done a good job with its wine list and selection of servers.

★ The Café at The Ritz-Carlton Atlanta $$ ✖

181 Peachtree St. (corner of Ellis). Map A. (404) 659-0400.
Daily 6:30 A.M. to 11:30 P.M. Reservations and all major credit cards accepted. Valet parking.

This clubby room with its dark green walls and safe hunting prints has no competition as *the* downtown public gathering place for the elite early in the morning. If you need to entertain an important client for a power breakfast, you'll find here the kind of pampering, attentive service normally associated with private clubs. If you have no big-time business to conduct but just want to get the day started right, you'll enjoy the luxury of having fresh juice and coffee poured for you by brisk but friendly professionals.

Lunch and dinner come closer to traditional hotel cooking, though some dishes have shown clever use of local products, such as a peppy black-eyed pea soup with salsa and sour cream.

★★ The Café at The Ritz-Carlton Buckhead $$ ⊗⊗⊗

3434 Peachtree Rd. (opposite Lenox Square). Map B. (404) 237-2700. Daily 6:30 A.M. to midnight. Reservations and all major credit cards accepted. Valet parking.

That there should be a big difference between the fancy dining room of a hotel and the café in the same hotel is something to be expected. With The Ritz-Carlton in Buckhead, however, there is less of a difference than seems desirable. The Café has always been a comfortable, elegant space, but its role as a safety net to catch the clientele that won't commit to the extremes of star chef Guenter Seeger one floor above may be redundant.

In other words, does The Ritz need two gourmet dining rooms? Perhaps yes. The Café is always on the look-out for interesting seasonal promotions, often playing host to chefs from other part of the country and abroad. It also is the best place in town for a white-glove power breakfast and its suave decor goes from day to night without losing any of its charm. It has an excellent pastry kitchen with dynamic and sophisticated young bakers. The wine list is eclectic and expensive.

★★ Café Diem $ ⊗

640 N. Highland Ave. Map C. (404) 607-7008.
Sunday to Thursday 11:30 A.M. to midnight. Friday and

Saturday 11:30 A.M. to 2 A.M. No reservations. V, MC, AE. Awkward small parking lot or street parking.

Not everyone is going to love Café Diem. If your standard is Café Intermezzo or if you have no tolerance for the inner-city wildlife, you will find this eccentric hip hole on the south side of Ponce inconsequential. But if you swim in Greenwich Village like a fish, if you miss the serendipity of the Latin Quarter and Europe on five dollars a day, you may gravitate toward this unlikely spot and find that it is just what you were looking for.

Lord knows on what frequency Café Diem is broadcasting its signals but the right clientele has been tuning in almost since day one. Wandering German students, writers with the tools of their trade spread on the table, artists with paint in their hair, and a significant representation of Inman Park neighbors have materialized on the formerly empty terrace, now filled night and day and protected by a fancy plastic enclosure. The inside of Café Diem is at least as nice as the terrace and the hand-painted tables give the generously proportioned room its final artistic definition.

The staff works more like a commune than a hierarchy and it is sometimes difficult to figure out who is customer and who is in charge. Everybody flies joyously by the seat of their pants. Café Diem, created in the spirit of carpe diem, is easier to describe as a happening than a restaurant. Part gallery, part coffeehouse, it has gained credibility with every passing month.

The menu, sandwiches on French bread, excellent fresh salads, snacks, and pasta dishes, plays more than a supporting role to the constant gush of espresso from two temperamental machines. There is a true kitchen and the young team does wonderful hot specials at unbeatable prices.

Café au lait means a big ceramic cup with a double shot of espresso and a little pot of steamed milk to mix your own. Café Diem serves imported beers and wine by the glass. There are cakes from a variety of suppliers and a small selection of Greenwood's ice creams. Brunch is excellent, from egg dishes to fresh-squeezed juices.

★ Café Intermezzo $ (X)

*1845 Peachtree Rd. (south of Collier Rd.). Map C. (404) 355-0411.
Sunday to Thursday 10 A.M. to 2 A.M. Friday and Saturday 10
A.M. to 3 A.M. No reservations. All major credit cards. Parking
lot in the back frequently overloaded.*

The original in Park Place was the first sophisticated European coffee bar in the city. Set in an older building, this South-Buckhead version is more glamorous, elegant down to the last crystal chandelier and the exquisite pastry cases whose softly rounded glass seems to dematerialize to offer a no-glare view of the regal sweets. The bust of Beethoven, reflected in the windows, looks like a hologram above Peachtree Street. Classical music pours over the loudspeakers.

An espresso machine as big as a pipe organ shines behind the pastry counter. Worshippers sip fancy coffees through clouds of whipped cream. Intermezzo has a proper bar trade as well, and a short menu of continental specialties. The hot food is not especially impressive (with the exception of the gnocchi), but the salads and sandwiches are usually fine. As a dessert bar, however, Café Intermezzo wins hands down over the competition.

Each day starts with approximately forty cakes gathered from a variety of sources. Some people make only one or two specialty desserts for the restaurant; others have a bigger output. While many of the baked goods have extraordinary eye appeal, few manage to stay within the rigorous European format their names frequently evoke. From Linzer torte with an unusual layer of marzipan to Sacher torte, Dobos torte, and more, all cakes are bigger and richer than their models.

Try to catch a marvelous banana chocolate cake with glossy chocolate icing or an Autumn flower chocolate cake with big shavings of soft chocolate. Indulge in an Ambrosia (intense flourless chocolate cake with stencils of powdered sugar) or a warm, gooey Derby pie. The variety of cheesecakes is mind-boggling (from a delicious discreet Dutch apple to a sick-looking Black Forest). A cream pie flavored with kahlua may be your ticket to paradise or you may want to bury yourself in a warm apple strudel. Don't deny yourself the huge lemon pound cake with fancy icing. Trust your eye more than your tour guide and discover your bliss. The quality is there for the most part.

The whipped cream, German style and slightly sweetened, is the best in the city.

★★ Café Nirvana $$$ ⓧⓧ

3081 E. Shadowlawn Ave. (near E. Paces Ferry Rd.). Map B. (404) 233-3890.
Dinner Monday to Saturday 6 to 11 P.M. Reservations accepted. V, MC, AE. Small, awkward parking lot or street parking.

Nobody can accuse this new offbeat restaurant of lack of ambition. A small house with a big agenda, Café Nirvana calls itself "Simply Divine," uses the Mona Lisa on the cover of its menu and wine list, and offers French-fusion cuisine at prices that compare with those of far grander and more accomplished restaurants.

The owners are young and forward thinking. The progressive decor is hip enough for a sophisticated crowd. With its electric colors, modern art, and mood-setting sconces, Café Nirvana has the feel of a late-night bistro. A sweet little barroom lit with twists of gold mesh is a dandy spot to hang out with a romantic friend. Each room has a different paint job and feel. Thick mysterious curtains and fireplaces add to the glamor of the interior.

Nirvana has a bit of a sense of humor. On the wine list, Mona Lisa sports an electric red line on her upper lip. On the menu, she has a splash of mustard yellow just between the breasts, as if she were one of us and the wining and dining had left telltale signs.

The menu is pretty serious, though, and there is often a gap between concept and execution. You may feel little enthusiasm for a guinea hen tasting unpleasantly of the grill and propped on saffron risotto cakes surrounded by an abundance of mediocre mud-colored sauce. But the quail appetizer on Asian slaw is charming and delicate.

From crawfish spring rolls with tamarind sauce to calamari stuffed with California roll (a faintly absurd and obscene process) and a gristly Thai-style namtok beef salad with lemon grass and lime juice, the appetizers are focused on Asia. The napoleon of smoked salmon on greasy potato crisps is too measly to justify the price. And any chef who serves a plateful of potato and leek sludge, tops it with an eighth of a teaspoon of caviar on a squirt of crème fraîche, and calls the result a Vichyssoise with Georgia caviar ought to be tarred and feathered.

The entrées are more mainstream: tiny lamb chops grilled in a mustard crust and propped over a few leaves of fresh spinach; pan-seared salmon with Japanese buckwheat noodles mixed with long shreds of cucumber; and a geometrically cut, bizarrely presented seared tuna over jasmine rice. The vegetarian tower with crisp potatoes and wrapped asparagus is much, much more unusual and sophisticated.

For dessert, you have only three choices. Frozen mango soufflé with blackberry sauce, ginger crème brûlée in a barely sufficient amount, and a flattish dark-chocolate terrine with raspberry sauce are all adequate, if, again, expensive. The wine list is small as well.

★★ Café Renaissance $$ ⊗⊗

7050 Jimmy Carter Blvd. (one block west of Peachtree Industrial in Peachtree Corner Center, Norcross). Map I. (770) 441-0291.
 Lunch Monday to Friday 11:30 A.M. to 2:30 P.M. Dinner Tuesday to Saturday 6 to 10 P.M. Reservations and all major credit cards accepted. Large parking lot.

Success stories such as those of Van Gogh's, La Strada, and the Brooklyn Café should be a comfort to Café Renaissance, in a corner of Gwinnett easily accessed from North Fulton or Buckhead. The restaurant occupies a prominent corner of its shopping center. The room is large enough to absorb a number of styles. The walls have been stuccoed in a pattern that suggests the Painted Desert. Rice-paper screens, heavy round mirrors salvaged from an old private club in Miami, tiny cacti, Hawaiian screens, art with and without frames, high-backed upholstered chairs, and a bar used only for service give a measure of the original owner's resourcefulness or eccentricity in collecting odds and ends. The old steamer trunk used to store the menus right by the host's Lucite stand is particularly nice.

The restaurant offers a seductive package: a menu full of character, an unusual decor, polished service, and a small but clever selection of wines including some rare varietals. Don't get your hopes up too high. There are a few gaps between concept and execution. But let's say you want a pretty slice of pâté (homemade with chicken, pork, veal, shiitake mushrooms, and sun-dried tomatoes, served with dill horseradish sauce), a few bites of pasta (with chicken, cream, fresh lemon, and rosemary), and a good salad (shredded duck and goat cheese over elegant greens). You are in luck!

Dishes are trend conscious but conservative enough for the average diner. Sautéed fresh salmon with ginger and lime is a frisky preparation. Black grouper stuffed with scorpion fish and shrimp comes with a rich béarnaise, a pretty stack of haricots verts, and a rich potato galette. In the same vein, chicken Oscar features fresh crab meat, pretty asparagus spears, and béarnaise on a grilled chicken breast. The management feels that crab cakes are obligatory and obliges with a light classic seasoned with vegetables. A hearty meat pasta with chunky mushrooms, beef, pork, and lamb in a highly reduced tomato sauce served atop fresh bowties is a rich, thirst-inducing experience. Desserts come from a variety of suppliers.

★★ Café Sunflower $$ ⊗⊗

5975 Roswell Rd. (at Hammond Dr., Sandy Springs). Map H. (404) 256-1675.

Lunch Monday to Saturday 11:30 A.M. to 2:30 P.M. Dinner 5 to 9 P.M. Reservations and all major credit cards accepted. Adequate parking lot.

Martha Stewart might have run through this new restaurant with an armload of Williams Sonoma conversation pieces and an assortment of pretty dried flowers. Café Sunflower looks more playful and sophisticated than the typical straight-and-narrow vegetarian restaurant. The theme, sunflowers and colorful accessories, unfolds without awkwardness. Seating is in booths almost tall enough to qualify as roomettes, each a private corner with classy ceramic pieces. A yellow sunflower pokes through a square opening cut like a window between booths.

There are other corners fitted with tables and chairs. The walls are busy with artwork and flower arrangements, some of them gigantic sunflowers made of various natural materials. Only the back counter (reserved for take-out orders, teas, and desserts) feels a bit plain, like a leftover from a sixties commune.

Café Sunflower draws from Asian, Southwestern and Mediterranean cuisines. Most of the dishes are vegan (no animal proteins whatsoever), with about 10 percent of the menu making light use of milk and cheese. The preparations tend to be complex, the presentations elaborate. Two of the very best dishes are the curried vegetables and couscous (presented as a timbale of raisin couscous pilaf surrounded by a fragrant stew of vegetables with cashews and drizzles of yogurt) and the creamed-spinach puff pastry (a rich blend of fresh spinach, mushrooms, and onions bound by light cream sauce and topped with fluffy triangles of elegant puff pastry). Bread is, of course, sunflower rolls.

The café is successful with soups (including a light cream of cauliflower), anything Mediterranean (a delicious eggplant and bell-pepper lasagna with a fresh marinara, a red-pepper hummus with crisp raw vegetables), and salads. The Asian flavors work least of all: blah rainbow pancake (a faintly greasy, crisp flour-vegetable pancake with soy dipping sauce), very oily Chinese-style eggplant in a brown ginger and garlic sauce served with brown rice. The Sandy Spring rolls (crisp fried, filled with shredded vegetables, rice noodles, and tofu) are the best of the Asian bunch.

Vegetarians say how much they look forward to dessert. You would too if you had given up almost everything else. Café Sunflower's vegan sweets are beyond awful. But the regular carrot cake and the chocolate cake (both of them from The Dessert Place) are luscious. Bad coffee, pretty fruit punches served in interesting goblets, herbal teas, and mineral waters are offered as beverages.

★ Café Tu Tu Tango $$ ⓧ

220 Pharr Rd. Map B. (404) 841-6222.
   Sunday to Wednesday 11:30 A.M. to 11 P.M. Thursday 11:30 A.M. to 1 A.M. Friday and Saturday 11:30 A.M. to 2 A.M. No reservations. V, MC, AE. Valet parking.

This Miami export is the quintessential theme restaurant. Artists, some of whom sport Keds, short shorts, and big hair, dab canvas as if they were paid to make it last forever. The walls are faux this and faux that. Pizza comes on a palette. Paint brushes (glued to the pot) are in the same container as the silverware. Matisse margarita, Leonardo lemonade, and Renoir runner are on the list of drinks. The staff is relentless. The name of your waiter (likely something silly) and the list of drinks are stamped enthusiastically on every possible surface. For all you know, you will be branded and sold as cattle too.

Everything comes in appetizer portions. The spiel is that you will order two to four per person and share everything, thanks to a stack of little plates balanced on the table. People who have lived in their attics for the last ten years will be glad to have a glossary place mat defining such terms as quesadilla, chili, marinara, plum tomato ("Little Pear Shaped Tomatoes"), Impressionism, ellipse, and opaque ("something you cannot see through—like meat").

We don't mind the "food for the starving artist." Some is moderately clever; some is not. On the first list is fried calamari; hummus with rosemary flat bread; cold frittata (a Spanish omelet) with chorizo, onion, and potato, garnished with red-pepper rouille and baby greens; thin-crust pizza with cheddar, goat, mozzarella, Manchego, and Parmesan cheeses; Barcelona stir-fry (shrimp, calamari, chicken, Creole sausage, mushrooms, and a side of awful rice); lamb and sweet-plantain skewer with sweet banana curry sauce and chutney; and cold eggplant caponata with prosciutto and rosemary flat bread.

On the second list is drunken shrimp cocktail, shrimp and pork dim sum, croquetas (ham and crab meat) with corn chive sauce, deflated duck and spinach empanadas, sweeter than sweet sun-dried tomato pizza; sourish mashed-potato pie with ground lamb, and Cajun chicken egg roll. Most everything is cold to the touch. The house red sangria tastes like pop but the white one is much better. Desserts are good for the most part (especially the plantain chocolate mousse and the guava cheesecake).

★★ Calcutta $

1138 Euclid Ave. (Little Five Points). Map E. (404) 681-1838.
Lunch Monday to Saturday 11:30 A.M. to 2:30 P.M. Dinner Sunday to Thursday 5:30 to 10:30 P.M., Friday and Saturday 5:30 to 11. Reservations accepted. V, MC, AE. Difficult street parking.

The original Calcutta in Cherokee Plaza pioneered in introducing Atlantans to the mysteries of Indian cuisine. Much has changed in Indian dining hereabouts since those early days. Now well established in Little Five Points, the restaurant has grown in scope and reliability.

The tandoori specialties, the shrimp dishes, and most vegetables and breads are routinely excellent. Ordering in an Indian restaurant isn't the easiest thing in the world. Most of us think in terms of appetizer followed by a substantial main course, followed by dessert. But here you must order vegetables, bread, rice, and relishes or you won't get any, and your entrée will seem dismally small, lacking an essential dimension.

The distinction between courses is elastic. Calcutta's delicious masala kulcha, a leavened bread stuffed with onion, can serve as an appetizer, as can such tandoori dishes as the ground lamb sausage flavored with cumin and fresh mint. On the other hand, the chicken tikka, seared in the tandoor and chopped off the bones, which is listed as a first course, makes a fine light entrée.

The restaurant serves a mild version of yellow lentils puréed with clarified butter, excellent fresh okra, firmly textured eggplant, and spinach mixed with potatoes, tomatoes and spices. Nan, a chewy wheat bread baked on the side of the clay oven, and plain paratha, a fried whole-wheat bread, are especially good. Splendid basmati is used for the plain rice, the peas pulao, and the biryanis.

Wonderful is a relative term. The dishes are good rather than exceptional. But what is truly wonderful is the fact that you can get either a simple meal or a number of courses for very little money.

★★ California Café $$$ ⊗⊗

3365 Piedmont Rd. (in Piedmont Plaza). Map B. (404) 816-8686.
Lunch Monday to Saturday 11:30 A.M. to 3 P.M. Dinner nightly 5:30 to 11:30. Brunch Sunday 11:30 A.M. to 3 P.M. Reservations and all major credit cards accepted. Valet parking.

The eye is more easily fooled than the palate in this sleek corporate product, a well-designed attractive restaurant that is part of the new eyesore plaza ruining the view of Tower Place. California Café has almost all the trappings of a fine-dining restaurant: valet parking, a glamorous executive chef (Daniel Malzhan), a wine room, a California wine list with cellar selections, an upscale creative menu, great visuals, etc.

While the restaurant is several steps up from its noisy neighbors and provides an exciting dining environment, the food is hardly worth the sixty or seventy dollars you will almost invariably spend on dinner for two. Meet your friends for a bottle of wine and a few nibbles, including excellent designer pizzas baked in a wood-burning oven, and the signature smoked chicken and tasso spring rolls over watermelon-jicama slaw. But be prepared for some of the gourmet dishes to disappoint.

Take the special of halibut served on a baby octopus stew, layered over couscous and under a salad of flat-leaf parsley with a tapenade of black olives garnished with shards of asiago cheese. Clever? Not really. Tasty? Not on your life. The swordfish displayed on a pedestal of eggplant and showered with crisp cellophane noodles has most people scratching their heads and wondering what the heck they ordered. The grilled lamb with honey-fig sauce, potato mushroom pie, and grilled radicchio is dry and grainy despite its red color.

The fried green tomato napoleon with pesto, Sonoma goat cheese, and olive tapenade is decently done but the spicy duck empanada seems filled with baby food. A rock-shrimp sundae looks fetching in a bright blue margarita glass but has a slimy, unpleasant feel in the mouth. The relentless trendiness is hard on the palate. Beet chips, Asian apple pears, focaccia croutons, hoisin barbecue sauce, and apricot and pine nut compote are treated more like cute accessories than elements in a coherent composition. If you are looking for simplicity, the penne pasta with caramelized onion, smoked bacon, and shaved Grana cheese is innocuous and the portobello mushroom pizza with roasted garlic is a winner.

There is a pastry chef on duty. Less convoluted than the rest of the menu, the dessert course includes panna cotta, almost a coeur à la crème only lighter and creamier, served with fresh berries, and a lemon bar served in a bowl with homemade fruit sorbet. The chocolate desserts aren't very special, with the exception of the hot-flavored Mexican chocolate ice cream served with crisp almond cookies.

The restaurant has been well designed with a large exhibition kitchen, oversize booths, and a clever set of lights trained on artwork and decorative groupings of jars and bottles. There is a lot of colorful Italian glass treated almost like a Modernist mosaic. The ceiling has swirling Calderesque shapes and a path of halogen pinpoint lights. The service is excellent.

★★ California Pizza Kitchen $ ⊗

Lenox Square (one level above the Food Court). Map B. (404) 262-9221. Other locations.

   In Lenox, Monday to Thursday 11:30 A.M. to 10 P.M. Friday and Saturday 11:30 A.M. to 11 P.M. Sunday noon to 10 P.M. No reservations. V, MC, AE. Adequate parking in mall lots; long walk required.

The U.S. Department of Agriculture defines pizza as a

dough-based product containing cheese and tomato sauce. Wolfgang Puck, inventor of the American (as opposed to Italian) boutique pizza, ran afoul of the bureaucracy when he tried to market frozen versions of his signature pies. If it hasn't got tomato sauce, it ain't pizza, said the Feds. Ha ha ha, laughs California Pizza Kitchen, a small chain out of Beverly Hills that uses pesto, barbecue sauce, spicy peanut sauce, and hoisin sauce on its wood-fired pizzas and offers cheeseless versions with chilled tuna or grilled eggplant. Tomato sauce is a rarity.

Owners Rick Rosenfield and Larry Flax have done for pizza what Baskin-Robbins did for ice cream: develop a large range of unusual flavors. Thai chicken, Peking duck, Caribbean shrimp, Hawaiian (with pineapple), and Cajun (with andouille) are a few of the options. The ingredients are exceptionally fresh, often homemade, handled with confidence, and spiced intelligently. Intense heat generated by imported wood-burning pizza ovens crisps the pies in three minutes flat, leaving the vegetables sweet and crunchy, the shrimp bursting with juices, the herbs unwilted.

But for all its creativity and impressive standards, California Pizza Kitchen has failed to design an impressive crust. The juicier the ingredients, the better the pizza, as in the combination of shrimp, fresh tomato, Greek olives, sun-dried tomato, and pesto or the option containing duck sausage, fresh spinach, sun-dried tomato, and sweet roasted garlic. There is more than pizza on the menu: fresh salads, homemade pasta, and desserts. Ambitions run high. The salads are of fresh greens tossed with monster croutons, shaved romano, goat cheese, imported olives, and/or sun-dried tomatoes.

The extremely high staff-to-customer ratio makes for frisky service. No sooner have you lifted your fanny off the seat than a determined team erases every sign of your earthly passage in less time than it takes you to reach the door.

★★ Camille's $$ ⊗

1186 N. Highland Ave. (near Amsterdam Ave.). Map C. (404) 872-7203.

> *Dinner only, nightly 5:30 to 11. No reservations. V, MC, AE. Parking in lot next door or on street.*

Before Camille Sotis acquired a small, obscure pizzeria next to the North Highland post office and opened her Italian-American trattoria, the only crowds in Virginia-Highland waiting on the street for a restaurant table had been in front of Capo's Café. Once people caught the first whiff of Little Italy, they started queuing every night for a seat indoors on a funky banquette or bar stool or at a worn picnic table on the sidewalk. Soon the clientele grew beyond the immediate circle of intown residents. To permit outdoor dining year-round, Camille's added a collapsible plastic enclosure in front of the restaurant. The restaurant eventually doubled its size by acquiring a commercial space in the back and grew cozier with every passing year. The most recent renovation, solid brick facade and substantial patio, has added a lot to the feel of the restaurant.

The food is plentiful, appealingly prepared in a style devoid of pretensions. Big platters of fleshy, lusty calamari crisped in fresh oil are served with cut lemon and a peppery Fra Diavolo sauce. Delicious rice balls studded with chopped salami, oozy provolone, and ricotta cheese roll around on a thick china plate. A tangle of marinated squid tossed with fresh celery shines under a gloss of good olive oil. The pasta comes in enormous helpings with chunky clams, steamed mussels, sautéed calamari, and an excellent tomato sauce.

Prices are higher than those commanded by comparable establishments in the streets of Little Italy. The pizza by the slice is particularly outrageous, with each "specialty topping" (fresh tomato, meatballs, anchovies, among others) adding up to a staggering total. Why one should pay more for fresh garlic (labeled "specialty") than for sausage (called "classic") is a vexatious mystery. Pizzas and calzones have no outstanding qualities, especially compared to the true specialties of the house, pasta and seafood.

★★★ Canoe $$$ ⊗⊗⊗

4199 Paces Ferry Rd. (at the river). Map G. (770) 432-2663.
Lunch Monday to Friday 11:30 A.M. to 2:30 P.M. Dinner nightly 5:30 to 11 (Sunday till 9). Reservations and all major credit cards accepted. Valet parking.

One could live one's whole life in Atlanta without so much as catching a glimpse of the Chattahoochee. The privileged few have the river in their backyards. Rafters bob on it and rowers dip their oars into the muddy flow. The banks belong to the state.

The new Canoe, one of only two restaurants on the river and with no prospect for competition, isn't any farther away from downtown Buckhead than, for example, Horseradish Grill, but one has a sense of a journey and a special place. The first thing architect Bill Johnson did was to go back in time, chip away the dubious improvements made on the original structure, and expose the natural materials. A bold change of floor plan has reoriented the restaurant to take full advantage of the view. There are some wonderful acknowledgments of the past, including a glamorous, vintage-look sign with individual light bulbs and some riotous hand-tinted photographs of Robinson's Tropical Gardens, a popular nightclub and restaurant, heir to the original Robinson's Chicken House founded in 1919 in the same location.

Nothing is left of the former tenure as the conservative Patio by the River. Important artists, including the metal sculptor Ivan Bailey, have been commissioned to fill the restaurant with creative details. The menu is also eclectic rather than thematic. The wine list is full of surprises. Chef-proprietor Gerry Klaskala and his crackerjack partners have pushed a grand yet gentle vision of a restaurant in synch with the nineties and the special location.

The food is delicious—casual, elegant, sensible, fashionable. Klaskala and his crew, headed by chef Gary Mennie, know how to keep all these concepts going. Moo shu duck with caramelized ginger and green onion pancake and tuna tuna tuna, an appetizer combination of seared, marinated, and sushied tuna, are two of the more spectacular appetizers. Rock-shrimp cakes with grainy mustard and yellow-tomato vinaigrette are visually more low-key but equally exciting to the palate.

House smoked salmon presented with shaved red onion, cucumber, dill cream, and toast is impeccably elegant. You can also go in a more rustic direction with an oak-roasted Vidalia onion soup with garlic chips or a simple tomato and bread salad with cucumbers and fresh basil. Roasted-corn risotto with grilled prawns and crisped ginger is a terrific alternative to some of the larger entrées. The goat cheese and potato ravioli with summer vegetable ragout are extraordinary.

Crispy duck, air dried in the Chinese manner, is paired with pungent, raspy mizzuna greens and a fresh plum sauce. Fall-apart-tender slow-roasted pork comes with an unctuous gorgonzola polenta and spicy escarole in another insightful pairing. Grilled lamb loin chops are sweet and tender on a bed of leeks and artichokes next to a cake of Parmesan-crusted potatoes.

Small pizzas have appeared on the regular bill of fare as well as the bar menu, which also features a witty pu pu platter. The restaurant bakes its own bread (including a spicy cracker bread), churns its own ice cream and fresh sorbets, and has a distinguished pastry kitchen. The chocolate hazelnut praline cake with Drambuie is a delicious signature dessert, bearing the name of the restaurant in filigree. Organic honey parfait with peach compote, caramelized warm banana brioche tart, and a new Cortland apple crisp with Grand Marnier dried-cranberry ice cream earn pastry chef Michael O'Connor the recognition he deserves.

Wine gourmets may reach for the reserve list. People who like to experiment will have fun with the organic selections and the "esoteric whites & blends" and the "esoteric red & Cal-Ital" sections on the regular list.

★★ Canton House $ ⊗

4825 Buford Hwy. (just before Chamblee Tucker Rd., Chamblee). Map D. (770) 936-9030.

Monday to Friday 11 A.M. to 3 P.M. and 5 to 11 P.M. Saturday 10:30 A.M. to 11 P.M. Sunday 10:30 A.M. to 10:30 P.M. Reservations accepted. V, MC, AE. Adequate parking lot.

There could be poems about dumplings. Be they Austro-Hungarian, Southern soul, or Oriental, they are all wonderful. There is something soft and mysterious about dumplings. You bite right through their yielding dough and, in many cases, they release a burst of juicy filling.

What is great about Canton House is less the exceptional

quality of its dumplings (good as they are) than their availability. Dim sum, served in a number of Chinese restaurants both on and off Buford Highway, is typically a weekend offering. The few restaurants that have dim sum during the week do not offer cart service. Canton House trundles noisy steel carts through the pink and garish dining room every day of the week. Granted, the selection is more exciting on Saturdays and Sundays, especially if you time your arrival for high noon, when everything is ready and none of the delicacies have run out. But how wonderful it is to show up for a Tuesday lunch, maybe even solo, and with a mean appetite for dumplings. Pork dumplings, shrimp dumplings, pork and shrimp dumplings, big slithery rice noodles filled with seafood or meat, bundles of sticky rice in lotus leaves, sesame rolls filled with sweet bean paste, egg custard pastries, and a few more selections pass by the tables at regular intervals.

The scene is more animated and the offerings twice as many on the weekend. Plump and glossy little shrimp cakes, potstickers, curried beef buns, big squares of a brown steamed cake that looks like a sponge from the bottom of the sea but tastes delicious, congee flavored with pork and thousand-year egg, pastries with lotus paste, fried taro dumplings, etc., are obviously fresh and well prepared.

Dinner is more average than dim sum. The inexpensive rice-bowl dishes (for example roasted duck over a mound of fresh rice) and the lighter side of the menu (steamed chicken with black mushrooms, spinach bean-curd soup) are good but the vegetables (delicate snow-pea vines collapsed under their own weight) and the not quite crisp salt and pepper squid disappoint.

★ Capo's Café $ ⊗

992 Virginia Ave. (just west of N. Highland Ave.). Map C. (404) 876-5655.
   Dinner Tuesday to Sunday 5:30 to 10:45 P.M. Brunch Sunday 11 A.M. to 2:30 P.M. Reservations not accepted. V, MC, AE, DC. Difficult parking on busy street.

When John Capozzoli refurbished an old neighborhood greasy spoon in 1977, he was charting new territory. The

Virginia-Highland intersection boasted nothing more than a few pungent old bars. New and casual, extremely inexpensive, the restaurant became an overnight success. Capo's still occupies a unique niche on the much expanded dining scene: priced above burger joints but way below intown chic, it is one of the most affordable dating spots in the city. Behind the old diner counter, frantic activities go on against a background of brushed stainless steel. The other parts of the restaurant display a comfy clutter of minor art against a blooming Country French wallpaper.

On the small menu, some very ordinary dishes have achieved cult status. The fettuccine Alfredo, tossed into an overcrowded cast-iron frying pan, remains an all-time favorite despite—or perhaps because of—its amateurish home-cooked flavor. Soups, salads, and freshly baked whole-wheat bread are decent enough, if not terribly distinguished. The much-beloved "Chicken Diable," two boneless breasts stuffed with mushrooms and cream cheese, spread with Dijon mustard, brown sugar, and chopped walnuts, may be enjoyed without guilt as the kind of dish one has outgrown but can revert to.

Among the desserts, the chocolate espresso pot de crème and an extremely sweet ricotta-cheese pudding are no disgrace to the genre and shouldn't be blamed for their lack of ambition. Much, much worse hides under whipped toppings in some of the most consistently praised gourmet restaurants. Watch for the (sometimes ambitious) specials on the blackboard.

☆ Carbo's Café $$$$ ⊗⊗

3717 Roswell Rd. (north of Piedmont). Map B. (404) 231-4433.
  Dinner only, nightly 5:30 to 10:30 (Friday and Saturday till 11:30). Reservations recommended. All major credit cards. Valet parking.

Open since 1980, Carbo's Café has become a tradition for some of the town's best-to-do. Inside, the clientele finds a decor combining features from the dens in their brand-new homes along the Chattahoochee with details befitting their lawyers' offices in the Candler Building downtown. In the fall of 1987, the restaurant underwent a major face lift, and now regular patrons have a whole new set of grandiosities to ooh and aah over. The expanded establishment includes an atmospheric cocktail lounge and a grand upstairs frequently used for private parties.

The kitchen has evolved at a much slower pace. The work of the most recent chef is unimpressive. Dishes aren't likely to show gross faults but still most of the cooking is no better than pedestrian, and the prices of everything far exceed the value delivered.

There are a few lighter options (tagliatelle with plum tomatoes and basil, more grilled and pan-seared seafood), but one still suffers through pretty little salads drenched in creamy dressing, heavy venison roulades tightly clamping a filling of dried cherries, and a thoroughly mediocre char-broiled veal T-bone steak rubbed with garlic, lemon juice, and cracked peppercorns.

The desserts, including classic soufflés, chocolate flourless brownies with Bailey's ice cream, homemade sorbets, and chocolate-mint tart, can be enjoyed full size or in petite portions as part of a Taste of Carbo's sampler platter.

★ Carey's Place $

1021 Cobb Pkwy. (U.S. 41, Marietta). Map G. (770) 422-8042. Monday to Saturday 11 A.M. to midnight. Sunday noon to midnight. Reservations and credit cards not accepted. Ample parking.

The walls of this grungy truck stop disappear under faded pictures of country and western singers, many of them bearing autographs beneath blurry, whiskered faces. New stars are pinned on top of old celebrities. The jukebox moans a sad blue-collar romance. Sitting at the bar, a man in a bargain suit feeds money into a vaguely obscene video game. Recreational opportunities abound: bowling machines await the shuffle of the puck; pinballs bump and twinkle.

Carey's looks like a place where you might have to step out and defend your manhood in the parking lot, but the joint is abuzz with harmless activities. Patrons who aren't drinking beer in a pumping motion lift serious hamburgers and monster hot dogs from their crowded plates. The burgers command a fanatical following. People drive all the way from downtown Atlanta for their choice of eight or twelve ounces of good, juicy beef, an oversize bun, a thick slice each of tomato and onion, and ketchup on the table.

What more could you ask? Good fries? Nope! Beaded with grease, they droop on the plate. But the hot dogs are delicious, especially slathered with grilled onions and mustard. A Buckhead location opened and closed without creating much of a stir.

★ The Chart House $$ (✘)(✘)

6450 Powers Ferry Rd. Map G. (770) 980-1671.
Dinner only, Sunday to Thursday 5 to 10 P.M. Friday and Saturday 5 to 11 P.M. Reservations and all major credit cards accepted. Ample parking.

Known nationwide (but better in California and Florida than anywhere else), The Chart House taps the familiar and presents it in a reassuring configuration. "Steaks. Seafood. Prime Rib," the menu plainly and squarely states. The architecture is massive contemporary with a touch of the Pacific Northwest. Heavy redwood beams radiate from the ceiling in an umbrella pattern. Some of the art looks more like craft but there is plenty of it, evoking various aspects of the sea. Laminated on each tabletop, beautifully detailed maritime charts pick up the leitmotif. The staff, a bunch of energetic young people, wears hot tropical prints.

There are several reasons you may want to try The Chart House. The restaurant accepts and honors reservations. Everything is very low stress. There are only a few cuts of beef, a few species of fresh fish. A tender chicken skewer brushed with teriyaki is big enough as an appetizer to be shared by two. A plump California artichoke boiled with hot spices and served with aioli makes a fun nibble. New England clam chowder is fair and hearty. A dark squaw bread (close to a soft pumpernickel) and a spongy but fragrant sourdough bread are supplied in generous amounts.

Some ideas are mediocre: shrimp rolled in coconut, fried to a boring crunch and served with three sauces; excellent sea scallops jammed in the kind of oval dish that makes everything look like slop at the diner; teriyaki sauce or Hawaiian glaze (ginger and sweet soy) slapped over many dishes. The impeccably trimmed prime rib, however, is worth the trip. When it comes to salad-bar choices, The Chart House doesn't stint on quality. Selections even include fresh tropical fruit and whipped cream, and chilled plates in an insulated drawer are a nice touch.

The wine list is pricy but if you are willing to part with your dollars, you can drink a 1988 Cabernet Sauvignon that goes the distance. Dessert, limited to a gigantic frozen Mud Pie or a Key Lime Pie, isn't what you'd call aesthetic but in both cases the taste corrects the first impression. Service is courteous and bright in the style of a Houston's. Recipe cards for some of the specialties are provided on the hostess's desk.

★ The Cheesecake Factory $$ ✖✖

3024 Peachtree Rd. Map B. (404) 816-2555.
  Monday to Thursday 11:30 A.M. to 11 P.M. Friday and Saturday 11:30 A.M. to 12:30 A.M. Sunday 10 A.M. to 11 P.M. (brunch served until 2 P.M.). No reservations. All major credit cards. Valet parking.

What makes this ostentatious California-style building lit up like some major historic landmark such a hot destination? And why did all the restaurants in the same bracket tremble at the idea of this successful chain invading their territory? Preceded by a terrific reputation, The Cheesecake Factory has exceeded almost anyone's expectations.

The design is very busy: columns that wouldn't be out of place in a Babylonian movie; lots of copper bent this way and that; hand-painted upholstery looking like Indian teepee hides; custom lighting in every possible shape; an immense open kitchen backing the bar; a pastry counter with every cheesecake known to man. The commotion is unbelievable.

The menu, a spiral-bound opus complete with advertising for products ranging from spas to Oriental rugs, compares to the average bill of fare the way the Encyclopedia Brittanica compares to a paperback novel. Name almost anything a person would want to eat and you will find it on the menu of The Cheesecake Factory. There isn't one restaurant in the metropolitan area that can compete in terms of sheer variety. Beyond that, the portions are enormous and the food, for the most part, is competently prepared.

The following are recommended: the best California artichoke ever (fire roasted, served with aioli and balsamic vinaigrette); a massive fresh herb and vegetable meatloaf over excellent mashed potatoes with gravy and grilled onions; Caesar salad pasta (hot linguine tossed with sautéed romaine, garlic, olive oil, and lemon zest, topped with croutons, Parmesan, and marinated chicken); sliders, which are upscale versions of the old Krystal miniburgers, served four to an order with excellent pickles.

The cheesecakes come in a staggering number of flavors—raspberry tropical passion, chocolate-chip chocolate cupcake, apple pie, peanut-butter-cup fudge ripple, fresh banana. Lemon mousse (tart and light) and double chocolate upside-down Jack Daniels are good. Everybody takes leftovers home.

★★★ Chefs' Café $$ ⊗⊗

2115 Piedmont Rd. (just south of I-85, in the Comfort Inn). Map C. (404) 872-2284.

Lunch Monday to Friday 11:30 A.M. to 2 P.M. Dinner Sunday to Thursday 6 to 10 P.M., Friday and Saturday 6 to 11 P.M. Brunch Sunday 11 A.M. to 2:30 P.M. Reservations and all major credit cards accepted. Ample parking.

Investors from California completely renovated a drab motel in the shadow of I-85, designed a clever little dining room, and hired a manager who had worked with Joyce Goldstein from Square One in old Fog City. The motel was subsequently bought by a national chain, and the restaurant has become independent. Atlanta people no longer view the location as a handicap, but visitors may need some convincing.

Managing partner Mike Tuohy has worked with a number of chefs without compromising his standards. His kitchen wouldn't turn out a tuna fish salad prepared with anything less than grilled fresh albacore or yellow fin, or a garlic mayonnaise that wasn't homemade. Potato pancakes are freshly grated and sautéed in sweet butter. Crab cakes have to have lots and lots of beautiful sweet meat.

The menu changes often, flashing tantalizing California-born dishes a few at a time. Polenta and grilled eggplant with a relish of tomato, garlic, and fresh basil; cornmeal chive cakes with black caviar and crème fraîche; sautéed crab cakes with tomatillo salsa; grilled chicken breast with black bean sauce; fresh pasta with green-lipped mussels and baby lobster tails—one dish after another has come to challenge the local taste for "things fried and sweet."

The kitchen has lagged a tad behind the concept at times, but Tuohy is there to push for greater accomplishments. His sensible style is evident in things ranging from fresh spinach and mushroom tarts to slowly braised lamb shanks and an assiette of grilled vegetables. The famous crab cakes with spicy remoulade have never been better and all seafood preparations are simple and forceful. Many of the dishes (including the Café Paella) are available in half-orders, which again puts Chefs' Café high on the list of trendsetters.

Brunch is exceptional, offering crab cakes with small, perfectly poached eggs and a light Hollandaise; admirable green-onion potato pancakes with fresh apple sauce; poached eggs and tomato Hollandaise; gorgeous carrot muffins; cheddar cheese grits; and much, much more.

Chefs' Café got its name from a series of naive paintings found by one of the general partners. Rubicund chefs gambol and juggle with food against a background of brightly colored landscapes. The small foyer welcomes guests with a display of interesting wine bottles set on a dresser next to an urn of fresh flowers. Seating has become far more comfortable after a well-handled renovation giving a softer focus to the formerly casual dining room.

The clientele, from surrounding neighborhoods of varying

economic power, feels no pressure to dress up or down. Diners come as they are, and so should you. Service is attentive, supervision excellent. Eminently drinkable wines by the glass and bottle and educated service add to the reasons for putting Chefs' Café on your agenda.

★★ Chin Chin $$ ⊗⊗

3887 Peachtree Rd. (in Cherokee Plaza). Map B. (404) 816-2229. Monday to Thursday 11 A.M. to 10 P.M. Friday and Saturday 11 A.M. to 11 P.M. Sunday 3 to 10 P.M. Reservations accepted. V, MC, AE. Ample parking.

From the outside, the restaurant is almost forbidding behind a heavy door. Inside, it's a different, friendlier story. The decor is geographically neutral: flowered tablecloths, Western art, comfortable chairs. The kitchen, fully visible behind a glass partition, is an obviously hygienic workplace for a busy, quiet crew in short-sleeve shirts and white caps.

The menu, Hong Kong gourmet with a promise of spicy heat, takes a while to read. The only dishes described are those in a section called Chef's Special featuring the most elaborate and costliest specialties. Everything else is crowded on two pages without a word of explanation.

Consider Chin Chin for two opposite reasons. The gourmet aspect means that you will find some unusual items such as Gold Coin shrimp patties (two cutie pies, lightly sautéed), scallion pancake (excellent with wine), lettuce cups stuffed with minced lobster or chicken and water chestnuts, and Three Cups Taiwanese chicken (a bracing casserole with cauliflower, black mushrooms, hot peppers, and three cups of rich soup in a hot pot).

The health aspect of Chin Chin means that you can avoid all the rich and repetitive sauces, the oil, the salt, etc., in favor of dietetic and tasty dishes served in a bamboo steamer. Steamed fish or steamed shrimp with a heap of healthy, unseasoned vegetables comes with brown rice and a gravy boat of soy-based sauce for a guilt-free treat. Four or five different styles of tofu (including a wonderful one with hot sauce and ground pork) can also be considered dietetic.

The unsuccessful dishes are the ones that involve an enormous amount of sauce—the black-pepper ministeak, for example, or the dumplings with hot sesame sauce. The pan-fried noodles are the greasy vermicelli kind but the toppings are good. At the opposite end of the spectrum, the salt and pepper calamari looks like dehydrated trail food. The dessert section is unusually long, including four different kinds of ice cream (green tea, coconut, mango, and fried in a shell of dough), banana fritters, and red-bean pastries.

★★★ Chops $$$$ ✗✗✗✗

70 W. Paces Ferry Rd. (in Buckhead Plaza). Map B. (404) 262-2675. Dinner only, Monday to Thursday 5:30 to 11 P.M., Friday and Saturday 5:30 P.M. to midnight, Sunday 5:30 to 10 P.M. Reservations and all major credit cards accepted. Valet parking.

Establishing a new standard of luxury is Pano Karatassos's invariable approach to doing business of any kind. Chops is no exception to the platinum rule. The usual image for a power steakhouse is low profile, conservative to reactionary in decor, service style, and menu. San Francisco designer Patrick Kuleto went for an unabashedly opulent look: exquisite, furniture-grade wood is everywhere, even on the coffered ceilings. Custom lighting sets a triumphant mood in the dining room. Not so subtle symbols of wealth can be seen in the diamond-shaped tips pointing downward from alabaster globes. Some sconces resemble cornucopias. Thick crystal oil lamps add jewel tones to the bar.

Where a greedy restaurateur might have squeezed in twice as much seating, Karatassos gave diners the luxury of exceedingly generous space between tables. Some of the most desirable spots include booths on a raised platform overlooking the open kitchen.

Everything is on display at Chops. The aging of the beef happens behind glass doors. Happy clams and oysters take a shower in an aquarium equipped for wave motion. Monster lobsters die for your pleasure in a gleaming sauna compartment.

You meet potatoes, tomatoes, steak, and salmon at the door, where they stand on a sideboard in a regal arrangement. The kitchen is fully open. Even the prep room can be watched behind a clear window.

Normal mortals don't usually have access to the quality of meat supplied to the restaurant. Select any cut—beef, veal, or lamb—and you can be assured of a first-rate product. The kitchen uses radiant broilers, thus avoiding the acrid fumes from dripping meat juices.

You may never have had as beautiful a veal chop as the one served over fresh spinach. Swordfish receives a royal treatment. Coated with coarse black pepper and crushed almonds, the delicate meaty fish is served over perfect mashed potatoes and moistened with natural veal juices. Size and quality are tops for the scallop and shrimp scampi.

The filet mignon steak tartare (listed as an appetizer) could easily become a light entrée. The quality of the meat is exquisite. The preparation happens tableside, with the just ground filet being tossed in a wooden bowl with all the classic condiments. A perfect course before or after the steak tartare would be the traditional chopped salad.

Salt sticks, raisin bread, and, most delicious of all, onion rolls are brought at the beginning of the meal with big pats of fresh sweet butter. Homemade sorbets and ice creams come in all shades of deliciousness. Chocolate melt cake with coffee-bean sauce is a wonderful treat.

★★★ Chopstix $$$ ⊗⊗

4279 Roswell Rd. (Chastain Square). Map B. (404) 255-4868.
  Lunch Monday to Friday 11:30 A.M. to 2:30 P.M. Dinner Monday to Saturday 6 to 10:30 P.M., Sunday 6 to 10 P.M. Reservations accepted. V, MC, AE. Ample parking.

If it weren't for Chopstix, some folks would never set foot in a Chinese restaurant. People who like to see and be seen, people who spend it as fast as they get it, come here. The purists, the Chinatown minglers, don't quite know what to do with this sophisticated, hyper-modern spot. Design chairs of perforated metal, pale greys and bare pinks as decorating colors, even inflated prices, wouldn't be out of place in a fashionable corner of L.A.

The prices on the menu are fully justified by the quality of the ingredients. Every shrimp, scallop, or oyster is of an extraordinary size. The preparations are rarely less than rich, whether one talks about a rare duck salad with mango, shiitake mushrooms, and greens dressed with sweet mango sauce or a terrific appetizer of chicken and pine nuts with flash-fried spinach. Beautiful satay noodles come garnished with an abundance of shrimp, scallops, and shiitake mushrooms. Black-pepper scallops paired with sugar peas are sweetly fresh and meltingly tender in their spicy sauce.

When this elegant uptown Chinese restaurant offers orange roughy stuffed with crawfish and garnished with a confetti of fresh mango on special, one feels almost silly attacking the rich, delicious dish with chopsticks. Chopstix offers classic Chinese delicacies: sliced calamari, steamed tender and briefly crisped in fresh, hot oil; homemade refrigerator pickles sprinkled with sesame seeds; shredded pon pon chicken served as a cold salad with julienne fresh vegetables; magnificent oysters bursting with juice under a barely glazed crust and served in a lush, dark sauce redolent of sesame and cracked black pepper.

The specials, posted daily on a chalkboard inside the door, emphasize light, healthy combinations of fresh ingredients. A nice wine list, Greenwood's ice cream (ginger especially suitable after an Oriental meal), and chocolate mousse cake aren't as much cultural clashes as pleasant bridges between East and West. You expect no fortune cookies. But, yes, "you will win a beauty contest soon."

Elegant host and owner Philip Chan knows how to coddle the clientele. The third stage in an extensive renovation has softened the look of the restaurant, adding touches of romance such as a piano bar and diffuse lighting. Sunday is a particularly cozy night to pick to experience the restaurant and its regular following.

☆ Chow $$ ⊗⊗

1027 N. Highland Ave. (at Virginia Ave.). Map C. (404) 872-0869. Lunch Monday to Saturday 11:30 A.M. to 3 P.M. Dinner Tuesday to Thursday 6 to 10:30 P.M., Friday and Saturday 6 to

11:30 P.M., Sunday 6 to 10 P.M. Brunch Sunday 11:30 A.M. to 3 P.M. No reservations. V, MC, AE. Difficult parking on street and in lot behind restaurant. Other location downtown.

Chow has dealt very elegantly with the legacy of two restaurants at the same location. Dramatic enough for a special engagement, sufficiently relaxed to accommodate the one-course meal on the run, equipped with a nifty little bar—Chow is happy to see you spend as much or as little as you wish. The restaurant likes to bill itself as "New American," which raises expectations too high. Chow doesn't map out new culinary territories, but it has assimilated most of the lasting trends. The target clientele is interested in low-guilt, moderately adventurous cuisine.

Every restaurant should have a signature dish, something it alone does or does better than anyone else. Chow has its baked whole head of garlic and feta cheese spread. The upper third of the garlic head has been neatly severed, allowing you to pick out the delicious, melting flesh with the tip of your knife prior to mashing it on a crouton spread with feta. The smoked mackerel au poivre with sour cream is another wonderfully loud appetizer. Compared to these beauties, the rest of the menu is pretty tame.

The restaurant has a pleasant air of overall thoughtfulness, but there are technical failures. Preparations that require more than basic skills aren't mastered by the kitchen. A limited repertoire and some problems in timing limit the seriousness with which one can take the place. Brunch—pleasant because of warm light playing off old bricks and because of brisk service—is dutiful rather than imaginative. Some desserts come from outside purveyors; some are made in-house. Most feature chocolate—good chocolate. All are reasonably competent.

A new location in downtown Atlanta has the same air of sophistication as the original.

★★ Ciboulette $$$ ⊗⊗

1529 Piedmont Rd. Map C. (404) 874-7600.
 Dinner only, Monday to Thursday 6 to 10 P.M., Friday and Saturday 5:30 to 11 P.M. Reservations and all major credit cards accepted. Ample parking.

A conservative French bistro for the American taste, this high-profile Ansley restaurant is the result of a cooperative effort between chef Tom Coohill (known through his work at The Abbey and City Grill) and his mentor Jean Banchet, who put in two good years at the restaurant before moving on to new projects of his own.

Divided by columns, the dining room seems wider and better balanced than it did during its previous incarnation. The open kitchen has been softened by a wide arch fronted with warm ceramic tiles. Posh banquettes with a rich leaf pattern occupy the long wall under a band of narrow mirrors. Stripped of all the copper pans, silver deer, realistic bronzes, and deadly oil paintings in golden frames, the room could be charmingly modern.

While some of the cooking is classic bistro (e.g., the thick Lyonnaise sausage served en croûte over a warm lentil salad; the pork chop rising over a clear jus on a delicious mound of crunchy macaroni; the fabulous cabbage confit rich in fatty pork nuggets served with a lean carved squab), there is a general lack of focus.

A lentil soup garnished with rabbit is exactly what you expect in a French bistro but why the hot smoked salmon on couscous (you'd rather smoke cigarette butts than have to eat it) or the roasted blue cod with chicken juices (not much better than a blue-plate special despite the delicious galette of potatoes placed rakishly on top)? The coq au vin (a capon) is just a double breast barely influenced by a thin, marginally acidic wine sauce.

The kitchen often falls back on anemic seafood mousses, imperfect pâtés, and far too much butter and cream. Because a restaurant is named Ciboulette ("chives" in French), does that mean that the kitchen has the right to cover your salad with that particular herb, chopped without particular finesse? The stuffed baby vegetables plunked on all entrée plates together with out-of-context black linguine are hateful additions.

Desserts, always one of Coohill's fortes, look less than inviting when presented in durable samples trundled around in a fancy cart and passed under your nose close enough for you to notice that the scoop of ice cream is really molded butter. Warm apple tart with calvados sauce and vanilla ice cream is an excellent, sensible choice. The gâteau Ciboulette (a classic

Opera cake) has one layer too many but lovely fresh-fruit gratins are highly recommended. The wine list is reasonable and reputable, with some excellent selections by the glass.

★★★ City Grill $$$ ⊗⊗⊗

55 Hurt Plaza (at Edgewood Ave.). Map A. (404) 524-2489.
Lunch Monday to Friday 11:30 A.M. to 2:30 P.M. Dinner Monday to Saturday 5:30 to 10 P.M. Reservations and all major credit cards accepted. Valet parking.

Inspired by some of the old clubs in Boston and Philadelphia, located in a historic building, this spectacular restaurant has been a big coup for the powerful Peasant Restaurants corporation. Extraordinary efforts have been lavished on the property. Entrance is through a gracious rotunda. A double staircase of Georgia marble curves up to massive brass doors. A first glance sweeps foyer, bar, and multiple-level dining room, travels up twenty-four-foot ceilings defined by intricate gilt moldings, and rests on pastoral murals filled with leafy boughs and blue sky.

The hiring of Roger Kaplan is much more than Band-Aid therapy for a restaurant that, although it is widely recognized as downtown's best and most powerful, lags behind its enormous potential as a destination place. Asked to bring the costs down and aim at greater accessibility, a lesser chef might have felt cramped and edited his own style. Kaplan, however, has the enthusiasm of youth backed by a very real talent. Transferring from the security of the prestigious Crescent Court in Dallas to this difficult position hasn't dampened his spirits.

Just about every version of City Grill over its short and complicated history has been likable, but the Kaplan regime is the most fun to date. Like a breath of fresh air, specials are being written into the menu each day. Summer is celebrated with what is essentially a classic Vichyssoise except that plantains have been used instead of potatoes and the chilled soup is garnished with a dice of ripe papaya, refreshed with a bit of lime, and perfumed with Jamaican allspice. Steak tartare becomes a big surprise: seared, julienne New York strip with hot sambal and cucumber relish in a cornucopia of thin, crisp dough. Black-pepper tuna sashimi comes with fried glass noodles, shiitake mushrooms, and the prettiest little jar of soy sauce.

Boned young quails are deep fried in a light buttermilk batter and displayed on an elegant sausage gravy with blackberry pepper biscuits no bigger than your thumb. Roasted chicken is divided into elegant slices next to a savory bread pudding topped with custard and studded with rhubarb and sweet onions. A nice small cut of salmon is cleverly balanced on a potato cake with fresh leaf spinach. You can cut actual wedges of the three-layer composition and drag them through an enchanting light caviar sauce. Side dishes such as spoon bread, polenta, truffled whipped potatoes, and black-bean stack are part of the repertoire.

Kaplan also creates intense sorbets (mango, blackberry, passion fruit, coconut) and sometimes ice perfumed with violet, lavender, or lemon balm for the restaurant. Lemon meringue pie, fresh peach crackle, a warm, oozing chocolate soufflé with pecan crust, and banana ice cream are other dessert options.

City Grill is still a long way away from being a totally relaxed restaurant, but you will see a few parties in colorful, open-neck shirts instead of the usual somber lawyerly attire. Service is at its peak, with well-rehearsed routines and a terrifically comfortable staff free from the burden of synchronized formality.

★ Claudette's $$ ⊗⊗

315 W. Ponce de Leon Ave. (in First Atlanta Bank building, downtown Decatur). Map E. (404) 378-9861.

Lunch Monday to Friday 11:30 A.M. to 2:30 P.M. Dinner Monday to Thursday 6 to 10 P.M., Friday and Saturday 6 to 11 P.M. Reservations and all major credit cards accepted. Ample parking.

The First Atlanta Bank building might seem like the least likely destination for a romantic date. Beyond the anonymous terrazzo-floored lobby, past the concrete walls, and up the stairs, however, a charming little French inn awaits. Dark wood paneling in the second-floor lobby prepares you for the enclosed, discreet, clandestine feeling of this cozy place. A narrow bar off to one side is a private place to sip one of the restaurant's inexpensive French wines. Fireplaces, multiple inoffensive landscapes, crocheted tablecloths, and narrow stained-glass panels help to set the mood for intimacy in the dining rooms.

Claudette's has no pretensions beyond being warm and welcoming. The restaurant, originally known for old-fashioned French dishes, like quiche Lorraine and coquilles Saint Jacques, has taken a surprising turn at the hand of a new owner from Russia. Pirozhkis and chicken Kiev (delicious) have appeared on the menu. The preparations are no longer the kind of "Country French" cooking that used to be standard back in the 1950s. Crab cakes and fresh asparagus are every bit as valid as onion soup or Vichyssoise on the new menu. The servers are solicitous and cheerful. Private parties may happen around the corner from your tête à tête but folding doors will give you some privacy.

★ The Coach and Six $$$$ ⊗⊗⊗

1776 Peachtree Rd. (north of Brookwood Station). Map C. (404) 872-6666.

Lunch Monday to Friday 11:30 A.M. to 2 P.M. Dinner Monday to Thursday 5:30 to 10 P.M., Friday and Saturday 5:30 to 11 P.M. Reservations and all major credit cards accepted. Valet parking.

After more than thirty years, The Coach and Six isn't Atlanta's most elegant restaurant any longer, nor is it its best steakhouse, as it once was. It is, however, an important traditional dining room with a culture of its own. One may regard it as a family heirloom, a carefully maintained, softly polished piece of silver to pass on to the next generation. While the quality of the actual dining has fluctuated up and down over the years, the restaurant has always been able to provide an impressive start with an abundance of free offerings and a grand finale with remarkable desserts from its own in-house bakery.

The old rooms are resplendent after the latest renovation under the previous management. Framed paintings, a fortune in mirrors, heavy chandeliers, and all the posh things money can buy uphold the tradition. Three-tiered dessert carts make their precarious way between tables. The bread basket is still a splendid offering with terrific New York style rolls (onion, pumpernickel, poppyseed) and the best challah with nuts ever baked. Fresh vegetables and olives on ice followed by the traditional spinach puffs stretch the cocktail hour and lower expectations of dinner.

In the capable hands of Sue and Frank Heavlin, the restaurant feels solid and well maintained. Tasty new appetizers include seared Cajun tuna bites, spicy, crusty morsels served with tangy mustard, corn relish, and an onion remoulade. The smoked salmon tart looks like a double order of biscuits but is actually made of puff pastry with fried capers and a pretty drizzle of cream-cheese dressing.

You are on safe ground with specialties from the grill. The traditional Coach strip weighs in at sixteen ounces, the center-cut filet mignon at eight or twelve ounces. The Coach serves as good a grilled veal T-bone chop as anyone else in town and the famous triple-cut spring lamb chops are still a cult item. The also famous black bean soup is better spiced than ever before. Chocolate mousse roll, champagne jelly roll, and other sweet treats for which The Coach remains famous are wheeled in at dessert time.

The dining room staff commits to its duties with various shades of proficiency and excitement. Overall, one could wish for more warmth, but the style is appropriate. In an age of disappearing amenities, The Coach still offers a coat check and a famously comfortable lounge still graced with local celebrities on Kouresh's who's-who mural.

★★ Colette $$ ⊗⊗

2157 Briarcliff Rd. (at LaVista Rd. in the Briar Vista Shopping Center). Map C. (404) 321-5538.

Lunch Monday to Friday 11 A.M. to 2 P.M. Dinner Monday to Thursday 5:30 to 10 P.M., Friday and Saturday 5:30 to 11 P.M. Reservations and all major credit cards accepted. Adequate parking.

In a French context the name isn't unusual enough for you

to identify the muse of this brand-new restaurant as the famous author of *Chéri*. There she is by the door, though, with her gamine haircut and her thin lips, painted somewhat awkwardly by someone related to the owners of Colette.

Inside, don't count on finding the period or the clutter in which Colette lived her life. The dining room is quiet and simple, the walls sponged a vibrant shade of yellow and natural linen shades drawn across the windows to obscure an undistinguished view of the parking lot. There are good tablecloths on the tables and a striped awning above the bar. The people in charge are very young and uniformly pleasant.

Viewed as an inexpensive neighborhood bistro, Colette is quite a find. Nobody knows how to make a proper salad dressing. The kitchen relies too much on cream and uses the same garnishes over and over again. But most of the food tastes good and there are healthy, low-fat dishes, some of them Moroccan. Colette, for example, offers a delicious vegetarian couscous and, on occasion, beef or butterflied lamb couscous.

The mussels are excellent, prepared à la marinière with white wine, garlic, shallot, and parsley and finished with a swirl of cream. One can easily eat about half a dozen tiny dinner rolls dipped into the delicious broth. Escargots, pâté de campagne with cornichons, and a few salads, including a clingy Caesar, sum up the starters.

There are better poulets Provençale (breast meat topped with tomatoes, onions, mushrooms, and green peppers) and more scintillating soles à l'estragon (creamy tarragon sauce and a bizarre garnish including red cabbage, pommes sautées, and onions) but you will enjoy the simplicity and abundance of both plates served with numerous fresh vegetables.

The desserts are homemade and include a perfectly nice crème brûlée and a fresh mocha cake served on too much dessert sauce. Service is polite and a cut above the prices.

★ The Colonnade $ ⊗

1879 Cheshire Bridge Rd. (near Piedmont Rd.). Map C. (404) 874-5642.

Lunch daily 11 A.M. to 2:30 P.M. Dinner Monday to Thursday

5 to 9 P.M., Friday and Saturday 5 to 10 P.M. Open all day Sunday 11 A.M. to 9 P.M. No reservations or credit cards. Adequate parking.

The purest examples of Ozzie and Harriet cooking survive in this large establishment popular with the blue-hair crowd and a younger generation nostalgic for the kind of bland fare Moms served up in the Eisenhower era. A change in management and a much publicized fire have brought a higher level of comfort into the elderly, undistinguished structure.

A cozy bar with large tables and sofas grouped around a working fireplace is a more pleasant place to wait for tables than the old crowded porch. Mixed drinks, boutique beers, and wines by the glass keep the waiting clientele in good spirits. French prints, matted and double matted, cover walls that used to stand bare. Some heavy round tables accommodate large parties.

With their red miniblinds and fresh new wallpaper, the dining rooms are spiffier but not significantly altered. Tables and booths are still jammed at funny angles, creating extraordinary opportunities for people watching and involvement in other parties' business. While many of the old waitresses work in a daze of boredom, their younger colleagues focus more sharply on their duties, establishing good rapport with the enormous clientele of regulars.

Despite some trendy additions such as grilled amberjack, the menu is mostly a throwback to the fifties. Meats and vegetables are starkly unseasoned. The soft yeast rolls are pure nostalgia. The crusty old staff has to tell you about new-fangled specials such as mahi-mahi; spare their feelings by ordering something more in keeping with the place such as fried chicken livers (excellent), roast pork with celery dressing, lamb shanks covered with brown sauce, or chicken pot pie with canned or frozen peas. You remember to dab mayonnaise on tomato aspic, and finish all your vegetables, whether you like them or not.

Your best bets are old-fashioned oyster stew made from scratch, fried chicken, tenderloin wrapped in bacon, and macaroni and cheese. The icebox pies are virtually indistinguishable from one another.

★★ Corky's $ ⓧ

1605 Pleasant Hill Rd. (east of I-85, Duluth). Map I. (770) 564-8666.
　Sunday to Thursday 11 A.M. to 11 P.M. Friday and Saturday 11 A.M. to midnight. No reservations. V, MC, AE. Ample parking.

There is no city in the U.S. that takes barbecue more seriously than Memphis, Tennessee. Barbecue in Memphis doesn't mean pork butts or hams the way it does in Georgia. Elvis may have lived on cheeseburgers but, by gosh, Memphis loves ribs! One can eat ribs in Memphis every day of the week for months on end without returning to the same place. The natives are divided into two camps: those who like their ribs wet and those who prefer them dry, dusted with a mixture of hot red spices. They are good both ways.

Long considered Memphis's #1 rib restaurant, Corky's is widely known out of state and the restaurant ships its famous barbecue anywhere in the U.S. The first thing you need to know about this new suburban franchise operation is that the ribs are worth the trip. The second draw is that Corky's is a real restaurant, not some rough BBQ shack. It lacks the picturesque quality of the original (woodsy, low ceilinged), but has a charm of its own. Built of warm solid brick like a Houston's, the restaurant feels substantial and comfortable. Large parties find space to spread out. The noise escapes in the direction of the high ceiling. The staff (including the bartenders dressed like young Mormons in shirt and tie) is first rate. Beale Street jazz and Tennessee whiskey are celebrated on the walls without taking over every available space.

You could order an appetizer before your ribs: decent fried onion rings pressed into a loaf, or a little dish of hot tamales, or, better yet, the same hot tamale over an excellent bean chili. But why bother? Don't you want to fall ravenously on a big slab of the leanest, meatiest hickory-smoked barbecued ribs you have ever imagined? The ribs, available in several sizes (regular order, large order, full slab "built for 2"), come wet unless otherwise stated. The best thing about Corky's ribs (besides their flavor, that is) is the fact that the barbecue sauce is baked on instead of slathered. The dry ribs are a totally different experience: spicier, more violent to the mouth, and totally addictive. The pulled pork is lean and a bit dry. To jazz it up, stuff it inside the delicious fresh-baked hot rolls served by the basketful and add some sauce and some crunchy coleslaw.

BBQ pork and spaghetti (a Memphis staple), BBQ shrimp, and BBQ chicken will have to wait until you are hungry again, but don't miss the apple caramel cobbler (yum) and the chocolate fudge cobbler (so close to a brownie à la mode, you won't be able to tell the difference). Drinks are replenished until you burst. Corky's has a drive-thru, a catering division, and a full bar.

★★★ Corner Café & Buckhead Bread Co. $$
ⓧⓧ

3070 Piedmont Rd. (at E. Paces Ferry Rd.). Map B. (404) 240-1978. Monday to Friday 6:30 A.M. to 10 P.M. Saturday and Sunday 8 A.M. to 10 P.M. No reservations. All major credit cards. Valet parking.

Isn't it like the Buckhead Life Restaurant Group to build a grandiosity trimmed with golden rolling pins and custom neon accessories and call it Corner Café? These are, of course, the folks who gave you a million-dollar Diner and a Fish Market to gawk at, and they can't help but be fancy.

From the outside, the building looks too impossibly grand to be a bakery, let alone a corner café. Once you are inside, however, especially in the crowded café side, you'll feel like bracing yourself and pushing walls and ceiling apart. The huge globe lambs, the neon graffiti on the mirrored ceiling, and the gigantic mural of a wheat farmer who looks like a Soviet production god all seem to belong in a much larger environment.

A lot is happening in the same space. It's a bakery, pâtisserie, espresso bar, breakfast place, busy lunch spot, and a dinner restaurant with a small but ambitious menu. Breakfasts, lunches, and dinners at the Corner Café are delicious but almost never relaxing. The most horrendous pressure seems to bear down on Saturday brunch, with weekday breakfasts being at the opposite end of the scale. Corner Café isn't equipped for scrambled eggs or omelets, but the organic eggs served either in the shell (five-minute egg with strips of grilled chive baguette, stone-ground grits on the side) or poached (the best combination includes grits mixed with finely ground corned beef and a side of fresh tomato salsa) are fantastic. Fresh-roasted granola (almond or currant flavor) is available for a healthy breakfast with yogurt and fresh fruit.

Brioche French toast, sourdough pancakes, and freshly made giant French crêpes satisfy the sweet-tooth brunch bunch, while more substantial items such as the portobello pancake and the eggs-and-things please the rest.

Lunch and dinner are the same: fresh soups (including delightful potato leek and fennel soup with fried mashed potatoes), creative sandwiches (grilled portobello mushrooms, roasted peppers, and arugula on olive-oil boule), and some excellent main course salads (crisp duck confit, haricots verts, and frisée lettuce with light creamy vinaigrette and duck jus, for example).

The Corner Café has very pretty hot entrées as well: roasted lamb top round with grilled vegetables and a risotto of couscous pearls; roasted breast of marinated chicken with twice-baked unstuffed potatoes; beef tenderloin with basil mashed potatoes and chile-corn relish. The style of cooking is reminiscent of the Diner across the street, but without the congruence between glamorous menu and glamorous decor.

Join the crowd admiring the fabulous new pastries created by wiz François Collet, some of which have golden canopies and cost more than twenty dollars. Look at the glossy Danishes and the hygienically wrapped sandwiches. Whatever you do, make sure that you buy a loaf or two of the Buckhead Bread Co. incomparable bread.

★ Country Place at Colony Square $$ ⊗⊗

1197 Peachtree St. (at 14th). Map C. (404) 881-0144.
  Lunch Monday to Friday 11:30 A.M. to 2:30 P.M. Dinner nightly 5:30 to 11. Brunch Sunday 11 A.M. to 2:30 P.M. No reservations. All major credit cards. Validated parking.

Of all the properties developed by the Peasant Corporation, this suave gathering place for the advertising and public relations firms that are major tenants in Colony Square tends to garner the fiercest adherents. Part of the appeal is the look and feel of the space. To one side of the entrance, a long, narrow lounge stretches beside the bar beneath a cheerful striped awning. A high wrought-iron fence marks the boundaries of this watering hole within the busy surrounding mall. The dining room, recently renovated, is a vast echoing hall with a tiled floor in large black and white squares, numerous potted plants, and a sense of ceaseless activity. Neutral, restful colors—oyster and soft grey tones—allow the eye to focus on the animated patrons and, after dark, on candles flickering from tabletops that seem to stretch off to the horizon.

The Peasant Corporation's chefs keep coming up with clever, flashy dishes to entertain their patrons. Under the sesame seeds, raspberry vinegar, and pink peppercorns one frequently finds neatly prepared basic items. Eat the whole basket of deep-fried sourdough rolls. After years of Peasant-style oral menus, the company has now switched to printed ones.

☆ Cowtippers $$ ⊗⊗

1600 Piedmont Rd. Map C. (404) 874-3751.

Monday to Thursday 11:30 A.M. to 11 P.M. Friday and Saturday 11:30 A.M. to midnight. Sunday 5 to 11 P.M. No reservations. All major credit cards. Adequate parking.

A try-too-hard Western steakhouse by the owners of Einstein's, this conversion of the old Hickory House a block away from Ansley has an amusing decor: cute light fixtures (prickly cactus and wrought iron), cow-print tables, Western paraphernalia. But it's not as if John Wayne were about to grab the entwined horseshoes that serve as door knobs, push the door open, and order Miss Kitty's K-bobs with a side of Tumbleweed Caesar.

While the young at heart may like to sit around with blue tortilla chips and spicy hot cheese ("Durango Dip"), or fried stuffed jalapeños ("Armadillo Eggs") served in a real egg carton with a side of fresh salsa and a funky beer such as Shinerbock from Texas, those who want a good steak are out of luck.

There isn't anything special about the cuts we have tasted. 'Tippers T-bone, "the biggest steak in the house," is kind of thin and flavorless. The Rustler's ribeye is fatty and tough. The small filet (Deputy's cut) can be gobbled up in exactly four bites and its diminutive size makes it unlikely that you will receive exactly what you wanted in terms of doneness. One whole scallion and a choice of potato (baked OK, Texas fries obnoxiously seasoned) complete the plate.

The vegetables of the day are plain good but even they could do without the butter sauce. The hamburger comes in a pleasant freshly baked roll. Dessert is strictly routine. If you want to drink something truly shocking, there is a chile beer (Cave Creek from New Mexico) that tastes like jalapeño juice. Service varies with the degree of seniority.

★ Dailey's $$

17 International Blvd. (just east of Peachtree). Map A. (404) 681-3303. Lunch Monday to Friday 11 A.M. to 2:30 P.M. (downstairs till 3:30 P.M.). Dinner Sunday to Thursday 5:30 to 11 P.M., Friday and Saturday 5:30 P.M. to midnight. No reservations. All major credit cards. Street parking almost impossible, nearby lot parking not validated.

"How can we get people to stay downtown after dark?" moan Atlanta's convention planners, city bureaucrats, and business leaders. They should ask the Peasant Corporation's founders! One after the other, dinnertime restaurants of all types and pretensions fail in the central business district, while Dailey's continues to pack local residents into its immense spaces. Once you're admitted to the dining room, suave, slick young waiters stand ready to give a neat performance. The Peasant Corporation trains them like chorus girls. They introduce themselves by name, these Marks and Christophers, then painstakingly trot you through the menu selections chalked on a little slate, detailing preparations and ingredients.

Dailey's is fun, especially if you don't take food all that seriously and have a big appetite. Menu developers work hard to come up with items like black bean chili, veal with Pommery mustard, amberjack au poivre, and all sorts of moderately trendy ideas. The kitchen does what it can to feed the masses. The simpler the dish, the higher the chances for success. Stick with the crackling, delicious grilled duck. Enjoy the copious fresh salads included with entrées. The deep-fried sourdough rolls, incompatible with everything else, are perversely marvelous by themselves.

Line up at the dessert bar for a spectacle somewhere between an auction and a fashion show as each enormous, silly cake is introduced to the wide-eyed audience. Or stay at your table and have fried ice cream in a gigantic snifter. Old merry-go-round horses, enormous ribbed-glass fixtures, massive doors, a majestic staircase that eight could climb abreast, a rain forest of vegetation, a busy wallpaper patterned like a flutter of dollar bills—all seem perfectly in scale with the gigantic space of this former warehouse. Downstairs acts as a bar and grill with a simpler menu.

★ Dante's Down the Hatch $$ ⊗

60 Upper Alabama St. (Underground Atlanta). Map A. (404) 577-1800. 3380 Peachtree Rd. (across from Lenox Square). Map B. (404) 266-1600.

Monday to Thursday 2 to 11 P.M. Friday and Saturday 2 P.M. to 12:30 A.M. Sunday 6 P.M. to midnight. Reservations suggested even for drinks (especially on weekends). All major credit cards. Underground parking lots downtown, ample parking and ramp access in Buckhead.

Dante Stephensen, the owner of these two nightclubs and entertainment centers, is one of Atlanta's great eccentrics. Throughout the 1970s, Dante's Down the Hatch anchored Underground Atlanta, to which he has now returned, and Stephensen used his position as head of the Underground business association to sound forth on a wide range of public issues. He moved his business to Buckhead in 1981, creating a new fantasyland, but was the first to be back in Underground.

Crocodiles (some born on the premises) swim in a moat surrounding the polished hull of an eighteenth-century sailing vessel. On the ship, a stellar jazz trio holds forth while folk singers croon in the area of the club known as "the wharf." Fun things to look at include stained-glass windows originally from Lloyd's of London. Female patrons must not miss the witch waiting to greet them with a cackle in the ladies' room.

Both locations are more watering holes than restaurants. Drinkers of flavored daiquiris get to take home decorative glasses as souvenirs, but wine is the beverage of choice here. The list is particularly strong in German offerings, while lovers of Sauternes and other sweet wines will find much to attract them.

The menu features various fondues, including a traditional beef fondue, Mandarin fondue, Chinese dumplings fondue, imported cheese fondue, and, more than just a dessert, a chocolate fondue. Tasmanian beef stu, a hearty soup served with French bread, may be all you need. Or you can order a cheese platter, mellow out with a bottle of Tokay or hock, and relax to the easy strains of jazz.

★★★ Delectables $ ⊗

Below sidewalk level of the Central Public Library, 1 Margaret Mitchell Square (accessible from inside library and from separate entrance on Carnegie Way). Map A. (404) 681-2909.

Lunch only, Monday to Friday 11 A.M. to 2:30 P.M. No reservations or credit cards. Difficult parking in nearby lots or department store garage.

Once upon a time, there was a drab little cafeteria here, close to the children's books department. Something happened to it. Something along the lines of the pumpkin turned golden carriage. "Delectables," glows a gemlike blue neon sign on a library wall that used to be bare. A few attractive tables are cordoned off in the downstairs lobby. A soft echo of big-band jazz filters through a doorway, pulling you toward a charming lunchroom filled with flowers: lush blooms on coated-chintz peach tablecloths; fresh buds on the tables; and, beyond glass doors, a patio attractively landscaped with trees and potted plants. Designer chairs (blond wood inside, perforated bright yellow metal outside), menus propped on music stands, and real china add to the atmosphere.

The patrons don't look like dusty intellectuals or semi-permanent residents of the periodical room. Indeed, few of them come from the library at all. They enter through the patio. You can imagine them just having buzzed their secretaries to say they were going to lunch. The format is still a cafeteria; but the heavy cutlery is wrapped in thick linen napkins. Two vertical cooling units are stocked with gorgeous edibles kept sparkling fresh under clear plastic film.

This is the kind of food you wish you had, and rarely get, at a garden party. Delectables, indeed: tiny asparagus, proud and crisp, served with a delicate lemon sauce flecked with cayenne pepper; sweetly fresh coral shrimp in dill sauce; twelve-layer salad in gorgeously colored strata, clearly visible through a pristine glass container. Light quiche, fluffy as a chiffon pie; new potatoes tossed with sour cream and fresh herbs; runny camembert baked in a rich egg brioche; and leek and potato soup, smashingly balanced, are other strong points.

Some of the best chili in town is here—medium-hot, its plentiful component of beef perfectly lean and tender, with coarsely grated cheddar and onions served in cups on the side, to be added at your discretion. Any restaurant would be proud to serve Delectables' quintessential cheesecake (perfect throughout), its airy lemon soufflé, its coarse carrot cake of restrained sweetness. The cookies are delicious, too.

★★ The Dessert Place $ ⊗

1000 Virginia Ave. (at N. Highland Ave.). Map C. (404) 892-8921.
279 E. Paces Ferry Rd. (at Peachtree St.). Map B. (404) 233-2331.
Monday to Thursday 9 A.M. to 11:30 P.M. Friday 9 A.M. to 1 A.M. Saturday 10 A.M. to 1 A.M. Sunday 10 A.M. to 11:30 P.M. No reservations or credit cards accepted. Lot around the corner or difficult street parking in both locations.

The well-named Dessert Place is Atlanta's best homegrown sweets parlor. Local and energetic management and an all-American straightforwardness keep the customers happy. The design of the original store (Virginia-Highland) has been successfully reproduced in later ventures: the entrance is like a march (and often a wait) through the corridor of temptations. The goodies are displayed on glass shelves at eye level.

The long counter is used for buffet service, with a young staff readying orders on a tray while you wait. The sitting area is low key and attractive: tables are close together, set against a background of exposed bricks, lush plants, and rampant ducts. Lights are turned down to facilitate intimacy. The Dessert Place in Virginia-Highland shares a charming backdoor space with neighboring establishments.

Many of the innocently shaped, devastatingly sugary cakes haven't changed one bit over the years. As opposed to many of its competitors, The Dessert Place bakes all of its products. This gives the dessert menu great homogeneity and a clear sense of style. Poppyseed loaf with delicious brown edges, terrifically tart lemon pound cake, crumbly Dutch apple pie topped with streusel, Italian cream cake (with pecan, coconut, and cream cheese icing), iced carrot cake, and a moist Quaker oatmeal cake are almost always available. Most look more like home-kitchen goods than fancy bakery products. The chocolate chocolate cake can disappoint people whose tastes have progressed beyond childhood. But with its pale, heavy icing, its flavor of chocolate lost somewhere between the butter and the sugar, it may be just your idea of regression therapy. There is a basic Key lime pie kept on ice and a wonderfully sticky caramel chocolate pie.

The Dessert Place is especially strong when it comes to cookies and small cakes. Thumb-print cookies (raspberry jam and a dusting of nuts), cream-cheese brownies, puffins (small, sugary cakes baked in muffin tins), baby bundt cakes with icing, and cinnamon-raisin stickies are good enough for a fancy tea (your place or theirs). White chocolate macadamia nut cookies, chocolate chewies, chocolate chip cookies, and whittakers (a bar bristling with chopped pecans, coconut, and butterscotch chips) are always fresh, and rich beyond belief.

Compared to these old-fashioned beauties, the various health muffins seem cast in concrete, clawing their way down your throat before resting heavily on your stomach. The Virginia-Highland location serves a simple continental breakfast; the

★★★★ The Dining Room at The Ritz-Carlton Buckhead $$$$ ✗✗✗✗

3434 Peachtree Rd. (opposite Lenox Square). Map B. (404) 237-2700. Dinner only, Monday to Saturday 6 to 10:30 P.M. Reservations recommended. All major credit cards. Valet and validated parking.

When chef Guenter Seeger appeared on our doorstep, only two other chefs living in America had been awarded stars by the world-famous Michelin guide. Why would a man like Seeger, who fought hard for success and recognition as owner of one of Germany's best restaurants sell out and come to America? He wanted to be great. He was one of twenty. He wanted to be one of five.

In Atlanta, Chef Seeger rose to the top of his profession. But for all the beauty of the new concept and all the talent, recognition came very slowly. The clientele accustomed to the Ritz's original safe hotel fare was distressed by the change. Some people were incensed, especially those who wanted half a cow on the plate and a baked potato. "The duck wasn't crisp!" "My fish wasn't cooked!" "Where is the food?" Seeger didn't budge. "This is the way I cook" was less a stubborn statement than the expression of an inescapable inner truth. Seeger never apprenticed under a great chef. He evolved very specific techniques, many of them involving cooking at unusually low temperatures, in a sustained effort to protect the essential qualities of the exceptional products he seeks.

Fat chunks of barely opaque lobster, beautifully silky filets of rouget barbet, quiveringly rare fresh duck liver, and supple saddle of veal aren't raw by any means. But you can't figure out how they have been cooked without a hint of stiffening. You rather fancy that the chef holds his hands above the flesh, lets the energy flow, and dispatches it to you, warm and gorgeous and magical.

Nothing is lush, complicated, or contrived. There is a

charming modesty about the lamb slices spread in a rosette, garnished with translucent turnip in paper-thin supple strands and an "eye of the cyclone" arrangement of minuscule vegetables. The fresh sea urchins, agape on a bed of seaweed, offer their warm creamy coral, gratinéed for a split second with little morsels of lobster. Sautéed spring onion and a concassée of sweet yellow peppers grace the admirable rouget.

In Seeger's hands, lobster, venison, squab, and oysters lose their deadly seriousness, not their intensity. Haute or nouvelle, cuisine can be so joyless, so "look at me now." But here, the lobster is thrown casually into a pumpkin soup that tastes of fall and harvest. Or it comes as a mock pancake, lighter than a mousse and garnished with beet ravioli in chive sauce. The sautéed oysters, strong, fleshy Belons raised in Maine, are served barely warm in a cucumber vinaigrette spooned gently into the deep rounded shell. The venison is rolled in a crust of fresh thyme and sliced and fanned out over a ravishing, slightly tart sauce.

Each of Seeger's plates is a gorgeous, asymmetrical postmodern composition. Tiny diamonds of green, red, and yellow pepper radiate from a silky cut of raw tuna set at an angle over a pool of ginger cream. Shiny, buttery snow peas fan out next to a disheveled softshell crab in bacon butter. A dotted poppyseed parfait sits rakishly on a film of strawberry coulis. Fresh caramel ice cream, shaped like a bullet, presses against a thin tart displaying a beautiful concentric pattern of pear slices.

The bill of fare is handwritten every day. On the left is a special four-course fixed-price menu with four matching wines by the glass. On the right are a dozen dishes, all unbearably appealing. The best way to get to know this exceptional chef is through a total surrender of your will to his. One member of your party must order the day's special menu. Then everyone else must get a full four courses, too. Sounds like a lot of money, a lot of food. Well, it's worth every earned, borrowed, or stolen penny.

With an expert sommelier and sixteen selections available by the glass from the two Cruvinets you've got a great chance to pick the right thing to sip. The unflappable Peter Krehan, a perfect gentleman of a maître d', materializes only—but always—when needed. You are in good hands with the discreet and well-trained staff. The decor is suitably posh, with tapestried furniture, rich wood, and nineteenth-century art. The only concession to modern days is a small show kitchen, a fascinating window into the domain of a chef of the very highest rank.

★★ Dominick's $$ ⊗⊗

95 S. Peachtree St. (Norcross). Map I. (770) 449-0096.
Lunch Monday to Friday 11:30 A.M. to 3 P.M. Dinner Monday to Thursday 5 to 10 P.M., Friday and Saturday 5 to 11 P.M., Sunday 5 to 9 P.M. Reservations for parties of six or more. All major credit cards. Small, crowded parking lot or street parking.

"A lotta fun!" is how most people would describe this Italian restaurant in downtown Historic Norcross. First of all there is the surprise element in arriving in this quaint strip of Americana that one can barely believe still exists in Gwinnett. Dominick's is a wonderful space, a roomy old store with a high pressed-tin ceiling. The walls are warm red brick with a zillion black-and-white photographs circling the room. There is enough space for a couple of street lamps with fat white globes. With a sizable back room and a generous bar, the place accommodates a crowd. White tablecloths overlaid with paper and small kitchen glasses for wine create a friendly, relaxed mood.

Dominick's is a unique phenomenon. In the suburbs but not of the suburbs, it has been able to attract a mature crowd, respectable professionals thirty and up. Even though the restaurant serves family style and is particularly well suited for group outings, most folks have made the decision to leave the kiddies at home.

Appetizers, hardly a necessity considering the scale of the entrées, are almost exclusively deep fried: calamari (solo or paired with shrimp), zucchini, mozzarella en carroza, and enormous stuffed mushrooms that look a bit like hushpuppies. The pasta dishes can be somewhat generic (e.g., the linguine with Bolognese sauce) but you won't eat anything you'll end up regretting. The ravioli di Dominick's in a light tomato sauce touched with cream are particularly fine. The chicken Dominick, tender boneless breasts sandwiched between melting mozzarella and a bed of fresh spinach, is delicious. There are also several versions of chicken scarpariello (cooked in chunks in a lemon and white wine sauce with potatoes, peppers, and sausage) and a bunch of homemade desserts.

Brace yourself for the check, although the more of you there are, the less expensive the meal.

★ East Village Grille $ ⊗

248 Buckhead Ave. (at Bolling Way). Map B. (404) 233-3345.
  Daily 11 A.M. to 4 A.M. No reservations. All major credit cards.
  Parking (often difficult) on street or in pay lots.

The determined upswim of spawning salmon is a civilized event compared to the bar scene in this former fire station. George Rohrig, also owner of Peachtree Café and Otto's within a block of East Village Grille, must spray the walls of his establishments with some powerful animal scent. Women pretend hard that they are interested in each other's conversation. Men posture and shop.

How absolutely extraordinary in these circumstances that the food should be old-fashioned, wholesome, and inexpensive. The style is retro-chic: between a meat-and-three and a diner. Forget the nymphomaniacs. Ignore the lechers. Who needs sex when you can have macaroni and cheese, steamed cabbage, fried okra, meatloaf, and apple cake?

In some ways East Village Grille is a throwback to the early, preyuppie days of Peachtree Café. The kitchen doesn't pretend to be fancy. The service doesn't try to be cute. The prices are better than reasonable, maybe because of the huge profit on beverages.

Perfectly nice hamburgers have the virtue of simplicity. The T-bone steak is well trimmed and well grilled. The meatloaf oozes with good juices. The chicken and rice soup has the flavor of your childhood.

The triangular dining room walled in industrial brick lacks coziness, despite the fire burning in a small fireplace, the TV set above the bar, and the baby-blue ceilings. Two terraces more than triple the space. The first one, on a level with the restaurant, has a trompe l'oeil boardwalk and a beer station

★★ Eats $

600 Ponce de Leon Ave. (across from City Hall East). Map C. (404) 888-9149.
> *Monday to Friday 11 A.M. to 10 P.M. Saturday and Sunday noon to 10 P.M. No reservations or credit cards. Street parking.*

The food concept for this new inner-city venture, an urban food court with character, feels rather like the result of an informal poll taken in and around Little Five Points. "What do *you* like to eat?" "And *you*, what do you like?" The answers, translated into plain, easily understood language, are pasta, vegetarian stuff, jerk chicken, very, very cheap.

Doing quality eats at rock-bottom prices is a trademark for owner Charlie Kerns, who also operates Tortillas a few blocks east on Ponce de Leon. Eats stands on a corner, a large bunker iced with what looks like thick white cream cheese troweled into waves. Indoors, the level of comfort emulates that of Tortillas' latest version: essential furniture, acoustic tile, linoleum floors except where a raised area shines with new parquet. There are some touches of bright colors and four individual counters succeeding one another in the shape of an *L*.

Put up with the bizarre traffic patterns and you will enjoy a healthy and tasty meal at a ridiculously low price. Take the pasta for example. Readied in individual portions, fresh fettuccine or linguine are tossed to order in a large pot of constantly boiling water. Spaghettini and ziti are ready in a jiffy as well. You pick one of four sauces (wonderfully garlicky marinara, marinara with peppers and mushrooms, alfredo, pesto). All pasta comes with garlic bread. All variations are decent to delicious. The price is $2.50 to $3.50, depending on the sauce.

There is nothing wrong with the vegetable station except

that the employees seem to consider the fate of each green bean instead of plopping the servings on the plate in the best cafeteria style. Corn freshly cut off the cob, spicy black beans, green beans cooked long enough for a Southerner, al dente broccoli, and a ragout of tomatoes, peppers, onions, raisins, and peanuts are cooked without animal fat and served with rice or couscous.

Creative types can purchase, for example, a side of broccoli ($.85) to boost the nutritional content of their pasta. Baked potato with/without sour cream rounds out the vegetarian counter. Held in a warming oven, the jerk chicken is fresh and spicy. Espresso, brownies, and draft beer (a few imports next to the common domestic types) have a sleek counter all their own.

★ Eat Your Vegetables $ ⊗

438 Maryland Ave. (Little Five Points). Map E. (404) 523-2671. Sunday to Thursday 11:30 A.M. to 10 P.M. Friday and Saturday 11:30 A.M. to 10:30 P.M. No reservations. V, MC. Insufficient reserved spaces in crowded parking lot.

Strict vegetarianism has a poor track record in a city that grew up on fried chicken and salt pork. A narrow customer base proved insufficient to keep alive the succession of mostly small establishments that pioneered the concept of meatless cuisine. Eat Your Vegetables has succeeded where many of its more competent predecessors failed, thanks to its location, its attractive decor, and the inclusion of chicken and seafood dishes next to macrobiotic entrées and vegetable plates.

People who have cut meat out of their diets on philosophical, economic, or irrational grounds abound in the surrounding intown neighborhoods. A tremendously loyal clientele uses the restaurant on a regular basis. In addition to its basic culinary orientation, Eat Your Vegetables provides calm, supportive surroundings for social intercourse. Softened by flowery café curtains, the woodsy dining room is comfortably furnished.

The kitchen has always had a wild streak of misdirected

creativity. Variations in kitchen personnel have been hard to deal with but avoiding the pitfalls of the gourmet fringe is easy if one stays in the narrow channel of true vegetarianism.

"Eat Your Veggies Salad" combines very fresh lettuce, sprouts, carrots, mushrooms, avocado, feta cheese, and sunflower seeds in a brimming arrangement that is enough for a healthy dinner. A creamy tofu vinaigrette adds just the right amount of lubrication to this crunchy salad. The Vegetarian Dinner is usually dependable, too, containing large servings of steamed vegetables and beans over nutty brown rice.

Heavily salted with tamari, frequently overspicy, the food is best consumed with plenty of fluids. Several nice wines are available by the glass, in addition to the iced zinger tea and apple juice favored by the eternal children of the age of Aquarius. Late-night entertainment and a new espresso bar have livened things up.

★★★ The 1848 House $$$ ⊗⊗⊗

780 S. Cobb Dr. SE (4 miles west of Dobbins Air Force Base, right turn on Pearl St., Marietta). Map G. (770) 428-1848.
Dinner nightly 6 to 9:30. Brunch Sunday 10:30 A.M. to 2:30 P.M. Reservations and all major credit cards accepted. Valet parking.

The year 1848 is of enormous importance to restaurateur Bill Dunaway. The stately mansion, which you may remember as The Planters, was built in 1848 and everything from the new name to the phone number and the date of origin for many recently acquired antiques has been coordinated to bring a startling new sense of congruence.

The food has caught up with the decor as well. If you remember the previous fare dulled by the passage of time and the annoying discrepancy between the noble Southern structure and its geographically incorrect menu, you will be glad to hear of the changes.

In the daylight of summer there is no prettier dining room than the larger of the two glassed-in porches. On blustery, cold nights, however, you will feel more attracted to cozier corners within view of a dancing fire. You will find abundant literature on the history of the house on the premises. Suffice it to say that the former residence of the mayor of Marietta has been given back to the public and that the food is enjoyable.

Slow-cooked duck leg with warm red cabbage and blue cheese melting into a sauce or a terrine of Southern vegetables wrapped in fresh noodle dough with a light sun-dried-tomato butter show plenty of technique. Less of a dare, but equally intense, a rich Charleston she-crab soup says good things about the region. Marinated grilled shrimp with peanut barbecue sauce is a fun idea for a light appetizer. Oysters in a salty crust of angel-hair potato need to be toned down to engage the palate fully, but who can resist their funny, frizzy appearance?

A fresh pumpkin soup with a tiny crawfish cake has been cleverly enhanced by a swirl of refreshing sour cream. The black bean soup is prime edible art. Rich with a taste of hot pepper and andouille sausage, it is served on a shallow plate with a pretty pattern of drizzled sour cream. Warm Georgia goat cheese salad is a must and the mixed field greens with toasted pecans should be sampled as well.

Downright outrageous is a strip steak of venison, served medium rare, sliced on a spicy Southern chili that includes black-eyed peas and corn. Lamb loin receives a pretty and delicious treatment, coated with crisp potatoes and carved over an acorn-squash ratatouille. Snapper in a crust of bran and crushed pecans is square and good served with fresh corn relish and leaf spinach.

The 1848 House has its own pastry chef and stylish desserts are part of the bargain. Tiny crèmes brûlées offered as a trio take on intriguing flavors such as kiwi or raspberry. Sweet-potato pecan pie is the best of the regional desserts. Two usually homey specialties are treated with unusual elegance, but while the white-chocolate carrot cake beautifully displayed on its own sweet sauce is a marvel, the banana cream pie loses some of its charm in the fancy translation.

Brunch is suave and more traditional than dinner. Wonderful biscuits with sausage gravy, homemade chutneys and chowchows, Southern entrées à la carte, and everything else comes as a reasonable-size buffet.

★★ El Charro $

2581 Piedmont Rd. (on the side of Lindbergh Plaza facing Cub Foods). Map C. (404) 264-0613. Other locations.

Daily 10 A.M. to 11 P.M. No reservations or credit cards. Ample parking.

The charro, a child-size department store mannequin equipped with a bull whip and a sombrero, stands near the door of what used to be a strictly Hispanic dive. Anglo customers and old clientele mix about as well as vinegar and oil. Mexican men straddle bar stools. They sit together in booths with their elbows on the tables and a small covered basket of tortillas next to their bottles of beer.

If you focus your eyes away from the gringos, you will have a feeling of total authenticity. The memorabilia tacked here and there on crudely painted walls seems less like touristy promo than genuine remembrances of home. Some of the staff don't speak a lick of English. There are hand-printed signs in Spanish warning the clientele that "persons who are inebriated will no longer be served" and a Hispanic taxi company is advertised nearby.

The menu is bilingual, chock full of unusual dishes such as liver and onions, tongue tacos, stewed cabrito, and pork-tripe soup. Tacos are not to be missed. Three to a plate (also available as a single nibble), the palm-sized tortillas de maíz are topped with various piquant, always well-prepared ingredients: a single piece of tender goat meat stewed with spices; marinated grilled pork showered with cilantro; crumbled chorizo sausage, onions, and salsa; julienne tongue with salsa and cilantro; chicken in dark mole sauce.

Once you have discovered how much you like the stuffings in the tacos, it becomes easy to trust the same preparations as a main course. Choose from stewed cabrito, liver and onions, and chicken or pork mole flavored with bitter chocolate.

Huevos rancheros and chiles rellenos (using delicious poblano peppers and a very light cheese) make perfect sense as light entrées. Changuitos (flour tortillas rolled around seasoned ground beef, potatoes, and pico de gallo, then fried in tight little bundles) and gorditas (thick corn tortillas stuffed or topped in several variations) are on the heavy side of finger food.

★★★ El Taco Veloz $

5064 Buford Hwy. (Doraville). Map D. (770) 936-9094. Other locations in Sandy Springs and Cobb County.

Daily 10 A.M. to 9 P.M. No reservations or credit cards. Small parking lot.

Velocity is just one of many positives for this tiny taco shack on a stretch of Buford Highway equally divided between Hispanic and Asian food cultures. There are other Mexican holes-in-the-wall nearby, but none as basic in meeting human needs for good food without any of the obligations of a sit-down restaurant. There are fewer than ten stools inside and only two wooden counters (one barely a ledge) on which to unwrap your goodies. Most of the business is drive-thru, nearly always conducted in Spanish.

The operation is simple: the cook (in full view at the original location) peels off a few corn tortillas from a stack, softens them wrapped in wax paper in the microwave, flips a piece of steak on the grill, and chops it furiously. He then ladles on homemade green tomatillo salsa, scatters cilantro and onion, rolls the bundle tight like a homemade cig, and passes it on. There is no room for errors and none are committed. This is as pure as it gets.

What makes the first bite (and the next) so special? The tacos (two per bundle) are soft and warm, the meat delicious, the fresh green sauce hotter than hell. From the cook's hands to your mouth, food takes only a minute to hit your sensitive taste buds. The job is perfectly streamlined. Each day the cook makes a big batch of terrific salsa, using fresh, tangy tomatillos.

There are only a few fillings: quickly seared steak, barbacoa (a tender, spicy beef stew), and (best of all) tongue (in soft, delicious chunks). An excellent small chile relleno wrapped in soft tacos is only available when the right peppers can be found. Chicken tacos have recently appeared. There are burritos as well as tacos—same fillings, different feel (tacos win).

As an alternative to soft drinks, you can try horchata, a sweet and slightly cloudy beverage based on rice water poured over crushed ice. More than likely you'll spend more on gas than on food when zipping to Taco Veloz. A recently opened second location on Roswell Road is larger and more comfortable, with plenty of seating and a slightly larger menu.

★★ Embers $$ ⊗

234 Hildebrand Ave. (off Roswell Rd. at I-285, Sandy Springs). Map H. (404) 256-0977.

Lunch Monday to Friday 11:30 A.M. to 3 P.M. Dinner Monday to Thursday 6 to 10:30 P.M., Friday and Saturday 6 to 11 P.M., Sunday 6 to 9:30 P.M. Reservations and all major credit cards accepted. Ample parking.

In the mideighties, when seafood grills were the big new fad, Embers rated far worse than Marra's, which it then strongly resembled. The restaurant seems to have headed in the right direction. The decor is still not particularly coherent; the building is less beachy but still not elegant by a long shot. Fancy window treatments and mirrors are downright bizarre in a casual and cluttered environment.

But decor be damned. If you lived in Sandy Springs, you would treat Embers as a better neighborhood joint. The clientele seems to be perfectly comfortable in business or casual dress. To raise your level of expectation, terrifically articulate servers volunteer detailed explanations of the menu, have an opinion about the wine, and work the dining room with confidence.

This is just the place you'd like to drop into without bells and whistles to dine on excellent little-neck clams steamed in white wine, perfectly textured crab cakes (snow crab, blue crab, and a bit of long-grain rice) with drawn butter, and a great salmon trout served grilled over garlic mashed potatoes. Embers offers a Havana Banana nightly, the fish of the day prepared in a Cuban sauce with gentle banana peppers and served with red beans and rice.

The garnishes are honest, the desserts homemade. The Key lime pie and the sorbets (vanilla, orange, and butterscotch) leave a clean taste on the palate. Service remains consistent throughout the meal.

★★ Evelyn's Café $

3853-F Lawrenceville Hwy. (2 miles outside I-285 in Brockett Square, Tucker). Map I. (770) 496-0561.
   Lunch Monday to Saturday 11 A.M. to 3 P.M. Dinner Monday to Saturday 5 to 10 P.M. Reservations accepted. V, MC, AE. Ample parking.

There really is an Evelyn behind the counter, rattling pans on the big stove and lifting frying baskets from clean, bubbling oil. Her place is immaculate: shiny checkerboard floors, cheery oilcloths (all in different patterns) smoothed on round tables, a pretty border rimming freshly painted walls with framed photographs of Greek landscapes.

The kitchen may be smaller than many a New York apartment's, but the little crew cooks up a storm and all the food carried by efficient waitresses in red polo shirts looks great. A big gyro tans and sputters on a spit. Freshly cut potatoes hit the oil with a resounding hiss. The restaurant does excellent specials such as stuffed peppers and tomatoes, pasticcio, and lamb ragout, but most of the lunch trade is salad, gyros, and Greek hamburgers. The latter are fabulous, served proud and juicy in a length of crusty bread with tzaziki sauce, lettuce, onion, and tomato.

Whether piled high on the plate with marinated onions, tzaziki sauce, golden fried potatoes, and wedges of plump pita bread or wrapped sandwich style in a twist of waxed paper, the gyro is excellent. The souvlaki plate, however, built along the same lines as the gyro plate, features meat of an occasionally tough nature. Greek salad comes in three sizes (Jr. included with the specials), abundantly dressed with red-vinegar vinaigrette and garnished with finely chipped feta cheese and good olives.

Evelyn's is well worth exploring beyond the lunch quickies. Lamb steaks mountain style (served au jus with herbed potatoes) are spectacularly delicious. Mild, loosely packed grape leaves in tart lemon sauce make an excellent appetizer. Batter-fried ripe tomatoes and beautiful crisp meatballs served with a pungent tomato sauce fall in the same category of great starters. Spanakopita, on the other hand, come one large, droopy triangle to the order and offer no special stimulation. Evelyn's sells a complete line of fresh Greek pastries, including a flaky, honey-scented chocolate baklava.

★★ Everybody's $ ⊗

1593 N. Decatur Rd. (in Emory Village). Map E. (404) 377-7766.
1040 N. Highland Ave. (at Virginia Ave.). Map C. (404) 873-4545.
Sunday noon to 10 P.M. Monday and Tuesday 11:30 A.M. to 10 P.M. Wednesday and Thursday 11:30 A.M. to 10:30 P.M. Friday and Saturday 11:30 A.M. to midnight. No reservations. All major credit cards. Ample parking.

Before Everybody's, pizza didn't exist in Atlanta as a worthy object of desire. Started in 1971 as a tiny hangout for students, this cult establishment has grown over the years, switching its focus to acquire a broader clientele while retaining the endearing qualities of the original. The purists groaned when a modern wing more than tripled the space, chasing some of the murky darkness away. "Oh, God, now it looks like a fern bar," complained some of the regulars, whose social life had been shaped by shared tables, long waits, and lack of parking. They clung to the old corners, leaving the brighter new space to young families and more elegant Druid Hills residents.

But even the grouches had to admit the pizza hadn't changed. Thick and chewy, the crust was still magnificently risen. A yeasty warm aroma rewarded every bite. Mushrooms, green peppers, sliced tomatoes, and pepperoni still tumbled into laps from the richly garnished "Everybody's Special."

The kitchen staff roared with laughter once when a prissy customer issued this astonishing criticism through clenched teeth: "My pizza wasn't neat." Few pies, indeed, look more gloriously messy than a bumpy, swollen Everybody's pie with a precarious balance of assorted toppings. Some of the combinations work much better than others, the Mexican pizza with Mexican spiced beef, sharp cheddar, and jalapeño slices occupying a lowly rank among the possibilities. Introduced as appetizer pizzas, some individual thin-crust pies use no sauce at all, only herbed oil, lemon juice, cheese, and fresh garlic.

The second store in Virginia-Highland is an architectural statement, a sophisticated elongated restaurant with sponge-painted walls and comfortable furniture. The outdoor area, shared with other businesses, is a wonderful balcony with lush plantings. The menu is forever adding new pizza variations, including spectacularly delicious pizza crisps (like chicken and pesto) and salad pizzas (a huge salad balanced on a pizza crust).

The sandwiches on fresh pizza bread are marvelous, the enormous salads overwhelming. The serving personnel is young, spirited, and full of good will.

★★ Fat Matt's Rib Shack $ ⊗

1811 Piedmont Rd. (at Rock Springs Rd.). Map C. (404) 607-1622. Sunday to Thursday 11:30 A.M. to 11:30 P.M. Friday and Saturday 11:30 A.M. to 12:30 A.M. No reservations or credit cards. Small, congested parking lot.

The words "barbecue" and "flair" are rarely, if ever, used in the same sentence. But the first attribute of this cue joint is a certain hip nonchalance not usually encountered in the good ole oinky world of Georgia barbecue. The rounded edges, deep violet colors, and funky beach-style patio make it highly unlikely that you will remember the building as the former Mr. Ching, a study in blandness. A marquee tickles your funny bone with unlikely self-promotions. J.J. of L.A. painted the windows in his usual hyperbolic style, transforming a mere chicken into a turkey from hell.

Inside, it's electric colors. One wall in pulsating cherry red is pinned with blues posters. The rest-room doors are chrome yellow. One says *Duke* above a huge painted key; the other says *Duchess* and has a picture of a lock. A steamy kitchen is visible behind a short counter. At the far end of the room, the piano from the old Royal Peacock is part of a small stage for nightly live blues music.

A chopped-pork sandwich has been added to the basic

ribs or chicken equation. Chicken and ribs each have their own merit: neat versus messy, lean versus fatty, both tender and flavorful. The sauce does an interesting balancing act between the ketchupy excess of Georgia barbecue and the thin vinegariness of its North Carolina counterpart. Served on the side instead of glopped on the ribs, the spicy red concoction can be doctored with Louisiana hot sauce.

The trimmings are limited to potato salad (heavily mayonnaised), coleslaw (very white, crisp, and clean tasting) and rum baked beans (sweet, almost caramelized, with a potent whiff of alcohol). Hot roasted peanuts and draft beer complete the menu. Perverse souls will be entertained by the notion of chewing on bones within a stone's throw of a cemetery. Fat Matt's Chicken Shack next door does a brisk business with fried chicken and fried fish sandwiches in two red-hot tiny rooms.

★ Feeders $

1999 Cheshire Bridge Rd. Map C. (404) 872-8488.
Monday to Friday 11:30 A.M. to 10 P.M. Saturday 5 to 10 P.M.
No reservations or credit cards. Small parking lot.

An unusual rough-and-tough barbecue spot next to a bunch of disreputable lingerie-modeling shops, this unprepossessing young business offers California-style BBQ to a clientele of devotees. There is a little deck where you will fry in the sun unless you move your table into the shade of the building. Inside, the space is kind of cramped.

Go to Feeders. You will find great pulled-pork sandwiches with an indecently hot sauce flavored with habanero peppers. The chili is made with real chile. The smoked prime rib is almost too bizarre for words. Greyish and wet, it seems to be a case study in how not to cook beef but some OK bites are to be found away from the fatty parts. The smoked chicken rubbed with Tex-Mex spices is excellent. You will find unusual side dishes (unusual for a barbecue joint, anyway) and you can pump the owner for information about his special "hall of flame" dinners for people who can take the heat. The restaurant does a fair amount of take-out business and delivers between 6 and 9 P.M.

★★ Fellini's Pizza $ ⊗

2809 Peachtree Rd. (at Rumson Rd.). Map B. (404) 266-0082. 422 Seminole Ave. (Little Five Points). Map E. 525-2530. Additional locations.

Monday to Saturday 11 A.M. to 2 A.M. Sunday noon to midnight. No reservations or credit cards. Crowded lots, street parking.

Not everyone can do the scruffy chic look. Too much, and you're a fright; not enough, and you're merely trendy. Fellini's original pizza parlor transformed a skinny, claustrophobic bar next to the Garden Hills movie theater into a piece of situational art, a Dada collage for hip clientele. Owners Clay Harper and Mike Nelson have since built an empire.

The last few years have seen a definite upward trend: original art, comfortable patios, and a maturing customer base in just about every location. Little Five Points remains true to the original and is one of the best hangouts in the city. Stuffy types might not be up to the clientele. If you feel like calling your lawyer when someone rolls over your toe with a skateboard, if your eyes bug out when you witness the entrance of a smashingly elegant young man in ankle-length skirt and beret, or if the punkettes with morbid lips give you the creeps, then send your kids to fetch the pie. They'll love it, as will anyone with sympathy for the Bohemian side of life.

Don't let the surface wackiness fool you. Deep down, Fellini's is tremendously organized. Only Pizza Hut serves you faster. Place your order at the little island of madness dammed by a high counter. You'll receive a photograph of an entertainer in a Lucite frame. This you plunk on your table. When the crew is done with your large sausage, olive, and double-cheese pizza, they go look for Nat King Cole. The medium Fellini's special with everything is for Elvis.

Fellini's pizza is New York style: thin bottom, light crust, very tender, with a sweet taste of fresh bread. This excellent dough tends to be overwhelmed when too many ingredients are requested. The best pizza in the house involves green peppers, olives, and mushrooms. Fresh mushrooms, lots and lots of them, are thinly sliced and scattered *at the last minute*, when the pie is nearly done. The mushrooms remain a light buff color and firm and crunchy, never reaching the limp greasy stage. The basic tomato sauce, thinly spread on the dough, is highly spiced with flakes of dried red pepper. Good cheese (not Crazy Glue) is used to bond the ingredients.

The white pizza, a fairly recent addition, and the calzone bulging with ricotta cheese, mozzarella, sweet sausage, and/or spinach are excellent, too. The salads have improved over the years. Fellini's serves beer and wine.

★★ First China $ ⊗

5295 Buford Hwy. (a half-mile inside I-285, Doraville). Map D. (770) 457-6788.
   Sunday, Monday, Wednesday, and Thursday 11:30 A.M. to 9:30 P.M. Friday and Saturday 11:30 A.M. to 10:30 P.M. Closed Tuesday. Dim sum Saturday and Sunday 11:30 A.M. to 3 P.M., Monday 11:30 A.M. to 2:30 P.M. Reservations and all major credit cards accepted. Small, cramped parking lot.

One of the best restaurants for the last ten years and one of the very first to offer a special Chinese menu as well as authentic dim sum, this well-run family establishment changed hands in 1994. The Mui family recipes are no longer listed on a separate section of the menu. The friendly, articulate brothers who have seen diners through many an awkward spot aren't there to guide you through the intricacies of Cantonese cuisine. But although the restaurant has a different feel, more rather than less authentic delicacies have appeared on the menu.

You must make sure that you don't get stuck with the ordinary Chinese-American menu automatically handed to non-Oriental patrons. Ask for the *Chinese* menu printed on *white* laminated sheets. Sea cucumber, fish maw, beef tripe, seafood hot pots, and myriad other far-out dishes appear in endless permutations on a bill of fare where Chinese ideograms are translated in Vietnamese as well as English.

The style of cooking is typically Cantonese: lots of fresh seafood and exquisite vegetables, mild seasonings for the most part. Particularly good is a clear soup with watercress, delicate shrimp balls, and slivers of crunchy ginger. Among the vegetables, something called kang kong vegetables comes by the platterful, a wonderful sauté of green leafy little plants with hollow stems and a vibrant, delicious taste.

Tender, floppy beef and sliced onion coated with a spicy satay sauce is another highlight on the menu. The salt-baked squid tastes as if it had been dusted with rice flour as well as salt and looks better than it tastes. Bean curd with ground pork and hot spices is too mild in a sauce way too thin. The room is clean and modern, the atmosphere pleasant, and the service eager.

☆ Florencia $$$$ ✗✗✗

75 14th St. (in The Grand). Map C. (404) 881-9898.
 Dinner nightly 6 to 11. Reservations and all major credit cards accepted. Valet parking.

The difference between an extraordinary tuna-fish sandwich and a merely average one is easy to perceive. But when one enters the realm of high cuisine, the judgment call is more difficult. One is so impressed by the shopping list (truffles, quail eggs, duck breast, rare mushrooms) that relatively weak preparations get the benefit of the doubt. Florencia's menu (five-course degustation on one side, regular list on the other) is every bit as expensive as, for example, that of The Dining Room at The Ritz-Carlton Buckhead. But instead of rare taste sensations and awesome mysteries, one experiences a lot of fancy work one will have trouble remembering in the morning.

Quail eggs meet pickled baby beets and tiny haricots verts in a pretty salad of oakleaf lettuce. The price of another salad described as Wild Greens reaches an astronomical $8.75 thanks to champagne vinegar and truffle oil. Shrimp are shoved into the gaping shells of whole fresh sea scallops set on a sauce in which cilantro and horseradish fight one another. Baby artichokes and asparagus so thin it is hardly worth eating aren't an obvious match either but they look pretty in a light tomato coulis. Risotto with grilled vegetables and leek juice is almost more cream than rice and becomes increasingly difficult to look at when rivulets of beet juice run through its whiteness.

A marvelously tart pomegranate granita (an upscale

slushie) comes next, a tiny moment of joy before an entrée course that could be hard to negotiate. Rare, even extremely rare, duck breast is no problem. But what is fanned out here on raspberry black-peppercorn sauce garnished with a hard, hard baby pear filled with chestnut purée looks and tastes almost like something you would carve out of a live duck!

The pastry chef shows off with extraordinary-looking concoctions such as a trompe l'oeil espresso cup made of chocolate and filled with a rich espresso mousse. The shadow of a spoon is even drawn on the plate in sifted cocoa. A fresh fig tart with Port Chambord sauce is more modest. Except for occasional parties of jolly Spaniards entertained by the general manager, there is never a crowd at Florencia. Having an excellent, intelligent waiter almost all to yourself ranks as a positive experience but hardly compensates for the sense of boredom and isolation.

★★★ The Flying Biscuit Café $ ⊗

1655 McLendon Ave. (at Clifton Rd.). Map E. (404) 687-8888.
Tuesday to Sunday 9 A.M. to 9 P.M. No reservations or credit cards. Small, crowded lot around the corner or street parking.

The biscuits *are* flying in this wonderfully cozy and cramped new intown café filled with the hot smells of baking. Big pans are forever being shoved into the oven, instantly depleted, filled again, and so on. Each fluffy, light, fragrant biscuit you break open and spread with homemade cranberry apple butter is a revelation. The Flying Biscuit Café is located in a neighborhood where folks take time to breakfast. Even better, it serves breakfast all day, a windfall for restaurant people whose shift may mean that they are ready for a plate of eggs at four in the afternoon.

In some ways the restaurant is very traditional Southern but in many others it is thoroughly modern and different. The sunny-side-up eggs come topped with salsa verde and sour cream on thin, crisp black-bean cakes. The scrambled eggs arrive Mexican style in a flour tortilla with warm red salsa. Even the basic Flying Biscuit Breakfast comes with a delicious turkey and sage sausage specially ground for the restaurant.

If eggs aren't on your agenda, there are organic oatmeal

pancakes served with fresh fruit salsa and pure maple syrup. The spicy scramble of tofu, ginger, onion, and red and green peppers spiked with crushed red peppers and fresh herbs has been toned down to accommodate the basic clientele but can be recreated in full force if you make your preference known. Eggs and tofu come with unusually good oven-roasted rosemary potatoes.

There are entrées, virtuous and otherwise. Lucero's Love Cakes, three black-bean and cornmeal cakes with tomatillo salsa and spears of raw onions, are too good to be true, especially with a fresh salad. From fresh pasta to salmon wrapped in rice paper, turkey meatloaf with puddle (mashed potatoes and sun-dried tomatoes), and macaroni and cheese pie, the kitchen has eased into sophisticated tastes.

The entrée-size house salad of organic field greens tossed to order in a fresh balsamic vinaigrette sparkles, especially with the addition of crumbled Maytag blue cheese. Desserts are all homemade: thin and rich espresso bar, sexier than a brownie; seasonal apple spice cake with vanilla ice cream; a cream cheese coffee cake good enough to take home.

The decor is homey: a comfortable counter, tables with matching tablecloths, sponged walls in a brilliant marigold color. A new room, painted like a field of flowers visited by golden bumblebees, has relieved some of the congestion of this popular restaurant. There is even a new wholesome bakery attached to the original storefront.

★★★ Fratelli di Napoli $$ ⊗⊗

2101 Tula St. (off Bennett St.). Map B. (404) 351-1533.
Dinner only, Monday to Saturday 5 to 11 P.M. (late-night menu till 2 A.M.), Sunday 4 to 10 P.M. Reservations for parties of six or more. V, MC, AE. Crowded parking lot.

The more definitely means the merrier in this new supercompetent Italian restaurant in the warehouse section of Bennett Street in Buckhead. If you are of the "two's company, three's a crowd" persuasion, you may not be cut out to appreciate Fratelli di Napoli. Your average picky gourmet couple who want to sample each other's dishes and demand many tastes for their money won't be able to make much headway in the enormous menu served family style in platters that easily feed three or four.

You may be caught in a crowd if you visit Fratelli on a weekend, but you won't get shafted in any way. The staff is on top of things. Owner Tony La Rocco, an experienced restaurateur with two previous places in Hilton Head, remembers everything. And the kitchen holds its own.

Take the pasta, for example. Picture your party passing around a huge steaming platter of penne al carciofi (quill-shaped pasta tossed with artichoke hearts, black olives, fresh diced tomatoes, chopped garlic, white wine, and herbs) or an incredible pappardelle e rapini, with broccoli rabe and little nuggets of sweet sausage. Another penne combination with escarole, white beans, and crumbled sausage is one of the best pasta dishes in the city.

The antipasto platter is a beautiful sampler of cold grilled vegetables (sweet fennel, spears of zucchini, and red peppers among them) with peperoncini, great shards of pungent Parmesan, and a splash of balsamic. The fritto misto and the grilled portobello mushrooms are perfect.

The chicken scarpariello comes on the bone, a mound of easy-to-grab sections of leg cooked in white wine with lots of fresh herb. Salmon romanesco couldn't be more beautiful, tender, and flaky in a rustic red-pepper pesto thickened with a considerable amount of pine nuts.

The desserts are a letdown, especially the awful strawberry mousse that tastes like a cosmetic product. The zabaglione over fresh berries is made in advance but at least it is pleasant tasting.

★★ French Quarter Food Shoppe $

923 Peachtree St. Map C. (404) 875-2489. Other location in Dunwoody. Tuesday to Thursday 11 A.M. to 10 P.M. Friday and Saturday 11 A.M. to 11 P.M. No reservations. V, MC. Small lot around the corner.

French Quarter Food Shoppe has a busy history. As Crescent City Café on Peachtree, it was a lunch extension of A

Taste of New Orleans. Sold once and then sold again, the place is now fully independent of Taste. This typical Cajun café, with a pocket-size patio looking out on the Peachtree traffic, functions as an unofficial clubhouse for Cajuns in exile. People hop tables and ask each other who their papa is. Many of the staff (and all the chefs) have impeccable Cajun pedigrees. The decor isn't much: small black tables, narrow ledges, strips of mirror, a few New Orleans posters, Mardi Gras beads here and Cajun staples there.

Considering the format of the restaurant, there is an amazing level of diversification in the cooking. Gumbo isn't an umbrella term. The seafood gumbo, for example, is radically different from the chicken gumbo or any of other delicious Cajun gumbos offered on a rotation basis. There are many recipes for étouffée as well, depending on the main, mostly seasonal, ingredients.

Although the kitchen looks barely big enough to slice bread for the po' boys, you can expect far beyond the basics. There are, for example, two remoulades: one warm and creamy served over shrimp, the other cold and more mustardy for the chicken tenders in the lagniappe salad. Count also on a strong and rich jambalaya and many interesting specials.

The messy po' boys dripping dressing and shedding lettuce are one of the restaurant's main attractions. Shrimp, oysters, andouille sausage, roast beef, or smoked turkey are equally worthwhile. The muffaletta sandwich comes with the typical oily, spicy olive-pepper-artichoke relish cooked and refrigerated overnight for better flavor. Red beans and rice flavored with andouille sausage are a mainstay, available as a side order.

At night one receives full table service; at lunch things are more hectic (especially on Fridays), with a likely traffic jam at the counter but efficient table delivery by number. A brand-new second location outside the Perimeter taps the suburban market.

★ Galletto Espress-oh $ ⊗

985 Monroe Dr. (at Virginia Ave.). Map C. (404) 724-0204.
Monday to Thursday 7 A.M. to 10 P.M. Friday 7 A.M. to midnight. Saturday 9 A.M. to midnight. Sunday 9 A.M. to 2 P.M. No reservations or credit cards. Small parking lot.

Some of you, perhaps most of you, live in beautiful comfortable homes. Café life, with its Bohemian focus and lack of amenities, may seem like a hardship barely worth the effort it takes to get out of the house. But whether your interior is a haven of peace and good taste or a temporary dump, you will be glad to know about this eminently civilized espresso bar, an easy walk from Piedmont Park and the Midtown cinemas.

Galletto, "cockerel" in Italian, hides behind an anonymous modern facade. Inside, it's a different story. The ceiling is out of sight, the room is framed with shelves like a library, and there is even a library ladder running on a rail. All accessories are expensive and harmonious: coffee cups for sale in an enchanting shade of yellow, great glasses shaped like horns of plenty for the iced coffee concoctions. The furniture is solid oak. Teddy bears and baskets are a bit much, but Galletto is enormously appealing, especially for meeting someone on business.

Galletto roasts its own beans. Particularly good is the iced coffee with a shot of espresso and the big foamy mochaccino. All coffee drinks and hot chocolates come with a tiny complimentary biscotti or cookie. Galletto has the usual choice of regular and low-fat muffins, some very expensive cupcakes, and pretty layer cakes. One of their enormous cookies is enough for a meal.

★★ Garam $$ ⊗⊗

5881 Buford Hwy. (1 mile outside I-285). Map D. (770) 454-9198. Lunch Monday to Friday 11:30 A.M. to 2:30 P.M. Dinner Sunday to Thursday 5:30 to 11 P.M., Friday and Saturday 5:30 P.M. to midnight. Reservations and all major credit cards accepted. Adequate parking lot.

Despair, rather than the excitement of discovery, may be the first emotion you experience at this important ethnic restaurant. One look at the menu, and you feel like the novice on a five-day package trip to the Orient—without a guide. Garam, meaning big river, is *the* big-deal Korean restaurant in town. The menu is gigantic in size and scope. Japanese cuisine is represented in a section of its own. The staff either sprint around as if you didn't exist or politely convey their heartfelt regrets at not being able to answer your questions.

Forge on. You are in a very pretty restaurant. Most dishes are good to very good. Any entrée will entitle you to a stunning variety of small plates and bowls containing delectable pickled items. Kimchee (fermented napa cabbage preserved in hot-pepper marinade—the glory of any Korean home kitchen) is particularly fresh and delicious. Chunks of crisp daikon radish, thin stalks of green vegetables, dried fish, small mild peppers, egg custard, fresh mung beans, assorted vegetables in cold vinegar broth—all become part of a wonderful taste mosaic.

Don't even try to order your meal in courses. Soups, sushi, pancakes, and main courses arrive mostly at the same time or in reverse logical order (yellowtail hand-roll sushi when you are completely riced out at the end of dinner). Fiery (as in "starch noodles mix with fiery") is a notion to be taken seriously. The calamari casserole is a good example of the highly spicy food you will encounter at Garam.

Some dishes are hot in a different sense. Yook-hwe b-bim-bop, a combination of rice, slivered vegetables, and marinated raw beef cut in a fine julienne, arrives topped with one egg in a red-hot stone pot. The heat may be so intense as to crack the plate on which the pot is resting. The rice is dangerously close to burning, the meat cooks in an instant, and you must work like a maniac with your chopsticks to toss, fluff, and mix for a spectacular treat.

There are a few bland items: grainy, starchy mung-bean pancakes (the least expensive item on the menu at $1.50); a strange, elastic confection offered as a freebie with a plate of sliced orange and fresh pineapple.

★★ Georgia Grille $$ ✘✘

2290 Peachtree Rd. (1 block south of Peachtree Battle). Map B. (404) 352-3517.

Dinner only, Tuesday to Sunday 6 to 11 P.M. No reservations. All major credit cards. Self-parking in surrounding lot.

When Karen Hilliard and son Billy Kennedy opened this spicy neighborhood bistro, the name seemed odd in a place that didn't feel particularly Southern. Ms. Hilliard, who was born in Atlanta but raised in Texas, dedicated her restaurant to artist Georgia O'Keeffe and thrived on the double entendre. The space (the former Gianni's) was stripped and redone in pleasant, sunny neutrals. The restaurant lost its air of askewness. Everything looks straighter, stronger. There is a new patio off to one side and the kitchen now is fully visible.

Georgia Grille has a strong Southwestern persona. Affordable, neighborly, the restaurant is a nice place to hang out with a glass of wine (many open selections on wine list and blackboard) and a plate of serious food. Quesadillas with crab meat and chunky guacamole, intensely flavored finely puréed black bean soup with fresh salsa, or meltingly tender swordfish with a hot pineapple glaze will give you a good feeling for Georgia Grille. Lobster enchiladas, fresh crawfish cakes, and Indian fry bread with meat and green chile sauce are among the strongest gourmet items.

Until you know your way around the menu, though, you may bounce from blandness to spiciness within the same meal. This can also be regarded as a positive in a restaurant that can fulfill different sets of expectations. The bread is homemade, and the salads tossed with bacon buttermilk dressing couldn't be fresher. Hurrah for the vegetable plate and most anything from the grill.

If there is a heaven for inspired dessert makers, Ms. Hilliard should be lifted skyward in a flutter of tiny white wings. Can you imagine an improvement on the concept of chocolate mousse? Georgia Grille's Triple Chocolate Mousse is a wonder of casual architecture. Finely ground chocolate wafers counteract the egginess of the mousse, giving it an invisible but deliciously felt inner structure. A fudgy sauce hits some spots and not others, providing further interest to the plate. Peach blackberry cobbler is another casual miracle, while Grand Marnier flan with berries is simply very, very good.

★ Good Old Days $

401 Moreland Ave. Map E. (404) 688-1006. Other locations.
   Tuesday to Friday 7 A.M. to 3 A.M. Saturday and Sunday 9 A.M. to 3 A.M. No reservations. All major credit cards. Small parking lot.

When the first Good Old Days opened near Emory University, nobody could have predicted how far the concept would reach. Flowerpot sandwiches and beer by the pitcher racked up a fortune for the original owners. Good Old Days moved into a different territory (bar business and live music) but the Little Five Points location is reminiscent of the early days.

The patio isn't what you'd call pretty. Its awning is aggressively bright and tight. But once you are seated, the view is great. The exact same row of stores and restaurants can be found inside as well, in a long mural faithfully documenting Little Five Points as it was in opening week. The room is paved with recycled marble and furnished with austere booths. Billiard tables add some fun to the barroom in the back.

The restaurant's claim to fame, its flowerpot bread used in wholesome sandwiches, has adapted readily to breakfast items. The Sticky Pot is the best thing on the menu. Cinnamon, brown sugar, and butter are added to the regular recipe for wholewheat flowerpot bread. As soon as the bread slips out of the flowerpot, it is split, spread with cream cheese, and topped with crunchy granola. Not nearly as good, but still pretty great, the same flowerpot bread becomes a McFlowerpot sandwich with scrambled egg, bacon, and a blend of two cheeses. In the eggs department, try the breakfast pizza (enough for two): a light deep-dish crust topped with scrambled eggs and cheese. Of all the ingredients that may be mixed into the eggs, small link sausage tastes particularly good. Eggbeaters as well as real eggs are available, with good sautéed red new potatoes, toast, homemade flowerpot bread, or decent flattish biscuits. Pancakes come in blueberry, trail mix, or chocolate chip flavors.

None of the other locations does breakfast but the patios are always jammed with young folks, most of them drinking beer by the pitcher and munching on light fare.

☆ Gorin's Diner $ ⓧ

1170 Peachtree St. (at 14th St.). Map C. (404) 892-2500.
 Sunday to Thursday 7 A.M. to 11 P.M. Friday and Saturday 7 A.M. to midnight. No reservations. V, MC, AE. Crowded parking lot.

Not so long ago one didn't expect much from a diner. Being there when one needed it, being cheap and forthcoming with stuff one didn't then call comfort food, that was just about it. Nowadays diners have come dangerously close to being theme restaurants. Synthetic nostalgia is easier to manufacture than quality, however, as demonstrated in this skin-deep operation, a disappointing step up for a popular operation known citywide for excellent ice cream.

Gorin's energy level mimics that of a true diner for less than an hour a day, when the surrounding offices disgorge their quota of lunchers. Then you can feed on the frenzy and snap your fingers to the rhythm of banging plates.

At any other time, you are bound to feel far less engaged. The cruelly shiny little spot with the pretty banquettes (lipstick red, royal blue, and the most joyous, throbbing shade of green) is a drawing-board kind of restaurant. Hyperbolic descriptions and cheesy promises are all over the menu. Burgers and chicken grills are among the better choices, but cheesesteak ("An authentic cheesesteak, Finally!" according to the house) consists of nothing more than thin flakes of meat topped with cheese on a squashed grilled hoagie. Anything vegetable is treated with the crassest disrespect. Overall, prices are no fun considering the quality.

★★★ Greenwood's on Green Street $ ⊗

1087 Green St. (at Cherry St., Roswell). Map H. (770) 992-5383.
Dinner only, Wednesday to Saturday 5 to 10 P.M., Sunday 5 to 9 P.M. No reservations or credit cards. Small parking lot.

Roswell's pride and joy and a great excursion from Atlanta, this small frame house off the main thoroughfare seems to be run by a granny with the energy of a lumberjack. Chef-owner Bill Greenwood isn't quite Southern (he was born in Baltimore), but he is a total believer in home-cooked comfort food. Taking the kind of fare one often sees half-dead on steam tables, making sure that it is well prepared (from scratch, with fresh ingredients) and well seasoned, Greenwood gives us back what we thought was gone for good.

Chicken pot pie with fresh chicken stock, garden vegetables, and a homemade crust; Baltimore-style crab cakes; a marvelous Georgia mountain trout secretly boned and reclosed; a tender filet of catfish; an exceptionally lean rotisserie duck; even potato pancakes stuffed with shredded duck come with hefty servings of fresh vegetables. There are no appetizers to ruin your appetite (the portions are huge) but good homemade soups (mushroom barley or split pea in the winter, fish soup served in a fish bowl in the summer) and fresh batches of corn muffins are just what you need to feel cozy.

Greenwood's is known for its pies. Apple, blackberry, cherry, strawberry/rhubarb, blueberry—the pies are the real thing, baked right in the kitchen and set to cool on the windowsill. Butterscotch pudding, chocolate pudding, banana chocolate-chip pudding, and homemade ice cream are available as well.

When it's cold, there is a fire burning in the fireplace, and when it's warm, you can swing on the porch. The property keeps improving and the number of knickknacks (candles, embroidery, stuff) keeps growing. The restaurant is entirely nonsmoking, with a down-to-earth staff and small wine list.

☆ Hal's $$ ⊗

30 Old Ivy Rd. Map B. (404) 261-0025.
   Dinner only, Monday to Saturday 5 to 11 P.M. Reservations and all major credit cards accepted. Crowded parking lot.

Invisibility seems to be less of a problem for this Creole/Italian schmoozing place than for its predecessors. Owner Hal Nowak, formerly of Vittorio's, has many friends in the city and you may have the feeling that you are the only one in the place who doesn't know just about everyone else.

The building has found a new level of attractiveness. Divided into a casual bar/open kitchen area and a more formal, atmospheric dining room, Hal's serves as a meeting ground for media luminaries and more prosaic Buckhead types. There is big talk at the bar and a pianist who croons old favorites.

The tables are draped with white linen; the lighting is

subdued. Handsomely dressed waiters attend a posh crowd against a background of dark, mellow brick and antiqued mirrors. Everyone seems at ease. Enjoy the feeling while it lasts.

The food is thoroughly mystifying: mediocre at best and especially shocking after the owner identifies himself as coming from New Orleans. Overcooked shrimp, hesitant spicing, heavily fried items, and a smattering of Italian dishes await you here. The entrées fare better than the appetizers as a general rule. Your bill will be too high for you to adopt a tolerant attitude.

★★ Hama $$ ⊗

2390 Chamblee-Tucker Rd. (off Chamblee-Dunwoody Rd., Chamblee). Map D. (770) 451-9883.
> *Lunch Tuesday to Friday 11:30 A.M. to 2:30 P.M. Dinner Tuesday to Saturday 5:30 to 10:30 P.M., Sunday 5:30 to 10 P.M. Reservations accepted. V, MC, AE. Adequate parking.*

Japanese families come to this demure spot to dine in peace, enjoying the moderate prices and the attention of an unpretentious staff. A minuscule entrance hall leads to a pleasant dining room with unremarkable furniture, a few latticed screens, and a minimum of decorative efforts. A well-scrubbed sushi bar occupies one wall, a row of tatami rooms another.

Behind the sushi bar, Chef Fukuhara works with nervous intensity. His style is breathtakingly fast, his demeanor sweetly considerate. His signature dish is an unusual "heaven roll": deep-fried soft-shell crab poking brazenly out of a delicious big roll wrapped in crisp seaweed.

The menu is relatively short: juicy steamed dumplings with varied shapes and fillings, grilled fish, barbecued slices of beef served sizzling with soft onions and sprouts, various tempura preparations, including unusual mini-pancakes made of finely chopped assorted vegetables, and seafood fried in crisp tempura batter. Hama serves combination dinners in large, compartmented bento boxes, nowhere near as elegant as the exquisite samplers offered in delicate lacquer in other restaurants. Various noodle dishes, hot and cold, buckwheat or rice based, come as daily specials.

★ Hard Rock Café $$ ⊗⊗

215 Peachtree St. (at International Blvd.). Map A. (404) 688-7625.
Daily 11 A.M. to 2 A.M. No reservations. All major credit cards. Parking in expensive downtown lots.

Suburban teenagers and aimless tourists never seem to mind the insufferable wait at this entertaining theme restaurant. The 2 to 3 P.M. time slot is rumored to be the only one without a debilitating wait. If you go in the evening, of course there is a line. Forty minutes and a rubber stamp later (to prove that you are old enough to drink!), you barely earn the right to stand in the bar area for the real wait. Every attempt to walk around is met with a figurative crack of the whip.

Noisewise, Hard Rock Café isn't as wretched as a cult concert at the Omni but every surface you come in contact with vibrates perceptibly as the bass passes through it. The room is grand, a sort of chapel of rock with Elvis and Little Richard in larger than life-size stained-glass windows and a beautiful cupola painted like an ideal sky with the sun, the moon, and the stars. The famous guitar-shaped bar is so big and so crowded that the only way to see its full shape would be to hang from the ceiling. If you have the misfortune of sitting close to some worthwhile artifact (Diana Ross's dress, a good picture of Jimi Hendrix), people will push their way into your booth. The staff is infernally cheerful.

The clientele gorges on heaps of French fries, bulging burgers, and mega nachos. Vegetarian items and some wholegrain munchies are available as well. The burgers require much effort, and the notion of a vegetable Reuben with the broccoli and carrots of the season fails to impress, although it has a place. Children and adolescents adore it.

★ Harold's Barbecue $

171 McDonough Blvd. SE (near Jonesboro Rd.). Map F. (404) 627-9268.
Monday to Saturday 10:30 A.M. to 9 P.M. No reservations or credit cards. Tiny parking lot in front.

Lunch time is your best bet for catching the curious mix of regular patrons at the trough. Harold's is a favorite of lawmen: city cops, state troopers, wardens from the nearby Atlanta Penitentiary. Bureaucrats from the Capitol join blue-collar workers from the big GM plant around the corner to sit at the counter in the front room or to gather at solid wooden tables in the back room, whose unpainted pine paneling has darkened to a rich patina.

Harold's barbecued pork and beef are not incredibly special but there's a strong gastronomic justification for sitting with Atlanta's finest here: this is one of the last city bastions to serve that great Southern creation, cornbread with cracklin's. Adding to good moist cornbread the crisp bits of rendered pork fat provides a delicious crunch that is one of the great pleasures of Dixie eating.

Two sauces for the barbecued meat sit on tables, one unpleasantly thin and tart, the other unpleasantly thick and sweet. The brunswick stew has a good chunky consistency, but almost no flavor. Decorations are limited to embossed metallic platters of the dime-store variety and plaques bearing religious and upbeat sayings. Individual packets of Alka-Seltzer are dispensed at the front counter, along with an impressive assortment of cigars.

★ Harry & Sons $ ⊗

820 N. Highland Ave. Map C. (404) 873-2009.
Lunch Sunday to Thursday 11:30 A.M. to 2:30 P.M. Dinner Sunday to Thursday 5:30 to 10:30 P.M., Friday and Saturday 10 A.M. to 2 A.M. No reservations. All major credit cards. Small parking lot behind Surin or difficult street parking.

With American bistros everywhere borrowing Asian dishes and adapting Asian techniques, it stood to reason that the reverse could, indeed would, happen. Harry & Sons, related to nearby Surin of Thailand, offers an unlikely Thai-Italian menu where, for example, pad thai and spicy basil noodles come in the same section as pasta primavera and rigatoni in filetti di pomodoro sauce.

The main interest at Harry's is the satay bar. At $1 apiece

and with a choice of pork, beef, chicken, lamb, or squid, the typical Thai skewers served with a beautiful spicy peanut sauce and sweet marinated cucumbers sound better than all the other appetizers put together.

When you can tear yourself away from the satay counter (you can also order the skewers while seated in the dining room), move on to the tom yam koong (a bracingly hot and sour Thai-style shrimp soup garnished with big slices of American mushrooms and beautiful shrimp). Fried calamari with tangy red sauce is perfect, done tempura style and in big chunks. Curry puffs with cucumber sauce, on the other hand, are a generic appetizer.

Entrées garnished with carved vegetables and served with brown rice define themselves in terms of their sauces. Panang (a red curry based on coconut milk, red chiles, garlic, and lemon grass), Kiev-Wone (a shrimp curry sauce), spicy Thai basil sauce, roasted cashew sauce, black mushroom and ginger sauce, and even an Italian-style white wine and garlic sauce can be combined with chicken, beef, pork, shrimp, or scallops. The pad thai (Thai noodles with shrimp, bean sprouts, eggs, and crushed peanuts) isn't especially memorable, but the spicy basil noodles pan-fried with onion, tomato, Thai basil, and your choice of meat are extraordinarily good.

Italian-style pasta is served crowded onto too small plates and, in the case of a linguine and clam, can be disconcertingly unorthodox (huge strips of something hard to identify as regular clams) as well as disappointing in taste. Harry's offers some good desserts (a carrot cake among them) and a pleasant choice of beers and wines. The dining room is small: apricot walls, vintage brick, plump banquettes a few steps up from the regular tables and chairs.

★★ Hashiguchi $$ ⊗⊗

3000 Windy Hill Rd. (The Terrace shopping center). Map G. (770) 955-2337. Other location in Around Lenox shopping center.
    Lunch Monday to Friday 11:30 A.M. to 2 P.M. Dinner Monday to Thursday 5:30 to 10 P.M., Friday and Saturday 5:30 to 10:30. Reservations and all major credit cards accepted. Ample parking.

Hashiguchi at The Terrace boasts of having the area's largest sushi bar, and it also offers an extensive and intriguing menu. Patrons greedy for exotica will have their hunger slaked here. In addition to the sushi bar, the restaurant offers small dining rooms with efficient and friendly table service. The look is crisp, clean, austere—polished light woods, a few handsome vases and porcelain trays strategically placed.

The sushi bar is an especially gregarious place. People quickly fall into conversation with their neighbors, exchanging favorite sushi memories of California, Pennsylvania, or Tokyo. Try the "Special California Roll," which adds to the basic ingredients of crab and avocado a generous beading of red caviar on the outside. For the most sumptuous texture contrasts, order a combination of quail's egg and flying fish roe—soft, slithery, crunchy, and crackly all rolling around in your mouth together. For a different kind of treat, ask for a "hand roll," any item or combination with rice inside a seaweed cone the size of a classic ice-cream cone.

A new, smaller version of Hashiguchi serves the same excellent fare across from Lenox Square Mall. The sushi rolls, served on an ornamental ti leaf, include a perfect spicy tuna roll, a special rainbow roll with beautiful layers of various fish, and a tempura-fried sea bass roll. Lacquered boxes of chirashi sushi ("scattered" sushi) and vinegared octopus with Japanese eggplant are great treats as well.

★★ Havana Sandwich Shop $

2905 Buford Hwy. (near N. Druid Hills Rd.). Map D. (404) 636-4094. Monday to Saturday 11 A.M. to 9:30 P.M. No reservations or credit cards. Small parking lot.

Don't look for romance at this counter-service spot irradiated by fluorescent lighting and decorated with beer emblems, a poster for *Gone With the Wind*, and another poster showing two pigs smooching. Order a Cuban sandwich (plentiful tender pork marinated in a piquant sauce, with ham, peppers, and mustard on a fine crusty hoagie) or the steak sandwich made from thin slices of excellent beef. Tangy grilled onions give a coquettish twist to the boliche sandwich (finely chopped pot roast, swiss cheese, pickles, and peppers on crisp Cuban bread). Another dependable sandwich is the Milanesa (heavily breaded steak, onions, lettuce, tomato, and tiny slivers of fried potato on Cuban bread—dry, but tasty).

Voracious eaters should order the magnificent thick, smoky garbanzo bean soup and the steak sandwich made from thin slices of really good beef. The pork platter comes with sautéed and browned thick slices of onion. The Cuban tamal flecked with ham has a fine strong corn taste. The black beans and rice that accompany dinner plates are almost always nicely textured and tasty, unlike the dull iceberg lettuce and pale tomato slices garnishes.

Pick up dessert orders at the same time you get main dishes. The thuddy cheesecake, average flan, and cinnamony sweet rice pudding are stored under refrigeration and need time to warm up for best savoring. Service is brisk but amiable.

★★ Haveli $$ ⊗⊗

2706 Cobb Pkwy. (just north of Cumberland Mall). Map G. (770) 955-4525. Other location downtown.
  Lunch Monday to Saturday 11:30 A.M. to 2 P.M. Dinner nightly 5:30 to 10:30. Reservations and all credit cards accepted. Ample parking.

This is the area's most elegant Indian restaurant, known for its lavish dinner parties and excellent lunch buffet. Haveli transformed a former stereo salesroom into a quiet, luxurious environment. A glassed-in tandoor oven operates in a tiled room at the rear of the main dining room. Soberly dressed managers walk the floor, supervising a cheerful and accommodating staff.

The name of the restaurant means "treasure" or "riches," a promising moniker for a menu that is more ambitious and, to a significant degree, better prepared than at Haveli's counterparts around Atlanta.

Haveli is a classic Northern restaurant, with great emphasis on fancy meat dishes. Chicken cooked in the tandoor emerges fall-apart tender. A particularly pleasant way to enjoy tandoori chicken is in a dish called murg tikka masala, a simmer in rich cream sauce spiked with spices. Lamb comes in small installments in finely tuned sauces. Nan bread, excellent plain, becomes magical when stuffed with minced lamb (keema nan). If your budget will allow it, order jheenga saagwala, shrimp served with onion, mint, and a purée of spinach and herbs.

The vegetarian preparations, excluding the dull biryanis, range from good to spectacular. An entire vegetarian dinner served in individual dishes on a round tray is an excellent and economical option. An eggplant preparation called baingan bharta is particularly good. The eggplant, first baked on skewers in the tandoor, is then chopped and simmered with tomato, onion, and spices in a fragrant sauce thickened with coconut milk.

The chutneys and breads are above average, the fried appetizers their usual heavy selves. Desserts, from irresistible pistachio ice cream to rice pudding cooked with rose water (kheer), a delicious cottage-cheese dish in milky syrup (rasmalai), and a confection of carrots and almonds in clarified butter (gajar ka halwa), are unusually agreeable.

Haveli celebrates special holidays with festive menus. A new location downtown is especially convenient to the Apparel and Gift marts.

★★ The Heaping Bowl and Brew $ ⓧ

469A Flat Shoals Rd. (at Glenwood Ave.). Map E. (404) 523-8030. Monday to Thursday 11:30 A.M. to 10 P.M. Friday 11:30 A.M. to 11 P.M. Saturday 8 A.M. to 11 P.M. No reservations or credit cards. Street parking.

Young patrons, some of whom come from neighboring Grant Park and Ormewood Park, join the business folks and residents of East Atlanta in this brand-new café. Art-statement tables painted by a well-known Atlanta artist, hip green walls with orange ducts and a giant map of the world, neatly folded copies of prestige newspapers (including the *Financial Times*), and a wall of pristine kitchen equipment give style to The Heaping Bowl and Brew. The menu is distinctive as well, a mix of vegetarian and casual fun dishes with a special emphasis on homegrown vegetables.

Were it not for his mother's organic farm and for a serious loan encouraging urban renewal, young chef-owner Todd Semrau wouldn't have been able to make nearly as large a contribution to his evolving neighborhood. Everything fell into place, though, down to the beer and wine license and the enthusiastic crew, including Mom, pressed into service as a short-order cook.

If you pop into The Heaping Bowl for munchies, you are in luck: baskets of skinny sweet-potato fries sprinkled with cinnamon pepper with cranberry-mustard dip, grilled sliced country bread available by itself or as an add-on to an appetizer sampler of grilled fresh vegetables with rice, Damn Big Turkey Leg grilled with lemon pepper, Polish-style noodle dumplings with sour cream and spring onion. All are unique to the restaurant.

The "Heaping Bowls" section of the menu offers sausage and sage perogies filled with cheese and potato, chicken and noodles with a tart lemon-herb broth and an assortment of chunky fresh vegetables, and the occasional delicious Chinese hot and sour pot over rice. All are served in heavy white bowls. The greens and beans stew includes red and white beans and assorted Georgia greens "from Izzy's garden."

Izzy, known to Atlantans in another life as Betty Semrau, the suave voice of the Peasant Restaurants, brings in an amazing variety of her vegetables: long green beans to be stir-fried with a Thai peanut and ginger sauce; skinny eggplant and colorful squashes for grilling; sweet potatoes, kale, okra, and tomatoes to use in many dishes. The homemade desserts are fresh and delicious. The peach-blueberry crumble and the custardy, light chocolate bread pudding are both served warm with ice cream.

If you want a beer with your (delicious) burger or bratwurst, there are big sixteen-ounce drafts and a small but upscale selection of microbrews by the bottle.

★★★ The Hedgerose Heights Inn $$$$ ⓧⓧⓧ

490 E. Paces Ferry Rd. Map B. (404) 233-7673.
Dinner only, Tuesday to Saturday 6:30 to 10 P.M. Reservations essential. All major credit cards. Adequate parking behind and on side of restaurant.

The restrained elegance of this small house and the refinement of its opulent dishes have set the standard for excellence in Atlanta dining since April of 1981. Bravado presentations of powerful dishes are the Hedgerose's stock in trade, but a light touch can be expected as well. The grand gestures are the telling ones.

Started as a partnership between brothers Heinz and Roland Schwab, the restaurant has enjoyed the finest of reputations. The recent death of Heinz Schwab (once the young and talented chef at Nikolai's Roof) has saddened the entire restaurant community, leaving Roland in sole charge of a restaurant that shows strong signs of surviving with no compromise of long-held standards.

The dining room is lovely. Flowers are everywhere, in giant sprays spilling from celadon vases, reproduced in low mirrors behind a row of banquettes, and in the stunning service plate that unites the basic colors in the restaurant's design. The wine selection, divided almost equally between California and Europe, is on a par with the food and atmosphere. No major restaurant in the city has more bad tables, however. Those lined up along the mirrored wall are much too close together, so that waiters and exiting customers are forever brushing up against your shoulder, and their conversation cannot possibly *not* be overheard.

The bar has been recently revamped. Wines by the taste as well as the glass or the bottle can be enjoyed in a sophisticated setting and the dining room has a charming new softness.

The Hedgerose can't ever replace its original chef. But Roland's first big move has been to hire young Steve Austin, who distinguished himself as the chef for Brasserie Le Coze. With Austin in charge, the menu has altered its course. There is a new emphasis on seafood. The style is less classic and more

American. Some of the dishes, such as the sautéed shrimp on seaweed salad with ginger vinaigrette and the exquisitely light fresh crab salad flavored with mint and chervil, are clearly Austin's.

The perogies with béarnaise are still on the menu, however, and so are the rich pâtés, the Swiss salad (a delicate assiette de crudités by another name), the game dishes, and the hot soufflés for which the restaurant is known. A delicious complimentary hors d'oeuvre, a gravlax tidbit over a paper-thin round of potato with herbed oil, may upstage such solid appetizers as a Mediterranean seafood selection (shrimp in mustard-herb sauce, calamari with tomato-zucchini relish, mussels with sweet peppers, and sea scallops in cilantro oil) and a timbale of puff pastry with escargots and creamed artichokes.

One could make a case against the soft-shell crab served in a messy way over lobster sauce and shreds of gingered carrot. The breast of pheasant is a bit neutral to the taste (if one has been spoiled by the wild intensity of game pheasant) although the preparation, with porcini mushroom sauce, celery mashed potatoes, and leek compote, has plenty of panache.

The desserts, from the individual baked Alaska shaped like an igloo to the impeccable crème brûlée and gorgeous soufflés, haven't suffered the least bit. The Hedgerose remains a fine European-style dining room and one of the great places to savor a special bottle of wine.

★★ Heera of India $$ ⊗⊗

Rio Shopping Center (at North Ave. and Piedmont). Map C.
(404) 876-4408.
> *Lunch daily 11:30 A.M. to 2:30 P.M. Dinner Sunday to Thursday 5:30 to 10:30 P.M., Friday and Saturday 5:30 to 11 P.M. Reservations accepted. V, MC, AE. Ample parking.*

A short passage through Rio's acid colors and crouching golden frogs will lead you into a contrasting world of quiet dignity. Enough architectural details have been added to Heera's basic modern space to create a sense of departure. Light cream-colored stucco was used like lavish icing on a cake. Some walls recess to provide for the display of delicately carved artwork. Overhangs soften the lines of the bar corner. The lights are gentle, the tables attractively set.

At the far end of the restaurant, a tandoori chef tends the fire behind a plate-glass enclosure. The tandoori combinations show an excellent range of flavors. Chicken tikka masala (boneless breast simmered in cream) and sheekh kabab wrapped with onions and lettuce in soft whole-wheat paratha are delicious appetizers. Meat and vegetable samosas are unusually light. Nan bread stuffed with minced lamb or onions and spices is a glorious first course.

Curries and vegetable dishes have distinctive spicings. The lunch buffet is an excellent way to sample to your heart's content. Dessert may be time to pass up the calories. Only the kheer (runny, perfumy rice pudding with sliced almonds and pistachio nuts) can be described as comparable in refinement to the rest of the meal.

★ Highland Tap $$ ⊗

1026 N. Highland Ave. (at Virginia Ave.). Map C. (404) 875-3673. Dinner Sunday to Thursday 5 P.M. to midnight, Friday and Saturday 5 P.M. to 1 A.M. Brunch Saturday and Sunday 11 A.M. to 3 P.M. Later hours for the bar. No reservations. All major credit cards. Small parking lot in the back or difficult street parking.

Patterned after the Midwestern steakhouses from the 1950s, this popular cellar is as famous for its world-class Martinis as for its much less memorable steaks and burgers. The dark room with massive stone walls is cozy and the bar one of the best in town. The stools hug you in the right places. The light is warm. Blue-collar beers and serious drinks attract a large crowd.

Take no notice of the froufrou appetizers such as escargots in puff pastry, but the basic meat and potato entrées are always at least OK. The kitchen has improved since the early days and one can now get a nicely charred rib eye or New York strip. When the burgers are on target, they are drippy and delicious. Big salt-crusted baked potatoes should be considered the vegetable of choice.

Brunch is a popular event with a great, old-fashioned menu including wonderful monster biscuits with gravy.

★★ Ho Ho $

3683 Clairmont Rd. (between Buford Hwy. and Peachtree-DeKalb Airport). Map D. (770) 451-7240.
   Lunch Monday to Friday 11:30 A.M. to 2:30 P.M. Dinner nightly 5 to 10 (Friday and Saturday till 10:30). Reservations and all major credit cards accepted. Adequate parking.

Like Atlanta, Ho Ho resurrected itself after a fire. Note the phoenix on the back wall of the small dining room, rampant above a Budweiser Light emblem and a double thermostat. During hours when other Chinese restaurants are closed, it is not at all uncommon to find their proprietors here, enjoying delicacies available at few other eating places in this city. Care in ordering is required here, however. Choose exclusively from among the fifty or so numbered items on the "Special Chinese Menu" inserted among the other pages.

The owners come from a coastal mainland province opposite Hong Kong known for its preparation of seafood. Distinctive specialties include handmade shrimp balls and fish cakes, fried oyster pancakes with bean sprouts, and a crunchy cold jellyfish salad.

Western palates may resist trying the wonderful braised pig nose served with cilantro and vinegar, but the cold chunks of roast duck with cilantro should present no problem. If you like the flavor of star anise, try either the beef stew pot with bean curd, or the beef stew noodles. Both are excellent, but very similar in taste.

★★ Hong Kong Harbor $$ ⊗⊗

2184 Cheshire Bridge Rd. Map C. (404) 325-7630.
   Monday to Thursday 11:30 A.M. to 1 A.M. Friday and Saturday 10:30 A.M. to 3 A.M. Sunday 10:30 A.M. to 1 A.M. Reservations accepted. V, MC, AE. Small parking lot.

Ease of use is a cardinal advantage this intown Chinese restaurant has over its competitors. You don't have to ask for "the special menu." You don't have to flag someone to translate ideograms pinned on the walls in a desperate effort to order what "they" are having. The kitchen is fully visible behind a large picture window hung with crisp brown lacquered ducks. Two large aquariums built into the back wall harbor a healthy population of fat lobsters and heavyweight crabs.

Hong Kong Harbor lists an enormous variety of dishes, true Chinese delicacies for the most part. Pay particular attention to the special sections on congee (many variations of rice soup) and Hong Kong hot pots. Concentrate on seafood. If you are informed, for example, that oysters are great on the day of your visit, you would be a fool to ignore the tip. Other "must-try" dishes include large shrimp in their shells, lobster casually hacked in pieces, tender salt-and-pepper squid with a good hot bite of freshly sliced hot peppers and marinated slivers of onion, and deep-fried whitebait mounded on a plate (an ideal snack with beer).

A mainstream dish to indulge in would be tiny Singapore noodles pan-fried with roast pork and shrimp and a dusting of curry. To round out the meal there are many fresh vegetables to choose from: cho sum, Chinese broccoli, braised mushrooms and bamboo shoots, and more. The one not to be passed up is pea vines with tender leaves and minute tendrils, cooked down like fresh greens.

Hong Kong Harbor serves excellent dim sum. The good Chinese tea lunch delicacies are served seven days a week until 3 P.M. (cart service on weekends, menu weekdays).

★★ Honto $$

3295 Chamblee-Dunwoody Rd. (off Buford Hwy., Chamblee). Map D. (770) 458-8088.

Monday 11 A.M. to 10 P.M. Tuesday to Thursday 11:30 A.M. to 10 P.M. Friday and Saturday 11:30 A.M. to 11 P.M. Sunday 10 A.M. to 10 P.M. No reservations. V, MC, AE. Adequate parking.

You can get the full Chinatown experience in the briskly lit square rooms of this popular restaurant. Don't expect much in the way of exotica. There are tables and chairs and people—most of them Chinese. Long strips of paper hang on the wall: the specials of the day in black ideograms. In a fish tank by the door lobsters or eels await their fate.

The dishes arrive, in rapid succession: roasted duck lacquered in a delicate shade of orange; meaty chunks of fresh bacon with crackling crispy skin; floppy slices of elephant clams sautéed with straw mushrooms and pea pods; squid in a light batter, fried with *hot* green peppers; strands of broad rice noodles intensely flavored with fresh ginger and little nuggets of beef; fresh shrimp dumplings and Chinese broccoli barely poached in clear stock.

All inhibitions lifted, you'll find yourself digging faster and faster into the food: huge, luscious shrimp, head, tail and all, dry-sautéed with coarse salt and fresh ginger; hog chitterlings, shaped like a baby's tiny ear, loud and pungent but with a very clean taste; fish ball soup of comforting blandness; whole grouper festooned with julienne vegetables and sprinkled with ground pork; chunks of tender chicken, hacked through the bone and flecked with salted black beans.

Atlanta has quite a large group of Oriental foodies, many of them in the restaurant business. They are a tough lot, uncompromising on authenticity. If you want to see them, go before 8:30 P.M.—the Chinese eat early. By 9 P.M., Honto's clientele is solid American. Whether you are interested in the fringes of edibility or like plain good food, you'll put up with the lack of decor and the marginally hostile service. Honto serves an excellent weekend dim sum.

★★★ Horseradish Grill $$ ⊗⊗

4300 Powers Ferry Rd. Map B. (404) 255-7277.
Monday to Friday 11:30 A.M. to 10 P.M. Saturday and Sunday 11:30 A.M. to 3:30 P.M. and 5 to 10 P.M. No reservations. All major credit cards. Valet parking.

Every coo and gurgle of this new restaurant has been attended to by someone whose fame has preceded him or her. Showered with gifts galore and a prestige location (the former

Red Barn Inn by Chastain Park), Horseradish set itself up for almost unreasonable expectations. Thanks to chef Scott Peacock, the restaurant offers a taste of the New South in an attractive, sensible package.

Architect Bill Johnson has done extraordinarily well, transforming the former old barn into something that could serve as a background for a Ralph Lauren ad. Beautiful wood, natural stone, great white surfaces, modern paintings—all are the epitome of comfortable good taste. The bar, attractive in its own way, is used as a secondary dining room. There are two outdoor areas, one used for drinks and waiting, the other a gracious dining terrace under spectacular old trees.

The menu is terribly clever: a modern, fashionable compendium of new regional dishes with plenty of references to Southern traditions. Some of the best dishes are hard to classify, which makes them great grazing material. The Georgia caviar (black-eyed peas, sweet pepper relish, homemade corn crackers), the Hot Georgia Browns (generously cut house-smoked turkey served on biscuits with a light cheese sauce and crumbled bacon), and the stylistically related Maryland-style chicken on hot buttermilk biscuits with tomato gravy all fall into this category.

The farm-style chicken salad is a sublime summer dish: fresh chicken pulled off the bones in luscious big strips, oven-roasted beets and potatoes, homemade mayonnaise. The roasted Vidalia onion with spicy greens, field peas, and tomato garlic sauce is one of the highlights among the starters, but would also be a great component of the vegetable plate.

For entrées, there is a definitive version of fried chicken properly done in a skillet; an impeccably trimmed fresh pork chop served with turnip greens and a fancy version of macaroni and cheese; pedigreed white Georgia shrimp lightly grilled, drizzled with garlic parsley vinaigrette, and served over an abundant salad of fresh greens; and delicious catfish, served as a filet over tomato, cucumbers, salad greens, and ginger pickled onions in a buttermilk dressing. The trout wrapped in bacon (also available without the bacon) has become a signature item for the restaurant.

Dessert time is the magic moment to lay all criticism to rest. Pineapple upside-down cake with rich homemade vanilla ice cream, chocolate chocolate layer cake, lemon chess pie with Bourbon cream, and fresh peach cobbler with a delicate sugary crust are some of the finest, most refined versions ever created. An incredibly creamy homemade chocolate ice cream served with fresh sugar cookies is something you would steal from the plate of your own child. Ditto the oven-warmed golden cupcakes with chocolate sauce and soft whipped cream.

Long waits and uneven service are typical of a hot new restaurant. Horseradish prepares picnic baskets to go to the park, the lake, a concert, or anywhere. A beautiful vegetable garden serves as a reminder of the seasons.

★★ House of Chan $$ ⓧ

2469 Cobb Pkwy. (U.S. 41, across from Loehmann's Plaza, Smyrna). Map G. (770) 955-9444.
   Lunch Monday to Friday 11:30 A.M. to 2:30 P.M. Dinner nightly 5 to 10 (Friday and Saturday till 10:30). Reservations accepted. V, MC, AE. Ample parking.

The apartment-dwellers who pour into this unassuming storefront might well be satisfied with the sort of fare that passes for Chinese at the scores of places lining the Marietta 4-Lane, but the Chans do not cut corners. The least educated of palates are treated like honored guests. The wide range of dishes is typical of the sort of nouvelle Chinese cuisine that has evolved in Hong Kong, where chefs from all the various provinces of China work together. In the case of this modestly charming place, the term is an invitation to cover a lot of culinary ground in a few short moments.

Have no fear of such common vulgarities as abuse of monosodium glutamate, garlic, cornstarch, or sugar. Sauces are scarce, subtle. Duck, for example, is stuffed with preserved plums, roasted, and hacked into delicious morsels. The plums turned into sauce are gently spooned over the luscious meat. General Tao's chicken, marinated with Szechuan pepper and vinegar, is exquisitely hot. Eggplant seasoned with minced pork melts richly in your mouth. Even the sweet and sour sauce is robust, not at all like the orange goo you may be used to.

Seafood preparations are particularly varied and distinctive. Don't miss the menu item of plump, juicy oysters stir-fried with green onion and ginger and barely filmed with a pungent sauce, or the shrimp in bird's nest with near-black, crunchy walnut meats and stir-fried snow-pea pods in a tangle of crisp shredded potatoes.

★ Houston's $$ ⊗

3539 Northside Pkwy. (at W. Paces Ferry Rd.). Map B. 262-7130. Other locations in Buckhead.
   Monday to Thursday 11 A.M. to 11 P.M. Friday and Saturday 11 A.M. to midnight. Sunday 5 to 10 P.M. No reservations. All major credit cards. Congested parking lot.

This enormously popular midrange chain specializes in straight-arrow American cuisine. The waits for tables are famous but so is the quality of the service (all servers go through a rigorous boot camp and management stays very close to the operations). The food is honest: gigantic fresh burgers, generous salads (the Southwestern-style grilled chicken salad with narrow strips of tortilla is particularly good), and, as a recent development, gourmet pizzas with creative toppings.

A good selection of homemade signature soups; freshly cut fish served with coleslaw, French fries, or couscous; oven-roasted chicken; and prime rib allow for substantial eating. People like the drinks and the "Chicago Style" spinach and artichoke dip. The decor, brick and brass, often imitated by other restaurateurs, is posh and comfortable. The clientele tends to be young and frequently single.

★★ Hsu's $$$ ⊗⊗

192 Peachtree Center Ave. (at International Blvd.). Map A. (404) 659-2788.
   Monday to Friday 11 A.M. to 10:30 P.M. Sunday 5 to 10 P.M. Reservations and all major credit cards accepted. Validated valet parking in the evening.

Hsu's location in the lower regions of Tower Place eventually defeated owner Raymond Hsu, who relocated downtown after years of struggle. Hsu's is a Hong Kong-style restaurant, the kind of establishment where, in the Orient, wealthy merchants retire for elaborate banquets. Patrons expecting a typical Chinese-American environment may lack a frame of reference for some of the arcane offerings and fancy edible carvings that are part of the repertoire of trained banquet chefs.

Trim tuxedoed waiters bring, carve, serve, and defer with elegant manners. A typical menu might include crisp large leaves of iceberg lettuce stuffed, taco style, with spiced hot minced pork, followed by small oysters on the half-shell, steamed and topped with pungent black bean sauce. Next comes a soothing tofu soup, then tender chicken sautéed with fresh mango, and a combination of grilled salmon and large prawns in a sweet orange-colored sauce. Last is ginger ice cream.

The quality of cooking varies. Cornstarch is used too freely in some dishes, and spicing is not always judicious. But you can order some of the choicest items à la carte: sesame roast chicken (carved tableside), anything paired with luscious slivers of mango, an exceptional fried rice, and some of the best oolong teas in town. The expansive formal dining room has enough class for business entertaining.

★★ The Imperial Fez $$ ✗✗

2285 Peachtree Rd. Map B. (404) 351-0870.
  Dinner only, nightly 6 to 10. Reservations accepted. V, MC, AE. Small parking lot.

To tell or not to tell? Describing the restaurant to your friends is almost as bad as revealing the end of a play or movie. There is an element of surprise that shouldn't be spoiled. Every inch of wall, ceiling, and column is padded with brilliant fabrics. Silver and gold threads trace complicated embroidery patterns everywhere. There are rugs upon rugs, piles of cushions around low tables, exotic vessels, cone-shaped baskets—a myriad of rich details. You must surrender your shoes. Barefoot and bedazzled, you will make your way to a dining nest of pillows.

Planned as a happening as much as a meal, the five-course dinner involves only one decision: your choice of an entrée. After a ritual washing of the hands above a gleaming basin, you will soon be digging into the food with slippery fingers. A basket of sweet honey-wheat bread appears first, followed by bowls of harrira, a rich red soup based on lamb and lentils. A combination of salads fanned on a platter poses quite a challenge as the marinated eggplant, fava beans, potatoes, carrots and raisins sprinkled with rose water, and other oily treats tend to slip between your fingers.

The next course is a b'stella, traditionally a sweet meat pie filled with squab, egg, almonds, and spices, here using succulent morsels of Cornish hen instead. The combination of meat and sweet can be repeated with the entrées (e.g., lamb glazed with honey and almonds). You should definitely try couscous, a healthy combination of grain (heart of the wheat), meat or seafood, and vegetables (turnips, eggplant, garbanzos). Already combined on a plate, the couscous is at its most delicious when sprinkled every once in a while with some of the broth over which it has been steamed and spiced with harissa (a fiery paste of red-hot peppers).

Dessert is a philo b'stella filled with chocolate and nuts. You'll receive a final aspersion with a mixture of orange-blossom and rose water. Owner Rafih Benjelloun will probably tell you about his many lives, his many friends, and his many dreams. Top belly dancers always.

★★★ Indian Delights $

1707 Church St. (at Scott Blvd., Decatur). Map E. (404) 296-2965. Tuesday to Thursday 11:30 A.M. to 8 P.M. Friday and Saturday 11:30 A.M. to 9 P.M. Sunday noon to 8 P.M. No reservations or credit cards. Ample parking.

Extraordinary. The word will form upon your lips again and again. The style of cooking, the balance of spices, the incredibly low prices have never been experienced before in Atlanta in this particular configuration.

There is nothing exotic whatsoever about the dining room,

a strictly functional arrangement of Formica tables and budget chairs contained in a plain storefront. Indian Delights is as much a carry-out as it is a restaurant. Service is at the counter, a glass top over some refrigerated shelves.

Strict vegetarianism prevails. Don't stop traffic while you ponder about the unfamiliar menu items. "A little bit of everything" will serve as an introductory sentence. The food is dirt cheap and everything is good. One dish is on nearly every table: an enormous pancake folded like an omelet and a small bowl of soup. This is called masala dhosa, and it is a crisp, faintly sticky pancake made with rice and lentil flour stuffed with curried potatoes. The soup is a hot infusion of vegetables and spices. On the plate is a line of freshly grated coconut chutney. The combination will leave you speechless with wonder.

Other mysterious items include squares of ground chick peas (not unlike unfried falafel) seasoned with black mustard seeds and served with an intense green chile sauce; a delicately spicy concoction based on unsweetened puffed rice, diced vegetables, and cilantro; and various bean and lentil dishes served either with fried puri bread or big round cakes of soft rice flour. You will recognize samosas (turnovers) and bhajhi (onion and vegetable fritters) but will be amazed at their lightness. Totally mystifying (as well as uncannily delicious), mini-puri breads the size of silver dollars have been opened at the top, filled with a delicious yellow vegetable curry, and drizzled with a tart yogurt sauce.

Among desserts, gulab jamun and ras malai are both round, sweet, and unpleasantly textured by Western standards. You may find a more rewarding experience in a pudding of grated carrots boiled in syrup, small fingers of baklava filled with pistachio nuts, or excellent crumbly almond cookies. Indian tea takes a while to prepare but the frothy mixture flavored with pods of cardamom and whitened with milk is a wonderful comfort drink.

★★★ Indigo Coastal Grill $$ ⊗⊗

1397 N. Highland Ave. (Morningside). Map C. (404) 876-0676.
  Dinner nightly 5:30 to 11 (Friday and Saturday till 11:30).

Brunch Sunday 9 A.M. to 3 P.M. No reservations. All major credit cards. Parking in small lot across the street (sometimes difficult), behind the building, and in a real estate company lot nearby.

This relaxed restaurant, a companion piece to Partners next door, offers coastal cuisine and an atmosphere of permanent vacation. Chic, relaxed touches are everywhere. Prominent wall space has been given to a tawdry papier-mâché depiction of "King Lobster and his Court" (reportedly salvaged from a Red Lobster). A gorgeous marine aquarium serves as a room divider. A Hemingway-sized sailfish dangles from the ceiling. The kitchen encroaches upon the dining room. Brown wrapping paper is stretched on the tables. A fabulous back porch, a new front porch, and a connected shop expand the space.

Waiting is a given, unless you come at opening time. People line up docilely at the bar for a glass of boutique California wine, old-fashioned ginger beer, straight or mixed with pineapple juice and Jamaican rum (ask for a Rastafarian), or a special margarita made with fresh Key lime juice.

The menu is full of good ideas: tiny goat cheese enchiladas with black beans; grilled chicken with fresh fruit salsa (papaya, pineapple, pomegranate seeds); crisp pork carnitas rubbed with achiote and rolled in soft flour tortillas; Yucatanean lime soup; deep-fried plantain chips with garlicky fresh avocado purée; double breast of chicken rubbed with jerking spices.

Many tastes can be accommodated. A steamer brought to the table with sea trout or baby cohoe and eight or ten perfect vegetables seduces some, while the new fusion dishes delight others. The vegetarians can have the steamer without the fish; or wrap crisp vegetables in warm soft flour tortillas, making generous use of bubbly queso fundido and onions marinated in lime juice to spice them up.

Nobody could resist owner Dan Carson's Mom's Key lime pie (no meringue, no whipped cream, a buttery graham cracker crust that never weeps), the Bahama bananas (with rum and Key lime sauce), or the warm chocolate chip cookie pie.

In keeping with the Indigo mentality, the new brunch is a trip from one hot spot to the next. There are Vermont-style cornmeal blueberry pancakes with eggs, maple syrup, and old-fashioned warm apple sauce. A low-country sauté of shrimp, country ham, peppers, and onions comes over creamy grits. There are good desserts, too: warm coconut pound cake, cool Key lime pie, and comfort cobblers.

★★ Ippolito's $ ⊗

1425 Kings Market (at Holcomb Bridge Rd., Roswell). Map H. (770) 998-5683. Other locations near Perimeter Mall (Map H) and in Alpharetta (Map H).

Lunch Monday to Friday 11:30 A.M. to 2:30 P.M. Dinner nightly 5 to 10 (Friday and Saturday till 11). No reservations. V, MC, AE. Ample parking.

If you believe that one rates restaurants as much with the heart as with the palate, you'll be doubly impressed by this hopping neighborhood joint, a pizza-and-pasta concept with a touch of the eccentric. Knowing nothing of the ownership, you may safely assume that Ippolito's is operated by a bunch of pack rats. Every inch of wall space, ceiling, counter, and bathroom stall has been claimed for pop-culture displays.

There always seems to be a wait at Ippolito's. Channeled between a wall of stacked beer cartons and a busy-busy bar, lots of people get friendly with one another, drink red wine in small kitchen glasses, or pass a handful of crayons to other folks' kids to color their own menus. If you are really, really hungry, you can get started with a snack at the bar: delicious fresh garlic rolls dusted with Parmesan; Italian sausage chunked in rich red sauce or wrapped in tender, puffy pizza dough.

Even though Ippolito's is more than a pizzeria, the open kitchen at the back sets the tone with its mad baking activity. The basics are excellent: fresh dough swelling into beautiful, tender pies; an excellent sauce, neither too dark nor too acidic; great ingredients aplenty. The calzone are, if anything, more remarkable than the pizza. How anything that large can be that light is a matter for consideration. The white pizza is another highlight of the menu, with garlic, olive oil, basil, sun-dried tomatoes, and fresh parsley.

You may play with the notion of selecting a shape of pasta and a sauce from a list of five (spaghetti aglio e olio, cheese tortellini with cream pesto, etc.) and pat yourself on the back for having made a good decision. The kitchen's idea of baked ziti doesn't meet general standards, though, and the ravioli are particularly thick and unappealing. All dinners come with an excellent crisp salad and an order of garlic rolls.

★ Jagger's $ ⊗

1577 N. Decatur Rd. (in Emory Village). Map E. (404) 377-8888.
Monday to Thursday 11:30 A.M. to 1 A.M. Friday 11:30 A.M. to 2 A.M. Saturday 11:30 A.M. to 1 A.M. Sunday 11:30 A.M. to 9 P.M. No reservations. All major credit cards. Parking in front or in back lot.

Bill Jagger, who earned his Ph.D. from Emory, has opted for pizza, burgers, and beer in preference to force-feeding cultture to youth. The town is full of lecturing professors, but only a handful of people know how to bake good pizza. And Jagger's is tops.

When the popular tavern opened in the early seventies, pizza was far indeed from Bill Jagger's mind. He turned pizza-maker as a result of a beer price war fought with Everybody's next door. When the archenemy started selling beer at a price Jagger was unwilling to match, he replied by selling pizza. The reaction was good. The pizza was here to stay.

The rectangular pie served on a round platter and cut into pieces of unequal size may offend your sense of geometry, but not your appetite. Excellent ingredients piled high on the dough stay together by virtue of plenty of good cheese. While most pizza-grade mozzarella melts into a thick lava bonding all ingredients it encounters, the Wisconsin brick used by this restaurant rests lightly on the pie and offers no resistance to the bite. More brick cheese is sprinkled in the pizza pan before the dough is patted in, giving the crust an interesting tang.

The hamburgers, on the other hand, are far from reliable. Sometimes the patties burst with savory juices. On other occasions, the meat is grey and gristly. Simple burgers are much to be preferred over fanciful combinations.

Faculty and students from Emory hang out in the mellow

old room darkened by age and cigarette smoke. A brightly modern addition to the restaurant failed to establish a separate identity, first as a deli, then as an upscale café. This less atmospheric section now serves the same pub food and pizza as the original tavern.

★ Jake's $ ⊗

931 Monroe Dr. (at Virginia Ave. in Midtown Promenade). Map C. (404) 874-0418.
Monday to Thursday 7 A.M. to 11 P.M. Friday 7 A.M. to 1 A.M. Saturday 10 A.M. to 1 A.M. Sunday 11 A.M. to 11 P.M. No reservations or credit cards. Ample parking.

Some people swear by Häagen-Dazs; others are devoted to Bassett's or Ben & Jerry's. One brand of ice cream, though, made right here in Atlanta, is every bit as rich and delicious as the better-known competition, with a large number of enthralling flavors. Greenwood's manufactures its confections in small batches and distributes them mostly to clubs and restaurants. Short of touring the Chamblee plant, the best access to a large range of flavors is at Jake's dessert and ice-cream parlor hiding behind an austere facade that bears an absurdly unobtrusive neon sign.

Original owner Jake Ingram has sold the business but the tradition goes on. At prime dessert time, the place becomes congested with a slow-moving line waiting for the crew to pack Viennese strawberry sherbet (flavored with orange peel), Bailey's Irish Cream, chocolate fetish (fudge, chocolate chips, and chocolate ice cream), hazelnut Frangelica, bittersweet mint, and English toffee into sugar cones and rolled-up waffle cones. When employees abandon the scooping of the rich ice cream in order to perform time-consuming tasks like operating the espresso machine or cutting and serving cake, traffic slows to a crawl. The baked goods, a choice of approximately a dozen, come from various local sources and carry reasonable price tags.

The cappuccino is prepared simply and correctly. Lipstick-red banquettes, sharp modern tables, and contemporary mirrors await you inside, while more mundane furniture is used outdoors.

★★ Java Jive $ ⓧ

790 Ponce de Leon Ave. Map C. (404) 876-6161.
Breakfast Tuesday to Friday 7 to 11:30 A.M. Brunch Saturday and Sunday 10:30 A.M. to 2:30 P.M. Lunch Tuesday to Friday 11:30 A.M. to 3 P.M. Dinner Tuesday to Thursday 6 P.M. to midnight, Friday and Saturday 6 P.M. to 2 A.M. No reservations or credit cards. Small parking lot or street parking.

If The OK Café and Johnny Rockets can do it, by gosh so can this new luncheonette/coffeehouse on Ponce across from the old Clairmont Motor Lodge. Java Jive isn't nearly as mainstream as the other two, but the principle is the same: a nostalgic trip back in time, food good enough for today's standards.

The building, a former Maytag laundry, is an electric shade of blue-violet. Inside, Formica and linoleum reign supreme. Off to one side, a space that could be used for expansion looks like a pool deck or the practice rink at the roller-skating place. This comes in handy for parking bikes or baby strollers but adds to the strangeness of the building.

The table lamps are of a style sought by collectors and pretty much despised by anyone else: typical odd ceramic bases and often two-tiered marbleized parchment shades straight out of the fifties. A grouping of period kitchen clocks and another of coffeepots have become art on the wall. "You'll like our big fluffy dryers," claims a sign painted in cheerful colors. The place is a bit bare but music fills the gap.

Java Jive has a pleasant lunch and dinner menu (mostly sandwiches and salads), bakes its own old-fashioned desserts, and even dips some pretty good ice cream. The brunch menu is particularly great: granola parfait, wheat germ pancakes, Peanut Butter and Jelly French Toast, scrambled eggs with cream cheese and fresh basil. The challah French toast is light and wonderful. The gingerbread waffle with homemade lemon curd may be too sweet for some but you can almost treat it as a fluffy and delicious dessert. Aunt Bernice's Fried Matzo dipped in egg batter will have you speaking Yiddish in no time. Oy! Especially good is the scrambled tofu prepared with mushrooms, onions, and red peppers. Weekday breakfasts are more limited, but you'll simply fall for the tender biscuits and pristine egg dishes.

★★ Jersey $

4920 Roswell Rd. (in Fountain Oaks Shopping Center inside I-285). Map H. (404) 847-0576.
   Monday to Friday 11 A.M. to 8 P.M. Saturday 11 A.M. to 7 P.M. No reservations or credit cards. Adequate parking.

New Jersey, no breakthrough state in terms of culinary invention, has given us at least one distinctive specialty: the submarine sandwich. Crammed with deli cuts and cheese and, in the case of the cold sub, piled high with shredded lettuce, sliced onions and tomatoes, and dripping with vinaigrette, a Jersey-style sub sandwich comes on a long, preferably crisp loaf of bread. Marinated sweet or hot peppers, pepperoncini, jalapeños, grilled onions, and even kosher dills can be added to boost the sandwich.

You may be under the impression that you don't like sub sandwiches. More likely than not, the versions you have been exposed to below the Mason-Dixon line have been mass marketed, served in fluff bread, and wrapped in paper printed with a corporate logo. Some chains are a lot better than others, but for a return to the source, stop at Jersey in Sandy Springs, where the art of sandwich making is taken seriously.

The bread, white or an amazingly good whole wheat, is oven fresh. The meats are sliced to order and the sandwich assembled while you watch, with possible last-minute interaction to customize your sub. The cold subs, such as the Jersey Special with cheese, roast beef, and pepperoni or the Jersey Original with cheese, boiled ham, prosciutto, capocollo, salami, and pepperoni, are best. Both are far lighter than expected with an excellent balance of finely sliced ingredients.

The steak sandwiches are fairly greasy but delicious. Give the shaved steak an occasional miss though and opt for the chicken cheese steak described as "a cheese steak without steak!" Owner Ken Celmer stands at the cash register, supervising a friendly, clean environment, where everything feels organized with the customer in mind.

★★ Joey D's Oak Room $$ ⊗⊗

1015 Crown Pointe Pkwy. (at Abernathy Rd.). Map H. (770) 512-7063.
 Daily 11 A.M. to 10 P.M. (Friday and Saturday till 11 P.M.). No reservations. All major credit cards. Ample parking.

Described euphemistically as "mostly true" by management, the story of one Joey d'Angelo as a source of inspiration for this self-confident restaurant is a clever composite picture aimed at winning approval from several sides. Bar, steakhouse, deli, New Orleans dining hall—Joey D's does it all under one roof.

Everything happens in a tall, wide room sprawling on several levels. The kitchen line is fully visible in a central location. The bar is a stunner, stocked seven tiers high with an inventory that includes more than four hundred brands. The dining room is informal. Set on acres of oak parquet, the tables are covered in white, well-padded oilcloth. Elegant picture windows and old-fashioned ceiling fans complete the picture. The staff does laps around the room, waiting on any table with a minimum of fuss.

Joey D's has done what folks said couldn't be done, bringing to Atlanta the ultimate in deli sandwiches and charging plenty for it. The Authentic Carnegie Deli Corned Beef Sandwich is a cheap ticket to New York, a fabulous amount of delicious brisket piled on flavorful, springy rye bread, served with deli mustard and a crisp pickle. The next aspect of the restaurant, the steakhouse angle, is fun as well. A hefty bone-in strip steak, a proud nine-ounce filet, and even the house special twenty-ounce bone-in rib eye are easily affordable. The quality is absolutely fair for your money, the grilling without surprise despite a cryptic warning on the menu that the cooking is "Pittsburgh-style" and that the meats "are cooked to classic temperatures which may be less done than you expect."

Excellent French fries, decent baked potatoes, or fettuccine

Alfredo are included in the price of a meat entrée, as well as a house salad or beefsteak tomatoes and onions. Joey D's seafood selection is limited to a few tasty items. Best of the lot are the New Orleans spicy shrimp, a wear-a-bib kind of dish, with deliciously hot, firm shrimp in their shells swimming in a punchy, oily bath. Broiled fish (one or two varieties a night) are available plain or Sicilian style (a light brushing with extravirgin olive oil, onion, and spices).

If you are a fan of *real* New York cheesecake (incredibly dense, cheesy rather than sugary the way Southerners like theirs), by all means cram in an enormous wedge. If suicide by cheesecake doesn't appeal to you, there is warm chocolate-chip pecan pie and grown-up milkshakes with booze and silly stuff.

★★ Johnny Rockets $ ⊗

6510 Roswell Rd. (at Abernathy Rd., Sandy Springs). Map H. (404) 257-0677. Other locations.
   Daily 11 A.M. to 10:30 P.M. (Friday and Saturday till 2 A.M.). No reservations or credit cards. Small parking lot.

If cleanliness is next to godliness, then this immaculate malt shop must be revered above all restaurants, old and new. Walls of white tiles are washed every night. Chrome sparkles. On the kitchen wall, stainless steel shows no smudge of human activities. The food area is kept obsessively clean, smoking prohibited throughout the restaurant.

The concept of Johnny Rockets (a throwback to the high-school malt shop of the fifties) comes from Los Angeles. This Sandy Springs unit was the first to open in the Southeast, followed by other locations. Decor and food show meticulous attention to details. Restored flip-tab jukeboxes gleam on the counter, swallowing nickels and crooning "Rama Lama Ding Dong" and "Big Girls Don't Cry." A life-size WAC found in the Coca Cola archives smiles at a uniformed WAVE on opposite walls of the restaurant. Covers from *Life Magazine* are displayed under glass. All soda pops come in long-neck bottles. Water is dispensed in red plastic paper-cone holders.

The burgers in their idiot-proof wrapping are delicious.

They are just the right size, the meat freshly ground, the buns baked especially for the restaurant. Tillanook cheddar, not some undistinguished processed yuk, graces the cheeseburger. The fries are stupendously good, either plain or with chili, cheese, and raw onion (the best junk food in the city).

Have a tuna salad sandwich made with pure white tuna and light mayonnaise. Don't miss the shakes (triumphantly thick) or the malts. The apple pie is a cult item: baked fresh throughout the day, it has been lightly brushed with egg wash (a secret stolen from the French) for an unusually delicious and crisp crust. Peach pie is available as well, plain or à la mode.

★★ Joli-Kobe $ ⊗

5600 Roswell Rd. (upper level of The Prado). Map H. (404) 843-3257.

Lunch only, Monday to Saturday 11 A.M. to 3 P.M. No reservations. V, MC. Ample parking.

This is a European bakery, except that it isn't. There are quiches, stuffed croissants, baked goods with French names, yes. But the bakers, standing on tiptoe or crouching to stock and unload gleaming steel ovens—how strange that the bakers should all be Oriental! And the cakes, whole at the bottom of the display case, in rigorously identical slices just above, they look—different. Nothing obvious, but you could swear . . .

You have just entered a *Japanese* European bakery. The Japanese take a look at our Western products and cheerfully decide they'll make better ones, but could it be that recipes for combining electronic components are easier to duplicate than blueprints for charlottes or cheesecake?

Operated by Kobe Steaks in the same shopping center, Joli-Kobe is a dazzlingly clean, beautiful little café that smells warmly of bread being baked. If you are the big burly type that likes to open your mouth wide and shovel, Joli-Kobe may be too dainty for you. But if you notice things like quality, freshness, and aesthetics, the salads and sandwiches are great.

The Japanese, like the French, consider American cakes much too sweet. Using all natural ingredients, half the sugar (and twice the gelatin), Joli-Kobe manufactures a number of mousse cakes, charlottes, and cheesecakes with a very dry sponge base and the palest, most otherworldly fillings you ever tasted.

★★ Kamogawa $$$$ ⊗⊗

3300 Peachtree Rd. (at Piedmont Rd. inside the Hotel Nikko). Map B. (404) 841-0314.
>Japanese breakfast Monday to Friday 7 to 10 A.M. Lunch Monday to Friday 11:30 A.M. to 2:30 P.M. Dinner Monday to Thursday 6 to 10 P.M., weekends 6 to 10:30 P.M. Reservations and all major credit cards accepted. Valet parking.

The Kamogawa company started with one ryokan (a traditional Japanese inn) in Tokyo, expanded its operations to modern resort hotels, and went into the restaurant business in the early eighties. Built by temple craftsmen from Kyoto, this handsome restaurant leases space from the hotel.

When you reach Kamogawa at the west end of the hotel building, you set foot in a different world. The entrance is delicately serene. With bamboo poles, rice paper, clean pale wood, and long, straight granite paths, the restaurant takes you on a journey to traditional Japan.

If you were in Tokyo, you wouldn't expect to eat sushi, tempura, noodles, and ceremonial kaiseki dishes in the same establishment. Wanting to provide the American clientele with a comprehensive Japanese experience without sacrificing the amenities that keep things legitimate for business travelers from Japan, Kamogawa has incorporated many cooking styles into its concept.

The sushi bar is a bit boring. The dining room looks a bit sterile as well, but offers some unusual delicacies. While salted bonito intestines may sound too authentic for you, you could venture into some delicious exotica such as a combination of delicate, firmly textured pickles made from burdock roots, a beautiful raw tuna served cubed in a thick, milky substance made from a grated mountain yam, or a little dish of blanched, rolled spinach served in sesame milk. A delicate custard with ginkgo nut and exquisite rice comes with the entrées, some of which disappoint.

The ultimate experience is that of a kaiseki dinner in one of four tatami rooms. When making arrangements for a kaiseki dinner, the only thing you may discuss is the price ($40, $70, or $100). The chef enjoys total creative freedom within the limits of the given budget. He is strongly moved by the influence of the seasons, considering the availability of certain ingredients as well as the aesthetic climate of a particular time of the year.

Eating a kaiseki dinner compares to a regular meat-and-potato meal the way esoteric science fiction relates to pulp novels. You could be on the planet Mars, where a stalk of asparagus feeds twelve delicate aliens, where the eyes are as important to gourmet appreciation as the taste buds, where unusual textures and poetic translucence matter passionately.

Make sure to look at the two-story-high Japanese courtyard, a massive arrangement of man-made rocks with three gushing waterfalls cascading into a landscaped pool. Were it not for a few charming trees and a dwarf temple, you'd expect to see Bam-Bam and the Flintstones.

★ King and I $ ⊗

*1510-F Piedmont Ave. (Ansley Square). Map C. (404) 892-7743.
4058C Peachtree Rd. (at N. Druid Hills Rd., in Windsor Station shopping strip opposite Brookhaven MARTA station). Map D. (404) 262-7985.*

> *Lunch Monday to Friday 11:30 A.M. to 2:30 P.M. Dinner nightly 5:30 to 10 (Friday and Saturday till 10:30). No reservations at Ansley Square, reservations accepted in Brookhaven. V, MC, AE. Ample parking both locations.*

The original King and I in Ansley Square has always been a modest establishment—humble in scale and looks, limited in menu selection. It bills itself as "Thai-Chinese," which is fair enough, given the small choice of Thai dishes. None of them ravishes, but the entrées featuring basil as the main seasoning for various meats are usually well balanced and tasty, the coconut ice cream with split peanuts always delicious. The appetizers of spicy chopped meat (larb) and pork on skewers with a peanut sauce (satay) are very reasonable, the staff friendly, and a dinner here can be a pleasant experience. Bas relief prints of Thai dancers constitute the sole decorative touches.

Far grander and more authoritative is the second location in Brookhaven. By ethnic restaurant standards, this is quite an elegant place, though the prices are unexpectedly low. Good tablecloths, lush window treatments, an elaborate portico of nonstructural columns, and a couple of original oil paintings that look more like objects from a modern gallery than an Asian five-and-dime contribute to the atmosphere.

No particular audacity or skill is required to pick pleasant dishes out of a well-translated menu. Spicing has been toned down to a widely acceptable level. Many dishes are served at an exceedingly pleasant warm temperature: rice vermicelli tossed with minced pork, shrimp, and lime juice, garnished with fresh bean sprouts (yum woon sen); larb, a salad of ground beef seasoned with lime juice, fish sauce, and fresh hot peppers; pad thai, flat rice noodles, gently elastic to the bite, stir-fried with lime juice, sliced chicken, and shrimp, garnished with raw sprouts and ground peanuts.

Even the hot dishes feel refreshing. The tom yum soup (chicken, mushroom, lime juice, and lemon grass) and the fisherman soup (much the same, but substituting shrimp, fish, and squid for the chicken) have a charming tart quality a world away from puckering sourness. The curries are light and flowery, with a teasing aroma of jasmine.

★ Kobe Steaks $$$ ⊗

5600 Roswell Rd. (in The Prado). Map H. (404) 256-0810.
Dinner only, Monday to Thursday 5 to 10:30 P.M., Friday and Saturday 5 to 11 P.M., Sunday 4:30 to 10 P.M. Reservations and all major credit cards accepted. Parking in crowded mall lots.

Some adults may balk at the idea of having their steak cut into bites, sautéed in rice wine, soy sauce, and "Japanese butter," but children of all ages will adore the clownery, not to mention the final product: tender, flavorful meat alongside heaped, delicious vegetables. The system is fabulously efficient—drinks, soups, salads happen in minutes. The chef trundles in his cart of goodies, rushes through a few jokes, and the food starts flying on the flat grill. An entire meal can take less than an hour.

The sirloin dinner is hands-down best, followed by filet mignon and shrimp. Tell the culinary ninja to go easy on the grease, the seasonings, and the soy, and you'll have a perfectly decent meal. Dessert and green tea are included in the price of dinner specials. The children's menu costs half the price of a regular entrée. Little children are offered chopsticks ingeniously tied together with rubber bands around a wad of paper. Even a three-year-old can manipulate the primitive contraption.

Reservations are essential, or you'll spend as much time waiting in the expansive lounge as you will eating. The formula isn't suited for intimate gatherings that permit all members to engage in conversation. Strung out in a line, diners focus on the show rather than each other. Since the light in each dining room is trained on the performing chef, the walls recede into darkness. The decor matches the concept: it looks much more American than Japanese.

★★ Kudzu Café $$ ⊗⊗

3215 Peachtree Rd. Map B. (404) 262-0661.
 Daily 11 A.M. to 11 P.M. (Friday and Saturday till midnight).
 No reservations. V, MC, AE. Congested lot.

Very, very, very clever. No one will ever fault Susan DeRose and Richard Lewis on account of taste or intelligence. Previous restaurant concepts, from Bone's and The OK Café to the gone but not forgotten Pearl's Fish Café and Trotters, have shown the same talent for slipping into a particular mode and developing a congruent menu.

Not as chef-driven as Buckhead Diner nor as plain as Houston's, this tasty new hybrid has a bit of both with a residual taste from The OK Café.

There is nothing Southern or caféish about the posh little

structure, which could be expected to hold its own in one of Dunwoody's moneyed shopping centers. Inside, imagine lots of daylight pouring into the brick and brass environment of an updated mainstream American restaurant.

There is a sharp horseshoe bar dead ahead with lots of fancy overhead storage. A sweet little rec room with sofa, fireplace, and game machines catches the overflow of the restaurant. A garden room with rattan furniture at the far end and a larger section with posh booths and a clever pattern of green-painted wooden uprights complete the picture. A ritzy kitchen stretches in the distance behind a clear glass wall.

Where is the kudzu? In the pattern of the carpet and on the vests of the servers; wrought in greenish metal and climbing on the walls; in whimsical Southern photographs; on the logo of the restaurant.

Southern culinary imagery serves as a point of reference only. Homemade jumbo saltines with fresh peanut butter, peachy exotic iced tea, chicken and dumplings that resemble amusing little wontons dotted with black mustard seeds entertain the senses. Frozen moon pie is a fun joke played on the white trash classic.

Crispy calamari with lime-caper tartar sauce or tuna burger with pickled ginger mayonnaise cannot claim any Southern affiliation but both are good, delicious even, in their own right. The burger uses freshly ground tuna, as dark and meaty as beef and more mysteriously delicate.

Roasted chicken basted with red pepper jelly is amazingly tender and flavorful served with a choice of vegetables. Fried green tomatoes, homemade mashed potatoes, split corn on the cob grilled on hickory, apple-cider slaw, and Brussels sprouts are favorites. Salads, served with homemade jumbo saltines, are topped with the restaurant's "secret kudzu recipe" (fried turnip greens or so they say). The Tomahawk Chopped Salad is a fine mixture of greens, smoked turkey, crisp bacon, salami, chick peas, green olives, hard-boiled eggs, tomato, and blue cheese cut in itsy bitsy pieces and tossed with Dijon vinaigrette. The Kudzu Smoked Turkey Salad has big chunks of lightly barbecued smoked bird on a beautiful mixture of lettuces, yellow peppers, marinated cucumbers, and more, dressed with balsamic vinaigrette.

Watermelon is served in season and there are shakes every day, but when it comes to dessert, you won't want to miss the frozen moon pie, an enormous ice-cream sandwich including everything from icy marshmallows to crème de menthe, hot fudge, and chopped salted peanuts. Expect to drink American wines and American beers. The servers are a bright bunch empowered to make decisions.

★★ Kurt's River Manor $$$ ✘✘

4225 River Green Pkwy. (between Hwy. 120 and Pleasant Hill Rd., Duluth). Map I. (770) 623-4128.
Lunch Monday to Friday 11:30 A.M. to 2 P.M. Dinner Monday to Saturday 6 to 10 P.M. Reservations and all major credit cards accepted. Ample parking.

From the cover of the menu and the restaurant's business card, he sneers, knowingly, rakishly, from under jutting eyebrows that arch like fish hooks. This caricature of sharp-nosed, goateed chef and owner Kurt Eisele endears and invites. Eisele used to head the kitchen at the Atlanta Athletic Club.

Chef Eisele's long stint in private clubs gives him a good grip on versatility as well as a perspective on the difference excellent service makes in the enjoyment of a meal. You will find some of the best possible waitresses at Kurt's and a good traditional menu with a rich German influence.

Spaetzle (a wonderfully textural starch that is a cross between a noodle and a dumpling) sautéed with ham, mushrooms, and fresh cream are particularly good as are the snails in red-skin potatoes and the variations on the Wiener Schnitzel theme. A sauté of shrimp and veal in curry sauce is the kind of preparation one rarely sees anymore but reconnects with easily. Soft-shell crabs absorb too much of their lemon-caper butter to be truly distinguished, but overall the kitchen inspires trust.

Excellent homemade desserts and an impressive list of European beers (treated as seriously as the wines on the wine list) are two further attractions. A beer garden with a more casual German menu is open three days a week (Thursday to Saturday).

Built in the ultima Thule of the Atlanta suburbs, River Manor appears at the end of a long driveway cutting through a featureless pasture. The river is in sight only if you can fly like the proverbial crow, but you don't need a view to dine happily among the suburban gentry in this large, low-ceilinged restaurant decorated in opulent middle-class style.

★★ La Fonda Latina $ ⊗

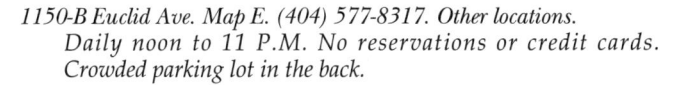

1150-B Euclid Ave. Map E. (404) 577-8317. Other locations.
  Daily noon to 11 P.M. No reservations or credit cards.
  Crowded parking lot in the back.

From day one La Fonda had all the makings of a cult restaurant: a funky location, a menu unlike any other, shockingly low prices. Who but Mike Nelson and Clay Harper of Fellini's Pizza would have taken a chance on a decrepit performing space with no street access? The one-room facility had the charm of a subbasement. Yes, but the rent was cheap and there was space to pour a patio.

Impossible odds being what pump Nelson and Harper full of adrenaline, the recycling battle was won in record time. The patio is a terrific space. On vacation from life, you enter a totally protected space covered with a corrugated translucent roof. You could be anywhere that's fun.

Frantic or sentimental, Latin music fills the air. Standing fans blow a strong breeze between walls of chipping old brick and a cinder-block restaurant with a curtain of plastic beads. Trashy and/or brilliant colors have been used with nonchalant disrespect for bourgeois taste. A second-phase blitz renovation created access from the street, an explosion of art, and a more comfortable dining room on the same level as the patio.

Mike Nelson was raised in Spain and his memory served him well on the paella. Nothing comes close to the price/quality ratio of this authentically flavored Spanish rice dish served directly in cast-iron frying pans. Paella for one is $5.50. In case you are still reading (instead of rushing out to grab one), paella for two is $10. Chicken and chorizo, calamari and shrimp, onion and garlic are buried in generously flavored short-grain rice. You know you've paid three times as much for something that hasn't been half as good!

Excellent quesadillas served with black beans and rice, a bocadillo (Cuban sandwich), a few grilled items, and an abundant salad round out the menu. La Fonda charges for chips and salsa but the price of draft beer is laughable. Sangria by the pitcher is fun and refreshing. And when you leave the restaurant, it is with amazement that the pebble beach you imagined behind the wall has turned into a cruddy parking lot. Subsequent locations have been more mainstream but all have kept the flavor of the original.

★★★ La Grotta $$$$ ⓧⓧⓧ

2637 Peachtree Rd. Map B. (404) 231-1368. Other location in the Crown Plaza Ravinia.

Dinner only, Tuesday to Saturday 6 to 10:30 P.M. Reservations essential. All major credit cards. Valet parking.

Maître d' Sergio Favalli and chef Antonio Abizanda had worked together at Bugatti in the Omni International Hotel downtown before deciding, in September 1978, to strike out on their own. The location they chose—the low-ceilinged basement of an impersonally modern apartment building—might have seemed unfavorable for their purposes, but they have turned the setting to their advantage. The most recent renovation has given us an even more intimate and charming restaurant with deep colors, large mirrors, and sophisticated photographs. The atmosphere crackles with electricity under the magnetic direction of Favalli.

The best Italian dishes at La Grotta exude a kind of frolicsome sensuality that is hard to resist. Beauty of composition is less important to chef Abizanda than unctuous textures and vigorous, earthy flavors. The three types of roasted peppers in an antipasto platter and the sun-dried tomatoes layered on top of a succulent grouper entrée caress the palate with rich oils. Risotto with wild mushrooms, black and white linguine with calamari and a touch of garlic, and the mixture known as "Rich and Poor" (shrimp and squid with Tuscan white beans) are deliciously rustic.

The menu focuses on classic dishes, but more and more contemporary touches show that the kitchen can master new tricks. The restaurant turns out veal preparations that are inventive and masterful, ranging from a house trademark served since opening day called Scaloppini Antonio, simply sautéed with rosemary and sage, to intricate daily specials. The tiramisù (a complex mixture containing Mascarpone cheese, Marsala, ladyfingers, macaroons, and chocolate) is one of the best in the city.

The wine list is extensive. You can find some fine bargains among Italian reds (especially the strong, rich Amarones), but California bottles carry hefty price tags. Ask Favalli for wine advice. The dining-room crew is among the town's most engaging and industrious.

A further enticement during temperate weather at the Buckhead branch is outdoor dining on a lovely enclosed patio. Flickering candles on each of seven tables add to a romantic and serene environment beautified by bedding plants. A second location in the Hyatt Ravinia has difficulty measuring up to the original but the setting is charming.

☆ Landmark Diner $$ ⊗

3652 Roswell Rd. (at Piedmont Rd.). Map B. (404) 816-9090.
Daily 24 hours. No reservations. All major credit cards. Ample parking.

It takes nerve for some guys from New York to arrive here and call what they built a landmark. Bristling with sharp angles and reflecting surfaces, Landmark Diner is cruel to the eye. Inside, it's sickly blue-green and mauve-pink colors. The serpentine roses etched on the glass dividers make you want to call the bad-taste police.

There are diners in New York with hundreds of items on their menus and everything available. Landmark's bill of fare is full of things you don't want to think about: crab cakes and macaroni and cheese as part of the same dish, Italian pasta prepared the French way, a bagel (with all the works) that costs $9.95.

The only decent meal is breakfast. The bagels aren't jumbo by Atlanta standards, but the omelets are nice. A peasant omelet (California peasant) with avocado, tomato, Monterey Jack, and sour cream and a spinach and feta-cheese omelet are prepared in the same style: ingredients mixed in instead of stuffed into the folded eggs. The corned beef is hateful, though.

The Greek specialties aren't bad. There is a loaded Greek antipasto platter that would easily feed two. If some little guy with red hair tells you that what the Landmark does best is seafood, run for your life. One bite of waterlogged broiled filet of sole served with awful rice and the kind of carrots and peas that make you hate vegetables is enough to want to chase the waiter up and down the aisles. Landmark Diner serves expensive cocktails and very ordinary sweets including Greek wedding cookies.

★ La Paz $$ ✗✗

6410 Roswell Rd. (Sandy Springs). Map H. (404) 256-3555.
Monday to Friday 11 A.M. to 11 P.M. Saturday 5 to 11 P.M. Sunday 5 to 10 P.M. No reservations. All major credit cards. Ample parking.

When restaurants decide to relocate for one reason or another, some move next door, others across town. La Paz moved to its own backyard. While a fancy new structure was being erected at the end of the parking lot, the original business hid the construction. The small original cantina was then bulldozed, giving a full view of the imposing new structure now sitting at a comfortable distance from busy Roswell Road.

The old La Paz looked like a Western fern bar. The new set is a wonderfully camp version of a frontier town's fanciest hotel as seen in countless John Ford and Sergio Leone movies. A balcony with wooden railings runs around the dining room. Massive wrought-iron chandeliers descend from the ceiling. A floor lamp with a silk-fringed shade is lit near the entrance. Slightly worn square tables seem ready to be cleared off for a sharp game of cards.

From the dining room, a steep wooden staircase shoots straight up between walls papered with a naughty purplish damask. You fully expect to be handed a big iron key and to walk into a room where a girl in a corset sits on a lumpy bed. You find, instead, a snug saloon and a small dining terrace.

La Paz pulls in a crowd for its walloping combinaciones of Colorado- and New Mexico-style dishes buried under salsa, guacamole, Jack cheese, lettuce, and sour cream. If you know what's good for you, you will make a wide detour around the zapnins (chimichanga-style deep-fried burritos in a mound of greenery) and the New Mexico enchiladas (corn tortillas layered, smothered, topped, and baked into some elastic goo) in favor of the simpler dishes.

Start with an excellent chile con queso enriched with either creamy spinach or chopped chorizo. The chiles rellenos are delicious: made with skinny New Mexico peppers, stuffed with mild Monterey Jack, dipped in thin egg batter, and fried just right. The fajitas, perfectly adequate when doctored with picante salsa and guacamole, are a nice option as well. The Mexican rice is flavorful, the refried beans chunky. Even the silliest combinations start with fresh ingredients.

For dessert, indulge in a big, crisp buñuelo à la mode, but resist firmly the chemical-tasting margarita pie, a sort of salted Key lime pie. Service is superfriendly and prices attractive enough to justify a family outing. Shield the kiddies from the souvenir panties emblazoned with La Paz's hot chile-pepper logo.

★★★ La Strada $$ ⓧⓧ

2930 Johnson Ferry Rd. (Marietta). Map G. (770) 640-7008. 8550 Roswell Rd. (Dunwoody). Map H. (770) 552-1300.

Dinner only, Sunday to Thursday 5 to 10 P.M. Friday and Saturday 4:30 to 11 P.M. No reservations. All major credit cards. Adequate parking.

When Tino ("Mister Charm") Venturi and chef Eric Hald left Capriccio to pioneer the far regions of east East Cobb, they had no guarantee the concept would fly. Taking over a basic structure just vacated by Ernie's Family Steak House, they packed it wall to wall with a warm, very personal clutter of black and white photographs, glass jars, ceramics, and assorted knickknacks. Instead of going for the exaggerated Italian look and the sentimental goo, the two men created exactly the atmosphere you would expect in a small trattoria on one of Rome's less touristy streets.

There is nothing remotely fancy about La Strada. In the original location, the floors are bare planks, the woodwork budget grade. People sit in comfortable wide booths lined up in an *L* pattern. There is white paper on the table. In Dunwoody, the dining room is slightly more elegant.

From the moment you get the first freebie (a little crock of minced olives mixed with garlic and extravirgin olive oil) to the finale of your meal (homemade goodies of a rare quality), you know that you are in a class operation. To be able to eat so well in such a casual environment and at such prices is almost too good to be true.

Don't go overboard with the hors d'oeuvres or you'll live to regret it. What if you ate too much bruschetta to make your way through delicious fried calamari, pasta e fagioli soup, delicate salmon in pesto sauce with crisp-tender vegetables, and the most heavenly spumoni you will taste in a long time?

Fresh rigatoni (big tubes of thin pasta) with sautéed escarole leaves, bread crumbs, pecorino cheese, and lean, tender Italian sausage makes a beautiful first course. Mussels fragrant with wine and garlic are another light option. Coins of sweet Italian sausage with roasted peppers, onion, and fresh tomato sauce are more dangerous but hard to resist. A hot antipasto with stuffed clams, mushroom, eggplant, and shrimp marinara stuffed in a clam shell will be almost too much.

Calamalone (available as an appetizer or an entrée) are the specialty of the house. Picture pearly medallions of calamari steak, every bit as delicious as abalone, which they resemble, dipped in light egg batter, gently sautéed with lemon butter, and served with fresh angel-hair pasta. Chicken cacciatore doesn't simmer one moment too long in a light wine, tomato, and mushroom sauce. Veal stew with marinara sauce is as tender as the chicken.

If you stop before dessert, you will have missed a most delicate (creamy rather than eggy) chilled crème brûlée. This beauty isn't topped with the often impenetrable sweet glassy lava but with a light dusting of almost burnt sugar. Chocolate soufflé cake, white or dark chocolate gelato, lemon sorbet, and zuppa inglese are also unbelievably good. The service is perky and friendly.

★★ Lawrence's $$ ⊗

2888 Buford Hwy. (just south of N. Druid Hills Rd.). Map D. (404) 320-7756.
  Lunch Monday to Friday 11 A.M. to 3 P.M., Saturday noon to 3 P.M. Dinner Monday to Thursday 5 to 10 P.M., Friday and Saturday 5 to 11 P.M. Reservations and all major credit cards accepted. Very small parking lot.

This small establishment is named for the British adventurer T. E. Lawrence. A romanticized painting of him in full desert regalia hangs on one wheat-colored wall. Wooden strips in a lattice pattern cover the windows, and one of the rooms has recently been outfitted like a fancy tent.

Ownership of Lawrence's has changed a few times but the kitchen retains its ability to prepare the ethnic specialties one hopes to enjoy in Middle Eastern restaurants. The eggplant appetizer, baba ghannoug, for example, has a luscious texture and an intriguing smoky flavor entirely lacking the burnt undertaste that too often destroys the balance of this dish. Garlic makes an authoritative but not overpowering statement in the fine hummus. The kibbi is engagingly spiced.

A blackboard chalked with many nightly specials sits by the door. Study it carefully. You're in luck if an entrée of cabbage rolls is listed. There's not a dish remotely like it in any area restaurant. Young, tender leaves of cabbage are wrapped tightly around beautifully lean forcemeat, making long cylinders scarcely wider than a pencil. A yogurt sauce adds another kind of tartness to a dish already carrying an element of sassiness reminiscent of Eastern European cooking.

Another entrée special, shawarma, combines beef and lamb with the distinctive seasonings of cumin and sumac to great effect. Nuts and fruits make their way into jumbles of rice and meat in several dishes, and matchsticks of still-crisp turnip, dyed red, accompany many platters. A rich couscous and a grilled fish with tahini sauce are divine.

The pocket sandwiches are superior. The falafel (small balls of chick-pea flour ground with spices and garlic, then fried) is served in a soft pita with chopped tomatoes, cucumbers, and lettuce, and drizzled with tahini sauce. An open-face pita sandwich called hashwee is an outstanding, complex mixture of spices, ground beef, onions, and pine nuts, topped with feta cheese and tomatoes. The Kafta Burger contains a layer of chopped tomato and lettuce salad, tahini sauce, and six ounces of kafta (ground chuck, diced onion, parsley, and Mediterranean spices).

A large selection of desserts is displayed on glass shelves under the front counter. Try harissa (cake, honey, raisins, and walnuts) or the custardy milk pudding, sahlab, delicately flavored with rose water and cinnamon. Top off your meal with strong Turkish coffee.

★★ Le Giverny $$ ⊗

1355 Clairmont Rd. (at N. Decatur Rd.). Map E. (404) 325-7252.
Lunch Tuesday to Friday 11:30 A.M. to 2 P.M. Dinner Monday to Thursday 5:30 to 10 P.M., Friday and Saturday 5:30 to 11 P.M. Brunch Sunday 11:30 A.M. to 3 P.M. Reservations accepted weekdays only. All major credit cards. Crowded parking lot.

Two short steps down from street level will take you to the kind of undistinguished restaurant you could have found on your own in Paris, a place that seems made for the romantic on a budget. Le Giverny reduces French cooking to a few tried and true potboilers with a side order of atmosphere.

Le Giverny will do well as a charming, inexpensive neighborhood spot. The dining room feels just right: cozy exposed brick in the style of a European cellar, white tablecloths, Monet posters, candlelight, tremulous French music. The prices are extremely reasonable and the restaurant even has a full liquor license.

If every item, or even most items, on the small menu were prepared with gusto, one wouldn't criticize the lack of ambition in the concept. The kitchen, however, gets away with murder. Every dish, even the grilled steak, is garnished with the same monster slices of carrots and the same converted rice topped with a Provençale piperade reeking of dried herbs. The crème caramel competes with the chocolate mousse in the "who's the palest of them all?" pageant, while the profiteroles look as if they are taking swimming lessons in a sea of dark chocolate.

You can, however, enjoy a perfectly pleasant entrecôte à l'ail, a strip steak with garlic-herb butter, or a robust country pâté showered with thinly sliced red onions. The house salad is delicious, a mesclun mixture with crumbled cheese and frisky vinaigrette. The boeuf bourguignon, a classic beef and red wine stew, is decently prepared. Not much can be said, however, in favor of the pork in green-pepper cream sauce or the sole nantaise in a pink cream sauce, both equally ordinary in taste.

Three prix-fixe menus bear startlingly low prices but may encourage you to taste some items you would have been perfectly happy never to encounter, such as a terrine of young vegetables that resembles ratatouille en aspic. The house red is decent, the service friendly.

★ Lickskillet Farm $$ ⊗⊗

Old Roswell Rd. at Rockmill Rd. off Georgia 140 (Holcomb Bridge Rd., Roswell). Map H. (770) 475-6484.
Lunch Tuesday to Friday 11:30 A.M. to 2 P.M. Dinner Tuesday to Sunday 6 to 10 P.M. Brunch Sunday 11 A.M. to 2 P.M. Reservations recommended. All major credit cards. Ample parking.

One of the area's most romantic settings is this nineteenth-century farmhouse long known for serving the classics of Southern home cooking. Part of the appeal is the surprise of coming upon so handsome an environment a short distance from cluttered Holcomb Bridge Road. You wind past storage warehouses and raw tract developments before spotting the restaurant's sign near the intersection of Rock Mill and Old Roswell roads.

Giant water oaks shade the low frame structure, and a brick path leads between neatly laid-out flowerbeds to the front entrance. The low-ceilinged, grey-toned interior features plain, wide floorboards and paneled walls—simple, straightforward, and soothing. Behind the house, a walkway leads down to a wooden platform overlooking a creek that ripples beside fields of waist-high golden grass.

Lickskillet's fame derives from the cornbread with cracklin's served in an iron skillet at the table. The menu used to offer old-fashioned Southern specialties exclusively—fried chicken, fried pork chop, steaks, and the like. Perhaps Roswell's new sophistication is responsible for the recent addition of fancy continental dishes. You'd do better sticking to the tried and true. Wines are stored in a large pantry, which you are invited to enter to make your selection from bottles displayed along a shelf. Sunday brunch features champagne cocktails and large crowds.

★ Lindy's $$ ⊗⊗

10 Kings Cir. (at Peachtree Hills Ave.). Map C. (404) 231-4112.
Lunch Tuesday to Friday 11:30 A.M. to 2:30 P.M. Dinner nightly 5:30 to 11 (Friday and Saturday till midnight). No reservations. All major credit cards. Small lot and street parking.

Nothing could be more unlike "A Neighborhood Italian Café" than chintz, employed as the unifying principle of decoration. The waiting area by the front door is outfitted like the parlor in an English bed and breakfast inn run by some dotty country matron. Lace curtains hang at the windows; Victorian lampshades cover bulbs. Black and white linoleum tiles support chintz armchairs and shelves holding decorative ceramic objects, books, a TV set, and quaint stuffed animals.

Seating on the ground floor is at tables and in bare wooden booths, which can absorb the din from the open kitchen and shouting serving personnel no better than the rugless floor. The covered roof, however, is one of the most pleasant outdoor seating areas in the city. Cabbage roses decorate the oilcloth on tables. Potted plants sway in the breeze from numerous fans in the ceiling.

There's nothing refined about the cooking but dishes are hearty and vigorously flavored. The kitchen gets considerable mileage out of some cheap and easy tricks, like including lots of onion in dishes and slathering ingredients in oil and butter. Elegant? No. Tasty? You bet. Entrée platters are preceded by a respectable Caesar-type salad, made with a little anchovy paste, romaine, and good crunchy croutons.

You're likely to fare best sticking to the least complicated dishes. Common sense in ordering will save you from the silly excesses, like chicken stuffed with pears and cream cheese, then topped with a Frangelico cream sauce and hazelnuts. Desserts come from a mix of suppliers. They're serviceable rather than distinguished, and, except for chocolate-dipped cannoli, have nothing to do with the self-styled "Italian" theme of the restaurant.

★★★ Little Szechuan $

5091-C Buford Hwy. (Northwoods Plaza, Doraville). Map D. (404) 451-0192.
Sunday through Monday and Wednesday through Saturday 11:30 A.M. to 10 P.M. Closed Tuesday. Reservations accepted. V, MC. Adequate parking.

Little Szechuan opens a wonderful new era. Authentic Szechuan cooking never got a fair deal until this originally microscopic business migrated from a booth in the Chinatown Square mall to a perfectly reasonable and comfortable storefront, where it could be spotted by a larger public.

Little Szechuan is a classic small-budget Chinese restaurant in terms of decor and atmosphere, a wildly different place as far as its menu is concerned. Instead of trying to describe exotic dishes in limited English, the restaurant supplies fifty glorious pictures on laminated stock. Twenty-five additional dishes are listed on the back. The more interest you show, the more responsive the staff will be.

Bean curd in black bean sauce (not on the menu) may be

the zenith tofu can reach. Silky and spicy, the dish is also deliciously complex. More forthright but just about as exciting, Mo Poo Tofu (tiny dice of tofu mixed with fiery ground pork) goes spectacularly well with the perfect fluffy rice served by Little Szechuan.

Fried chicken roll (a spectacular, pan-fried treat) is really tofu skin in disguise. Shredded pork, either with young chives or garlic sauce, is among the most wonderful dishes on the menu. Stir-fried pork kidneys with garlic sauce are a revelation. If you have high blood pressure, stay away from the madly salty but wickedly fascinating baby anchovies (barely bigger than plankton) mixed with roasted peanuts and sliced hot peppers. Dreary mealy squid and well-seasoned but frozen shrimp aren't the restaurant's best effort but everything chicken is delicious.

Among the vegetable dishes, eggplant in garlic sauce, stir-fried sweet pea leaves, and Szechuan long beans with ground pork aren't to be missed. And if you take leftovers home (the portions are enormous) you will be amazed at their intense fragrance and intricate spiciness even if you eat them cold out of the carton.

★★ Lombardi's $$ ⊗⊗

98 Pryor St. (Underground Atlanta). Map A. (404) 522-6568.
Monday to Thursday 11 A.M. to 10 P.M. Friday 11 A.M. to 11 P.M. Saturday 5 to 11 P.M. Sunday 5 to 10 P.M. Reservations and all major credit cards accepted. Parking in Underground pay lots.

Highly visible from the street, more difficult to find through Kenney's Alley, this thoroughly professional operation (Alberto Lombardi's first out of Dallas) admits a good flow of traffic. The decor is an elegant Italian bistro: large picture windows, beveled glass partitions, walls painted in appetizing colors, and an open kitchen trimmed in gleaming copper. This is good enough for a business lunch. From sophisticated wood-oven pizzas to pasta dishes and hearty Italian specialties, the menu has something for everyone. The recipes work well in most cases.

Especially good is the house focaccia, plain or in sandwich form. The trittico di pasta, a daily three-pasta combination, is a smart way to work through the menu. Fresh bow-tie pasta with peas and prosciutto, gnocchi with gorgonzola, green cannelloni with veal stuffing, and an unusually light lasagna are often part of the deal.

Marinated rabbit with tomato and black olives, white sea bass with tarragon lemon sauce, and juicy Italian sausage on polenta are solid choices. Bad dishes are the exception and service is better than average as well. The only thing Lombardi's can't do is compete with the big boys when it comes to using a great deal of finesse. But as corporate packages go, things feel on target.

★ Longhorn Steaks $$ ⊗

2151 Peachtree Rd. (Buckhead). Map B. (404) 351-6086. Other locations.

Monday to Thursday 11:30 A.M. to 11 P.M. Friday 11:15 A.M. to midnight. Saturday 4 P.M. to midnight. Sunday noon to 11 P.M. No reservations. All major credit cards. Awkward parking in small lot.

The head of a massive Texas steer fitted with a cocky little shower cap sits above the bar. An armadillo walks upside down on the ceiling. A duck pushes his wings out of a red life jacket. The rear end of a deer moons from a rough wood partition. World War I model planes, frozen in midloop, seem on a collision course with taxidermy gone mad. Autographed cocktail napkins, old license plates, sports pennants, snapshots, and business cards plaster every surface.

The clever corporate owners weren't born anywhere near Texas, but these kings of cowboy cuisine build fun restaurants for the casual market. The more than fifty Longhorns (some of them out of state) are carbon copies of one another: affordable steaks, honky-tonky funk, cool longnecks, tamed rowdiness and fun. The crowds are determined to forget cholesterol's link with coronary disease. From filet to porterhouse, all steaks, unless otherwise requested, swim in dark lemon butter. Onions are sautéed in it, mushrooms are basted with it, and chunks of baking potatoes are glazed with it. Only the jalapeño peppers and the salad escape the treatment.

Cleverly positioned between the no-chic family steakeries and the outrageously expensive power steakhouses, Longhorn serves a dandy little filet for a low price. Most other cuts, sautéed on a flat top, feel fatty, but the filet trades its usual lofty blandness for a more robust flavor. The hamburgers are decent in size and freshness, yet their buns cling to the roof of the mouth. The chili errs on the sweet side, but the meat melts on the tongue and the broth has been degreased. Seafood has appeared on the menu. Service (usually by cute, bubbly waitresses) is a plus.

★★★ Luna Si $$ ⓧⓧ

1931 Peachtree Rd. (across from Piedmont Hospital). Map B. (404) 355-5993.

Dinner only, Monday to Saturday 5:30 to 10:30 P.M. Reservations and all major credit cards accepted. Ample parking in back lot.

Started by the eccentric Paul Luna, known since his Bice days by his waist-long hair tied into an unruly ponytail and his red karate jackets worn instead of chef's whites, Luna Si is a black and white restaurant for colorful types. Now operated by Luna's brothers, Luna Si serves exceptional food you can actually afford.

You will have to do without the comfort of upholstered chairs (white aprons are tied cleverly to inexpensive wooden chairs in lieu of cushions). Instead of romantic lights, it's theatrical spots set at dramatic angles. Graffiti art is the only wall treatment and casually twisted canvas hangs in front of the windows. The bread is plunked directly on the white paper covering the tables. But, by gosh, the food has enough presence to stand up on its own!

When Luna said "simplicity" (the restaurant's motto) he really meant it. Most dishes include very few flavors. Each is left to its own seductive powers. The menu, a clever and inexpensive file folder used as a binder for an insert, changes every week. The restaurant is still fluctuating in its prix-fixe concept, but basically you can choose between three chef-chosen menus ($12, $15, or $17) or make your own selections from a short list of specialties. Former Bice customers can't believe their luck. The same wonderful smoked salad greens, cold spaghetti squash with aged ricotta and toasted walnuts, salmon in ginger crust, and cold marinated seafood with enchanting infusions of fresh herbs have been transferred to this, much more casual, setup without any loss in the process.

Still light by Atlanta standards, the portions are much larger than at the beginning. Creamless carrot soup with Maine scallops and carrot mirepoix and Ashland Farm greens with goat cheese and black olive croutons (both wonderful) have remained on the menu while spaghetti is combined with sashimi tuna and chive oil one week, shrimp or scallops and arugula oil other times. Roasted monkfish is stacked in pearly slices on whipped potatoes drizzled with thyme vinaigrette. New York strip comes over Mediterranean couscous seasoned with basil oil. Rare lamb is paired with a delicate ratatouille. The permutations all make sense and the flavors remain genuine.

Dessert keeps pace with the other courses: whimsical chocolate lasagna, light coconut sorbet, intense blackberry gelato, or strawberry consommé with cinnamon ice cream. The wine list follows the same path as the menu: simple, inventive, fair priced. An early-bird special menu and occasional gourmet wine dinners are offered.

★★ Magnolia Tea Room $$ ⊗⊗

5459 E. Mountain St. (off Main St., Stone Mountain). Map I. (770) 498-6304.

Lunch Tuesday to Saturday 11 A.M. to 2:30 P.M. Dinner Friday and Saturday 5:30 to 9 P.M. Brunch Sunday 11 A.M. to 2:30 P.M. Reservations suggested. No credit cards. Adequate parking.

Magnolia Tea Room is the kind of place vacationers look for in vain in downtown Atlanta: breezy porch, white columns, flowers everywhere, and a menu fresh and appealing enough for a proper garden party. The owners have resisted the temptation of prettying the place to death.

When the mother and daughter team bought Gormley House, a finely detailed but somber 1854 residence, they were careful to preserve the beautiful heart-of-pine floors, the granite fireplaces, and the wooded lot through which they made space for a skinny driveway and parking lot. Everything else had to be gutted. Now white with white trim, the dining rooms sparkle with joy. Audubon and botanical prints have been used discreetly, and there are no curtains to interfere with the light.

Magnolia Tea Room serves lunch during the week, dinner on weekends only, and brunch on Sunday. While the place is anything but froufrou, it is such a natural for bridal showers and special celebrations that your path may cross that of a giddy, beribonned party.

Sophisticated menu choices such as cold rare tenderloin of beef rolled galantine-style around chicken breast and pâté, served with caper mustard sauce, or a light and natural Florentine tomato soup, are possible but the restaurant also makes the most of the owners' Southern heritage. There are velvety flowers strewn on garden salads, cheese wafers, and a heart of puff pastry garnishing the kind of chicken salad and frozen fruit salad that suggest white gloves tucked into a purse. Small, fresh muffins are served with strawberry jam. The restaurant does its own sweets: chocolate-syrup cake, banana cheesecake with praline sauce, lemon curd with fresh fruit.

Brunch is served buffet style in a large new addition to the original house. Traditional and gourmet, it includes lunch entrées, omelets made to order, and a beautiful array of brunchy treats and sweets.

★★ Maharaja $ ⊗

3900 LaVista Rd. (one-half mile inside I-285 in Northlake Plaza, Tucker). Map I. (770) 414-1010.

Lunch Monday to Friday 11:30 A.M. to 2:30 P.M. Dinner nightly 5:30 to 11. Brunch Saturday and Sunday noon to 3 P.M. Reservations and all major credit cards accepted. Ample parking.

Brunch is in many ways more special than dinner in this elegantly appointed newcomer, the crown jewel in a small commercial strip occupied by a variety of Indian businesses. The idea of skipping eggs Benedict for an exotic spread may not appeal to you, but if, for example, you are the kind of person who regularly goes out to dim sum and can take spicy cuisine on an empty stomach, join the Indian community in a brunch that focuses on the fare of South India.

The formula is a buffet, and every time you get up, some new offerings seem to have materialized: fresh fruit in a carved melon, tiny rice pancakes to drop into a spicy soup, soft dhokla (squares of mashed chick peas sprinkled with black sesame), a sweet dessert between a porridge and a pudding. Dhosa (lentil-flour pancakes folded around spicy potatoes) are brought freshly cooked to the tables at regular intervals.

Also look for bhel puri (unsweetened puffed rice mixed with roasted nuts) with mint sauce, sambar (a dark vegetarian soup) with rice pancakes, tandoori chicken with fresh nan bread, many different curries, half of which are vegetarian, basmati rice pulao, the makings of a fresh salad, enough chutneys and sauces to set your mouth on fire, and a mysteriously delicious sweet rice pudding colored with turmeric.

Dinner means that you have to commit rather than sample. Recommendations from the staff always tend to be the same: combinations of fried appetizers (bad for the appetite), mixed specialties from the tandoor (too much of a good thing), and the more common vegetables. Make up your own mind.

☆ Majestic Food Shop $

1031 Ponce de Leon Ave. (west of N. Highland Ave.). Map C. (404) 875-0276.

Daily 24 hours. No reservations or credit cards. Adequate parking.

The old-fashioned diner came in for a new, classy revival in the late eighties. Mashed potatoes, meatloaf, succotash—the basic American fare of the depression and World War II eras has been rediscovered and marketed in neon-glittering interiors for the yuppie generation by smart entrepreneurs. To experience the ungentrified original come to the Majestic.

It's all here—street-wise waitresses, stools at a counter facing a sign on the wall advertising "Best Apple Pie in the World," a clientele that ranges from bums with stubble and trembling hands to hard-boiled working women to tweedy pipe smokers and dapper young professionals—local color forever. The short-order cooks churn out pecan waffles; eggs this way, that way, and over easy; platters of Southern meats and vegetables; and a famous apple pie probably made with canned apples.

★★★ Malaysia House $ ⊗

5945 Jimmy Carter Blvd. (at Norcross Tucker Rd., Norcross). Map I. (770) 368-8368.

Monday to Thursday 11 A.M. to 9:30 P.M. Friday and Saturday 11 A.M. to 10 P.M. Sunday noon to 4 P.M. Reservations accepted. V, MC. Adequate parking.

Your landmark to find Malaysia House is a big Hooter's less than a mile from I-85 on Jimmy Carter Boulevard. While the masses presumably carouse over chicken wings at the larger establishment, the crowd is minuscule in a dining room that has barely changed between occupants. The chairs are modern high-backs. The atmosphere is quietly pleasant.

The restaurant is well worth your time. Malaysian food is neither too weird nor too hot but, rather, clean and delicate, with strong ties to Indonesia. There are tofu dishes for the vegetarians and beef stews for the hearty eaters. One can't imagine anyone not liking the tiny, refined chargrilled satay skewers (chicken, beef, or combination) presented with a wonderfully complex, light peanut gravy, and, in separate dishes, molded cubes of rice and fresh cucumbers. The young waitress is more than willing and able to help you discover her mom's cooking.

The only thing you may not want, at least at first, is a salad called Malaysia rojak, a mix of chunky cucumbers, mango, pineapple, and bean sprouts strongly flavored with dried shrimp paste. This aside, everything is delicious. The flavorings are always complex. A nasi lemak, for example, combines fragrant coconut rice, shrimp sambal cooked with tamarind juice and chile paste, mildly sour pickled vegetables, peanuts and cucumbers, and half a hard-boiled egg topped with a sauce on a plate. It is up to you to eat a little bit of this and a little bit of that to challenge your palate. Beef rendang, splendidly cooked in an herbed marinade enriched with coconut milk, comes as a rich entrée or a side for a mound of delicate rice surrounded by cucumber.

Curry laksa, a choice of noodles (rice or wheat) topped with shredded chicken, shrimp, bean sprouts, and dried bean curd in a big bowl of curry gravy, is one of the best dishes on the menu. Curry sotong, made with long, tender slices of squid cooked in a delicious coconut gravy, and a tender bone-in chicken curry with potatoes are other dishes to fall in love with.

Malaysia kang kong, long-stem leafy vegetables in a beautifully spicy light gravy with bits of other sautéed vegetables, goes spectacularly well with any dish you care to order. The kitchen runs specials such as shrimp Asam, spicy but sweet, wonderfully paired with a sort of Asian ratatouille including mild, firm eggplant. Dessert is on the house and seems limited to fresh sliced oranges or a small taste of big-pearl tapioca in a glass bowl. Listed as a beverage, a grass jelly mixed into a glass of ice water is an interesting, faintly medicinal treat one wouldn't mind at the end of the meal.

★★ Mambo $$ ⊗

1402 N. Highland Ave. (at University Ave.). Map C. (404) 876-2626.

> *Dinner only, Monday to Thursday 5:30 to 10:30 P.M., Friday and Saturday 5:30 to 11:30 P.M., Sunday 5:30 to 10 P.M. No reservations. All major credit cards. Parking in congested lot next door.*

Once the owners of the hot hot Babalù in Decatur, Lucy Alvarez and Joseph Hilton are now full participants in the life of Morningside. The neighborhood is responsive to their brand of chic and their pitch for tropical sizzle. The space is long and narrow with the kind of café tables (a Formica top and a foot) that will barely accommodate a couple of plates, with no room for elbows. An exuberant Carmen Miranda figure scowls fiercely in an enormous mural reflected on the opposite wall by a line of mirrors. With flying limbs and fruity breasts, the character serves as a logo for the restaurant. Traffic flows easily between the tiny enclosed patio and the restaurant.

Transcending a culture for entertainment value is what Mambo does best. Whenever the kitchen lets loose, the food is marvelous: lime-marinated ceviche with big chunks of very white fish; spicy fried calamari with a beautiful cilantro sauce; black rice with mussels and squid; boiled yuca topped with garlic, lime, and marinated onions. Chickadillo, a variation on picadillo (a Cuban dish based on chopped beef, onions, peppers, olives, and raisins), is a guilt-free, spicy treat.

Mambo serves a creditable paella and has experimented with Chinolatino (Hispanic and Oriental fusion) successfully. The tapas (appetizer bites served with sherry) and the fresh tuna salad are worthwhile, Cuban croquetas (a different variety each day) are not.

Service is consistently friendly and the delicious sangria (an unusual version that resembles cold mulled wine) will help you over the few rough spots on the menu.

☆ The Mansion $$$ ⓧ

> *179 Ponce de Leon Ave. (at Piedmont). Map A. (404) 876-0727.*
> *Lunch Monday to Saturday 11 A.M. to 2 P.M. Dinner nightly 6 to 10. Brunch Sunday 11 A.M. to 2 P.M. Reservations and all major credit cards accepted. Valet parking.*

In a city not noted for preserving its architecturally significant residences, the Peters Mansion is especially noteworthy. Saved by a massive citizens' effort in the early 1970s, the High Victorian structure has been renovated with considerable sensitivity and care by restaurateur Bill Swearingen. The once-gloomy rooms have been brightened by sophisticated plum and smoky rose tones in keeping with the elaborate wood and leather paneling that gleams throughout the house.

Come and admire the building's frolicsome, overripe eccentricity, but since the food is not as enticing, limit your commitment. In recent years, this establishment, which always aimed for the tourist and private-parties dollar, has fallen behind. It can be near empty, with routine preparations and a lack of subtlety in its kitchen.

★ Manuel's Tavern $ ⊗

602 N. Highland Ave. (at North Ave.). Map C. (404) 525-3447.
Monday to Saturday 11 A.M. to 2 A.M. Sunday 3 to 11 P.M.
No reservations. V, MC, AE. Ample parking.

Former DeKalb County chief executive officer Manuel Maloof is no ordinary publican, and his squat building fronted with Stone Mountain granite is no ordinary neighborhood bar. Local journalists bring their colleagues from the national press here, and the big guns then produce columns hailing Manuel's as the quintessential Atlanta dive. The literary lions come, too. Former Emory theologian Tom ("God Is Dead") Altizer used to expound on his theory between these thick, smoke-stained walls.

The bar (rescued from a family pub in downtown Atlanta) is worn smooth by more than a century of human traffic. The tables are massive under a low ceiling. Lights shine yellow and soft to the eye. Faded collectible beer cans, brittle photographs, and darkened oils are everywhere. The TV plays sports and news only, below audible level. The bartenders know most of the patrons. A scent of old wood and drink hangs in the air. A rumble of conversation issues from every room. Construction crews, politicians, and students feel comfortable next to one another here, and women need not fear the drunks.

Even when nearby Ponce de Leon was skid row, before Poncey-Highland became a reclaimed neighborhood, Manuel's was an intensely cozy place to pass the time of day with a cool draught, a shot of whiskey, and some solid tavern food. Since the 1950s, Manuel's has served the same Oscar Mayer hot dogs at ridiculously low prices, topped with chili, slaw, onion, kraut, and relish at no extra charge. The hamburgers and cheeseburgers are reasonably sized, predating the invention of the quarter-pound gourmet burger. They fit nicely in your hand and don't drip.

Some of the sandwiches are named after the tavern's best-loved bartenders. A McCloskey contains thinly sliced roast beef and swiss cheese, served hot with lettuce and tomato on a kaiser roll. The chicken wings are good and hot, offered with celery and blue cheese dips.

Recent changes have addressed the needs of vegetarians and introduced healthier items. Not every dish comes automatically with French fries. The tavern now offers some chicken, smoked pork chops with apple sauce, and a few other solid new entrées.

★ Marra's $$ ⊗

1782 Cheshire Bridge Rd. Map C. (404) 874-7347.
Dinner only, nightly 5:30 to 10 (Friday and Saturday till 11). Reservations for 6 or more only. All major credit cards accepted. Valet parking.

This little house, whose dining areas were once cramped and awkward, has been elegantly transformed by major renovations. Walls in neutral tones rise, unbroken, to cathedral ceilings. Three-dimensional cutouts of fish hang in the void and jut from walls, mouths agape. Within this imposing space, you may be seated at either of two levels, while small parties have a choice of three new private dining rooms, paneled in dark wood like corporate board rooms and embellished with fancy cut-glass mirrors. The waiting area is now commodious, with seats both at a bar and at small tables placed along a wall. Sophisticated, contemporary, swanky, but comfortable, the redesign and decorating are an unqualified success.

Ah, but the French bromide that the more things change the more they stay the same was never truer than at Marra's. Plume yourself as much as you like on having chosen this tasteful place for dinner, you'll still only eat well if you restrict your choices to the grilled fish entrées, just as in the restaurant's old, squeezed days. Avoid anything complicated, anything sauced or fried or brothed.

Since you can run up a hefty bill ordering three courses, bypass appetizers and soups altogether. You'll still have a substantial meal. Tear off hunks of the good, heavy bread, smear it with the house's version of taramosalata (salty, heavily garlicked, not unctuous, but addictive), ask to accompany your lightly grilled fish with slices of buttery, garlicky potatoes, and finish off with the intense nut-topped chocolate mousse pie with a crumbly texture similar to an excellent brownie's. You'll feel just fine about your evening.

The barroom does a disservice to the restaurant. Frequently empty and glum, it is but the antechamber of a vibrant restaurant filled to capacity. Fair prices distinguish the wine list. As you'd expect at this seafood grill, white wines predominate among the 150-plus selections. A surprise, though, is the strength of the Italian offerings, more than half of which are red.

★ Mary Mac's $ ⊗

224 Ponce de Leon Ave. (at Myrtle St.). Map C. (404) 876-1800. Lunch daily 11 A.M. to 3 P.M. Dinner Monday to Saturday 5 to 9 P.M. Breakfast Saturday and Sunday 8 to 11 A.M. Reservations and credit cards not accepted. Street and lot parking sometimes difficult.

There's been a restaurant at this location since the early 1930s, and it's been called "Mary Mac's" since 1951. Most famous owner Margaret Lupo took over the business—a one-room establishment where the first of the present four dining rooms stands—eleven years later. A well-publicized sale and failed expansion had everybody worried, but a new successor has been found, and Margaret Lupo is back behind the scenes helping longtime family friend John Ferrell to get the restaurant back on track.

Mary Mac's isn't as busy as in its heyday, but the dining rooms are fresh and clean, newly repainted. Everything works in the same old way, with customers writing their own orders from an essentially unchanged menu. This is still the place to get a quick lesson in Atlanta sociology: orderly groups of tourists mix with locals in business attire and the usual assortment of eat-alone characters and small parties. No visit to Atlanta is complete without taking time to crumble the area's best cornbread into pot likker—a saporous liquid extracted from turnip greens.

The menu is printed anew each day and contains a wide assortment of entrées as well as ways of putting a meal together. Your best bet is to eat Southern all the way, picking a meat that is a regional staple (fried chicken, for example) and three or four side dishes. All of the breads are good—sweet cinnamon buns, nicely chewy biscuits. Mountain trout is a favorite of regulars. The catfish is among the best in town, but the smothered country steak is one of those indeterminate mealy meats that people addicted to the taste of flour in every bite seem to adore.

The large, continually changing vegetable assortment contains both treasures (stewed corn, pickled squash and onions, pickled beets) and bores (dressing for chicken, green beans without fatback, overly stiff soufflés). A number of dessert items are included among the side dishes you pick from. Unless nostalgia impels you to experience again the wholesome, nearly flavorless custards and creams of cafeteria lunch lines, you'd do best to stick with vegetable selections. You write out your own order on a meal ticket, which one of the establishment's famously friendly waitresses will pick up and expeditiously attend to, perhaps addressing you as "Dear" and administering a pat or rub on your back. You are in iced-tea heaven, but the restaurant also serves drinks.

★★ McKinnon's Louisiane $$$ ⊗⊗

3209 Maple Dr. (just south of Peachtree). Map B. (404) 237-1313. Dinner only, Monday to Thursday 6 to 10 P.M., Friday and Saturday 6 to 10:30 P.M. Reservations accepted in the main dining room; no reservations in the Grill. All major credit cards. Small parking lot in front, often inadequate.

For years and years McKinnon's Louisiane restaurant was an immutable Atlanta institution on Cheshire Bridge Road. Owner Billy McKinnon could have droned on from there, basking in his own success, but he wanted out of the rut. Early in 1986, the restaurant completed a major move that enhanced its image without trauma to the clientele. McKinnon's became two restaurants under one roof: a formal dining room on one side, and a casual grill on the other.

In the dining room proper, the menu keeps a rigorous balance between hot-tempered dishes and mild, creamy ones. On the hot side you will find delicious little crawfish tails fried with spices and similarly seasoned coconut shrimp Cajun style, both served with a cold sauce dominated by hot mustard and the pleasant bite of horseradish. Other spicy items are an assertive gumbo, and a loud and lusty Cajun bean soup.

The hot peppered shrimp will burn your fingers, burn your mouth, ruin your chin and your clothes, and you'll love it. McKinnon's blackened redfish might not be the blackest you ever had, but it has a distinctive flavor, unmarred by the usual acidity of powdered garlic. The remoulade is the best in town. Vibrantly orange, flecked with dark herbs, the unctuous sauce beautifies impeccable shrimp or sweet, fresh crab meat. Under "stuffed eggplant," you'll discover a pleasant melange of eggplant, shrimp, and crab bound by a light béchamel.

For dessert, the praline cheesecake and caramel custard are as good as they've ever been. Coffee will have you bouncing off the walls and counting crawfish all night, but it's worth it. The faithful staff is trained in good manners, prices are just a tad below the other expensive restaurants, and the owner knows how to bend over backward to accommodate the clientele.

The Grill room is jolly and colorful and the service is more casual. Whole sizzling catfish done à la Wolfgang Puck with fried ginger and a sweet sauce, Yucatan-style double breast of chicken, black bean tostada with shrimp and goat cheese, and a fresh bayou salad (romaine lettuce, fried crawfish, Creole mustard dressing) are among the specialties.

☆ Melear's Pit Cooked Barbecue $

6701 Roosevelt Hwy. (U.S. 29, south of College Park, Union City). Map F. (770) 964-9933.
 Sunday to Thursday 6 A.M. to 9 P.M. Friday and Saturday 6 A.M. to 10 P.M. Sunday 7 A.M. to 9 P.M. No reservations or credit cards. Ample parking.

This long-established barbecue house is the pride of the Southside. The price of all-you-can-eat meals and humongous platters—served on plastic trays, as in school cafeteria days—helps to explain the appeal. All orders come with plentiful potato chips and pickles. Gigantic glasses of iced tea sport big fat chunks of lemon. No desserts are served, but you're not likely to have any gaps to fill after chowing down on mildly flavored barbecue and thick brunswick stew that has been run through a food mill. Breakfast offerings fill one entire side of the two-page menu.

The barnlike interior is decorated with a frieze of commemorative plates tacked to plywood paneling, photos of hunting dogs, and pig paraphernalia.

★★ Mel's Steaks and Hoagies $ ⊗

4403 Fulton Industrial Blvd. (3 blocks south of I-20). Map F. (404) 696-2111.

Monday to Friday 11 A.M. to 2:30 P.M. No reservations or credit cards. Adequate parking.

When the original Mel's burned down in the mideighties, Alan Sheron seized the opportunity. The restaurant, operated by a former employee of his family's fine-fabric store, had little physical charm. Reborn as a bright and attractive restaurant with sleek, contemporary decor and a popular wooden deck, Mel's is more than a regular sandwich shop.

People who work nearby have made Mel's an unqualified success. Neither raucous nor dull, the lunch crowd provides a nice din against which to enjoy quality food. Quick decisions are expected by Sheron and staff; your order is frequently taken before you reach the counter.

The concept of an *elegant* hot dog is hard to entertain. And yet, when you order a "Chicago," you will get something so well put together that the word leaps to mind. There is nothing sloppy or excessive about Mel's hot dog. A shiny, juicy, all-beef Vienna lies snug in its steamed poppyseed bun. Pickle, tomato, onion, relish, and hot pepper fit neatly on top.

The hot dog is no lucky fluke either. The hamburger (especially the five-ounce "Big Mel") scores big. The Philly Cheese Steak is flawless. From Gourmet Chicken Salad (a richly deserved name) to corned beef sandwich, everything is just what it should be. There are even cream-cheese brownies from The Dessert Place.

If you need food for a small corporate party, call Mel's. If you want to sit in the sun with a cold beer or if you are on your way back from Charlie Brown airport, stop at Mel's. It's even on the way to Six Flags!

★★ Mexico City Gourmet $$ ⊗

2134 N. Decatur Rd. (at Clairmont Rd.). Map E. (404) 634-1128. 5500 Chamblee-Dunwoody Rd. (Shops of Dunwoody plaza). Map H. 396-1111.

Monday to Thursday 11 A.M. to 10 P.M. Friday 10 A.M. to 10:30 P.M. Saturday noon to 10:30 P.M. Sunday 5 to 9:30

P.M. Reservations and all major credit cards accepted. Ample parking in Dunwoody, adequate in Decatur.

A pioneer in terms of regional Mexican cooking, this modest operation paved the way for latter day gourmet restaurants committed to the authentic cuisine of Mexico. First-rate ceviche and guacamole dip appetizers are always on hand. A bowl of jalapeño bean soup, with or without meat, makes a substantial and delicious meal all by itself. Sirloin instead of the traditional skirt steak is used to make the excellent fajitas rolled in flour tortillas and served with a pungent pico de gallo sauce of onion, tomato, and cilantro. Sauces throughout are individually tailored to the meats they accompany. Side dishes of refried beans and fluffy rice have clear consistencies and nicely pointed flavors.

The mostly familiar tacos, burritos, and the like are dependably pleasant—but the best values are the daily specials, especially any of the soft tacos encasing various meats or the chicken Michoacana (lightly grilled supremes in a red tomato sauce with chipotle pepper, topped with cheese). The nearly omnipresent use of cilantro is a guarantee of authenticity. For dessert have a grandly heavy flan in a rich, syrupy caramelized sauce or an outrageously rich ice cream cake.

In Dunwoody order an "upside-down margarita" to show off your bar prowess (it has to be downed in a single gulp, and the staff of both kitchen and dining room will gather to monitor your performance).

★ Mick's $ ⊗⊗

557 Peachtree St. (at Linden). Map A. (404) 875-6425. Other locations.

Downtown location daily 11 A.M. to midnight. No reservations. All major credit cards. Validated parking in small lot off Linden and, when full, a block east on Courtland.

Casual and hip, with a well-researched and well-implemented menu, Mick's was a diner before diners became the cat's meow. The Peasant Corporation prides itself on riding the crest of the wave rather than anticipating new trends, but the first Mick's was a foray into uncharted territory for the Peasant people and a radical departure from their previous concept of affordable elegance. The target clientele was the fast-food generation grown into fickle adulthood. Amusing easy edibles, fountain drinks, and good California Chardonnay proved powerfully attractive to very diverse crowds.

The original Mick's in Midtown is a frisky but not disrespectful renovation of an old building: sky-blue pressed-tin ceiling, luncheonette counter with aqua-blue stools and neon art, dark half-paneling with neoclassical details, Pompeiian mosaic floor, and plenty of mirrors to watch yourself (and your neighbors) having fun. People squeeze in at all hours for huge fresh hamburgers, well-prepared chicken grills, amusing snacks, great big desserts, soda fountain drinks, and more.

Not every dish is 100 percent consistent, but by and large the menu works. The hamburgers, served on excellent, slightly sticky sesame buns, come in some interesting variations, including a particularly good "au poivre" preparation. Grilled chicken is a worthwhile alternative to the omnipresent burgers. Pasta dishes such as fresh linguine, supple and slithery, tossed with kernels of sweet corn and little chunks of fresh tomato are often better than those offered in the average Italian restaurant. Fun sandwiches include Greek salad in pita bread and fried green tomatoes on pumpernickel. Chicken pot pie and pork chops are there for more serious eating.

The desserts are entertaining to the max: delicious cheesecake with Oreo cookie crust and a very light filling, slightly grainy with crushed Oreos; old-fashioned cream pies in chocolate or butterscotch flavors; malts, sundaes, and floats.

Children are treated like important guests, receiving a menu of their own illustrated by other little tykes who developed the graphics as a school project. Tiny, tiny ones can be fed on Cheerios (plain or honey nut) while older ones devour excellent hamburgers, scaled and priced to their level. Service is uniformly spirited and pleasant at all locations.

★ Mirror of Korea $ ⊗

1049 Ponce de Leon Ave. (at N. Highland Ave.). Map C. (404) 874-6243.

> *Monday to Thursday 11 A.M. to 10 P.M. Friday 11 A.M. to 11 P.M. Saturday noon to 11 P.M. Reservations and all major credit cards accepted. Difficult parking in front of building, easier in the back lot.*

From the time it was Song's, a hole in the wall a few doors down from its present location, to its recent expansion with a sushi bar, this well-run neighborhood restaurant has been on a steady course of planned improvements. Using government funds available for rehabilitation of the city's oldest shopping center, Mr. and Mrs. Song rented a larger space, installed some tatami rooms, and used a lot of unfinished timber to create a look that is between Oriental spareness and rustic Americana.

Mirror of Korea is a hospitable place. The cooking, though altered to please the American palate, is serious enough. Some Chinese dishes appear on the menu, but mostly this is solid, medium-spicy Korean fare. The pancakes of ground fresh mung beans, minced pork, ginger, and sprouts are particularly delicious in a unique, lightly starchy way. The choice of pickled vegetables, from pungent cabbage to crunchy daikon in red pepper paste, cold spinach marinated with sesame oil, and vinegared lily-flower stems, is pleasant.

Soups play an important role in the gastronomy of Korea. Try cod roe and scrambled tofu in a cloudy broth seasoned with mild red pepper, or a variety of boiled beef soups. For a main course, you can enjoy a Korean barbecue of marinated short ribs, or a simple chicken breast brushed with soy. B-bim-bop is a basic bowl of rice layered with raw vegetables, sliced beef, the yolk of an egg, and hot sauce. Toss, toss, and toss again.

★★ Mi Spia $$ ⓧⓧ

4505 Ashford-Dunwoody Rd. (in Park Place Shopping Center). Map H. (770) 393-1333.

Lunch Monday to Friday 11 A.M. to 2:15 P.M. Dinner nightly 5 to 10 (Friday and Saturday till 11). Reservations and all major credit cards accepted. Ample parking.

This suburban upscale trattoria occupies a beautiful space: wide-open floor plan, friendly bar, subtle faux walls, a world of exposed ducts and dropped soffits high overhead. A dark wooden molding diffuses hidden lights. Behind expensive French doors, the patio could be a charmer were it not for the live music throbbing out of the establishment next door. Fashionable notes include the presence of herb-spiked olive oil on the tables and staff distributing bread out of handsome, market-size baskets. The oil could be fresher, the bread crustier, the staff more even (although usually pleasant), but all things considered, the restaurant makes a positive impression.

One of the best ways to experience Mi Spia is to go for the lighter items: a pretty wedge of tomato and roasted eggplant tart with basil sauce; a plate of black-pepper linguine with fresh clams, olive oil, leeks, and basil; saffron fettuccine with grilled chicken, leaf spinach, and wild mushrooms. You can also do extremely well with a few tiny slices of grilled lamb loin served with lamb ravioli over a pretty ragout of white beans with rosemary-scented jus and baby artichokes. Sampler plates such as the asparagus, prosciutto, and veal are excellent.

The menu begs for some editing: better mussels served in the delicious broth with fresh sweet fennel; less salt in the saffron mashed potatoes found under a beautiful piece of oak-grilled grouper topped with tomato-leek Mascarpone and surrounded by plump sugar snap peas; true penne (thin and quill shaped) rather than larger ribbed pasta in a heavy-handed dish with smoked duck, roasted eggplant, bitterly burnt radicchio, and Fontina cheese.

The risotto of the day (Swiss chard and chicken, for example) has a delicious flavor but a heavy texture. The grilled portobello spread with something that is either aged ricotta or gorgonzola becomes a bit deflated in the cooking, but the sautéed wild mushrooms with extravirgin olive oil, garlic, lemon, Italian parsley, and grilled brioche are plump and slick.

★ MOCHA $ ⊗

1424 N. Highland Ave. (at University Ave.). Map C. (404) 881-8008. Other location in Cabbagetown.

Monday to Thursday 7 A.M. to 11 P.M. Friday 7 A.M. to 1 A.M. Saturday 8 A.M. to 1 A.M. Sunday 9 A.M. to 10 P.M. No reservations or credit cards. Congested lot or difficult street parking.

The name is pretty, the place prettier still. MOCHA, the Museum of Contemporary Humorous Art, describes itself as Atlanta's first humor gallery/coffeehouse. You will eventually look at the art (fun) and the postcards (great) but the first thing to impress you about MOCHA is its exceptionally clever way of using a minuscule space and claiming an interesting view of Morningside.

MOCHA is perched high on the hill, directly across the street from the offices for 14 West Realty. Cheerful dark-green umbrellas shade just enough tables on a pocket-size terrace overlooking North Highland Avenue to qualify MOCHA as a cozy outdoor spot. You will see all that's happening at this busy corner. You will delight in the landscaping with lush blueberry bushes and vigorous herbs.

Inside, each tabletop is a colorful piece of art, either collage or painting. The *L*-shaped counter displays attractive sweets you haven't seen all around town. Not only is MOCHA thoroughly enjoyable on account of its atmosphere and choice of desserts, but—miracle of miracles—it has long hours. This means that you can show up at 7 A.M. for a café au lait and muffin quickie and that it will still be open when you get out of a movie and want a place to hang out.

The best dessert at MOCHA is a big, fluffy slice of lemon surprise (a tall layer cake with fresh blueberries and a tart lemon icing). Also good are the signature mocha cake, the sour-cream chocolate cake, and the blueberry pound cake. Skip a rhubarb strawberry pie of an unnamable color. Lunch and snacks are a recent addition, and with the acquisition of a storefront next door and another space in Cabbagetown, MOCHA is becoming a more serious food operation.

★ Morton's of Chicago $$$$ ✗✗

Ground floor of the Marquis Tower, 303 Peachtree Center Ave. (in the One Peachtree Center Bldg.). Map A. (404) 577-4366. Other location in Buckhead.

Dinner only, nightly 5 to 11 (Sunday till 10). Reservations accepted only until 7 P.M. All major credit cards. Valet parking.

Morton's is an expensive, showy, all-American steakhouse in the old tradition. The local power lunchers gorge themselves on beef from tartare to well done. The bar gets its quota of hard-liquor men. You may have to wait forty-five minutes without a reservation. Morton's is a formula that can be, and has been, duplicated successfully. If you've seen one, you've seen them all. Whether in Chicago, Philadelphia, or Atlanta, you'll find the same menu chalked on the wall. The employees do the same song and dance as they parade fancy cuts of raw meat, huge fish steaks, jumbo vegetables, some entrée platters, and one live lobster from table to table.

Morton's colossal steaks aren't likely to disappoint you: huge slabs of sirloin, double-cut filets the size of Rambo's fists, Porterhouses bigger than a regular dinner plate. Requests for varying degrees of doneness are honored. If your appetite gives up before you reach bare bone, don't be ashamed to ask for a doggie bag. This is one place where you almost have to.

If you order beef, a salad of thickly cut beefsteak tomatoes and Bermuda onion, and a slice of cheesecake, you'll never know Morton's shortcomings. But if you want an honest potato, a good shrimp cocktail, or a worthy black bean soup, you're out of luck. Morton's famous hash browns disappoint, as do the onion bread and the not-so-special soufflés. Ditto the beautifully thick veal chop, encased in a disagreeable batter flavored with Parmesan and garlic powder.

The wine list has remained strong, but the service has fallen apart since the early days. The decor leans more toward the functional than the dramatic: open kitchen, cream walls without much adornment, snapshots of celebrities, big red flowers in hefty vases.

☆ Moscow $ ⓧ

2581 Piedmont Rd. (in Lindbergh Plaza). Map C. (404) 237-2417.
Monday to Thursday 11 A.M. to 10 P.M. Friday and Saturday 11 A.M. to 11 P.M. Sunday 3 to 9 P.M. No reservations. All major credit cards. Ample parking.

If this really were Moscow, it might well be a relief to find such a restaurant. The decor would seem charming, the voluble woman in the fetching fur hat and fitted boots would be fashionably dressed, and the limited English of a waiter in an embroidered tunic would make you feel welcome. You'd be interested in the bouncy Russian pop tunes. The food, measured by Eastern-bloc standards, might well exceed expectations: cute dinner rolls instead of dense black bread, a menu open to Western influences, almost everything ordered actually available.

But this is America, and Moscow can feel endlessly dreary. The restaurant is cozy enough with its red curtains, cheerful pillows, and Russian memorabilia. It is, however, not nearly as engaging as the now defunct Maison Gourmet in the same location and the service can be sternly uncommunicative.

The menu does very little to inspire confidence. Awful continental standbys have been given a new pseudo-Russian identity. Who wants more salmon with Hollandaise? And how did scampi get to Russia? The eggplant salad, served hot or cold, and the borscht (a beef concoction without beet) are good enough, but not so the heavy pirozhki of the day (meat, fish, or vegetables) or the greasy stuffed pepper. The stuffed cabbage, dense with meat, rice, and tomatoes, is a better value than the dry chicken Kiev garnished with cold vegetables.

Desserts, presented like relics on a tray, seem uniformly stale and likely to choke you with hard, hard crumbs. Readying the check will take more time than dismantling the Russian empire.

★ Murphy's $ ⊗⊗

997 Virginia Ave. (at N. Highland Ave.). Map C. (404) 872-0904. Daily 8 A.M. to 10 P.M. (Friday and Saturday till midnight). No reservations. All major credit cards. Small parking lot, a few additional validated spots at night, street parking often difficult.

Anxiety ran high in Virginia-Highland as soon as rumors started about the impending move of this favorite institution. How could Tom Murphy do that? His cramped, jolly café was like an extension of everybody's living room. The fresh patio with its pretty planters, the low-ceilinged dining room, the always crowded counter were sure to be sorely missed.

The new Murphy's is far grander than the original. Some of the funky charm is gone, but the new place is wonderfully attractive in its own way, and a worthy successor to the old digs. Even with the expanded capacity, a wait for tables is common during prime breakfast hours as Virginia-Highland's young professional cadre stokes up for the day ahead. One still enters by squeezing past the deli counter and patrons ordering bakery products, salads, and sandwiches for takeout.

Breakfast is always great fun at Murphy's. The selection is imaginative and well prepared. A few of the wilder flights of fancy are French Brie Eggs and New Mexico Breakfast Tortilla (scrambled eggs, tomatoes, onions, and green peppers wrapped in a flour tortilla and covered with salsa, sour cream, and scallions).

The basil chicken-salad sandwich still makes a superb lunch. A recent, far more sophisticated menu has done away with some of the previous dubious gourmet preparations. Baked garlic and goat cheese with grilled levain bread, "Five O'clock" roasted chicken with mashed potatoes and gravy, and catch of the day with pesto sauce are a step in the right direction. The desserts are great, wine is served in too small glasses, and the service is always cheerful. Murphy's has developed its catering enormously and the takeout aspect of the restaurant is a success.

★★ Nakato $$$ ✗✗

1776 Cheshire Bridge Rd. (close to Piedmont Rd.). Map C. (404) 873-6582.

Dinner only, Monday to Thursday 5:30 to 10 P.M. Friday and Saturday 5:30 to 11 P.M. Sunday 5 to 10 P.M. Reservations and all major credit cards accepted. Valet parking.

If you are going to do sushi intown (as opposed to more exotic suburban locations), Nakato wins hands-down over many of its competitors. Even after the move to considerably fancier digs, the dull and respectable space could be part of a correct hotel in any number of Asian countries, but just surrender your car to the valet and head straight for the sushi bar.

You will never fail to receive a yummy little tidbit when sitting down at Nakato. The bartender is kind of slow with the martinis but they are worth waiting for. Chef Suzuki loves nothing better than a challenge. Say "chef's choice" and he may start chopping green-lipped mussels and nori (dried seaweed), adding smelt roe and tartar sauce to the mixture before depositing it in front of you with a big grin. The next time, it may be a spectacular bouquet of asparagus and crab legs in a cucumber skin.

Also excellent are the natto roll, pickled-mackerel hand roll, spicy tuna roll, and, in season, anything having to do with mushrooms. Order hot dishes with confidence and count on a great deal of socializing.

★★★ Nava $$$ ✗✗✗ 9:30

3060 Peachtree Rd. (at W. Paces Ferry Rd. in Buckhead Plaza). Map B. (404) 240-1984.

Lunch Monday to Friday 11 A.M. to 3 P.M. Dinner Monday to Thursday 5:30 to 11 P.M., Friday and Saturday 5:30 P.M. to midnight, Sunday 5:30 to 10 P.M. Brunch Saturday and

Sunday 10 A.M. to 3 P.M. Reservations and all major credit cards accepted. Valet parking.

The Southwestern research project leading to a new architectural and gastronomic style must have been a lot of fun for *Buckhead Life*'s Pano Karatassos, who, as usual, has spared no expense to add another jewel to the glittery crown. Craftsmen from New Mexico have worked for months on end under the direction of architect Bill Johnson to transform the previous airy, Mediterranean restaurant into a sort of cliff dwelling for the beautiful people.

Nava is a far cry from the sparse, peaceful design one associates with the Southwest. Think folk art and dramatic lights, some of which look like quivers for magic arrows. Think massive doors and swelling walls of softly rounded stucco. Think rough timber and daylight filtering through Indian blankets and sombrajes (shades) of skinny willows. The energy of the design and the organic feel of the uncured logs radiating on the ceiling in the traditional pattern of vigas and latillas are especially wonderful.

This pueblo for the rich is, of course, quite a scene. Chef Kevin Rathbun, formerly of Baby Routh in Dallas, is on track with a creative American menu largely influenced by but by no means limited to the Southwest and the cuisine of the native Americans. The presentations are frisky and the portions, of course, generous. Rabbit tostadas with an intense chipotle-flavored sauce, delicate little crawfish tacos with cilantro grits, blue-corn-crusted live soft-shell crab cooling its bottom in a beautiful green pureé of cilantro, and iron-skillet mussels in chipotle broth with sunflower-seed bread are among the most brilliant appetizers. The Sonoma jack fritters with red chile jelly and goat cheese are more of an all-purpose crowd pleaser and the shrimp and scallop tamale is astonishingly blah.

Most presentations are dynamic. The salad springs out of a timbale of thin, crisp, and unusually dark lavosh cracker bread. The rare tuna is sliced in the style of a London broil and paired with an exciting Thai-basil coleslaw. Chile-seared scallops achieve a vivid hue and a potent flavor on a background of tomato grits.

The corn-crusted snapper on Southwestern mashed potatoes

is fair and square rather than dashing. Meat entrées (few and far between) have a sort of campfire flavor fresh from the grill. The wood-roasted pork tenderloin with tamarind bean glaze and great arches of crisped plantains is almost a Jamaican oddity on the menu.

Pastry chef Kirk Parks has delightful flights of fancy (frozen tequila passion fruit cream with hibiscus-rhubarb salsa, taco split with Nava ice creams and candied bananas, strawberry crème brûlée between phyllo wafers) and classy clever versions of comfort desserts (warm chocolate-mousse cake with sour-cream ice cream and spikes of chocolate pastry, peanut-butter pie planted with caramel cacti).

You will like the well-grounded wine list and the prestige margaritas. Lunch is far quieter but every bit as interesting as dinner; the bar menu is appropriate for chic grazing.

★★★ Nickiemoto's $$

247 Buckhead Ave. (at Bolling Way). Map B. (404) 842-0334.
Dinner only, Sunday and Monday 5 to 11 P.M. Tuesday to Thursday 5 P.M. to midnight. Friday and Saturday 5 P.M. to 1 A.M. Reservations and all major credit cards accepted. Valet parking.

California is very much on everybody's mind in this sophisticated Japanese-American concept located in the same fancy compound as Azio and Café Tu Tu Tango. The dining room isn't laid out for comfort. Long and narrow, with windows on both sides and a wall of water straight down the middle (a backdrop for sushi activity), it offers no peaceful vista. Only the back wall, with inverted *V*s of metal thrust into beautiful wood and colorful bromeliads spurting against its rigor, qualifies as something relaxing.

The place feels with-it and chic. The crowds dress well in a relaxed manner. Many patrons schmooze around or flirt with their tablemates. The best social scene is around the sushi bar. On Tuesday nights, when the price of the nigiri sushi (the basic sushi finger with some juicy morsel on top) drops to $1 apiece, the crowds can be awful. The sushi is quite good (warm eel, spider roll, and chopped-yellowtail hand roll among the best), but it's the cooking that makes the place special.

The restaurant has had a number of chefs, none of them less than good. Under the current regime (chef Alena Pyles, sister of the famous Stephen Pyles) things are on track. If you could have only one thing at Nickiemoto's it would have to be the catfish. Easily shared as an appetizer or jealously guarded as an entrée, the fish looks triumphantly mustachioed and macho, slightly crusty from a quick swim in frying oil but cleansed and refreshed by big chips of crisped ginger inserted in its back like the bony plates in a stegosaurus.

Ahi tuna is sushi-grade perfect, its edges rolled in a mixture of black peppercorns and sesame seeds, served flesh up in a tangle of barely fried fresh spinach leaves. Seared sea scallops are melt-in-your-mouth tender over mixed greens in a racy citrus bacon basil dressing. Beautiful stir-fried baby calamari with a fresh purplish tinge are paired with a terrific black bean sauce and sliced stingless jalapeño peppers. Fresh salmon cakes dusted with Southwestern spices come on a vibrant yellow tomato salsa. And for dessert there are marvelous choices such as Pyles' family-recipe buttermilk pie with unusually intense blackberry and raspberry coulis or a crème brûlée of the day. The menu changes often, renewing the pleasure and the faith in cross-cultural cuisine.

★★ Nicola's $ ⊗

1602 LaVista Rd. (near Briarcliff Rd.). Map C. (404) 325-2524.
 Dinner only, nightly 5:30 to 10:30. Reservations and all major credit cards accepted. Small parking lot.

In this town, you won't find a more bustlingly cheery proprietor than Nicola Ayoub. His smile spreads all the way across his round face at the sight of patrons—no matter whether they're regulars or complete strangers. He begs to be of service, to suggest dishes he's particularly proud of that day.

Order without constraint any of the standard Lebanese items, several of which come on a combination plate called Mediterranean Delight: hummus, the paste of chick-peas, tahini, and lemon juice, flavored here with a hefty jolt of garlic;

falafel, mealy patties of ground chick-peas; tabbouleh, a salad of soaked cracked wheat (bulghur) tossed with fresh tomatoes, onions, and heaps of parsley. All of Ayoub's salads are inventive and fresh. The "Mediterranean" version comes with crumbled feta, artichoke hearts, olives, onions, iceberg lettuce, parsley, and good tomatoes in Nicola's inimitable sweet-tart dressing. Fattoush, a tossed salad containing bits of crisp pita bread, offers especially pleasurable texture contrasts. The "broasted" artichoke hearts are delicately battered and sautéed.

Some of the entrées on the menu look misleadingly "continental," but Ayoub gives a distinctive Lebanese flavor to, for example, "Chicken à la beef," which mingles white and dark chicken meat with nuggets of ground beef and strands of vermicelli. Add to these ingredients an herbed wine sauce and rice seasoned with cinnamon, and you'll understand why the taste is beguiling and complex. "Beefsteak Nicola" is a kind of wonderful pot roast created from marinating and cooking the meat long and slowly with wine and raisins. Other delights are lamb and beef in sesame sauce, braised lamb shank, and baked and raw kibbi.

Lovely pastries include harissi (squares of gently flavored farina cake) and nut mahmool (crumbly cookies filled with walnuts or pistachios). The Turkish coffee flavored with cardamom is good and strong. The sparse decor features exuberantly colored paintings along with prints of sailing ships and flower prints.

★ Nikolai's Roof $$$$ ⊗⊗⊗

Top of the Atlanta Hilton and Towers, 255 Courtland St. Map A. (404) 659-2000.
Daily seatings at 6:30 and 9:30 P.M. Reservations mandatory. All major credit cards. Validated parking in hotel.

Once upon a time, the ultimate proof of power and prestige in Atlanta was the ability to command a table at Nikolai's Roof without the seemingly obligatory six-month wait. Nikolai's reputation still has a lot to do with the work of its initial chef, Heinz Schwab, who established this kitchen as the most daring and inventive in town. Schwab left the Hilton in 1980 and a succession of corporate employees have basked in his reflected glory since. Some have plodded; others have shone briefly.

Nikolai's has always been known for showy bravado. Two standbys since opening day have been the Ukrainian borscht and the puff-pastry pirozhkis. The classic beet soup is always dependable. The pirozhkis remain as good as they've always been, served rolled up inside cloth napkins, whence you are instructed to extract them with your fingers and dip them in an undoctored béarnaise. If money is no concern, Russian caviar is served with all the trimmings. Flavored vodkas are available as an alternative to champagne.

Despite occasional strengths, a full dinner at Nikolai's (and that is your only option: five courses in rigid succession) is far from a stunning value. The fixed cost is high, exclusive of wine, tax, and tip. One improvement over the old oral menu routine is that the entrée choices are presented first, separately, giving patrons a chance to focus on a single option before straining ears to remember all the other possibilities of appetizers, soups, salads, and desserts.

All waiters perform graciously. Some have a natural talent for making the most of a lucky happening, adding their own special touches and sense of the unexpected to the job requirements. Others are stiffer and more afraid to deviate from the scenario. With a new French chef and an updated decor, Nikolai's Roof is making a big play for the Olympics.

★ Nino's $$ ⊗

1931 Cheshire Bridge Rd. (at Lenox Rd.). Map C. (404) 874-6505. Dinner only, Tuesday to Sunday 5:30 to 11 P.M. Reservations and all major credit cards accepted. Adequate parking.

Through many changes of owners and staff, Nino's has been able to keep the favor of the public, not because it is a particularly good restaurant, but because it is warm and fun, a nice place to hang out. Always busy, always noisy, the restaurant oozes Italian sentimentality. Yes, there are fat candles thrust in Chianti bottles. The wood paneling is dingy; the walls are dark from age and cigarette smoke, overladen with bizarre curios. The waiters zip around bearing generous portions of food to a faithful clientele.

Nino's isn't a cheap neighborhood trattoria. The wine list is expensive and the menu has some pretensions to elegance. This is the "tourist" side of the restaurant. But you are no fool—you'll have a carafe of perfectly nice house wine and something like a simple stracciatella soup, a nice green salad, and some old-fashioned pasta dish.

When the time comes for dessert, you needn't be specially careful or lucky. By and large, the choices are good: the sorbetti and gelati come from a premium supplier; the crema caramelle (a Mexican flan, really) and the runny zuppa inglese are homemade.

★★ Nuevo Laredo Cantina $ ⊗

1495 Chattahoochee Ave. (between Howell Mill and Marietta St.).
Map B. (404) 352-9009.
   Monday to Thursday 11:30 A.M. to 10 P.M. Friday and Saturday 11:30 A.M. to 11 P.M. Sunday 3 to 10:30 P.M. No reservations. V, MC. Small parking lot.

The middle of nowhere is the perfect setup for this atmospheric new hideaway by Chance Evans, creator of the original U.S. Bar y Grill. The only neighbors are warehouses along Chattahoochee Avenue. The building is attractively trashy: ochre-painted cinder blocks, vegetation spurting from fake rocks, roof redder than the blood of a bull. Pulling into a weed-infested front yard, you can feel the fun center of your brain responding to the challenge.

The interior is pure blue-collar romance: bump-your-head low ceiling, painted wooden chairs, diner-style bar with round red stools. The photographs on the wall document old Mexico in black and white. The music is furiously sentimental. A doorway offers a panoramic view of a pleasantly crude lower party room, the Cadillac Room, with a jukebox in a bright-green alcove.

The clientele is much more upscale than expected: connoisseurs of ambiance, rich folks from Buckhead out on the town, and Mexican workers from the surrounding industrial areas as well. Evans hustles among his staff, the only obvious Anglo in the cast.

Three fresh sauces (a frisky salsa cruda, a creamy avocado, a green chile and tomatillo) come in a relish holder on every table. The chips are thin, dry, and very fresh. With only a beer and wine license, Nuevo Laredo Cantina is able to offer tasty margaritas based on agave wine and a fresh Key lime mix. Excellent small soft tacos are offered two to an order at a low, low price. Use the salsas liberally on the various fillings (carne asada, chicken, chorizo, or tongue, scattered with fresh cilantro) for a delicious authentic flavor.

The ceviche resembles a seafood gazpacho served in a footed glass. The caldo de camaron, shrimp simmered in hot red-chile broth, has a more aggressive charm. From huevos rancheros to homemade tamales (especially delicious with green sauce) and an excellent chicken mole in a dark, rich sauce, you will find plenty to satisfy your taste for South of the Border at Nuevo Laredo Cantina.

★★ Oasis Café $

618 Ponce de Leon Ave. (across from the old Sears Building). Map C. (404) 881-0815. Other locations.

Lunch Monday to Saturday 11 A.M. to 3:30 P.M. Dinner Monday to Saturday 5:30 to 10 P.M. No reservations. V, MC. Ample parking.

On Ponce de Leon Avenue, almost anything qualifies as an oasis. Displaced from its original location, a tiny stuccoed building down the street, Oasis Café is now stretching out in a much larger space. This is a family operation. One brother works in the kitchen. Another waits on tables and has been known to tease the clientele with impromptu belly dancing. Other relatives operate a location in Sage Hill Shopping Center on Briarcliff Road and a third one on Windy Hill Road in Cobb County. The food is healthy and delicious, the atmosphere hospitable enough.

There are subtle differences between the dishes cooked Palestinian style at Oasis Café and those of its nearest, usually Lebanese, competitors. Everything feels startlingly fresh and light.

The flavors, especially in the sauces, tend to be pleasantly tart.

While complete dinners may feel expensive considering the location, take advantage of the daily lunch specials. A terrific falafel sandwich with fries or salad and a soft drink becomes the ultimate bargain at $2.99. Most of the other sandwiches rotate as specials but you won't mind paying full price for a lamb kabob wrapped in light, warm pita bread with tahini sauce, onions, and tomatoes or a marvelous baked kibbi stuffed with beef similarly wrapped as a sandwich.

Is the pita bread homemade or imported from New York? Who cares! It is just about the best, lightest, freshest you've ever had. Enjoy a basket of pita and a bowl of wonderful hummus or baba ghannoug, fava beans puréed with olive oil or soft fresh cheese retrieved from a jar of olive oil, stuffed grape leaves on the side, and a terrific salad seasoned with mint and fresh lemon juice. Other excellent specialties include shawarma beef gyro, beef and chicken kabob sandwiches, and homemade fries sprinkled with sumac. If you want to try something different, ask the kitchen to fix a grape leaves and hummus sandwich.

★★ OK Café $ ⓧⓧ

1284 W. Paces Ferry Rd. (at Northside Dr. and I-75). Map B. (404) 233-2888.

> *Daily 6 A.M. to 4:30 A.M. (Friday and Saturday 24 hours). No reservations. V, MC. Ample convenient parking.*

When Susan DeRose and Richard Lewis, creators of swank eateries for the expense-account set (e.g., Bone's), decided to do a diner for the same clientele, they couldn't have picked a better name, a better location, or a better look for their tongue-in-cheek treatment of mythical America circa 1950. Separated from Pano's & Paul's by a few hundred yards of parking space, the long, calculatedly plain building defies its chic neighbors by a show of saucy commonness.

A yellow between mustard and legal pad, trimmed in green, has been used for the exterior. Striped red-and-white vinyl awnings project stiffly from small windows. A narrow waiting hall fitted with comfortable banquettes opens onto a pandemonium of running waitresses, showing the backs of their knees in white polyester-blend smocks. White sneakers, bobby socks, a blue kangaroo pocket, and a fluted cloth tiara complete the uniform. Short-order cooks scramble wildly between a white tiled wall and a stainless-steel counter. They pause long enough to tilt back their narrow caps. People slide in and out of rows of bouncy vinyl banquettes, red with yellow piping. The windows are slatted with wooden blinds, framed by violently patterned curtains.

Everywhere you look, there is color and there is art. Wonderful art: modern folk bestiary crouching on shelves; trompe l'oeil ceramic platters depicting garish burgers and pies; a flag of Georgia in relief; a woodcut of a spotted dog near some painted, carousing English bull terriers; a few extremely strong photographs documenting the middle class and white trash in their weird habitats.

The food, from meatloaf to tofu burgers, is better than a throwback to road food. One of the strengths of the restaurant is its baking. Wonderful loaves of crusty bread, freshly and thickly sliced, are used for the sandwiches with fillings like a chunky chicken salad flavored with celery seeds. On the breakfast menu, the French toast is a unique version. Magnum slices of multigrain bread are dipped in eggs and milk and quickly deep-fried before being dusted with confectioners' sugar and brought with a pitcher of syrup. The egg batter foams up, solidifying in crisp, delicious curlicues. The biscuits are good, the classic egg preparations frequently greasy.

Breakfast is peaceful and businesslike during the week but a big social event on Sundays, when the Northwest crème de la crème skips in. Dinner is very much a family affair, too. One can't take the kids to Bone's, you know. Check out the new OK-To-Go and bring the goodies home.

★★ Old South Bar-B-Q $

601 Burbank Cir. (at the intersection of Cherokee Rd., Smyrna). Turn west off Atlanta Hwy. (Georgia 3) at Belmont Hills shopping center. Map G. (770) 435-4215.

Tuesday to Sunday 11 A.M. to 9:15 P.M. No reservations. V, MC. Small, steeply raked parking lot.

This quaint log cabin sits back from the road, making it difficult to see from a distance. Keep your eyes and nose alert for the aromatic smoke pouring from a wide brick chimney during prime cooking hours. The meat is smoked the slow old-fashioned way, in a specially designed hearth, and the meat tastes of that painstaking process.

For some of the best Georgia-style barbecue, ask for sliced outside pork. You get irregular chunks of beautifully butchered pork (not a trace of fat), one surface blackened from the fire. All of the juicy, tender flesh is thus impregnated with an intense wood-smoke flavor. If you've given up on Atlanta barbecue after your umpteenth slab of baked or stewed meat slathered in sauce and masquerading as the smoked stuff, drive to Smyrna and put some *real* South in your mouth.

Old South's sauce is also not too sweet, not too tart—a good balance between vinegar, ketchup, and steak sauce. The brunswick stew has a deep, fresh flavor. The atmosphere is low key, the walls covered with rec-room paneling on which smarmy, folksy illustrations of the Norman Rockwell school have been hung.

☆ Old Vinings Inn $$ ⊗⊗

3011 Paces Mill Rd. (downtown Vinings). (770) 438-2282. Map G. Lunch daily 11:30 A.M. to 2:30 P.M. Dinner nightly 5:30 to 10 (Sunday till 9). No reservations. All major credit cards. Small, awkward parking lot.

The days of "cute" are numbered for what used to be an idyllic community sandwiched between Buckhead and suburbia. The location of the old Old Vinings is to be bulldozed soon to make way for progress. The building across the street, formerly the bar of the Old Vinings, has been bought by a real-estate developer who has snatched the name and the concept, flaunting the curb appeal of this valuable property, while cleared land right in the back is being readied for nine new homes.

The new Old Vinings faces incessant daytime traffic. Dinner is a bit quieter in the charmingly decorated multiple rooms of the revived restaurant. The front dining room and an enclosed back porch are especially prim and pretty. The kitchen, a barely adequate galley affair, hints at a lack of sophistication but the menu promises plenty.

You won't mind the appetizers. The carpaccio isn't as thin as it could be, but the meat is beautifully tender under a light drizzle of horseradish cream and capers. Smoked salmon comes with tiny cold corn cakes, crème fraîche, and caviar. A fresh tomato soup swirled with cream is garnished with diced fresh tomato and a chiffonade of basil.

The shortcomings aren't far behind. A crab cake, massively overseasoned and full of fillers, masquerades as a softball on the plate. The pretty salad of organic field greens is garnished with blue cheese (good idea) and Christmas-style spiced walnuts (bad idea). Three entrées show the same combination of insufficient skills and poor judgment. An overcooked salmon filet with unbelievably awful, nearly raw green lentils and a saffron sauce, pathetic curling tidbits of snapper garnished with a bad pilaf and red cabbage, and soggy angel-hair pasta with chicken and a vegetable pesto cream show the chef in the same grim light.

When one finds the entrées inedible, one is neither placated nor amused by a single complimentary dessert of fresh berries with cream. Lunch is barely less aggravating than dinner. Chicken livers on toast points look like a repast for a cannibal: huge, massive halves still connected by nasty stuff swim in a dark and obnoxious gravy hiding two thick slices of disintegrating baguette. The turkey club sandwich is a pretty good way to eat 2,000 calories in one sitting. In the swordfish salad, you'll have trouble distinguishing the chunks of fish from the chunks of potato. The double chocolate cake is a commercial product.

All servers are young and eager in an attractive way but there is little evidence of strong management.

★★★ 103 West $$$$ ✗✗✗✗

103 W. Paces Ferry Rd. (just west of Peachtree). Map B. (404) 233-5993.

Dinner only, Monday to Saturday 6 to 11 P.M. Reservations essential. All major credit cards. Valet parking.

With all their major restaurants close to the center of Buckhead, Pano Karatassos and Paul Albrecht have played a key role in making this district the region's center for fine dining. All of their establishments merit visits, but for that big night out when you want to be coddled at the table and surrounded by—swaddled in—sensual enticements, this must be the choice. Every inch of the gigantic interior is gilded or embossed or luxuriously padded or painted to look like something it isn't. Baroque antiques loom from corners and frolic in midair. Marbleized columns, Aubusson tapestries, an eighteenth-century Italian porcelain of Zeus in action, trompe l'oeil murals, and a glittering gold espresso machine are a few of the diversions for the eye. The new facade and the opulent porte cochère, not to mention the immense new ballroom, boost the attractiveness of the restaurant.

The food stimulates one's lust for luxury as well. Even the menu descriptions excite. Caviar pearls, tartare of sea scallops, sautéed American mushrooms in puff pastry, sautéed fresh foie gras with warm asparagus are offered as appetizers. Truffles are sprinkled everywhere. Champagne-glazed Long Island oysters flavored with beluga caviar and smoked salmon are served at a teasing, warm temperature. Plump fresh Gulf-shrimp ravioli bathe in a languorous lobster bisque.

Juicy venison, chicken pot-au-feu, pink veal steak over basil-scented linguine, and ardent salads with unexpected color combinations (yellow cherry tomato, red Belgian endive, white chicory) will leave you flushed with a sense of well-being rather than deadened impulses. Enormous New Bedford sea scallops combine with bow-tie pasta and fresh spinach in a light garlic cream. Batter-fried lobster tails, sautéed tournedos of beef with four peppercorns, roasted duck breast, and confit of legs are some of the enduring specialties.

Delicious in-house desserts available individually or as a combination include apricot chocolate torte, baby truffles in a cookie basket, crème brûlée, and chocolate terrine and fresh sherbet sharing a plate dusted with confectioners' sugar.

The staff hovers and scrambles and whisks and bows and scrapes. Wines are high priced and classy. 103 West's wine room is a particularly pretty space for an elegant private party.

★★ Oriental Pearl Restaurant $$ ⊗⊗

5399 New Peachtree Rd. (Chinatown Square, Chamblee). Map D. 986-9866.

Lunch daily 11 A.M. to 3 P.M. Dinner nightly 5 to 10:30 (Friday and Saturday till 11). Reservations accepted. V, MC, AE. Ample parking.

Though not as easy to locate as in New York or San Francisco, Atlanta's Chinatown is a reality. Upper Buford Highway has attracted enough businesses over the years to qualify as the main drag. A right turn on Chamblee-Dunwoody Road will take you past Honto and to the cultural mecca of Chinatown Square, which includes the Chinese community center, a food court, a major Oriental grocery, and a variety of Chinese-owned stores. Anchoring the center, posh Oriental Pearl offers, among other things, the most varied and arguably the best dim sum in town.

The dining room seats a crowd but you needn't fear the infernal din sometimes associated with dim sum. Though large, the space is broken up. Carpets and tablecloths muffle the noise. Trundling and rattling are kept at a civilized level compatible with the feel of a room painted in creamy pastels and decorated with handsome etched glass and strips of mirror fanned out in a style oddly reminiscent of Art Deco. A large window gives a full view of prep pandemonium. Instead of curtains or valances, toasty brown ducks and strips of barbecued pork hang from hooks, as appetizing a still life as you could want to see.

Trying to spot snacks never encountered before is as interesting an exercise as looking for old favorites. In the first category, you may put deep-fried dumplings around fruit salad, a stunning plate of roast duck, chicken over a sort of Chinese version of Boston baked beans made with soy beans, trembling square cakes made with chunks of fresh water chestnuts, shredded jellyfish and chicken salad, and two versions of duck rolls served with Worcestershire sauce.

The selection of sweet dim sum items is particularly rewarding, including thick, tender almond cookies stuffed with sweet bean paste, flaky egg-custard tarts, red and yellow bean paste combined with nuts and molded into fat little rolls, steamed sweet buns, and steamed sponge cake. Keep your eyes peeled for a heavenly tapioca pudding handled almost like a crème brûlée.

Oriental Pearl is frequently the scene of wedding receptions and special parties. Dinner can otherwise feel very quiet compared to dim sum, but the quality is excellent and the offerings varied. As befits a Hong Kong establishment, seafood and vegetables reign supreme. Chef Chan is widely acknowledged as the finest banquet chef in the city and a true gourmet with a love for challenge.

★★ The Orient at Vinings $$ ✖✖

4199 Paces Ferry Rd. (in Vinings Square). Map B. (770) 438-8866. Monday to Thursday 11:45 A.M. to 10 P.M. Friday 11:45 A.M. to 11 P.M. Saturday 6 to 11 P.M. Sunday noon to 10 P.M. Reservations and all major credit cards accepted. Ample parking.

Built on an elevation above the flood level of the Chattahoochee, The Orient shines over a massive flight of concrete steps. Drama and sophistication have been planned into the small, intimately lit dining room. A halo of neon suffuses the bar with a soft purplish color. Three life-size ceramic god figures in elaborate Chinese robes occupy a large vitrine jutting into the dining space. Designer chairs, designer flatware, and ultramodern wall treatment (nuances of grey sponged and blended) await the posh Vinings clientele.

The kitchen breaks free from Chinese traditions with a creative menu that stops just short of fusion. Take the spectacular winter clam soup, for example, an intensely flavored stock with beautiful gaping shells and little bits of browned purple onions floating on the surface, or a special sole with pine nuts, filleted, slivered, briefly sautéed with Chinese vegetables and toasted pine nuts, and served on top of its very skin and bones fried crisper than crisp.

For appetizers you may choose from razor-thin slices of cuttlefish served with a light soy-based dipping sauce, fried

"Portuguese triangles" filled with curried beef, fresh lobster and chicken wrapped Shanghai style in a large egg-roll skin, and delicious chicken wings marinated in soy ginger sauce. Technically an entrée, minced chicken and water chestnuts in lettuce leaves can be shared as a first course.

Most dishes bear poetic names borrowed from natural phenomena or the jewelry trade. Presentations can be so intricate that you almost don't want to disturb them. Harbor shrimp for example resemble little boats with a full load of finely minced cuttlefish and a prow made with a thin stalk of asparagus. Sometimes, however, you could give up all the enchantments of these delicately prepared treats for a more definite taste. Low fat, low cal, low spice, the new style of cooking occasionally recalls an exotic spa operation.

The owner is in the kitchen; his wife runs the dining room with true grace. Your name will be remembered and your special needs will be taken seriously by the staff.

★ Otto's $$ ✗✗

265 E. Paces Ferry Rd. (at Peachtree Rd.). Map B. (404) 233-1133. Dinner only, Monday 5 P.M. to 1 A.M. Tuesday to Thursday 5 P.M. to 2 A.M. Friday and Saturday 5 P.M. to 3 A.M. Reservations and all major credit cards accepted. Difficult street parking or in several pay lots nearby.

The ability to make people feel a desired way is a key factor in the success of a restaurant. George Rohrig, owner of Otto's as well as Peachtree Café directly across the street and East Village Grille around the corner, has made a fortune zeroing in on a specific clientele. Otto's is cool, more elegant than a singles bar although frequently serving the same purpose. Hunters, hunted, and amused spectators of the hunt rub up against one another on highly sophisticated grounds.

Beautifully designed by Bill Johnson to take advantage of a deep, narrow space, the restaurant is mysteriously seductive, like a long glove or a slim cigarette holder. A small jazz combo is parked under the window. A long walk through a densely packed bar leads to a glamorous raised dining room.

Men wear fancy shirts, no ties. Women flash a shoulder, or a length of leg from under expensive garments. Dramatic halogen lights isolate modern flower compositions in tall urns. Glossy black surfaces contrast sharply with walls of soft stucco raked with razor-sharp horizontal lines like a Japanese sand garden.

When the restaurant started, the menu tried to match wits with the decor. But being at Otto's was enough for the clientele. Nobody wanted potentially embarrassing encounters with fiddlehead ferns. Out went the chef. Out went nouvelle cuisine.

After some bleak times devoted to cream sauces and other dull offerings, an agreeable list of easy specialties was put together. Many, many people feed on steaks: nicely scaled, perfectly tender, and darkly prime. The New York strip au poivre is especially appealing. Fish is more average. The new upstairs and the Library room see some of the most glamorous parties in town.

★★ Our Way Café $

303 E. College Ave. (near Agnes Scott College, Decatur). Map E. (404) 373-6665.
  Monday to Friday 11:30 A.M. to 2:30 P.M. No reservations or credit cards. Small parking lot.

With Agnes Scott on one side and the railroad tracks dead ahead, the location of this family-style restaurant is easy to pinpoint. Small-town cuisine, small-town setting—everything feels right. Appetizing smells greet you in the parking lot, becoming stronger and more delicious as you near the small counter set for cafeteria operation. Home cooking, threatened by the gentrification of Decatur, has found a friendly new hearth.

The menu is classic meat-and-three, although, judging by the reasonably healthy standards (no frying, no bacon grease, very little salt), the owners are probably fairly young. There are usually three entrée choices and plenty of delicious vegetables. Baked chicken, almost always fancy with lemon pepper or orange slices and almonds, tastes wonderful. Roast pork shredded in a rich gravy, boiled corned beef, and an excellent meatloaf in hefty, well-seasoned slices rotate on the menu.

The vegetables are worth the trip: unmistakably fresh corn cut and creamed; translucent, beautiful rutabaga tasting as if it belongs in an upscale restaurant; boiled cabbage; mild collard greens in their own cooking juices; real mashed potatoes; lima beans; heavenly squash casserole; dressing better than your mom's; fresh beets; carrots in big, crisp-tender slices. Frisky cornbread with jalapeño peppers is a treat with any vegetable plate.

The only disappointing thing is the desserts: so-called chocolate pound cake most probably made with vegetable oil; standard cobblers with slimy dough; chocolate cake with canned cherries. The decor is friendly, and with a large community table set in the front room, there is no need to sit alone and be depressed.

★★ Palisades $$ ⊗⊗

1829 Peachtree Rd. (at Palisade Dr.). Map B. (404) 350-6755.
  Dinner only, nightly 6 to 10:30. Reservations and all major credit cards accepted. Valet parking.

When people talk about cursed restaurant locations, they tend to blame geography rather than the entrepreneurial flaws that result in visible, repetitive failures in a particular spot. There is no reason, however, why the right kind of effort shouldn't meet with success, especially in the context of a restaurant-friendly neighborhood used to the Buckhead overflow.

If one had to describe Palisades in as few words as possible, one could call it a "better neighborhood restaurant" and be understood. Quieter than a bistro, less intimidating than a full-blast gourmet restaurant, this new dining room hits an interesting note.

The restaurant has been turned into something charming and European, no small feat considering its recent past. Carefully chosen original artwork, expensive lights, and café tables (some of which display their marble tops in casual style, while others are covered with fresh white linen) fit between pretty brick walls and classic French doors. The owners, a mature German-born couple perfect in manners and wardrobe, seem in total control of the front of the house.

The cuisine, poised between new continental and fresh American, knows where the boundaries of good taste lie. The opening chef set a trendy tone: grilled vegetables and polenta cakes splashed with balsamic vinaigrette; roasted leg of lamb served on mashed potatoes with roasted garlic, rosemary, natural jus, and dried cherries; seared salmon with tomato-cucumber relish and fried leeks; grilled pork chop with plum ketchup and juniper sauerkraut; ragout of rabbit with apricots, wild mushrooms, and Cabernet Sauvignon. The kitchen has gone more mainstream under his successors but the restaurant is still enjoyable.

★★★ Palm Restaurant $$$$ ✗✗

3391 Peachtree Rd. (across from Lenox Square in the Swissôtel). Map B. (404) 814-1955.

Monday to Saturday 11:30 A.M. to 11 P.M. Sunday 11 A.M. to 11 P.M. Brunch Sunday 11 A.M. to 3 P.M. Reservations and all major credit cards accepted. Valet parking.

And to think that it all started with a misunderstanding. "Parma, Parma," said John Ganzi and Pio Bozzi, two Italian immigrants, who wanted to name a restaurant after their native city. "Palm? Palm?" the Americans would ask. The local pronunciation prevailed and Palm Restaurant, which, unlike the competition, didn't even start as a steakhouse, was on its way to becoming a New York legend and a place that has stayed in the family and survived since 1926 in the same Second Avenue location.

The Atlanta restaurant is odd in the progressive architectural environment of the Swissôtel. Palm Restaurant feels rather like a bustling tavern, with comfortable booths and white tablecloths. There is a big mural with national cartoonists paying homage to the restaurant. There are also the faces of local luminaries and visiting celebrities captured in caricature form and applied to the walls by a process that recalls the kind of decals one used to find in bubble-gum packages.

Full every night, the restaurant is also a big scene at lunch. What's the big deal? Quality and plenty of it. An appetizer portion of fried calamari looks like dinner for four on a turkey platter. This also happens to be some of best, crispest, freshest calamari you have ever seen and it comes with a vivid and delicious marinara and cut-up lemons. Palm Restaurant's famous chips and onion rings are on the same level of abundance and excellence.

The steaks are massive and wonderfully cooked: dark on the outside and as red as you wish on the inside. There are no gimmicks in presentation and no letdown in quality. Just pick your favorite cut. The vegetables are, of course, à la carte. Most of them are straightforward (baked potatoes, big chips, string beans, spinach aglio e olio) and good—which makes it hard to understand why the plate of steamed vegetables, an entrée option, should be so blah, so overcooked, and so unworthy of the South.

The Palm's lobsters are famous for their size (three pounds, four pounds, and up) and preparation (split, basted with seasoned butter, and broiled, claws boiled and on the side). Two can easily share a four-pounder but most tables seem to get a lobster apiece, perhaps more as a status symbol than out of fear of not having enough.

But let's say you don't eat red meat. Or you don't feel up to running up a major tab. Palm Restaurant has some of the greatest and most fun salads ever. At lunch, for example, you may discover that the special features three perfect little pieces of filet mignon on sliced beefsteak tomatoes and Vidalia onion with a simple balsamic vinaigrette. Salad Gigi, named after one of the original managers, is a steakhouse-style chopped salad, a wonderful mound of lettuce, tomato, onions, diced jumbo shrimp, green beans, and crisp bacon with a mild dressing. The Monday Night Salad (available every day of the week) is almost like a solid-state gazpacho, a plate of finely minced greens, tomato, onion, and radishes with minced anchovies.

Palm Restaurant offers beautiful swordfish steaks, fabulously dense and fresh crab cakes (pure, solid crab meat, just seasoned, mounded, and finished in the oven), a crab-meat cocktail that could use some going over for bits of cartilage, and an insanely boring appetizer called shrimp Bruno and featuring contorted jumbo shrimp dipped in an egg wash and served over a Dijon mustard sauce. There are many Italian dishes on the menu: six veal specialties, a bunch of pasta, and a rustic pasta fagioli soup at lunch to name a few.

The apple pie is doughy and cold, the blueberry cake a horror, the Key lime pie merely average, but the New York cheesecake is a classic.

The waiters, Philadelphia and Jersey's finest, exude personality. The wine selection, which in the olden days used to be red or white only, has caught up with the times and offers mega-names at O.K. prices.

★★★ Pano's & Paul's $$$$ ⓧⓧⓧ

1232 W. Paces Ferry Rd. (at Northside Pkwy. and I-75). Map B. (404) 261-3662.

Dinner only, Monday to Friday 6 to 11 P.M. Saturday 5:30 to 11 P.M. Reservations required. All major credit cards. Valet parking.

There are restaurants that begin with a glow of light, streak into the public's consciousness like a comet, and as quickly disappear from sight. There are others that easily attain a nice cheerful sparkle and content themselves with the modest light they cast upon society, never striving for greater brilliance. Both types are common enough. Far rarer are the places that immediately establish preeminence and maintain it, against the challenge of upstarts and changing fads.

The opening in 1978 of this elaborately decorated venture by chef Paul Albrecht and general manager Pano Karatassos marked a milestone in Atlanta restaurant history. Richly textured fabrics, swirls of paisleys, and swaths of stripes dazzled patrons used to more restrained decor. The food was richly bewildering, the atmosphere full of bustle and excitement.

Albrecht and Karatassos have since gone on to launch many other ambitious and successful enterprises in town, and their first operation has kept up with the times. The menu at this temple of velvety fabrics reflects a far more daring sensibility than the original bill of fare. Some dishes remain from the old days: the batter-fried lobster tail is a solid classic with its accompanying sauce of honey mustard and drawn butter.

Ah, but one can so easily ignore the old favorites! Chef

Albrecht makes sure you will never be bored. Terrine of fresh foie gras and artichoke with truffle vinaigrette, sautéed sweetbreads with fried capers, and tournedos of Atlantic salmon in ginger pepper crust are captivating combinations. Extraordinary specials have included freshwater prawns poking extraordinary long antennas into the trembling flesh of deep-sea scallops steamed in soy ginger butter and garnished with fried baby spinach leaves.

A double breast of chicken served with tiny green beans, blanched garlic, sun-dried tomatoes, and crisp grilled onion shows the new restraint of a kitchen that used to overburden basic preparations with heavy sauces, crusts of pastries, and other fancy tricks. Fried mashed potatoes, gratin of fresh vegetables, orzo pasta primavera, angel-hair pasta cake, and spicy corn butter are but a few of the many garnishes accompanying the increasingly fashionable dishes.

Pano's & Paul's prides itself on filling requests for items not on their extensive menu. The service is mature and responsible. Don't miss a visit to the bar, done over in tones of plum and cinnamon and violet to evoke the self-indulgent exoticism of Paris in the 1920s.

★★★ Partners $$ ⊗ ⊗

1399 N. Highland Ave. (in Morningside). Map C. (404) 876-8104. Dinner only, nightly 5:30 to 11 (Friday and Saturday till 11:30). No reservations. All major credit cards. Parking across the street, behind the restaurant, or in real estate company lot up the street.

Call it flair; call it taste. Partners is nothing but a smallish rectangular room with three rows of chairs and tables. Yet it is visually exciting and beautiful, with many poetic details. On the street side of the restaurant, panels of lace effectively block out the sights of busy North Highland while creating the illusion that, if they were to open, a charming scene would unfold.

At the far end of the dining room, a casually pulled-aside curtain reveals a picture window into a busy kitchen, where a crew in whites seems to perform a hyper-realist work of modern choreography. The bar was put together out of various antique pieces. Near the entrance, the host has just enough space to place a tiny notebook on a clever stand acting as a desk. Extraordinary paintings of trees by Louis T. Sloan engage the imagination.

The menu shows some preoccupation with culinary fashion, but also a desire for simplicity, in keeping with the size of the place. A bubbling tomato fondue with fresh basil, Vermont goat cheese, and bruschetta; a plate of sophisticated lobster ravioli with shiitake mushrooms and dried flying-fish roe; and a pound of oven-roasted mussels with buttered bread crumbs have been among the best appetizers.

The catch of the day is always worth looking into. Lamb and couscous, bistro chicken on cannellini beans, and Tuscan pork misted with sambuca are well-balanced, creative entrées. The pasta is outstanding. Gumminess and over-elasticity, the two most common pitfalls, have been conquered. The dough, cut in ribbons of varying thickness, behaves perfectly. The house salad is a crunchy and assertive Caesar.

Glorious homemade desserts end the meal on a clear, positive note. If you have fallen in love with the gooey wedge of chocolate chip pie or a buttery Georgia peach pound cake, you will be able to buy them on impulse from the carry-out next door that packs food to go from both Partners' and Indigo's kitchens.

The owner has a strong interest in award-winning California vintages, planning interesting selections for the restaurant. The staff knows the food; service is friendly and expeditious. Despite recent changes in the kitchen, Partners remains a sophisticated and romantic bistro with a solid food scheme.

★ Paschal's $ ⊗

830 Martin Luther King Jr. Dr. (between Ashby Ave. and Atlanta University). Map F. (404) 577-3150.
   Daily 7 A.M. to 11 P.M. No reservations. All major credit cards. Ample parking in rear.

This motor hotel is situated in the heart of what used to be Hunter Street, one of Atlanta's two major black business districts in the old Jim Crow days. A block or two closer to downtown begins Atlanta University, the largest complex of black colleges in the nation. Paschal's has served as a nerve center for activists seeking, first, to change the old order and, subsequently, to consolidate the gains brought by integration.

Nostalgia may overwhelm you during a meal in its window-walled dining room. The menu, with its litany of all-American standbys, could have been printed in 1954 (except for the prices). The mostly black clientele goes just about as far back. You'll see veterans of Atlanta's civil-rights and political wars, neighborhood leaders, and corporate and governmental power brokers sitting in booths or at the counter, chatting from table to table, standing in the aisles to lean over the shoulders of old acquaintances. Right in the heart of the city is this community center with the feel of a small-town café.

Your taste buds, too, will call up auld lang syne. This is, authentically enough, the food of the fifties, as formerly dispensed at countless hotels and diners across the land. The Southern fried chicken is a perfectly sound, unassuming version of the classic. At all meals, not just breakfast, you may order a chicken liver omelet—and should. Different cooks reveal varying mastery of this delicacy, but at its best here, it is unsurpassed, the eggs a great creamy, puffy, frothy envelope for giant livers still pink in the middle and deeply impregnated with pan juices.

Breakfast served in a much more casual room—a bustling fifties luncheonette—is the meal of choice at Paschal's. The staff in crisp blue serge provides excellent service. All egg dishes and delicious Southern classics (fried pork chops the best) are reliably good.

★★ Pasta da Pulcinella $ ⊗

1027 Peachtree St. (at 11th St.). Map C. (404) 892-6195.
Lunch Monday to Friday 10:30 A.M. to 2:30 P.M. Dinner Monday to Thursday 5:30 to 10 P.M., Friday and Saturday 5:30 to 11 P.M. No reservations or credit cards. Small parking lot in the back or street parking.

It matters not how many people didn't make it in the same location. This is fresh and different, even sophisticated in a

Greenwich Village kind of way. Fresh homemade pasta, interesting regional recipes, a savvy urban environment, and not a thing on the menu higher than $6.50 set Pulcinella apart from the competition. If you work close to Midtown, you may as well drop everything and go see for yourself what this charming young place has to offer.

Pulcinella, the jester in the Italian *Commedia dell'Arte,* smiles on the window of this highly unusual pasta café. Opened on a shoestring by young people, the restaurant manages to be hip and clever as well as thoroughly original. No one's menu comes close to Pulcinella's short list of fresh pasta culled from various provinces of Italy. The signature dish, and one of the best pasta combinations anywhere, is an elegant-beyond-its-price tortelli di mele, round ravioli filled with browned Granny Smith apple, sweet sausage, and Parmesan elegantly topped with brown butter and fresh sage.

Buckwheat tagliatelle with sautéed rapini, Ligurian triangular pansotti with greens and pecan sauce, and Sardinian eggplant ravioli with fresh mint will broaden your pasta horizon. Traditionalists may opt for the basic fresh linguine with a choice of tomato sauce, pesto, or roasted-garlic sauce for a mere $3.95 (mixed vegetables and smoked chicken extra). Are you dreaming or what? Two fresh salads (including a low-fat Caesar) and a daily special complete the menu. Everything is delicious.

There is counter service only, but a fun dining room with artistically crumbling plaster and interesting things on the wall.

★ Pasta Vino $ ⓧ

2391 Peachtree Rd. (in Peachtree Battle Shopping Center, Peachtree Battle Ave.). Map B. (404) 231-4946.
  Monday to Thursday 11 A.M. to 10 P.M. Friday and Saturday 11 A.M. to 11 P.M. Sunday 5 to 10 P.M. No reservations or credit cards. Large but crowded parking lot.

Formerly a cold, unfriendly space with too many windows, this Buckhead pizzeria with trattoria ambitions has warmed up considerably, swathing itself in chintz fabrics and acquiring proper tablecloths. The effort paid off and even though one is still conscious of being in a corner storefront, the emotional temperature has gone up a few degrees. One is more willing to spend some time in the dining room instead of running home with a hot box of pizza.

Pasta Vino still serves New York-style pizza and calzone in the tradition of Broadway Danny's. Both are still good, although the white pizza seems to have taken a turn for the worse. Pasta is prepared according to simple recipes: linguine with pesto and pine nuts, a basic version of linguine in clam sauce fragrant with garlic, ziti with fresh broccoli and whole cloves of roasted garlic, eggplant lasagna. Nothing stands out spectacularly among the pasta dishes but the option is satisfying nevertheless, especially with a glass of inexpensive Merlot.

Pasta Vino offers a small menu of dinner entrées (several of them chicken) and runs daily specials. The window by the entrance now serves as a showcase for a colorful display of antipasti: roasted red peppers stuffed with marinated tomatoes, cold frittata studded with onion and potatoes, cold vegetables (mushrooms, onion, zucchini) stuffed with bread crumbs. The option of lingering for coffee is hard to pursue when lines of customers ogle the tables from a prime vantage point between the front door and the pizza counter.

★★ Peachtree Café $$ ⊗⊗

268 E. Paces Ferry Rd. (at Buckhead Ave.). Map B. (404) 233-4402. Sunday and Monday 11 A.M. to 10 P.M. Tuesday to Thursday 11 A.M. to 11 P.M. Friday and Saturday 11 A.M. to midnight. No reservations. All major credit cards. Parking on street or in congested pay lots nearby.

Back in 1982, Peachtree Café was just a little hole in the wall across the street from its present location. Baked potatoes, hot dogs, burgers, and a few soups and salads were the staples of a small, unsophisticated kitchen. The food was wholesome, the desserts delicious, the clientele low key. But by 1984, the operation had moved to spiffy new quarters. Prices were up, quality was down, and the singles were fighting to get in.

Peachtree Café had become the hottest Buckhead bar. Things have calmed down and the restaurant has reached a comfortable maturity.

The decor is attractive. Dining happens on two levels on dazzlingly white tablecloths. The posh bar is set in a bright, airy room where a baby grand piano lends a touch of class to the frenzy. Two amusing trompe l'oeil canvases simulate windows on a blind wall facing the entrance. Real windows open onto a delightful terrace shaded by large umbrellas.

Owner George Rohrig has hired a real chef and the menu has taken a turn for the better: homemade café chips with melted blue cheese, comforting seasonal soups (e.g., lentils in the wintertime), wood-grilled portobello mushrooms with basil oil, fresh salads with tony ingredients, lightly handled fresh pasta, and more complex entrées than ever before. At lunch, go for a nice big sandwich containing a whole grilled breast, havarti melted on top, lettuce, tomato, and mayonnaise on good French bread.

The list of homemade desserts has shrunk and the quality is up.

★★ The Peasant $$ ✗✗

3402 Piedmont Rd. (at Tower Place). Map B. (404) 231-8740.
Lunch Monday to Saturday 11:30 A.M. to 2:30 P.M. Dinner nightly 5:30 to 11. Limited reservations. All major credit cards. Valet parking.

The Trio concept, upscale contemporary dining, did a belly flop in this suave location. A campaign orchestrated by Fitzgerald & Co. ("Peasant Uprising") wiped out the notion of failure and launched the idea of victorious revolution when the local Peasant Restaurant company decided to dismantle Trio and redo it as a Peasant for the nineties.

A task force was quickly assembled and the transformation proceeded with surgical precision. Original designer Stan Topol introduced a new softness, murmuring messages of relaxation to the returning clientele. A decorating SWAT team managed the changes in a few days.

The facade sprouted a fetching awning. The entranceway

shed some of its intimidating elegance. New fabrics, big pillows tossed on the banquettes, and residential pieces (soft-looking antique wooden furniture, old lamps with textural flaws, marvelous obese pottery, and select knickknacks) did the trick. Some areas are close to formal (the back wall with new mirrors). Central to the restaurant, the bar/lounge is for mingling and waiting.

Ingredients viewed as too clever by half by some of the people who turned up their noses at Trio are still part of the food concept, but they sneak up on you instead of being listed on a too descriptive menu. Also typical of the nineties, enormous salads incorporate healthy protein in the form of grilled shrimp, grilled chicken breast, or grilled fresh tuna.

Failings in technique are few and far between. A summer gazpacho seems to involve no more than two steps: swirling a can of tomatoes in the blender on slow and tossing in a vast amount of thick-skinned, coarsely cut cucumber. A grilled-shrimp salad short on dressing and assembled with no particular authority is not especially lovable.

People starve for weeks so they can have dessert at The Peasant: apple walnut pie with cinnamon ice cream, warm peach and blackberry pie, frozen lemon pie with warm strawberry sauce, and the occasional big gooey chocolate dessert. The staff to customer ratio is impressive and the service polished. The downstairs private parties facility is an especially agreeable spot.

★ The Peasant Uptown $$ ⊗⊗

3500 Peachtree Rd. (upper level of Phipps Plaza). Map B. (404) 261-6341.

   Lunch daily 11:30 A.M. to 3 P.M. Dinner nightly 5:30 to 11. No reservations. All major credit cards. Parking in mall lots.

Suave decor, excellent management style, and a good ratio of price to quality give the Peasant restaurants a competitive edge all over town. A move within Phipps Plaza and a clever renovation have focused attention on this popular favorite. The green and white color scheme creates a lovely illusion of summery outdoors. The entire restaurant now feels like a garden room separated from the hustle and bustle of the mall.

Some dishes have been on the menu for years. Others rotate with the fashion. If you like one of the Peasant restaurants (including The Country Place, The Pleasant Peasant, Dailey's, and The Peasant), you like them all, including this one. Big, silly desserts will transform your party into giggling sinners.

The chorus line of talkative servers has been screened for pleasant personality traits and trained in genuine care for the customer. Waiters and manager pick up and deal perceptively with the faintest manifestations of unhappiness. Three cheers for the staff's professional aplomb.

★★ Pho Hoa $

5150 Buford Hwy. (Asian Square, 1 mile inside I-285, Chamblee). Map D. (770) 455-8729.

Daily 10 A.M. to 9 P.M. (Friday and Saturday till 10 P.M.). No reservations or credit cards. Ample parking.

A delicious complete meal (soup, one adequate serving of meat, one starch, fresh vegetables) just short of four dollars is almost too good to be true, especially at a speed that could compete with the average fast-food restaurant. Of course, your entire meal comes in a bowl—described as small on the menu but enormous by most standards—and if you aren't any good with chopsticks, the specialty of the house may remain literally beyond your grasp.

Pho Hoa is a chain, a smooth corporate version of the traditional Vietnamese pho house offering dozens of variations on the same beef and noodle soup. Everything has been made easy for Americans. The menu, for example, provides a section for beginners, discusses the fat content of some of the meat cuts, and tastefully urges the clientele to be adventurous or seek the more fortifying soups with the maximum of ingredients.

Basically the kitchen maintains big simmering vats of an aromatic, light-bodied beef stock permeated with the flavor of five-star anise and other spices. Each bowl of pho contains fresh rice noodles, a choice of meat, a light topping of cilantro and onion and comes accompanied by a large platter of crisp sprouts, basil leaves, and thinly sliced jalapeño pepper. Look for nuoc mam (a clear, pungent fish sauce) in a small cruet on the table.

Pho Hoa offers a few nonsoup items such as charbroiled pork chops or shrimp over vermicelli, traditional beef stew (too sweet and oily), and average spring rolls. Juices, crushed-ice desserts, homemade puddings, and strong coffees round out the menu.

★ Pilgreen's $$ ⓧ

1081 Lee St. (between Donnelly and Avon, West End). Map F. (404) 758-4669. Other locations.
 Tuesday to Thursday 11:30 A.M. to 9:30 P.M. Friday 11:30 A.M. to 10:30 P.M. Saturday 5 to 10:30 P.M. No reservations. All major credit cards. Ample parking.

This moderate-priced steakhouse began operations on the north side of downtown in 1932, but moved to Lee Street in the West End in 1949. It has been a staple on the south side ever since. Scanning the many license plates with Douglas, Fayette, and Clayton County tags in the parking lot reveals the loyalty of former city dwellers to a place they have been frequenting for a generation. Inside, these old-timers gasp in astonishment at signs of even the smallest change (such as the substitution of standard cocktail glasses for Pilgreen's distinctive tall tumblers). They come here for old favorites—fried onion rings, fried cauliflower, T-bones in three sizes. Novelty is the last thing they're looking for.

You have to put yourself in the faithful's frame of mind to derive full enjoyment from a visit to Pilgreen's. Dinner at Pilgreen's is a bargain. Begin your meal with a cup of vegetable soup, more for the old-fashioned cornbread hoecakes that accompany it than for the rather thin liquid itself. Dinner platters come with a salad, a heap of onion rings, and a potato of your choice. Big-deal steakhouses offer bigger, juicier cuts, but their prices are comparably heftier. Pilgreen's T-Bone is almost always decent and you will enjoy the notion of Pot Luck Steak (butcher's choice).

The original Pilgreen's sports an environment that induces nostalgia, albeit of a somewhat wacky sort. The cheaply paneled dining rooms strung out in a row off a narrow corridor, the garish landscapes and sentimental oil paintings, the brusquely efficient servers are a world away from Buckhead. Other subsequently opened outlets have never come up to the eccentric feel of the original.

★ Pittypat's Porch $$ ⊗⊗

25 International Blvd. (between Peachtree and Spring). Map A. (404) 525-8228.

    Dinner Sunday to Thursday 4:30 to 9 P.M. Friday and Saturday 5 to 10 P.M. No reservations. All major credit cards. Parking in pay garage next door.

Started in the midsixties by the Anthony family, and currently under new management, Pittypat's courts the first-time visitor with Southern clichés. A narrow, unremarkable entrance next to a parking deck leads to an astonishing fantasy of an old plantation porch. This house of illusion is built inside out, with the entire top floor meant to represent gracious outdoor living. Dozens of rocking chairs bob against wooden railings. Clutching a Scarlett (billed as "our own version of a strawberry daiquiri") or a Moonshiner's Punch, people wait docilely for their names to crackle over the loudspeakers.

No gracious Southern home opens beyond the porch. One descends instead into a teeming rathskeller hung with quaint rural and industrial implements and a few heads of game. There will always be a clientele for tourist restaurants. At times the bad rap has been richly deserved. But in recent years, closer supervision has elevated the food experience to a higher level.

The menu is printed on both sides of a cardboard fan. There are plenty of regional touches, but some questions go unanswered. Aunt Pittypat's sideboard no longer groans under displays of inferior food, but why pasta salad next to rice salad on the way to the more interesting sweet-potato salad, watermelon-rind pickles, and crisp marinated cucumbers? Why lavish crackers with the hot crab dip, reminding you of a hundred parties you didn't want to go to?

Black-eyed pea cakes with a spicy fresh Southern salsa (tomatoes, onions, peaches) are a good appetizer. Pecan-coated catfish fingers are fish sticks by another name. Among the entrées, the coastal venison pie topped with a thin cornbread crust qualifies as a signature entrée, but you may not want its "souvenir skillet." (Will it fit in your garment bag? Is that really the one you ate from?) Grilled pork tenderloin with curried peanut sauce is pretty dry, on a bed of sweet potato and apple purée. Grilled grouper tastes like the most innocuous of plated banquet food. Pecan pie, "the South's most famous dessert," and Pittypat's black-bottom pie aren't especially great specimens.

★ The Pleasant Peasant $$ ⊗⊗

555 Peachtree St. (at Linden). Map A. (404) 874-3223.
Lunch Monday to Friday 11:30 A.M. to 2:30 P.M. Dinner nightly 5:30 to 11 (Friday and Saturday till midnight). No reservations. All major credit cards. Validated parking in lot around corner on Linden or a block away, across Courtland.

In the context of the 1990s, it may be difficult to comprehend how this restaurant could have heralded a major change in the way Atlantans ate out. Back in 1973 residents had to choose between fancy, often downright pretentious restaurants with high prices and holes-in-the-wall with little or no charm. The Pleasant Peasant aimed for middle ground and achieved instantaneous success. Regular patrons trumpeted their favorite tables, favorite waiters, favorite dishes. Others prided themselves on working methodically through the list of items chalked on blackboards and described in detail by cheerful, carefully trained young men.

Enormous helpings, reinforced by generous garnishes and free side dishes, go far to explain the Peasant's great popularity. A recent renovation has added much charm to the room. Romance is in the air. Charming chandeliers descend from the ceilings. The mirrors reflect the decor rather than the customers. A new skylight has opened in the pressed tin ceiling.

The bad news is that the food is far too heavy for the health-conscious nineties. Dishes one expects to be light (bruschetta, for example) arrive loaded with fat. The bread (something cheesy and possibly fried) looks like twice-baked potatoes. The salads are drenched in dressing. Unless your appetite is Rabelaisian, you can probably forego appetizers. The details of seasoning often create problems. Even something as easy as a filet mignon aux champignons gets to be heavy.

It's hard to get upset in such a pleasant context, though, and the desserts are still grand.

★★★ Pricci $$$ ⊗⊗⊗

9:00

500 Pharr Rd. Map B. (404) 237-2941.
Lunch Monday to Friday 11 A.M. to 5 P.M. Dinner Monday to Thursday 5 to 11 P.M., Friday and Saturday 5 P.M. to midnight, Sunday 5 to 10 P.M. Reservations and all major credit cards accepted. Valet parking.

A definite qualifier in the glamor sweepstakes, this sexy Italian has more to offer than a great bod and a clever culinary concept. Like Buckhead Diner (another Pat Kuleto design), Pricci starts to sex up after dark. The blinding white building fills with magic as the switch is thrown and electricity flows through the striking array of glass-art fixtures.

The phases of the moon shine in an architectural canopy waving above the back wall. Precious glass shades dangle above the bar like gay Chinese lanterns, each with its own individual shape and sunset color. Strips of various metals wrap themselves around opalescent globes. A sculpture of heavy colored-glass wedges acts as a partition defining one of many dining areas.

Each step you take is on rainbow-colored terrazzo. Precious woods, deep booths, open kitchen, and chic pizza hearth will have your eyes rolling in your head. You want to see everything: the bottles of olive oil standing at attention on a satiny counter, the thick-crusted breads piled in an elegant wood-and-glass case, the fabulous bakery behind a picture window, the frantic chefing and expediting of highly decorative dishes.

Although no Italian by birth, chef John Carver masters the culinary language with tender potato gnocchi in fresh tomato and cream sauce, frisky salad of arugula with purple olivata vinaigrette and shingles of asiago cheese, custardy grilled polenta with baby veal sausages, and bomba (bomb) of pizza dough rising from the plate under rosy slices of prosciutto. All starters are beautiful. Risotto and pesto balls over melted fresh tomatoes and a beautifully plated vitello tonnato (veal in tuna sauce) are triumphs for the kitchen.

Rustic and sensible, pasta Pricci style is a must. From hand-rolled tortelloni with radicchio, ricotta, and walnuts to orrecchiete (ear-shaped pasta) with wild broccoli di rape, garlic, and pecorino cheese, this part of the menu is a winner.

The entrées are on target: lamb shank in an intense rosemary-infused barolo sauce; grilled quails and polenta surrounded with baby veal sausages, fried pancetta, and rosettes of baby artichokes; snapper in parchment with Calamata olives, oven-dried tomatoes, blanched garlic, and split baby artichokes; grilled marinated baby chicken on rosemary potatoes and roasted cloves of garlic. Duck breast, thickly sliced and heaped on marinated lentils with onions and wilted greens, becomes a real peasant feast. The flavors are well blended, the visual impressions always stimulating.

Dessert sustains the mood. Chocolate semifreddo with walnut pralines, meringue filled with lemon curd and candied lemon peel, Italian cheesecake with golden raisins, and a chunky, rustic upside-down apple cake with sweet polenta crust end a harmonious meal. Lunch, far quieter than dinner, is a good introduction to the restaurant.

☆ The Public House $$ ⊗⊗

607 Atlanta St. (U.S. 19, on the Roswell town square). Map H. (770) 992-4646.

Lunch daily 11:30 A.M. to 2:30 P.M. (Saturday and Sunday till 3 P.M.). Dinner Monday to Thursday 5:30 to 10 P.M., Friday and Saturday 5:30 to 11 P.M. No reservations. All major credit cards. Street parking in front, parking lot in rear.

The Peasant Corporation has specialized in turning abandoned commercial brick buildings into warm and lively arenas where the consumption of food is just a facet of the entertainment provided by the surroundings. This Roswell property features a cozy piano bar and lounge upstairs, a startling contrast to the immensely wide and open dining room on the ground floor. An illusion of intimacy is conveyed to diners by the bustle of gregarious waiters reciting menu selections from a blackboard placed at each table. Stand on the staircase leading to the piano bar and glance across the great expanse of the dining area at the candles twinkling on every table: as romantic a sight as a harbor filled with lighted fishing boats at night.

An evening here can be most agreeable if you don't catechize the dishes too closely and thereby spoil your pleasure in the environment. Servers lead patrons verbally through the menu items chalked on blackboards. The wine selection is small, sensibly chosen, and fairly priced.

★★★ Pung Mie $

5145 Buford Hwy. (just below Northwoods Plaza, Doraville). Map D. (404) 455-0370.

Daily 11 A.M. to midnight (Sunday till 11 P.M.). Reservations accepted. V, MC. Small parking lot, more space in the back.

Seen from the street, the name of the restaurant, written in Korean, resembles *OH HO,* but a smaller poster identifies the business as Pung Mie. If you have any reluctance about entering an operation that obviously doesn't count on much of an American clientele, you may be missing some of the best dumplings in the city. The restaurant, staffed by a Taiwanese family who lived in Korea before emigrating to the U.S., advertises itself as a dumpling house, and a Chinese restaurant for Koreans.

This is one of the best Chinese restaurants of all time. Language is no problem in the dining room. The servers may have a limited vocabulary, but their communication skills are adequate. The menu is trilingual: a column in Chinese, one in Korean, and the third a translation into (often funny) English.

Pig "funkles," "braiesd" five shreds, and house special "moot bell" are among the captivating mysteries.

Order a marvelous plate of plump, fragrant pot stickers, called fried dumplings on the menu, and you shall become a convert. Hugely swollen, their thin glossy dough masterfully stretched and crinkled, the pan-sautéed dumplings are stupendously good with a juicy pork and Chinese chives filling. The same beautiful dumplings are available steamed or boiled.

Beef dumplings (also listed on the menu) are named for a particular shape and type of dough (like a child's pincushion made of puffy, slightly sticky batter), not for their delicious filling made of pork. Flower rolls are fluffy clouds of white dough shaped like huge seashells, marvelously useful to sop sauces and clean the last bits of kimchee off your bowl. They are also available fried in an off-the-menu option.

Putting your faith in starch, you may also go for the noodle dishes. For a bracing main course, order san shan noodle soup: long egg noodles served in a bowl of fiery, oily broth with an assortment of delicious seafood including shrimp, tender morsels of squid, and gelatinous pieces of sea cucumber (an edible slug with limited appeal for most Westerners). For a lighter treat, consider chow shan si, a plateful of clear cellophane noodles seasoned with bits of pork, huge mushrooms, and chives.

Cold salads play an important part on the menu. Available individually or in combinations of up to six ingredients, they are mostly glorious. Cold spicy chicken in large round slices cut right through the bone, tender beef flavored with star anise, and shredded jellyfish tossed with lemon, cilantro, and julienne greens have the look and the taste one treasures on a hot summer night.

Exceedingly tender and pleasant-looking cold marinated tripe in firm, tangy strips may require a bit more courage, and you may draw the line at pig feet (the mysterious "funkles" on the menu), boiled with soy sauce and divided into crunchy, bony chunks. Garlic, lavishly sprinkled on some of the cold salads, is a constant, both in the aroma and the taste of dishes. It adds bite to the kimchee and can be felt in the other form of pickled vegetable (the stem of a leafy green, sliced and marinated) served with all meals. You will notice it in the delicious

Mongolian beef served rare with bok choy and in the hot braised fish, a tough customer with a mouthful of sharp little teeth and an unnerving blank boiled eye.

Two of the best dishes bear a striking resemblance to familiar Western combinations. Moot bell (read meatballs) may remind you of an exceptionally fine version of country sausage, cooked in big loose patties with hot sauce and green vegetables. Hot pepper chicken has the same pungent, vinegary bite as Buffalo wings, delicious as (messy) finger food or over snow-white plump rice. Shredded beef with pickled mustard greens tastes delicious as well, with acidic, crunchy morsels mixed in the julienne beef and barely cooked onions. Mounds of fresh green vegetables (including sweet pea vines and a mysterious leafy vegetable called nida) are to die for.

The heaviness and oiliness of some combinations may be too much for some and the garlic vapors may turn others off. But the obvious rapture of the Asian clientele is well worth sharing for the sake of an original and potent food experience.

★ Rainbow Natural Foods $

2118 N. Decatur Rd. (at Clairmont Rd.). Map E. (404) 633-3538. Monday to Saturday 10 A.M. to 8 P.M. No reservations or credit cards. Adequate parking.

A popular vegetarian hangout, this clean and cheerful cubbyhole of a dining room is located in the back of a meticulously scrubbed vegetarian health-food store and grocery. Seating is at plain wooden tables and chairs. Prints of plants provide spots of color in an interior otherwise monochromatically beige. Limited table service is provided.

The basic menu of salads, sandwiches, and rice with vegetables is supplemented by daily specials, printed up on weekly menus. Monday might offer seven beans soup and polenta with Italian vegetables, Wednesday potato soup and zucchini risotto, Thursday golden squash soup and Bulgarian cheese casserole, and so on.

The regular soups are always good, too: mushrooms mixed in with split peas, corn and cauliflower, miso with lima beans, and more. The filling for the whole-wheat vegetable quiche is as agreeable as the crust. The salad bar has improved markedly over the years. As at many health-food restaurants, only a dyed-in-the-wool fanatic could love the gummy cheesecakes, made with honey instead of sugar.

★★ Raja $$

2919 Peachtree Rd. (south of Pharr Rd.). Map B. (404) 237-2661. Lunch Monday to Friday 11:30 A.M. to 2:30 P.M. Dinner nightly 5:30 to 10 (Friday and Saturday till 10:30). Reservations accepted. V, MC, AE. Small parking lot.

This often overlooked hole in the wall features unusual specialty dishes invented by owner Raman Saha. Raja has grown to include tandoor preparations (a deliciously seasoned chicken tikka, an excellent shish kabob) but what you really want to try are the homespun, quirky preparations not obtainable anywhere else.

Don't be put off by the weird-sounding descriptions of the "Raja Special" and stuffed bell pepper main courses, both of which contain homemade cottage cheese, nuts, and raisins. The former dish is listed under chicken specialties, but lamb is in it, too, wrapped inside chicken strips. The lamb picks up succulent overtones from its accompanying ingredients (unlike the meat in the lamb curry, which is just dull cubes). The stuffing for the bell pepper has no meat and no need for it. Like Raja's version of saag panir (spinach sautéed with cheese), it's a coarse, hearty dish.

Raja's moghlai paratha (thin-layered stuffed bread baked on a hot plate) is quite unlike counterparts elsewhere in town. Egg and onion instead of meat and vegetables form the teasingly subtle stuffing. Even if you've always found the puffed-up bread called puri a bore, try it again here. Raja's has a delicate and refreshing fragrance.

The dining room is a poorly lit box hung with a scattering

of Indian fabrics. Harsh hanging lights stab sensitive retinas, yet gloom lingers in the corners of the room. A tape deck, however, plays soothing music from the subcontinent. Tea is strong and forcefully flowery. A few beers, including Eagle from India, are available.

★ Ray's on the River $$ ⊗⊗

6700 Powers Ferry Rd. (at the Chattahoochee). Map G. (404) 955-1187.

> *Lunch Monday to Friday 11 A.M. to 3 P.M. Dinner nightly 5 to 10 (Friday and Saturday till midnight). Brunch Sunday 10 A.M. to 3 P.M. Reservations and all major credit cards accepted. Large parking lot.*

This low, rambling building sits on an enormous parking lot overlooking the Chattahoochee. Entrance is by way of an easy ramp lined with wooden benches. Lounge, oyster bar, multiple dining areas, and patio—the restaurant can accommodate up to nine hundred people. The crowd is not all bunched up and noisy, however. Patrons sit peacefully, with plenty of space to spare. With its show kitchen and its tiles, brass, and marble in the dining room, Ray's looks like a more expensive place than it is.

With a solid background in food distribution and franchise operation, the owners pay close attention to details and packaging. Dinner unfolds without snafus: the bucket of spiced eat-and-peel shrimp hits the table in five minutes flat; the calamari are fried light and crisp; the only thing wrong with the mostly seafood entrées is your feeling of having seen and tasted it all before. A new chef has been hired, though, and one can hope for a more ambitious approach in the foreseeable future.

No, there is nothing startlingly new or original here. Like Rio Bravo Cantina, with which it shares owners, Ray's on the River generates good feelings in the clientele, thanks to its accommodating staff. The weekend jazz brunch, a lavish and popular event, is a particularly good way to experience the restaurant.

★★ The Restaurant at The Ritz-Carlton Atlanta $$$$ ⓧⓧⓧ

181 Peachtree St. (at Ellis St.). Map A. (404) 659-0400.
Dinner only, Monday to Saturday 6 to 10 P.M. Reservations and all major credit cards accepted. Valet parking.

An astonishing number of people talk about The Ritz, emphasis on *The*, as if there were only one (either uptown where they live or downtown where they work). There is a major difference, however, between the cutting edge of The Dining Room and the safer approach of The Restaurant.

There are physical resemblances between the two upscale Ritz dining rooms: upstairs location, clubby atmosphere, conservative hoopla, some identical pieces of furniture even. The original menu was terrifically ambitious, but downtown's business travelers weren't ready for it. The menu was cut severely. After four years at the helm, The Restaurant's chef Daniel Schaffhauser is infinitely more willing to stick his neck out with delicate and delicious preparations that integrate his French background and his world consciousness. More than likely, you will be able to recognize Asian and Mediterranean influences in many of the dishes.

Regale yourself with a light shellfish fricassée; enjoy a pure earthy taste of wild mushrooms used in a risotto with truffle oil and asiago cheese; be confident about the grilled loin of swordfish as firm and meaty as a sturgeon, served splashed with Niçoise vinaigrette over a white-bean purée and the delicate pink veal chop sliced off the bone like a flank steak with a fricassée of matsutake mushrooms over spicy yellow corn grits. The seared Maine scallops come on a julienne of mango, cucumber, and red pepper with a bit of Vietnamese nuoc mam sauce and a miso amaranth vinaigrette. There are fabulous sautéed purple potatoes under the impeccably seared filet of striped bass with roasted sesame seed ginger soy vinaigrette. Sous-chef Marcos Rodriguez contributes Latin flavors such as a dessert combination of guava-paste puffs and roasted-banana soufflé cake with dark-chocolate ice cream and fresh-fig confit.

Sommelier Bill Harris is into France, culture, and unusual wines. Not for him the usual pouring of Cabs and Merlots.

Gewürztraminer, Semillion, Sangiovese, Malvasia, and other unusually styled wines are introduced with a wealth of technical information and offbeat factoids. The rest of the staff needs to come up with a coherent style instead of each marching to the beat of his own drummer.

★★ Resto Nax $$ ⊗⊗

6025 Peachtree Pkwy. (GA 141, north of Holcomb Bridge Rd., Norcross). Map I. 416-9665.
  Monday to Thursday 11:15 A.M. to 10 P.M. Friday 11:15 A.M. to 10:30 P.M. Saturday 5 to 10:30 P.M. Sunday 5 to 9 P.M. Reservations and all major credit cards accepted. Ample parking.

Who's taking culinary risks in the suburbs? Where do the Swiss colony and the staff of the Swiss consulate hang out after hours? Would you drive to Gwinnett for a good meal in a substantial restaurant if you knew the price would be half what you could expect for a comparable experience in Buckhead? Are Swiss men ever wild extroverts?

Resto Nax, named after its owner's birthplace, a village in the Valais, can supply almost all the answers to the above. The restaurant looks like a transatlantic vessel, an ocean liner anchored in the sea of suburbia. A large free-standing structure with rounded corners and posh windows, Nax flies the Swiss flag but pipes insufferable muzak into the atmosphere. The same tunes wait for you inside.

Inside, with its ample bar and spacious dining room, Resto Nax reinforces the impression that you are on a cruise ship. With sophisticated linen shades and individual lamps, the booths look deep and intimate. Thick, soft white paper covers the tables. Heavy flatware awaits in a cleverly folded real napkin. The sandy colors match the use of natural materials. A splendid wood fire burns in an enclosed area, tall flames leaping toward a row of plump brown chickens.

The proprietor, jaunty, oversexed André Constantin, doesn't sport the gold braid and epaulets of a Cunard captain, but he takes his duties as a host seriously—down to flirting with the female clientele. Constantin, who used to own restaurants in

New York, knows that moderately innovative good food and plenty of it appeals to a suburban clientele fed up with the ubiquitous, indistinguishable restaurants pushing the same brand of casual cooking.

There are things that jump at you when you read the menu: polenta lasagna layered with Italian sausage, fresh mozzarella, Mascarpone cheese, and a tomato basil sauce; mixed field-green salad with smoked tomato dressing; warm spinach salad with herbed Georgia goat cheese, pine nuts, pancetta, and balsamic vinaigrette; grilled Tuscan toast with melted gorgonzola, red and yellow tomatoes, basil, capers, and onions. In each and every case the presentation is as polished as the taste.

Add Maryland crab cakes studded with fresh corn kernels on a cool, creamy remoulade; a rotisserie chicken with grilled polenta and a chunky salsa fresca; lots of steaks; and some seafood and pasta dishes. A Chilean bass special displays an exceptional fish on a heavy-duty orange butter sauce enriched with massive amounts of cream. The garnishes tend to be abundant but mundane and the kitchen has its weak moments.

Resto Nax has a strong wine list including a couple of Swiss selections. The lunch menu is well thought out and the restaurant would be an excellent choice for a special event.

★ Rio Bravo Cantina $$ ⊗

3172 Roswell Rd. (at Irby Ave.). Map B. 262-7431. Other locations. Daily 11 A.M. to 11 P.M. (Thursday to Saturday till midnight). No reservations. V, MC, AE. Congested validated parking lot.

Lovers of big crowds, deafening noise, and inspired junk food will be happy gulping down fajita-laden nachos in this cement barn. Don't expect ceremony or gentility. But you can have plenty of fun with, for example, the nachos al carbon topped with generous hunks of charred, juicy skirt steak. No other menu item stands up to such crispy, cheesy splendor, although the appetizer of quesadilla con pollo comes close.

All the fajitas—whether grilled and served whole or cut into strips for wrapping in soft flour tortillas—are good. The salsa on the table, a lusciously fresh mixture of good tomato with plenty of cilantro, is not particularly picante, but vibrant and delicious enough to eat with a large spoon. The chiles rellenos, although the peppers are proper poblanos, are stodgy and disappointing. The oversize desserts lack common sense.

The cavernous interior is noisy, but numerous alcoves provide some refuge from youthful beer-guzzlers. The cheerful young staff is eager to help and quick with orders. Mariachis sometimes serenade patrons on the patio. Fake graffiti and intentionally misspelled menu items decorate the walls; a bicycle hangs from the ceiling. An industrial machine flattens tortillas on metallic rollers, then bakes them—not exactly the way you remember seeing it done in Old Mexico. There are many clones of the original operation, pushing forth the same experience in suburban locations.

The new Rio Bravo Grille downtown is a more upscale version of the original. The immensely long bar is a great place to hang out for lunch with your co-workers.

★ Rio Vista $

3425 Moreland Ave. (south of I-285). Map F. (404) 361-0707.
  Monday to Thursday 11:30 A.M. to 9 P.M. Friday and Saturday 11:30 A.M. to 9:45 P.M. Sunday noon to 8:30 P.M. No reservations or credit cards. Adequate parking.

What "vista"? Of automotive-parts dealers? Trailer parks? No, you don't go to this old blue-collar café for the view, but for the catfish, all you can eat. Watch the experts twist the tail of the fish, detaching in one easy motion the succulent flesh from the bones. The frying of fish is messy and smelly, something very few people like to conduct in their kitchens. Bless the dear souls who stand over big vats of frying fat, tending wire baskets full of fish, potatoes, or hushpuppies.

Rio Vista's kitchen does a dandy job of keeping the fat fresh and sweet tasting. The catfish are light and crisp, the hushpuppies well seasoned. The chicken livers are as good as any in town, fresh and rosy, ensconced in a hissing flour batter.

Eating biscuits, rolls, and salads will only prevent you from filling up on the main edibles. Rio Vista's special salad dressing, sold in bottles at the counter, acts as a powerful appetite suppressant, unless you like ketchup, vinegar, and sugar on your salad greens. Beyond fried food there are honest deviled crabs, a decent center-cut ham, and an unpleasant oyster stew yellowed with margarine.

The decor relies mostly on knotty pine, green paint, and manmade greenery. Minimal decorative touches include a trivet here, a hook there, and a carved fish looking at a painted gull. The staff are attentive and friendly.

★★★ Riviera $$$ ⊗⊗

519 E. Paces Ferry Rd. (near Piedmont Rd.). Map B. (404) 262-7112. Dinner only, nightly 5:30 to 10 (Friday and Saturday till 11). Reservations and all major credit cards accepted. Valet parking.

Chef Jean Banchet's new Riviera is very much his old Ciboulette with a slight Mediterranean accent. The chef de cuisine worked for him at Ciboulette. Half the crew has one connection or another to his former restaurant. From the giant pepper mill to the copper pans and the collection of roosters posted in the dining room, the accessorizing is the same, although the space, a cozy small house with warm red walls and posh striped banquettes, feels more personal. The china, with a pattern of ripe olives and a bright yellow rim, is stunningly pretty.

The famous Banchet may be under the impression that he is finally running a simple little bistro, a place to have fun with and keep his hand in the kitchen. Riviera, however, looks at everything through a gourmet prism. Complicated terrines, fancy pâtés, demiglace in dishes one would expect to be rustic, and time-consuming garnishes for every plate are part of the package.

The cooking is rich and carried out in a mostly traditional way. A little galette of crisp potatoes here, a potato case there, sauce or jus with everything, cream swirled in the soup, croutons in the salad, and other fancy touches add a lot of calories to each and every item. The wonderful foie gras, for example, comes with a rich confit of cabbage, crisp potatoes, and a sauce of its own. The duck confit with green lentil salad is plated with a sauce too.

The free-form ravioli of the day is always a triumph of ingenuity: sweetbreads and wild mushrooms with demiglace or lobster with wild mushrooms and saffron beurre blanc are barely covered by an undulating tricolor sheet of pasta dough. The Mediterranean mussels, served on the half-shell around a nest of black linguine, are finished with a touch of cream. The traditional pâtés are excellent as well and far more accomplished than the bouncy bouillabaisse terrine, a complicated aspic thing tasting like a firm saffron Jell-O.

A simple soup of watercress and squash or a Belgian endive salad with Roquefort are rewarding alternatives to the prestige appetizers. Vegetarians and cholesterol watchhounds will be happy with the plate of well-seasoned Mediterranean grains around a vegetable tagine. One of the most splendid dishes on the menu is a skin-on filet of salmon pan seared and served with a ragout of white beans and an eggplant compote. The fish cooked skin down achieves a magic texture, with a crisp crust and barely opaque flesh. The roasted cod Monegasque is more conservative but excellent.

Beware of the fancy samplers of game served in a divided plate and of the symphony of fish Riviera—an upscale bouillabaisse with cream swirled in its saffron broth—both of which are endlessly boring. The stuffed capon breast is generic fancy cuisine.

The pastry kitchen does a triumphant, paper-thin individual tarte Tatin cooked à la minute and a fetching warm chocolate cake. The frozen parfait cake and the cappuccino tiramisù are less exciting. Riviera has a chic little bar downstairs and an upstairs appropriate for private parties.

★ RJ's Café $$ ⊗

870 N. Highland Ave. (at Drewry). Map C. (404) 875-7775.
 Dinner only, nightly 5:30 to 10:30 (Friday and Saturday till midnight). No reservations. All major credit cards. Tiny parking lot and difficult street parking.

With its charmingly designed, brick-enclosed dining room, its gay little patio, and its claustrophobic cellar, RJ's maintains its position as Atlanta's sweetest, coziest wine bar. The premises are a center of constant activity: tastings, seminars, wine dinners, brunches, and then some. The food concept has always lagged behind, however, and now creativity seems to spin out of control instead of narrowing its focus to the crucial pairing of food and wine.

In a whirlwind of self-expression, the management has initiated such events as International Nights (the cuisine of India, Germany, and Ireland within a short time) and posh wine dinners. The regular menu has seen little or no improvement.

Some dishes are spiced to a point of confusion baffling in the context of a wine bar. A baked seafood and artichoke dip is the sort of Junior League cookbook item not worthy of serious consideration. There is nothing about Thai beef with water chestnuts, snow peas, and a poisonously salty black bean sauce that will complement the wine at hand. Ditto for the bayou smoked catfish spread with Creole corn relish, shoestring onions, and horseradish sauce. Tapenade chicken, a dry breast tightly clamping a filling of sun-dried tomatoes, provolone cheese, black olives, garlic, and basil, doesn't discourage the enjoyment of wine while the better-prepared Catfish Jambalaya relapses into wine-hostile flavors.

The wine is far and away the star attraction. Some forty different bottles are uncorked at any one time for sampling by the taste or glass. An intriguing bonus for inquisitive wine fanciers is an arrangement of "flights" consisting of four tastes each of a single varietal or of related types. The system is easy to understand, clearly printed, and full of interest and variety. The serving staff knows the merchandise and has been well primed to answer questions.

★★ Rocky's Brick Oven Pizzeria $ ⊗

1770 Peachtree St. (north of Brookwood Station). Map C. (404) 876-1111. Other locations.

Lunch Monday to Friday 11 A.M. to 2:30 P.M. Dinner Monday to Thursday 5 to 11 P.M., Friday and Saturday 4 P.M. to midnight, Sunday 4 to 11 P.M. Reservations not accepted. All major credit cards. Adequate parking on side of building.

Bob Russo, longtime town character and pizza man in Athens, Georgia, left for New York one good day only to resurface in Atlanta and dedicate a new restaurant to his father. Even without any boosterism, Rocky's Pizzeria stands out as a high-energy sort of place. The boss has ideas to burn. To his credit are the well-risen crust with a tangy, oaky flavor; the mellow, handmade cheese; the clever pies; and the hip servers. But less than half of the various pizza combinations truly work. Most ingredients have a way of disappearing from sight and taste into a maelstrom of bubbling cheese.

One of the best pies, the Pastore, has two fresh eggs cracked on top of red and green bell peppers, sweet onion, and crumbled mild Italian sausage. The Pizza Bianca (with sun-dried tomato, fresh garlic, and virgin olive oil) is sensible. The potato pizza, originally made with freshly sliced spuds, has slipped in recent years. The wood heat is difficult to control, and some pies come with burnt edges. The menu says this is a plus, but you may disagree.

The various calzone are wonderfully light and less cheesy than the pie, with fillings ranging from wind-cured prosciutto, roasted chicken, fresh pesto, and whole milk ricotta to fresh spinach and crumbled sausage.

A large patio occupied by stacks of oak logs for the oven and tubular furniture doubles the capacity of the restaurant. Inside, the latest decorating effort has replaced the Italian green and red theme with a new tropical color scheme.

Cloned in Virginia-Highland and a few other locations, the original concept now includes home delivery.

★★ R. Thomas Deluxe Grill $ ⓧ

1812 Peachtree Rd. (south of Piedmont Hospital). Map C. (404) 872-2942.

>   *Daily 24 hours. No reservations. V, MC, AE. Awkward parking in too-small lot.*

This post-culinary-revolution diner markets eccentricity, inside and out. Lush, well-tended plantings all but obliterate the surrounding sidewalks. Brick planters hold pink flamingos and exotic flowers. Owner Richard Thomas tends the cotton plants, sweet potato vines, and herbs around all four sides of the restaurant. Nearby, a tall, steel-grey Statue of Liberty holds what appears to be the taillight of a car instead of a torch. Birds are known to tweet from a multitude of cages. At the end of a meal, patrons receive, instead of mints, packages of Bazooka bubble gum.

Inside the small building you'll find silver streamers, black marble, dazzling shades of neon, a billiard table, and a small open kitchen. The rest rooms are shrines to Marilyn Monroe and Elvis.

Over the years, the restaurant has slowly moved to the now fully climate-controlled patio and in the most recent bold move, all seating has been moved outdoors. The menu is easily manageable by a smallish team of short-order cooks: omelets, burgers, grilled chicken breasts, sandwiches, a few entrées that can be put together in a matter of minutes.

R. Thomas is no ordinary diner, however. The owner is extremely health conscious. The juicy hamburgers are served on a marvelous rough nine-grain bread. The chicken is roasted instead of fried. The vegetables are fresh. A new juice bar offers delicious combinations, attributing cosmetic or health benefits to the freshly squeezed product served with nine-grain toast points. Top off all that healthy stuff with ice cream or bread pudding.

★ Ru San's $ ✘✘

1529 Piedmont Ave. (across from Ansley Mall). Map C. (404) 875-7042. Lunch Monday to Saturday 11 A.M. to 3:30 P.M. Dinner Monday to Thursday 4:30 to 11:30 P.M., Friday and Saturday 4:30 P.M. to 1 A.M., Sunday 4 to 10 P.M. No reservations. V, MC, AE. Crowded parking lot.

Sushi should be inexpensive and fun, and this is the main idea behind this engaging California-new-wave restaurant. Ru San's explodes with color. The walls are a brilliant aqua undiluted by any tinted details. The only art, bold black ink on white background, is a series of originals by Ru-San (main chef and owner) himself. The lights are as bright as a clear California morning. An enormous sushi bar provides plenty of seating on three sides. The rest of the dining room is much more like a modern West Coast café than a traditional Japanese restaurant.

Expect to spend less than half what you normally would in a traditional sushi bar but be prepared for some shortcuts. By and large, people, especially young people, can be extraordinarily relaxed about exploring Japanese cuisine. Here, fresh and pleasant tastes abound, from tuna (spicy or regular) to yellowtail, sweet shrimp (head on the side), grilled smelt (bulging with roe, hand roll style), sea urchin, quail egg, and the like. Rare beef, snails, pickled garlic, and even cream cheese play an unusual role in Ru's sushi language.

The appetizer menu is a ride on the wild side. Fresh water eel baked with pesto and mozzarella cheese, Tiger Beef marinated with Oriental spices, sushi burger, Hawaiian-style raw marinated tuna with hot sesame oil and flying-fish roe (very authentic), and much more will provide you with months of experimentation. Japanese udon noodles, served Italian style with clams in the shell and shredded basil, are disconcerting and flavorful.

Tempura by the piece is a bummer, neither crisp nor light enough. Ru San's has a big yakitori menu but everything seems to have been coated in thick, sweetish black sauce probably straight from a bottle. You try desperately to taste the chicken, duck, beef tongue, squid, and other goodies grilled on a stick. The kushiage menu (breaded and fried items on a stick) is disappointing as well, with everything tasting greasy and crunchy and not at all like the main ingredient.

★ Ruth's Chris Steak House $$$$ ⊗⊗

Atlanta Plaza, 950 E. Paces Ferry Rd. (across from Lenox Square). Map B. (404) 365-0660. Other location in Sandy Springs. Map H.
Monday to Friday 11 A.M. to 11 P.M. Saturday 5 to 11 P.M. Sunday 5 to 10 P.M. Reservations and all major credit cards accepted. Valet parking.

Steakhouses do extremely well in Atlanta. People twist their tongues recommending Ruth's Chris Steak House to their moneyed friends. Back in Louisiana, where the business started, it's joked that state troopers should use the name of the restaurant, fast-mouthed three times, as a measure of sobriety. When Ruth Fertel from New Orleans bought a tiny restaurant called Chris Steak House, she grew tired of being asked if she was Chris and decided to tack her name to that of the purchased operation. More than twenty years later, Ruth's Chris emporium has grown to many franchises.

What's the ticket? Beef. U.S. Prime only, corn-fed, slaughtered, dry-aged, and shipped to exact specifications. The individual franchises receive huge slabs of meat, which they butcher to a customary one-and-one-half-inch thickness. Ever seen an eighteen-ounce rib eye? It looks like a small roast.

All Ruth's Chris steaks are massive, with the exception of the petit filet (nine ounces), and arrive preceded by an angry sizzle of butter. The waiter warns about spatters as little particles of hot fat dance halfway across the table. Why the fireworks? The high broiling temperature locks the juices in, while the hot butter poured on the lovely brown crust protects all surfaces against cooling and desiccation.

The restaurant flaunts its regional affiliation with appetizers and desserts. Shrimp remoulade and barbecued shrimp, tame by New Orleans standards, use good, fresh shellfish and an embarrassing amount of garlic. Mushrooms stuffed with crab contain mostly a big wad of garlicky bread crumbs. Faced with the bread pudding, you won't know whether to laugh or cry at the rectangle of what looks like tofu Newburg. Better to have a slice of the excellent pecan pie or the fluffy cheesecake with cascading blueberries.

Ruth's Chris has two locations in Atlanta: the first in the bowels of a marmoreal office building, the most recent in the huge space vacated by Lark and Dove in Sandy Springs.

★ St. Louis Bread Co. $ ⊗

2274 Peachtree Rd. Map B. (404) 351-7999. Other locations. Monday to Thursday 6:30 A.M. to 9 P.M. Friday and Saturday 6:30 A.M. to 10 P.M. Sunday 6:30 A.M. to 8 P.M. No reservations or credit cards. Congested parking lot.

The name may mislead you. If you are comparing St. Louis Bread Co. to the top-of-the-line gourmet bakeries, places where distinctive hand-crafted loaves are traded for piles of cash, you may find this new, prosperous-looking chain operation, a Missouri export, on the pedestrian side. What you must compare St. Louis Bread Co. to instead is the average sandwich shop or corner deli. Yes, the St. Louis Bread Co. bakes fresh loaves throughout the day, but it functions essentially as a casual restaurant with a limited menu of soups, salads, and sandwiches. The place looks more or less like an upscale food court, down to its cute indoor umbrellas and its cheerful furniture.

The sandwiches, most of them mainstream deli combinations, are unbelievably fresh. St. Louis's most popular bread, a huge loaf of medium-tangy, soft San Francisco sourdough, is an excellent vehicle. The French strip (a squat, compact baguette) is much better than a croissant if you want a chicken salad sandwich. Nine-grain bread goes with veggies and pumpernickel with salami.

Soups and salads (available in combination with half a sandwich for just under five dollars) each come in three variations. Especially good is the well-made, flavorful vegetarian lentil soup and the fresh and abundant Greek salad with a thin dressing. The chicken and wild rice soup served on Tuesdays (all soups are scheduled; there is a vegetarian selection each day) is your average pot of glue. An excellent sourdough roll comes with the soups and salads, but dessert time is unhappy time.

★★ Sakana-Ya $$ ✗✗

6041-A Peachtree Industrial Blvd. (in Friday's Plaza). Map D. (770) 458-0558.

> Lunch daily noon to 2 (Saturday and Sunday till 3). Dinner nightly 6 to 10:30. Reservations and all major credit cards accepted. Ample parking.

Japanese restaurants, unlike other operations, demand a bit of mental preparedness on the part of their customers. It won't do to stand by the door and fumble about when the hostess asks where you want to be seated. Sushi bar, dining room, tatami room, and, in this case, an authentic robata/kushiage counter are best decided upon on your way to dinner if not sooner.

Sakana-Ya is an exceedingly modern and attractive restaurant. No attempt has been made to introduce architectural preciosities. With a totally open floor plan, a gigantic expanse of beautiful blond wood underfoot, the dining room is as dynamic an experience as any available in an ethnic context.

Japanese customers tend to favor the robata counter over the sushi bar, and since you can order from the sushi bar or the kitchen anyway, you may as well join them and benefit from the interaction. Robata (broiled items) and kushiage (skewered items) can be selected, a few pieces at a time, by communicating directly with the chef. Many of the exotic delicacies are displayed sushi style on a ledge behind the counter. There is also a very amusing laminated menu with goofy-looking illustrations such as a slightly cross-eyed squid, a naive strutting chicken, a dear little green pumpkin, and various bizarre fish seen in full profile.

Specials such as broiled eel liver (delicious) supplement the menu. From mushrooms to tiny peppers, scallions, corn, and garlic, vegetables are well represented. Chicken comes as skin (very good), wings (even better), gizzard, white meat, and liver (parboiled and tough). Meatballs, tender short ribs, fish cakes, and skinny little sardines skewered head to tail are all highly recommended.

From the hot kitchen, the gyoza (pork dumplings) are especially impressive, almost off the chart in terms of tender juiciness. The best discovery is Shirataki Tarako-Ae, described as "strings of vegetable roots with cod roe," tasting like a fat version of glass noodles with tiny salty pearls of orange roe.

★★ Salar $ ⊗

5920 Roswell Rd. (Parkside Shopping Center, Sandy Springs). Map H. (404) 252-8181.

Monday to Thursday 11:30 A.M. to 10 P.M. Friday and Saturday 11:30 A.M. to 11 P.M. Sunday 11:30 A.M. to 9:30 P.M. Reservations and all major credit cards accepted. Ample parking.

Salar Persian restaurant and the adjacent Super Bahar grocery store are proof of sustained fertility in a suburban shopping center long known as a gourmet destination. The space is a simple storefront. A good floor (a thick vinyl that resembles stone) cushions the comings and goings. The pale walls display agreeable paintings. The tables are topped with glass and set attractively.

The clientele, mostly elegant men pursuing intense conversations, with an occasional mother or wife bringing up the rear, seems always very polished: silk shirts, good belts encrusted with silver, fine leather shoes. The waiters all wear soft long-sleeved shirts with the logo of the restaurant on the back.

At the far end of the dining room, cooking and baking take place in plain view behind a counter. An energetic fellow with rolled-up sleeves bakes fresh bread throughout the evening in a traditional open-mouthed oven reminiscent of an Indian tandoor. Rushed to the tables with fresh onion, crisp radishes, and bunches of fresh herbs, the bread is worth the trip to the restaurant.

Conveniently enough, many appetizers come in the form of thick dips. Homemade yogurt, tangy and rich, serves as a base enriched with either finely diced cucumbers, cooked fresh spinach, or minced shallots. Snipped fresh herbs and intriguingly tart spices are also part of the dips. The ultimate combination, though, involves no yogurt but mashed fried eggplant (no skin) topped with cream of whey and fried mint.

Ashe jo, a delicious soup based on finely minced greens, barley, rice, yellow lentils, and tiny beans, is a rich experience. A swirl of cream of whey with fried onion and fried mint adds further complexity to the bowl. Other first-course options range from a platter of feta cheese served with green onion, radishes, mint, basil, and watercress to an offering of tender grape leaves stuffed with rice, ground beef, and herbs, served with yogurt and sliced fresh tomatoes.

Sumac, a pulverized dried berry, sits on every table in a shaker with large holes. Its vigorous tartness perks up the taste of the meat and rice that constitute the bulk of the menu. Typically, chello (a pilaf of basmati rice flavored with saffron) tumbles loosely on the plate, crowned by a triumphant skewer. Abali doogh, a homemade carbonated yogurt drink, freshens your taste buds between delicious bites of spicy, tender meat.

Traditional Persian desserts have a seductive quality. There is a lush sweetness, a unique sensuality that makes you think of harems and beautiful courtesans, in the precious frozen dessert (a combination of starchy wheat and rose water) called faloudeh. Exquisitely sentimental recorded music played on combinations of strings delights the soul.

★ Savannah Fish Company $$$ ⊗⊗

Below sidewalk level of Westin Peachtree Plaza Hotel, 210 Peachtree St. (at International Blvd.). Map A. (404) 589-7456.
   Lunch Monday to Friday 11:30 A.M. to 2:30 P.M. Dinner nightly 5:30 to 10. Limited reservations. All major credit cards. Validated parking in hotel.

Yes, this is a hotel dining room, but nothing like the common garden variety. The concept is seafood with a menu printed like a tabloid. The outlines of fish appear next to menu items, stamped daily either "FRESH" or "DIDN'T BITE." The day's price for each of the former is inked inside the fish's outline. That price (identical at lunch and dinner) includes a large helping of fish stew. Julienne vegetables sautéed in olive oil, plus plenty of fish added at the last moment, enrich a delicious golden stock perfumed by saffron, wine, Pernod, and fennel.

The cooking is not performed by finicky, ego-ridden chefs adding last touches while the fish dries out. The people at the broiler and flat cooking top behave like short-order cooks. The fish is excellent for the most part, with a side of steamed vegetables. For dessert, Savannah Hot Puffs are little balls of dough, deep-fat fried like New Orleans beignets, sprinkled with sugar, and served with vanilla and chocolate sauce as well as whipped cream.

An enormous, tempting display of shrimp and various mollusks is heaped by the restaurant's entrance. A towering waterfall just outside the bank of windows is matched by oversize masonry columns between the tables, but these heavy trappings are softened by casual furniture and extensive greenery.

Banners with stylized China-blue catfish billow overhead. The servers are amiable and unstuffy.

★★ Seoul Garden $ ⊗

5398 Buford Hwy. (one-half mile outside I-285, Doraville). Map D. (770) 452-0123.
  Daily 10:30 A.M. to 2 A.M. Reservations accepted. V, MC, AE. Ample parking.

The new trend on Buford Highway seems to favor crisp, modern restaurants, places one can enter without the usual anxieties about violating some private ethnic world. This exceptionally bright and attractive Korean restaurant may answer its phone in Korean and flash only sharp ideograms on the sign nearest to the highway. Your business is welcome, nevertheless, in its well-designed, spacious dining room.

There is no mystery, no darkness. The air is clean; the dishes sparkle. The staff works in uniforms. A spotless sushi bar adds to the general air of prosperity. Seoul Garden is busy enough for you to be comfortable. You can observe the parties next to your table having just the kind of food you hope to get: big hearty bowls of soup, grilled meats served with platters of lettuce leaves, and the most gorgeous array of side dishes (included in the price of your meal).

For an excellent first impression, go for lunch. As a child you may have been lucky enough to take a lunch box to school and unpack the goodies from home with ever renewed anticipation. The $5.95 lunch special of Seoul Garden is like that, only much, much better. Your lunch, preceded by an array of pickled goodies, arrives in a large, beautiful lacquered box together with a bowl of miso soup. The surprises arranged in compartments of uneven sizes include a small salad with fresh apple, a few chunks of chicken in red sauce, rice mixed with vegetables, three golden pan-fried dumplings, and your main entrée (ineffably tender marinated beef ribs, for example). Fresh honeydew melon ends the affordable feast.

Dinner is more complex. The number of condiments at the beginning of the meal has increased to twelve, including tiny pickled whitebait and a spectacular pancake made of ground mung beans. Pan-sautéed squid with vegetables and red-pepper paste, Korean rice noodles with beef, blue-crab stew in a stone bowl, barbecued eel, and a wide assortment of grilled beef items are some of the highlights on the menu. Note that Seoul Garden keeps late hours every day of the week.

★ Sfuzzi $$ ⓧⓧ

2200 Peachtree Rd. (north of Brookwood Station). Map B. (404) 351-8222.

> *Lunch Monday to Friday 11 A.M. to 5 P.M., Saturday noon to 5 P.M. Dinner Monday to Wednesday 5 to 11 P.M., Thursday to Saturday 5 P.M. to midnight, Sunday 5 to 10 P.M. Brunch Sunday 11 A.M. to 5 P.M. Reservations and all major credit cards accepted. Valet parking.*

On one side, you have the fine dining establishments: Pricci, La Grotta, Abruzzi, to name a few. On the other, you've got the chains such as The Olive Garden and their many imitators. When you reach the level of a Cheesecake Factory or a Macaroni Grill, identifying a restaurant as a sleek corporate package rather than an individual effort becomes more difficult.

There are people, no doubt, for whom Sfuzzi, a Dallas-based group, will seem like a big deal. The building, a Hollywood set with a touch of the Sicilian grandiose, mixes the faux with the real and aims at high drama. Clever and loud, the dining room generates its own brand of energy. The parquet floor mixes light and dark wood to create the illusion of luxurious wide boards. The open kitchen is backed by beautiful tiles. Repetitive frescoes cling to the walls. There is even a wine room and an incredible carved limestone fireplace worthy of a palazzo.

Clever, too, is the menu with its well-worded contemporary Italian bistro specialties. Fashionably accessorized with portobello mushrooms, grilled asparagus, goat cheese, and basil broth, the dishes court an above-average dining crowd. Concentrate on the lighter options and you can eat reasonably well for a price you won't regret. A large, single ravioli stretched over a filling of lobster and porcini mushrooms, served in fresh basil broth; a light grilled pizza with a confetti of peppers, eggplant, and marinated tomatoes; a pretty salad of arugula and radicchio topped with grilled tomatoes and Reggiano Parmesan; a seasonal country soup made with fennel and red pepper topped with fried leeks—all are enjoyable choices.

It is much better to pay $12.95 for a fantastic grilled free-range chicken stuffed with goat cheese, roasted rosemary potatoes, and wild mushrooms than waste $19.95 on a mediocre veal chop milanaise in high-grease Parmesan crust, even though you may enjoy the potato-mushroom torte and roma-tomato vinaigrette provided with the hunk of meat.

The ravioli excepted, the pasta tends to be below par: limp angel hair nicely flavored with a fresh pomodoro and basil sauce; low-fat but dreary rigatoni with grilled chicken, way too much herbs, and oodles of pesto broth. Sfuzzi doesn't do too well with some classics such as fried calamari (too much batter but two great sauces) or attempts at sophistication (greasy roasted portobello mushrooms and asparagus with tomato vinaigrette, served on a pretty platter).

The desserts not shown (cappuccino ice cream pie with caramel sauce, fresh fruit sorbeti and gelati) are better than those brought to your table for inspection. Monthly wine dinners, a busy calendar of special events, and a room for private parties elevate Sfuzzi above the norm.

★★★ Shiki $$ ⊗⊗

1492 Pleasant Hill Rd. (Market Place shopping center, Duluth). Map I. (770) 279-0097.

Lunch Monday to Friday noon to 2 P.M. Dinner Monday to Thursday 5:30 to 10 P.M., Friday and Saturday 5:30 to 10:30 P.M. Reservations and all major credit cards accepted. Ample parking.

Owner Yukio Watanabe is known to many as the grand master of classicism. True to type, mature in age and vision, he expresses tranquil authority in this new restaurant in a posh free-standing building. Large in terms of square footage, the restaurant feels intimate and personal, like a much smaller operation.

The two sushi chefs operate more like dignified professionals than whiz entertainers, each concentrating on his sphere and his customers. Beauteous arrangements of sashimi are fanned around tangles of daikon radish and pickled spaghetti squash. Complex sushi rolls are meticulously pressed into the proper shape, decisively cut, and displayed in various flattering ways.

Georgia roll, involving barbecued eel, avocado, and tiny pearls of roe, comes as a large flower, almost mirroring the family crest of the restaurant exhibited on the back wall. The spider roll (soft-shell crab) is particularly spectacular. When you feel almost jaded from so much beauty, Alaska roll with crab inside and delicate shingles of salmon and avocado outside squeezes yet more emotion from you.

A seat at the sushi bar won't limit your access to cooked dishes. Authentic treasures include superior gyoza dumplings; salted grilled squid scored with the tip of a knife; homemade tofu with slivers of beef and a thin soy dipping sauce; another variation on tofu topped with near-transparent fish flakes; slow-roasted bonito fish wrapped in seaweed; silvery sardines rolled in rough, minty leaves; and a slurpy mixture of vinegared seaweed topped with grated mountain potato, a snow-white and pleasantly slimy substance with great health benefits.

If you can tear yourself away from the sampling of so many exquisite small servings, you can seek the comfort of noodle dishes or the familiarity of fried food tempura style. Both are superlative. For an unusually comforting taste (and maybe a relief from exotica), try gyu-kakuni. Described as cubes of beef braised in Shiki's special sauce, the dish reminds one of pot-roasted short ribs. Service is sensible all the way.

★★ The Showcase Eatery $ ⊗

5437 Old National Hwy. (College Park). Map F. (404) 669-0504.
Monday 5 to 10 P.M. Tuesday to Thursday 11:30 A.M. to 10 P.M. Friday 11:30 A.M. to 11 P.M. Saturday 1 to 11 P.M. Reservations and all major credit cards accepted. Adequate parking.

This sophisticated African-American operation on the Southside couldn't care less about fried chicken and soul food traditions. Showcase does an outstanding job with borderline health-food recipes and fresh seafood. It also has a splendidly entertaining decor and books live jazz acts on weekends.

The restaurant is one of a kind. Entrance is through a corridor framed by wooden panels with lead-glass inserts. One emerges into a warm-toned dining room filled with art, including press-clipping collages, original oils, and decorative musical instruments. Tables rest on mortared brick and the middle section features two long varnished tables set end to end, ready to seat sixteen or eighteen at a moment's notice. There is a small music stage and a visible kitchen. Everyone eating or waiting on tables seems to be worth knowing.

The dish that will hook you on Showcase is the "Chef's Seafood Surprise Salad." With a name like that a dish could be anything. Instead of the cold, mayonnaise-bound scoop of generic seafood one might have imagined, one feasts on a small piece of perfectly grilled fish of the day (amberjack, mahi-mahi, swordfish) over a plate of lettuce as pretty and as well dressed as in any fancy restaurant.

The vegetarian lasagna is right out of a good health-food cookbook. Champagne shrimp, Sassy Salmon (fresh grilled salmon chopped and mixed with sour cream, cheese, and herbs), and Chef's Special chicken breast stuffed with linguine and broccoli are all fresh and well prepared. A great seafood soup touched with cream is the best appetizer. Entrées come with rice or pasta and salad or a fresh vegetable such as wonderful golden cabbage.

The desserts look as if they have been made for a family gathering rather than for the restaurant trade: an electric-colored red velvet cake, a more somber but also excellent chocolate praline cake. Showcase Eatery is the kind of restaurant where people like to take their time. Don't go in breathing flames and demanding wham-bam service but enjoy the great hospitality.

★ The Silver Skillet $

200 14th St. (just west of I-75/85). Map C. (404) 874-1388.

Monday to Friday 6 A.M. to 3 P.M. Saturday 7 A.M. to 3 P.M. Sunday 8 A.M. to 2 P.M. No reservations or credit cards. Small parking lot.

With its pea-soup walls, vinyl luncheonette stools and booths, and cheeky "I-chew-steel" waitresses in nylon smocks with kangaroo pockets, the Skillet is the ultimate in diner nostalgia. "Sweet milk," "buttermilk," "fried chicken," "icebox pies," say the old signs. A fiercely loyal clientele eats here every day, writing the same order on little slips of paper. Buckheadites in business suits on their way downtown and academics from nearby Georgia Tech chow down on classic Southern eats at tables adjoining grease monkeys and white-haired matrons. The food, average or below, shouldn't dissuade anyone from the comforting sense of time stood still.

Country ham slices may look like rejects from a shoe factory, but by the time they get to the dining room, those ham slices are supple and mighty tasty. They come with a decent redeye gravy and good, thick grits. Go for breakfast for platters of eggs with white fluffy biscuits. Lingering is rarely an option and the staff is very good at reclaiming your table.

★★ Slocum's Tavern $$ ⊗

6025 Peachtree Pkwy. (Norcross). Map I. (770) 446-7725. Other locations.
Monday to Thursday 11:15 A.M. to 11 P.M. Friday and Saturday noon to 11:30 P.M. Sunday noon to 10:30 P.M. No reservations. All major credit cards. Ample parking.

Suburban restaurants don't have to be sterile. Taverns can serve good food. Anyone doubting these two statements should see Slocum in Peachtree Corners. Imagine a cross between Manuel's Tavern and a seafood restaurant. This rambling Gwinnett County neighborhood spot provides a lot under one roof.

Some folks show up to watch sports events on the big-screen TVs. Families are there for relaxed dining with their kids. There is a general feeling of belonging. People like to hang out at Slocum's; they don't rush through their meals; they don't wipe their beer mustaches and scoot. The food is good and the help is friendly.

Although it may feel like a bar, Slocum's is very much a restaurant. Owners Janis and John Slocum fly in fresh fish from Florida. You can see the big yellow-fin tuna steaks (the house specialty) marinating behind a glass counter. Cuts of beef, chicken, and fish look in blooming health, ready to hit the grill. From happy-hour buffets to kiddie menu to serious food preparation, including fresh vegetables, a house salad with Dijon mustard and tarragon, and a rich chocolate mousse, Slocum's gives excellent value. Other branches have sprouted in the suburbs.

★ Snack 'n Shop $

3515 Northside Pkwy. (at W. Paces Ferry Rd. and I-75). Map B. (404) 261-4737.

Monday to Friday 7 A.M. to 5 P.M. Saturday and Sunday 9 A.M. to 6 P.M. No reservations. V, MC. Adequate parking.

Snack 'n Shop has been an Atlanta institution since 1953, moving several times from its original location on Ponce de Leon. The physical appearance of this deli, almost the last of a dying breed, is unprepossessing. A sign atop the meat case advertises "Mama's homemade chicken liver." Refrigerated counters hold kosher meats, krauts, and knishes. Plain tables and chairs and a few thin banquettes are set in an unflattering light.

Although not every item can be counted on day in and day out, Snack 'n Shop provides a good range of traditional deli experiences. The corned beef sandwich and the Reuben are strong classic material. Other sandwiches, clever variations on old favorites, like the "Dutchman" (spicy pepper beef and Muenster on a crusty hard roll) and "Admiral Knockwurst" (hot pastrami and melted swiss on fresh rye), taste wonderful every day of the week. Good pickles, kraut, and two kinds of mustard provide the fixings needed to complete any sandwich.

Other pleasures include the rich matzo ball soup, and the beefy stuffed cabbage in tomato sauce. The quality of the brisket platter varies and the potato pancakes with commercial apple sauce are a big disappointment. The potato salad is one of the best anywhere.

Breakfast, a relatively new addition, is also one of the best anywhere with such specialties as One Eyed Jack (fried egg dead center in a slice of challah) and Salami Eggs and Onions. Heart Smart Breakfasts using Eggbeaters have also appeared on the menu. Thumbs up on the bagels and the friendly atmosphere. The old-fashioned staff is pretty matter of fact about delivering, and sometimes forgetting, your orders.

★★★★ Soto $$ ⊗⊗

3330 Piedmont Rd. (across from Tower Place). Map B. (404) 233-2005. Dinner Monday to Thursday 6 P.M. to 12:30 A.M., Friday and Saturday 6 P.M. to 1:30 A.M. Reservations and all major credit cards accepted. Crowded parking lot.

To describe Sotohiro Kosugi as an exquisite craftsman doesn't do justice to his stature. Sushi chef, son and grandson of sushi chefs, brother and nephew to yet more sushi chefs, Soto-san has the sure touch and the intensely personal, delicate vision of an artist.

The first sashimi platter ordered is a revelation: transparent slices of flounder like the petals of a white rose, brilliant salmon striated like a rare jewel, tuna belly fat enough to be almost hazy, mackerel of a precious grey, other mysterious and precise cuts arranged with a bold disrespect for symmetry. Soto-san prepares dozens of sashimi platters without ever repeating himself in the composition.

If the only sushi you know is the dollar-a-piece popular with the young crowd, and even if you have had sushi at each and every sushi bar in town, you will be whisked to a new level. You may not get it on your first visit. You will most probably never see the best of Soto if you order from a position in the dining room or deal with the new assistants rather than the master. The rapture comes when you stop ordering your favorite sushi and totally surrender to Soto-san's creativity.

You will feast on mysterious scrapings of the fattest part of the tuna belly wrapped in a parchment-colored soft kelp, transparent fish eggs and chopped calamari mixed with fresh wasabi and rolled tightly in kelp, pressed sushi in every shade of the rainbow, extraordinarily fresh uni (sea urchin) served on matchsticks of crisp daikon, tuna tartare mixed with green onion, and rolls made with salted plums and others with freshly plucked leaves from a plant grown in the kitchen.

A sushi master isn't a robotic creature with a high output. You have to be able to wait out the busy moments when the chef is working on someone else's behalf. Dishes ordered from the kitchen are just about as extraordinary as the sushi. Tiny squid, big as your pinky nail, are marinated in their own ink and served with grated daikon. Soft-shell crawfish arrive in a minuscule basket with shrimp stuffed with shiitake mushrooms. Calamalone (calamari steak) is sliced in a delicate white sauce with shiitake mushrooms and served on a sea-scallop shell.

There are pearls of salmon roe mixed with pungent finely grated daikon, broiled toro (fatty tuna) richer than a steak, boiled salted soybeans to refresh the palate with their faintly bitter austerity, geoduck clams cut like sea anemones, blue-fin tuna that costs the chef thirty-two dollars a pound, snow-crab dumplings wrapped in rice noodles, and an extraordinarily delicate crab salad with slices of pencil-thin cucumbers. The chef hands you a bowl of matsutake mushroom soup and a tiny dish of some chewy marine substance followed by a form of seafood as smooth as custard. Take it, take it!

The dining room, clean and serene, leaves room for the imagination. Premium sake is available at Soto but no desserts.

★★ Soul Vegetarian $

879-A Ralph David Abernathy Rd. (just south of I-20). Map F. (404) 752-5194. Other location in Poncey-Highland. Map C.
Monday to Saturday 11 A.M. to 11 P.M. Sunday 9:30 A.M. to 1 P.M. and 5 to 11 P.M. Reservations accepted. AE. Adequate parking.

Run by Black Hebrews, the lost tribe of Israel, this modest storefront restaurant offers the gastronomical equivalent of a spiritual retreat. There is wholesome, delicious food prepared in a strict vegetarian sense (no animal flesh, fat, or by-products), unhurried service by perfectly poised young women wrapped with dignity in full-length African fabrics, and time-warp decor framed by unpainted wood.

The restaurant, moved in 1985 from its original small shop at the busy intersection of Peachtree and Ponce de Leon, was well liked by Midtown apartment residents and the local work force. The present clientele comes from surrounding West End and neighboring Grant Park.

Soul Vegetarian has a distinctive style of cooking and flavoring nobody could call bland. The kitchen uses a considerable amount of turmeric, paprika, basil, garlic, and nutritional yeast in sauces, salad dressings, and high-protein meat substitute. The dominant flavor is that of nutritional yeast, fresh, slightly bitter, and reaching the back of your nose fast, like cumin or curry powder. It is particularly spectacular with creamy scrambled tofu broken into big curds or mixed into a light vinaigrette poured over fresh greens.

Without meat, eggs, butter, cheese, or any kind of dairy product, the cooks achieve a great variety of tastes and textures. The basket of lightly fried vegetables, dipped in a thin batter dotted with cornmeal; the crisp, sweet onion rings and soft tofu in the same fragile crust flavored with nutritional yeast; the cabbage rolls stuffed with rice and peas, served with thoroughly nice, fresh green beans and carrots—you need no special eating philosophy to appreciate their honesty. Ditto the creamy split pea soup.

Even more amazing are three kinds of burgers, a "hot dog" with relish and natural mustard, a gyro with yogurt dressing, and a fried tofu sandwich that puts many fish sandwiches to shame. Much of this delicious mock fast food is based on kalebone, a high-protein gluten produced in the restaurant by soaking and kneading whole-wheat flour. Only a vegetarian could claim that it resembles meat, but the product is attractive and firm, lending itself easily to slicing, shaping, and saucing.

Soul Vegetarian is attached to a cultural center and includes a boutique with natural beauty products, hair oil, and literature on various spiritual matters, including how to stay away from the evil pig.

★★ South City Kitchen $$ ⓧⓧ

1144 Crescent Ave. (near 14th St.). Map C. (404) 873-7358.
Daily 11 A.M. to 11 P.M. (Friday and Saturday till midnight).
Brunch Sunday 11 A.M. to 4 P.M. Reservations and all major credit cards accepted. Parking in nearby lots (some free) and on congested street.

Fresh out of Magnolias in Charleston, the two young owners found a charming spot for an Atlanta project. Gutting and updating an old house, pushing for modernism where quaintness previously prevailed, they clearly established South City Kitchen as a restaurant for the nineties. Decorwise, the place is a hit. Clean lines, light neutral colors, smashingly handsome furniture, and an open kitchen fronted by a lively bar make an excellent impression. South City Kitchen is as noisy as it is chic, connecting to the street with a sleek, urban patio.

After a weak beginning, the restaurant has become the kind of place one likes to show to any visitor: young, playful, but also sophisticated in a clever New-South way. The menu is tons of fun. The kitchen hasn't buckled under the strain of high volume. For versatility, the menu is divided into First Flavors, From the Stockpot, New South Salads, Sandwiches & Inspirations, and a relatively small entrée section entitled Skillet, Grill & Sauté.

Imagine walking into South City latish in the evening and falling ravenously on poached eggs and country ham over skillet-browned grits with black-eyed-pea relish, or a crab hash with roasted potato, poached eggs, and herb Hollandaise. Jalapeño-cheddar cornbread served in big chunks with creamed lump crab is comfort made three dimensional.

A round of grilled herb flat bread with collards, chicken, and smoked provolone is the Southern pizza you didn't know existed. What can you call a small seared catfish filet over red pepper and basil-studded grits cooked in pure cream other than an inspiration?

Low Country seared scallops over sautéed braising greens (some of them multicolored Savoy cabbage leaves) could use a classier Hollandaise but who's to quibble with the flavors? The entrées, easy to neglect on account of the preceding sections, include a wonderful grilled Atlantic salmon with scallop succotash, a rare grilled pork tenderloin on parsnip cakes with pecan-peach compote, spiced shrimp and scallops over creamy stone-ground grits and garlic gravy, and lamb loin with Jack Daniels sorghum sauce and sweet potato hash.

The pastry chef knows his chocolate bread pudding, his warm chocolate soufflé with Chunky Monkey ice cream, and a few other pretty tricks. The wine list is serious, the glasses beautiful. The downstairs room (open kitchen, double-wide bar, marvelous furniture) can be extraordinarily noisy but the itsy bitsy upstairs may not be an option if you are prone to vertigo. The patio is a suave alternative in good weather. Sunday brunch, expensive but classy, is an event for the well-to-do.

★ The Steamhouse $

3041 Bolling Way (off Pharr Rd.). Map B. (404) 233-7980.
Monday to Friday 11 A.M. to 4 A.M. Saturday 11:30 A.M. to 3 A.M. Sunday noon to 2 A.M. No reservations. All major credit cards. Small lot or difficult street parking.

How long since you've been to the coast? This is a fun place to fritter away an hour or two with beer and distinctive finger food. Like Vickery's in Midtown (owned by the same people), the operation has a strong sense of style. The free-standing building has a fun, ramshackle appearance, as if hastily constructed at the end of a pier. A discreet door lets you into an exceptionally well designed shelter.

There is nothing makeshift about the bolted steel beams, the long bar of blond wood curving smoothly at one end, the custom finish on the walls (a radiant ochre glaze air-brushed with a flotation line on which bottles and flagons seem to bob around the room). Tables and chairs are bar-height. A useful ledge runs along the walls, so you don't have to toss your material possessions on the floor beyond reach. In clement weather, a solid mass of humanity carouses upstairs on the terrace under the skies.

Beyond the bar, behind the tin pan full of ice and beer, the kitchen is visible. It's nothing fancy—big pots to boil water, some counter space to shuck oysters and assemble a few items. The shrimp are best enjoyed hot in a mist of bay leaf and peppercorn. The oysters come helter-skelter on painted metal trays. They are fresh. They are good. What more can you ask? You want them all the same size, preferably big? Not for this price, folks!

The house special is amusing to share. Frogmore Stew is like a paella without the rice, or a clam bake without the clams. Steamed oysters, shrimp, red potatoes, Polish sausage, and short stubs of corn on the cob fill a small iron skillet. Slices of garlic bread are provided to sop up the creamy, briny broth that gathers at the bottom of the pan.

★★ Stringer's $ ⊗

4484 Shallowford Rd. (at Buford Hwy., Chamblee). Map D. (770) 458-7145.

Monday to Thursday 11 A.M. to 9 P.M. Friday and Saturday 11 A.M. to 10 P.M. Sunday 2 to 9 P.M. No reservations. V, MC. Adequate parking.

One of a very few non-Oriental restaurants in its neighborhood, this original fish camp in the middle of Chamblee feels uncontrived and in tune with its surroundings. The specialty of the house is frying, frying, and some broiling. Solo or in combinations, fried oysters, fried shrimp, fried whole catfish and flounder, and more are excellently prepared. The cornmeal batter is thin enough to cling without adding much extra weight to the seafood.

The hushpuppies are sweet, the fries crisp. Corn salad is a delicious relish on the side. The clam chowder has a pleasant texture and an average taste. The Key lime pie is much too thin by gourmet standards but, hey, this is hardly a gourmet restaurant!

The menu is a kick. *Overlooking the Lake* printed at the top and *Overlooking the Ocean* at the bottom is just a typical witticism from eccentric owner Bob Edelhertz, who has recently expanded his operation outside of the city near a huge outlet mall in Commerce, Georgia.

★★★ Sundown Café $$ ⓧ

2165 Cheshire Bridge Rd. Map C. (404) 321-1118.
Lunch Monday to Friday 11 A.M. to 2 P.M. Dinner Monday to Thursday 5:30 to 10 P.M., Friday and Saturday 5:30 to 11 P.M. No reservations. All major credit cards. Ample parking.

"I make seventeen different salsas" is the kind of statement you expect from Dean Ferring or some other wizard of Southwestern chic, not from the part owner of a Mexican restaurant on Cheshire Bridge Road. And yet chef Eddie Hernandez doesn't brag for bragging's sake. The pursuit of the ultimate salsa is just one of the serious culinary games he plays even while commuting between Atlanta and Morrow, where he and partners operate the wonderful Azteca Grill. Don't settle for the (good) hot sauce served with crisp corn tortillas (light and dark). Sample your way through roasted jalapeño gravy, chayote salsa, sweet pico de gallo (amazingly fresh and pungent), and any of the other fabled salsas.

With the kind of graphic garnishing one finds in star restaurants, Sundown's dishes could compete in another league. But you don't need fancy to drive the prices up when you can enjoy a jolly trout pan fried in an elegant blue cornmeal batter served with poblano tartar sauce and chayote salsa, garnished with green rice and jicama salad. Eddie's Pork (grilled tenderloin with roasted jalapeño gravy, home-style potatoes, charro beans or Southwestern-style turnip greens, and handmade tortillas) has tons of comforting power.

A traditional Mexican shrimp soup strong with the flavor of roasted shrimp shells, onions, tomatoes, garlic, and jalapeños has an undercurrent of sophistication present in other areas of the menu. Grilled chicken cutlets on poblano and banana peppers with fresh tomato and Mexican rice shares a plate with a chicken enchilada in lemon cream sauce. Shrimp sautéed with chile de arbol come in a similar preparation, minus the enchilada, plus a basket of fresh flour tortillas.

The green chile stew is pure perfection: soft potatoes and yummy morsels of pork melting in a creamy blend of green chile peppers. Poblano corn chowder balances the sweetness of corn and shrimp with the cumulative heat of poblano and chile de arbol. The side dishes could use some savory language on the menu beyond a mere listing. The words "turnip greens" may not send you into orbit, but the exquisite Southwestern heat of the preparation will. Same thing for the charro beans, simmered with pork and onion.

It is a clever restaurant that ends on a strong note, such as a signature dessert or two. The sweet-potato cheesecake has a magnificent and mellow taste, best by far among desserts that also include an excellent bread pudding with a sweet lemon sauce and a fun chocolate chimichanga with tequila cream sauce.

Lunch is an entirely different concept: six or seven kinds of authentic soft tacos (fish, barbecued smoked pork, chicken, and green chile) and a few side dishes. This is a stupendous value, not to be missed. Plain by Atlanta standards but with excellent service always, the dining room is friendly and comfortable and the bar a fun spot to patronize.

★★ Suntory $$ ⊗⊗

3847 Roswell Rd. Map B. (404) 261-3737.
Lunch Monday to Friday 11:30 A.M. to 2 P.M. Dinner Monday to Thursday 6 to 10 P.M., Friday and Saturday 6 to 10:30 P.M. Reservations and all major credit cards accepted. Valet parking.

The Suntory Corporation, an entity comparable to Anheuser-Busch in this country, has developed a strong restaurant concept easily implanted in such diverse cities as Paris, Mexico City, Sydney, and many others, including now a North Buckhead location in Atlanta. Built in the shape of a *U* around a charming Japanese courtyard, the restaurant has five different dining rooms. With the exception of the sushi bar, all look at one another and at a scene of gurgling waterfalls emptying in a serene body of water. The poetic setting is somewhat undermined by the fact that some of the rooms are lit and furnished in a manner suggesting a particularly dull convention hotel.

Despite the claim of utmost authenticity, the concept is neatly tailored to suit the Western market. What makes Suntory special, however, is the extreme care applied to styles of cooking such as teppan yaki (show-cooking on a flat grill) or shabu shabu (Japanese fondue cooked in broth), which have been vulgarized beyond recognition in other contexts. Shabu shabu is a prime experience at Suntory, particularly in the form of a complete shabu shabu dinner with a variety of set small courses.

The ingredients for teppan yaki are excellent too: salmon, scallops, shrimp, lobster tail, live lobster, and several cuts of steak. In other rooms, a special Japanese menu is available to those who claim acquaintance with such Japanese delights as maguro yamakake (tuna in grated white yam), uni (sea urchins), and chasoba (buckwheat noodles flavored with tea).

The sushi bar is cozy and private, with fine selections. Private dining rooms are available for precious kaiseki dinners. The service overall is excellent.

★★ Surin of Thailand $ ⊗

810 N. Highland Ave. Map C. (404) 892-7789.
   Monday to Thursday 11:30 A.M. to 10:30 P.M. Friday 11:30 A.M. to 11:30 P.M. Saturday noon to 11:30 P.M. Sunday noon to 10:30 P.M. No reservations. All major credit cards. Two small parking lots or difficult street parking.

Surin Techarukpong, former chef-owner of Thai Restaurant of Norcross, has two American partners in this new venture. He, obviously, spends most of his time in the kitchen, while they handle the front of the house with the somewhat nervous candor of new restaurateurs.

Surin may well be the most successful ethnic restaurant in the city of Atlanta. Despite a rapid expansion into the space next door, the restaurant is nearly always filled to capacity in the evening, with would-be diners cooling their heels on the narrow sidewalk. The wait for a table is no problem for the docile intowners who are used to worse. The restaurant extends a fresh blue awning into the street, relies on the same shade of blue inside in the form of tablecloths, and takes a bistro rather than ethnic Thai approach to decorating its space. Young, slim Thai servers scurry between tables on a bright parquet floor.

You may want to preview the restaurant at lunch time. Not

only will you get a representative sampler, bargain prices, and a quiet atmosphere, but you will discover rich and wonderful combinations such as duck in red curry or a chicken and rice pot to remember. Fabulous soups with floating fresh mushrooms become part of your database of great food experiences.

To have a great dinner is a slightly more complex proposition. The fresh basil rolls, the spicy Thai spaghetti, the Thai sausage tossed in lime juice with cucumbers, and most of the curries are excellent and full flavored.

The main section of the menu is strictly modular in its approach. You pick the main ingredient (beef, pork, chicken, or shrimp), you pick the secondary flavor (Thai basil, ginger, broccoli, cashew nuts, garlic, red Thai curry, baby corn, etc.) and you enjoy the result of your creativity or the luck of the draw. Excellent ice creams (coconut, ginger, and green tea) bring the meal to a happy conclusion.

★★★ Sushi Huku $$ ⊗⊗

6300 Powers Ferry Rd. (just inside I-285 opposite Holiday Inn). Map G. (770) 956-9559.

Lunch Monday to Saturday 11:30 A.M. to 2:30 P.M. Dinner Monday to Saturday 5:30 to 10:30 P.M., Sunday 5 to 10 P.M. Reservations and all major credit cards accepted. Adequate parking.

Most of Atlanta's Japanese restaurants are good to very, very good. Each has its own following. The trend lately has been toward bigger, flashier, more modern, which is lots of fun. However, for sushi, you don't need a side order of stress. Many Westerners and Japanese can agree that Sushi Huku is the absolute essence of what to look for in a small Japanese restaurant. It is also one of the finest sushi experiences in the city.

Since 1987 Kimio Fukuya, his wife, and his daughters have run an impeccable place. A recent move to a new building has raised the level of comfort by several notches. The busy but by no means frantic classic dining room has an intimate feel, a close-knit atmosphere.

The Fukuya family, all of them exceedingly friendly, has

worked hard to achieve the current comfortable status. The exquisite quality of everything seafood is to be trusted at all times. Watch the special sashimi platters being readied out of impossibly beautiful cuts of assorted fish and other creatures from the sea in wonderful, healthy colors. Don't bother Mr. Fukuya too much with your questions but catch him between tasks to find out if he has caught and brought back some little mackerel from Panama City or if the grouper is at its peak.

Use the order sheet as suggestions to be discussed with the chef. Chopped yellowtail and green onion hand roll is spectacularly fine. The scallops melt in your mouth; ditto the sweet shrimp and the pearly grouper. The tuna is pure luxury. There is a wonderful crunch to a crazy-horse roll (avocado, cucumber, crab, and flying-fish roe beading the outside of the roll), and a firm, pleasant bite to an oshinko roll (pickled daikon inserted in the delicious vinegared rice).

You do well to rely more on the daily specials inserted in a small Lucite frame than on the menu. Of course you can't read the list. Draft the daughter of the house as translator, or just look dumb and say that you will eat anything. Goodies come in the form of shrimp croquettes (a whole shrimp inserted into a small ball of mashed potatoes and deep fried) or a special tempura of squid and shiitake mushroom caps. You can also look for a mentor among the Japanese businessmen at the bar. They will steer you toward baby octopus (fork tender and cooked with light soy), skewers of grilled clams (fabulous), or comforting bowls of soup containing fish cakes, a whole hard-boiled egg, and some marine mysteries. Everything is delicious.

★ Taco Mac $

1006 N. Highland Ave. (at Virginia Ave.). Map C. (404) 873-6529. Several other locations.
  Monday to Saturday 10:30 A.M. to 2 A.M. Sunday 11 A.M. to 2 A.M. No reservations. All major credit cards. Difficult parking on congested streets.

Success hasn't spoiled this widely cloned neighborhood institution. The clock is still broken above the front door. The restaurant still looks like a shabby package store with an awkward patio full of uncomfortably high stools and tables. Instead of dolling up the premises, the owners invested their sizable profits in the construction of fancier locations including Dugan's on Ponce de Leon Avenue. Taco Mac remains ugly—and proud of it.

People wait long at times for a chance to hang out here, jammed into a few square inches of undecorated space. Many are beer snobs. A big upright cooler with glass doors displays more than two hundred beers from all corners of the world.

Taco Mac's other claim to fame is chicken wings. "Chicken is chicken—but the wing is the thing" is Taco Mac's war cry. Not only was this the first restaurant to introduce Buffalo wings to Atlanta, but to this day it serves a delicious authentic version. Both principal owners were born in Buffalo, New York, where the pairing of wings, celery sticks, and blue cheese first occurred. The wings used to be bigger, but they are still very, very good lightly glazed with a thin *hot* sauce. They have no taste of grease. The celery is perfectly peeled and trimmed before being cut in skinny sticks. Real blue cheese is crumbled in abundance for a thick, lumpy dip.

★★ A Taste of New Orleans $$ ⊗⊗

889 W. Peachtree St. (at 8th). Map C. (404) 874-5535.
Lunch Monday to Friday 11:30 A.M. to 2 P.M. Dinner Monday to Thursday 6 to 10 P.M., Friday and Saturday 5:30 to 11 P.M. Reservations and all major credit cards accepted. Cramped, awkward parking.

From the street, the building's original function as a fast-food takeout stand is not entirely camouflaged in its current avatar as a New Orleans restaurant of distinction. Even once you're up the steps, through the teensy foyer, and into the *L*-shaped room with dining tables on the long side, bar stools on the short, you might miss the subtle signals that this is an important restaurant.

The sensibly small bill of fare is better than it reads. One secret is a light hand with seasonings. Another secret is combining mild flavors with strong ones in a manner that gives full marks to both experiences. The gumbo, the seafood baked eggplant, and a wonderfully strange spread called "Seafood Pâté" all demonstrate this skill.

Fish Moutarde (catch of the day brushed with Creole mustard and hot New Orleans spices) and Chicken Rockefeller stuffed with oysters are usually excellent. The seafood cakes (could be crab, crawfish, shrimp, or any combination of fresh seafood) rival some of the best crab cakes in town, creamy under a delicate crust. A spectacular crawfish étouffée full of fat, soft little critters in a sauce richer than many a beauty product dares you not to surrender to its outrageous but balanced spiciness. The platter of shrimp remoulade is a midsummer night's dream. The po' boys are excellent.

Unfortunately, not every taste satisfies. The New Orleans-style gumbo is very dark, very tomatoey, with a pervasive feel of flour possibly due to a rushing of the roux, and the (formerly delicious) seafood baked eggplant has become too heavy, too messy, and much too oily. Salmon (on special) doesn't take kindly to its brush with hot spices even with the mitigating influence of a good dill remoulade. Two of the desserts are exemplary, though. "Cajun Velvet Pie" and "French Silk Pie" are both delicate and light, yet rich. Combine the two in "Velvet on Silk Pie."

★★ The Tavern at Phipps $$ ⊗⊗

3500 Peachtree Rd. (in Phipps Plaza). Map B. (404) 814-9640.
  Daily 11 A.M. to 10 P.M. (Friday and Saturday till midnight). Reservations unavailable at lunch, very limited at dinner. All major credit cards. Self-parking in mall lots or complimentary valet.

There is something virile about a tavern, something about guys drinking whiskey and beer. The menu of this handsome restaurant supports but also corrects the initial impression. This is a place where a guy in a business suit could take a woman all dressed up and both could have a good time for a reasonable price. The Tavern is about steaks: a few cuts but all impeccable, topped with freshly chopped garlic in just-melted butter. It's also about great variety: extravagant salads, po' boy sandwiches, roasted fresh salmon, deli meats from the Carnegie Deli, desserts that are easy to eat, fresh-baked croissant rolls.

Although the restaurant offers many signature items, the Tavern Chips are the best thing on the menu. Imagine a plate heaped with fresh-cooked, thin, crisp tortilla chips layered with Thai chicken, red and yellow peppers, bean sprouts, cilantro, and peanut sauce or a traditional chili with cheese, fresh tomatoes, and sour cream. You may also fall for the Italian chips with chicken-basil sausage, peppers, fresh mushrooms, olives, mozzarella, and marinara sauce!

Greg Greenbaum's first success story (with Joey D's Oak Room) helped to refine his strategic thinking. Whether you choose "The Best Steak Deal in Town" (porterhouse for two served sliced, giant Caesar salad, two loaded baked potatoes and a 500-milliliter bottle of Buena Vista Cabernet Sauvignon for $49.00), or tap into New Orleans-style good times with oysters remoulade served in shooter glasses and then an authentic fried soft-shell crab po' boy, or ignore your doctor's advice and tackle thirteen ounces of spicy, fatty pastrami on Carnegie rye bread, you are dealing with a tried and true formula.

Mahogany-tinted varnish has been used by the bucket on everything from the bar to the service counters, the booths, and the many trompe l'oeil windows backed by mirrors. An enormous prep kitchen services the centrally located show kitchen with the big grills and the pretty salads. The bar, open to the outside in good weather, is a fun place to be.

★★★ Terra Cotta $$ ⊗⊗

1044 Greenwood Ave. (at N. Highland Ave.). Map C. (404) 853-7888.
   Dinner only, Wednesday to Sunday 6 to 11 P.M. Reservations and all major credit cards accepted. Small parking lot or difficult street parking.

If imitation is the most sincere form of flattery, then this charming newcomer pays homage where homage is due. Terra

Cotta will remind you of both Partners and Indigo just up the road. Sophisticated bistro cuisine, spicy little numbers that are fresh and inventive, clever vegetarian dishes and delectable desserts have a charm of their own, though, and no one would accuse the two chefs, one of whom trained under Alix Kenagy, of being copycats.

Terra Cotta has flair and chutzpah. The restaurant also has the energy of youth. Who but young people would have taken a risk on a potentially difficult location in a small house behind Dark Horse Tavern? Who else would have come up with a radical design, a great name, and a more advanced gourmet concept than has typically been the case in Virginia-Highland? The dining-room staff is young, too, and includes popular faces from Partners and Indigo.

The transformation of a little brick house into a modern restaurant without interior walls is unexpected. A vibrant terracotta paint job has done wonders for the exterior. A myriad of Christmas lights hang from the roof line like luminous bangs framing a pretty face. Inside, steel tension cables stretched overhead have replaced the bearing walls removed from the small A-frame. The colors are dark and sleek, the hopefully temporary artwork too aggressive for the small space.

The menu engages the imagination and rewards the taste buds. The crab-cake appetizer is unique and delicious: Thai style with lemon grass, scallions, and a chile-soy aioli, each plump patty is dusted with Japanese bread crumbs and garnished with seaweed and wakme red cabbage. Rope cultured mussels steamed in white wine, a pretty grilled eggplant with herbed cheese and tapenade, and a carpaccio of beef with wasabi and shaved-fennel salad complete the short list of starters.

For an entrée you can go the comfort route with lamb shanks over mission figs, Spanish peanuts, and couscous or diet tastefully with a perfect Alaskan halibut prepared in parchment with a julienne of assorted vegetables and a grapefruit-basil beurre blanc. Carnivores will beg their vegetarian friends for a taste of grilled haloumi cheese stacked with eggplant, portobello mushrooms, potatoes, and poblano peppers in an Italian-style fresh green sauce. From pork tenderloin with white peppercorn and shiitake jus, to Spanish risotto with free-range chicken, to grilled portobello mushroom and roasted vegetables in Thai pesto over linguine, you will appreciate the vision of this dynamic, fresh kitchen.

The desserts are delicious, the service accomplished. The bartender knows his wines and his customers.

★★★ Thai Chilli $ ⊗

2169 Briarcliff Rd. (at LaVista Rd. in Briarvista Shopping Center). Map E. (404) 315-6750.

Lunch Monday to Friday 11 A.M. to 2:30 P.M. Dinner nightly 5 to 10. (Friday and Saturday till 11). No reservations. All major credit cards. Adequate parking.

The same people who used to go out for Chinese every so often now go routinely to Thai restaurants. So many places have opened in recent years that it has become difficult to distinguish one from another or decide why you should make an effort to go here instead of there. Thai Chilli has an immediate impact and one can't recommend it highly enough.

Chef Robert Khankiew (remembered through Surin and Hot Pepper) has a cult following in the city. Now that he is his own boss, working with his own family, he has simply jumped to a higher level of cooking. The fresh basil roll appetizers are light and delicious. Nam Sod, a ground pork salad with an abundance of peanuts and shredded ginger, and larb, a pungent ground meat salad, have fantastic flavors.

Green curry, made with pork, is so amazing you want to stand up and tell everyone that you don't think you ever had a better one. From every table around, spectacular aromas hint at equally delicious food. Squid, whether as a salad or a traditional panang curry, is splendid.

The always popular pad thai (Thai noodles with sprouts, lime, egg, and shrimp) is a little too sweet and tends to require heavy doctoring with hot sauce. The vegetarian tofu is excellent.

Thai Chilli is neither especially attractive nor uncomfortable. The location, a shopping strip anchored by several kosher operations, is easily accessed from a variety of neighborhoods.

Success has hit rapidly for this fine operation. The waitresses, most of them family members in traditional Thai attire (a cropped top and long cotton skirt), sometimes buckle under the strain but their sweet nature reasserts itself in less pressured moments.

★★ Thai Restaurant of Norcross $ ⊗

6065 Norcross-Tucker Rd. (in second block south of Jimmy Carter Blvd.). Map I. (770) 938-3883.
  Lunch Monday to Friday 11 A.M. to 2:30 P.M. Dinner Sunday to Thursday 5 to 10 P.M., Friday 5 to 11 P.M., Saturday noon to 10 P.M. Reservations and all major credit cards accepted. Adequate parking.

Lovers of the intricately spiced food of Thailand had a kind of rollercoaster ride through the 1980s in Atlanta. Tame and limited versions of this fare were available throughout the decade close to downtown. In such diminished circumstances, the arrival of this quaint and friendly spot immeasurably widened the horizons for lemon grass fanatics. Chefs have come and gone, but regardless of its change in personnel, Thai of Norcross has remained consistently above average.

If you can't stand incendiary cooking, you'll miss some of this establishment's greatest glories, the "hot and sour" soups. Lemon grass is a principal ingredient in both the chicken coconut soup and the spicy soup made with your choice of shrimp, beef, or chicken. A satisfactory mild alternative is the bean cake soup, containing shrimp, pork, and vegetables. Tell the amiable servers your spicing requirements, and they'll try to accommodate, bringing great fronds of pungent cilantro on a plate or an assortment of condiments in individual containers: shredded peppers, Thai fish sauce, tiny rounds of jalapeño-like firebrands in vinegar.

The pricing of Thai dishes is something of a mystery, since most appetizers cost slightly more than the items marked "entrées." Order freely all across the board: it's almost impossible to spend a great deal. Among appetizers, don't miss the "Fancy Thai Sausage"—crisp, flat slices in a sauce tangily contrasting lime juice with sweetness. Satay, Thailand's most famous dish (strips of pork on skewers, served with peanut sauce and cucumber salad) is fine, if a little safe.

More intriguing, though not to everyone's taste, is meekrob: shrimp, egg, and bean sprouts on a nest of crisp noodles so thin, so fine, chomping on them may make you think of hay. Also recommended for spice-tolerant palates is the classic larb—ground beef mixed with mint, green onion, lime juice, and hot peppers—a moderately piquant dish. You may find more finely tuned and authoritative spicing in other Thai restaurants but this restaurant is an excellent way to get acquainted with its national cuisine.

★ Thelma's Kitchen $

867 Marietta St. N.W. (at Means St.). Map A. (404) 688-5855. Monday to Friday 7 A.M. to 5 P.M. No reservations or credit cards. Pay parking lot surrounding building.

Olympic construction nearly proved fatal for one of the most beloved soul-food restaurants in the city. The building on Luckie Street has been demolished, but Thelma Grundy and family have relocated and all of downtown breathed a sigh of relief. Compared with the old place this spot is a palace.

The kitchen has its secrets: marvelous okra cakes of squeaky-fresh, still raspy pods; delicious twice-baked potatoes; a famous baked chicken. What makes the collard greens, macaroni and cheese, or boiled okra so special? The place is popular with the business crowd, so come early to avoid finding every table crowded and a long line between the vegetables and you.

A few disappointments lurk among the pleasures: the cornbread is stiff and cold, the fried chicken not special in any way. But a taste of the greens studded with chopped turnips, the first forkful of black-eyed peas or creamy macaroni bonded with cheese, wipes away all memories of such peccadilloes. In the summer, ripe wedges of watermelon are bedded on a tub of ice. Otherwise, Thelma bakes lemon meringue pies and pound cakes. Breakfast is a Southern classic.

★ Tiburon Grille $$ ✗✗

1190-B N. Highland Ave. (at Amsterdam Ave.). Map C. (404) 892-2393.

> Lunch Tuesday to Friday 11:30 A.M. to 2 P.M. Dinner Sunday to Thursday 6 to 10 P.M., Friday and Saturday 5:30 to 11 P.M. Reservations and all major credit cards accepted. Congested parking lot or difficult street parking.

If John Beck, chef-owner of A Taste of New Orleans, is satisfied with running his latest endeavor as a popular hangout with a good wine list, who's to complain? Tiburon Grille has a pleasant look, a good location, wonderful breads, and nice things to drink, but it will take a serious culinary effort to convince one of its relevance as a contemporary American bistro.

Tiburon's bread basket is a splendid offering: Italian country bread, pane integrale, walnut baguette, spinach bread, focaccia even, all fresh from The Bread Garden down the street and cut in thick slices. There's no more delightful way to ruin an appetite than a tête à tête with the bread basket and a good glass of Merlot or Pinot Noir. But do all the soups, for example, have to be not only cream based but so incredibly rich in highly reduced cream as to feel more like dips? God forbid you should get to the bottom of a plate of roasted rosemary chicken soup or potato and leek soup! Much better to soak up the good flavor by dragging a chunk of fresh bread through their quagmire.

The appetizers tend to be wimpy. The Vietnamese spring rolls (lobster and fresh vegetables, Asian dipping sauce) are the best of the lot. The vegetable terrine (layers of oven-roasted vegetables glued together with goat cheese) and the pear napoleon (crunchy Bosc pears, Stilton, walnuts, and port in a barely baked puff pastry) are equally uninspiring. The Caesar salad with fried oysters doesn't feel special in any way.

In each of the entrées (with the possible exception of the New York strip with shiitake mushrooms, roasted potatoes, and spinach) one ingredient too many derails the overall impression. The grilled sea bass melts in your mouth just as the waiter said it would, but the combination of soy-lime marinade, citrus beurre blanc, and lime-currant rice becomes mildly obnoxious after a while. Ditto the excellent grilled Atlantic salmon "brushed" (covered, really) with a wasabi champagne mustard sauce garnished with bok choy. The stuffed pork chop (eggplant and andouille sausage) is paired with Stilton grits and collard greens. Scallops pasta ("very creamy," says the staff) and a vegetarian stir-fry round out the menu.

The desserts are uncomplicated and, for the most part, taste better than expected at the end of a heavy meal. The pear tart (shaped like either a thin-waisted pear or an amoeba) is best described as wussy, but the white chocolate and sweet potato cake and the chocolate mousse in an almond basket are delicious in their own right.

Tiburon is big and noisy, with an open kitchen, a cozy fireplace, and a chic faux wall with a barely discernible mural that looks like Japan in the mist.

★★★ Tom Tom $$ ⓧⓧ

3393 Peachtree Rd. (in Lenox Square Mall). Map B. (404) 264-1163. Monday to Thursday 11:30 A.M. to 10 P.M. Friday and Saturday 11 A.M. to 11 P.M. Sunday noon to 9 P.M. No reservations. All major credit cards. Ample parking.

Business partners, like married couples, are sometimes driven apart by new goals on which the involved parties fail to agree. The unlikely suitor who came between Tom Catherall and Todd Kane, the power tandem behind Azalea, was none other than the Lenox Square management team. Chef Catherall, Tom Tom to his intimates, was ready to cut a deal and launch a new, highly visible venture: the American bistro he carries within and of which he would be sole owner.

If you hate malls, you don't even have to set foot on the shopping floor. Tom Tom has a direct entrance one level above the Food Court (turn at the pedestrian overpass off Lenox Road). The restaurant is a soaring, modern space complete with bakery, to-go counter, and visible kitchen behind a handsome bar. The colors are very natural: sand, stone, light-colored clay, exotic wood. There are interesting architectural features but the overall feel is uncluttered. The exuberant and colorful food mural is a work of art by Catherall's wife, Leigh Smith Catherall.

More bistro and less fusion oriented than Azalea, Tom Tom has something for everyone: bistro bites, salads, fun pizzas, sandwiches on freshly baked breads and rosemary focaccia, rotisserie specials, lots of seafood and fresh pasta, and enough to satisfy the vegetarians. The menu is strong all around.

A whole sizzling catfish with Chinese black beans and chile dip lets itself be admired before being carved into luscious bites by the waiter. The bistro pâté with red currant port wine sauce is a wonderful rich slab. Calamari crisped in rice-flour crust come garnished with fresh peppers and a tomato basil and cilantro dipping sauce. Pizza bread with feta cheese, olives, garlic spread, and black-bean hummus just begs to be shared.

Marinated free-range chicken on mashed potatoes, rosemary and garlic studded lamb leg also on mashed potatoes, bistro fish stew with garlic croutons, and grilled fish of the day on balsamic-vinegared lentils with sun-dried tomatoes are exactly at the comfort level one expects from bistro cuisine. Specials can be bistro classics such as seared cod over mashed potatoes in a ring of white-bean cassoulet but fusion cuisine may also assert its rights in an extraordinary duck à l'orange reinterpreted Szechuan style with purple Chinese eggplants.

When the restaurant is busy, which is most of the time, the staff may not push the dessert menu, but you want it any way. Prunes soaked in Armagnac served over ice cream, trio of crèmes brûlées in sake cups, sesame lace baskets filled with brittle ice cream, and luscious daily specials are too good to miss. The wine list is full of fresh, interesting selections at affordable prices. A satellite operation, Tom Tom Too, just around the corner offers a quality experience at teeny-tiny prices.

★★ Top of the Plaza $ ⓧⓧ

250 E. Ponce de Leon Ave. (top floor of the First Union Bank, Decatur). Map E. (404) 377-7371.

Lunch only, Monday to Friday 11:30 A.M. to 2 P.M. Reservations recommended. All major credit cards. Validated parking next to building.

Old Decatur has always known about the Sky Room atop

what used to be the Decatur Federal building. Formerly used as a private dining room for the bank directors and the partners from the resident law firm of McCurdy and Candler, this venerable, clubby room has recently thrown open its doors to the public.

Feeling like a tourist in a foreign land, you ride the elevator to the Top of the Plaza. Walking in without reservations and lacking hair set by an approved salon, you look at the white-glove crowd (old ladies who chew nails as easily as they munch on dainties, well-groomed young matrons, a scattering of business suits) and feel a faint cold sweat of insecurity.

You aren't the kind that turns tail. Also you immediately love the grand old room—the wallpaper that looks like end papers for leather-bound volumes, the magnificent windows with the Atlanta skyline unfolding like a painted panorama. When the food comes, you can't believe it.

Far, far better than the Swan Coach House or the Magnolia Room ever were, the Top of the Plaza serves clever and delicious lunches. Tradition and new trends receive equal billing, with chef Paul Conway giving everybody their due. Of course Conway would offer cheese straws and frozen fruit salad. Both are delicious as components of a Magnolia Room Plate, which also includes chicken salad garnished with cucumber, tomato wedges, and hard-boiled egg. Of course there would be a honey-pecan chicken breast and a perfect grilled chicken club sandwich.

Having tipped his chef's hat to Southern traditions, Conway is free to explore more recent alleys. A three-cheese grits patty (smoked cheddar, Fontina, and Parmesan) on a light sage cream sauce, grilled slices of portobello mushroom served on a tomato-basil coulis garnished with crumbled Georgia goat cheese and crisp bacon, and a basket of homemade Idaho and sweet potato chips dusted with ground pecans served with a sour cream praline dipping sauce demonstrate a more playful side of his personality.

Savannah shrimp and red rice, a perfectly tender char-grilled pork tenderloin sliced thin and served with a red pepper jelly, a choice of Thai chicken or Thai beef salad, and a variety of Southwestern appetizers reveal a young chef who isn't afraid of spices. Genuine, made-from-scratch soups, freshly baked rolls and whole-wheat biscuits, homemade chocolate chip cookies, and a range of delicious desserts (apple and pear crisp, crème brûlée of the day, brownie nut sundae, rice pudding with cran-raspberry sauce) show very solid work.

There are several private rooms, each of them appropriate for special events, and the Top of the Plaza is available at night for private parties.

★★ Tortillas $

774 Ponce de Leon Ave. (at Ponce de Leon Pl.). Map C. (404) 892-3493.
   Daily 11 A.M. to 11 P.M. No reservations or credit cards. Parking in back.

Atlanta used to define a taco as a crisp fried object filled with ground beef, iceberg lettuce, and cheese. When the original glass-walled hut of this establishment opened in 1984, the city learned a new form: the soft taco, wrapped blanket style around pork carnitas, tender chunks of chicken, or beans, and green chile. Was there any way—other than dribbling and squirting all over one's front—to eat the delicious gargantuosities? One learned fast. Peeling back the aluminum foil that insulates the made-to-order tacos and burritos was an art. Not far enough, one ate tin. Too far, the whole darn thing unraveled into one's bosom.

Undaunted by technical difficulties, braving the tough urban surroundings (the panhandlers roaming the sidewalk, the drunks rapping at the windows), the vegetarians came first. They had heard that the food was prepared without animal fat. A steady flow of customers followed, attracted by the ridiculously low prices and the fresh, made-from-scratch honesty of the food.

A move to a larger building a few yards away hasn't changed a thing. The place has a cohesive, hip energy. A hardworking staff assembles tortillas behind a high counter. The tables and painted hard wooden booths are jammed. The new rooftop is a fabulous place to watch the life of the city. Takeout is now conducted out of a new building next door.

Tortillas is not a Mexican restaurant, but rather a San Francisco-style taqueria. The tortilla reigns supreme. You can have it folded into a splendid quesadilla, oozing melting Monterey Jack, chicken, and guacamole, or rolled into monster burritos bulging with beans, chile, cheese, and chunks of meat. Fat shrimp and healthy broccoli have been added to the quesadilla or burrito menu. Freshly made salsa (red hot or green hotter) is available in squeeze bottles. A basket of chips and a styrofoam cup of chunky guacamole flavored with cumin and fresh cilantro will keep you quiet while your order sizzles on the grill. Beer is available on draft.

★ Touch of India $$ ⓧ

962 Peachtree St. (at Peachtree Pl.). Map C. (404) 876-7777. Other location in Buckhead.

> Lunch Monday to Friday 11:30 A.M. to 2:30 P.M., Saturday noon to 2:30 P.M. Dinner nightly 5:30 to 10:30. No reservations. All major credit cards. Difficult parking in congested side streets.

The restaurant's name is humble, and properly so. This is not the place to plumb the deepest mysteries of the subcontinent's cuisines, but you can eat well here for very little money. If your idea of Indian restaurants has been formed by haughty or indifferent servers doing their utmost to make you feel inferior and foolish, this friendly, intimate spot will change your mind entirely.

Crystal chandeliers dangle above long rows of closely set tables. Thin colorful rugs and wall hangings depicting Indian beauties with enormous eyes are plastered on both sides of the long, pink room. A small service bar shaped like a festive tent protrudes from the far wall.

Order papadum (crisp wafers of lentil flour) to munch on while your food is cooking, then a variety of appetizers from the small list. Chicken tandoori comes next: marinated with violently red but gentle spices, it is seared in a primitive clay oven and heaped on a dish, splendidly hot and fragrant. Chicken tikka masala starts in the tandoori, but the juicy flesh is pulled off the bones and simmered in a thick creamy sauce richer than anything a French chef would concoct.

For a hot hot dish, try the pungent beef dhansak cooked with puréed lentils. For a mild alternative, the lamb pasanda, prepared with nuts and fruit, is fun. A mound of fluffy basmati rice and several vegetable dishes (especially the spinach with homemade curd and the dry vegetable bhaji) complete the feast. The kitchen has a tendency to oversweeten sauces, and the breads are often too doughy. A second location on Piedmont Road lacks some of the charm of the original.

★★ Toulouse $$ ⊗⊗

2293-B Peachtree Rd. (1 block south of Peachtree Battle). Map B. (404) 351-9533.

Dinner only, Monday to Thursday 6 to 10 P.M., Friday and Saturday 6 to 11 P.M. Reservations before 7:30 P.M. only. V, MC, AE. Ample parking.

Karen Hilliard, co-owner of this new restaurant with her son Billy and partner George Tice, has been loosely inspired by France in this project. The space, which you may remember as Bosco's or Blues Harbor, has changed dramatically. Totally gutted and redone like a huge loft, with the open kitchen and the bar set as two separate islands on a sea of wooden flooring, the restaurant is chic and stark. Tables draped in white stand at a comfortable distance from one another. Most of the energy comes from the kitchen, operated by a bunch of hip young chefs.

Ms. Hilliard, blond and unruffled, acts as her own executive chef. The menu, like the room, forgoes artificial separations. One scrolls through a list of dishes without having to jump from appetizers to soups, salads, main courses, and desserts. The effect is more liberating than confusing. The attractive wine list, put together by "the wine committee" (friends, consultants, and even competitors), comes on a separate sheet, but recommendations appear next to the dishes on the main menu.

You will like the wine (some great bargains, fun choices, a majority of the selections available by the taste and the glass as well as the bottle); you will want to stuff the homemade bread into your pockets (it's soft and fresh and fragrant); you will go gaga over the desserts; and you will fare well with most of the menu. Everybody orders salad for an appetizer. You can add baked goat cheese, grilled portobello mushroom, shrimp, or chicken livers to the basic mix of tender leaves tossed with a light vinaigrette.

Vegetarians, rejoice. Toulouse offers a marvelous platter of roasted vegetables with a pungent garlic rouille. The rustic potato soup, a scoop of mashed potatoes plunked into a bowl of creamy potato soup, is fun and casual. Also enjoyable is a big bowl of hot roasted-tomato and bean soup that makes one think of the American Southwest, while the light country pâté over greens asserts delicious French characteristics.

Among the entrées, the roasted chicken is absolute tops. Available for two, the plump organic bird is carved over a mound of fresh arugula dressed with pine nuts, currants, and toasted bread. The leg of lamb served over a delicious whitebean simmer and an undercooked ratatouille disappoints but the fish entrées are very good. A turbot au beurre noir is offered with huge spears of roasted potato and tempura green beans. A firmer and more ordinary halibut benefits from its pairing with a compote of beets and a rich beurre blanc. The salmon is superb.

Saving room for dessert is a clever thing to do. You will enjoy the golden, firm oven-roasted pears with honey ice cream, the flourless warm gâteau royale with Cointreau Chantilly, the lemon-rum frozen soufflé with a streak of cocoa at the bottom, and the profiteroles "Femme Fatale" served rolling about in a big bowl. Service, rough in the beginning, is maturing.

★★ Toyo Ta Ya $

5082 Buford Hwy. (across from Pinewoods Plaza, Doraville). Map D. (770) 986-0828.

Lunch daily 11:30 A.M. to 2:30 P.M. Dinner nightly 5:30 to 9:30. No reservations. V, MC. Small parking lot.

This recently opened Japanese buffet house promotes a new style of dining in a simple environment. Toyo Ta Ya seems to have been especially created for those who are uncomfortable ordering in an ethnic restaurant. You don't have to speak the sushi lingo. You don't have to ask what comes with the noodles. What you see is what you get, all fresh and attractive.

The dining room consists of four long rows of tables divided by a half-wall. Each place is already set with a plate, a bowl, a spoon, and a set of chopsticks in a paper sleeve. You could be in an exceptionally pleasant refectory. Minimal contact with the staff occurs, mostly the ordering and pouring of drinks. You are immediately in charge of your own dinner. Mimeographed sheets on the wall ask that you do not take more than you can eat.

What can you expect to see on the buffet? Miso soup with silken cubes of tofu; springy, fresh udon noodles next to a clear hot broth and a small container of green onion; wonderful dumplings shaped like beggar's purses; stuffed tofu glazed with soy; thin noodles mixed with vegetables; tender sliced beef with onion; delicately sauced teriyaki chicken; various forms of seafood including shrimp and calamari; crisp-tender long beans; medleys of vegetables; a very Chinese-looking bin of fried rice; Japanese red beans boiled down to the consistency of a relish.

Tempura items can be less than crisp but the sushi is a terrific deal. The constantly replenished and straightened supply will tempt most anyone. There is, of course, no expensive tuna belly or anything particularly rare. Yellowtail, octopus, salmon roe, omelet, shrimp, salmon, crab legs, avocado roll with flying-fish roe, and a few others rotate every few minutes. You have definitely had more exotic and luxurious Japanese food, but at $11.95 per person ($8.50 for children) Toyo Ta Ya is an experience you won't want to miss.

★ Uncle Tai's $$$ ⊗⊗

3500 Peachtree Rd. (in Phipps Plaza). Map B. (404) 816-8888.
 Monday to Thursday 11 A.M. to 10 P.M. Friday and Saturday 11 A.M. to 10:30 P.M. Sunday noon to 10 P.M. Reservations and all major credit cards accepted. Ample parking.

Atlanta as a whole has shown precious little enthusiasm for highly elaborate Chinese restaurants. Call us vulgar, call us coarse, but we'd rather sit somewhere with our elbows on the table than dine in the mahogany splendor of the new Uncle Tai's in the west wing of Phipps Plaza near the AMC theaters.

Initiated in New York, successfully transplanted in Houston and Dallas where people have lots of disposable income, the Uncle Tai's concept promises spicy regional cuisine in an upscale environment. The menu is well written and attractive. The symbol for *Hot & Spicy,* a jalapeño pepper apparently, graces many unusual-sounding dishes. You get to watch while the staff meticulously divides all dishes, scooping infinitesimal servings onto fancy plates.

Special Hunan Vegetable Pie (for two) would please a macrobiotic saint. Thin, crisp, and unidentifiable, two rectangles of compressed vegetable matter are wrapped mo shu style in thin wheat pancakes. Szechuan dumplings are clammy and hard. Hacked chicken in spicy sesame sauce and sliced prawns in peppercorn sauce can be combined as a classier, texturally correct appetizer.

Shredded pork and pickled cabbage soup is inexpensive but insipid. A crisp soft-shell crab with a dab of garlic sauce may be the best appetizer unless you consider munching on the restaurant's signature Crispy Walnuts (deliciously caramelized with honey), an acceptable first course.

The entrées tend to be murky. Shredded lamb with young gingerroots has an almost fetid taste while boneless frog legs with eggplant feel richer and more focused in a sauce that includes millions of sesame seeds. Shredded or sliced beef with broccoli is a totally routine preparation except for its devastating saltiness. Uncle Tai's Fried Rice has ten ingredients, all of them boring. Plates are garnished with the kind of infuriating watery baby carrots you associate with the hotel trade. If you want to see a more affordable side of Uncle Tai's, there are early-bird specials and inexpensive cooking classes including a seated lunch.

★ Urban Coffee Bungalow $ ⊗

1425-B Piedmont Ave. (just south of Monroe Dr.). Map C. (404) 892-8212. Other location in Garden Hills. Map B.

Monday to Thursday 7 A.M. to 11 P.M. Friday 7 A.M. to midnight. Saturday 8 A.M. to midnight. Sunday 8 A.M. to 11 P.M. No reservations or credit cards. Small parking lot in back, a few spots in front.

The connection between South City Kitchen, an elegant progressive restoration of an old residence, and this wacky, wonderful coffeehouse isn't obvious in any way. The commitment is much smaller, the visuals, a collage of bright materials assembled in a colorful room, eclectic and funky,

Flyers inform you of the monthly partnership between Urban Coffee Bungalow and a cause selected by the staff. A family shelter for homeless men and women started the charity drive during the opening weeks.

All baking operations for South City Kitchen have been transferred to the bakery downstairs. Homemade nut and raisin bread, toasted seed bread, and a variety of muffins and cookies are good for the most part. The scones are truly awful, but you can start the day with a fresh fruit cup and homemade granola already packaged with yogurt.

If you're looking for something substantial at lunch or dinner time, there are sandwiches on fresh round focaccia loaves. The salmon and cream cheese sandwich is particularly delicious hot; so is the hummus sandwich with roasted peppers and asparagus. Sweet-potato salad and marinated vegetables have a spot in the cooler. The espresso drinks and the basic coffee, awful at first, have come a long long way and this charming spot is Ansley Park's secret hangout.

★★ Van Gogh's $$ ⊗⊗

70 W. Crossville Rd. (next to Crabapple Square, Roswell). Map H. (770) 993-1156.

Monday to Saturday 11:30 A.M. to midnight. Sunday 5 to 10 P.M. Limited reservations accepted. All major credit cards. Ample parking.

Flowing into the many recesses of a generous free-standing building, Van Gogh's looks as prosperous as the big houses of surrounding Crabapple. Despite the name, the concept is American and eclectic. Regional cuisine interpreted by two opinionated chef owners who happen to be married has proven attractive to people who are interested in contemporary ideas but can't bear to give up the big portions typical of Southern hospitality.

Why are Chris and Michelle Sedgwick fulfilling their dream of "keeping the people up here" as opposed to losing them to Buckhead and beyond? Brushed with virgin olive oil, garnished with shaved asiago and toasted capers, sautéed in annatto oil, finished with a cool tomato concassée, the dishes are fashionable and abundant.

Thank God everything is delicious or you might feel overwhelmed by soups that fill a deep plate, salads climbing four inches high above their platter, and massive entrées boosted with enough pasta and vegetables to fuel an Olympic athlete. For an immediate introduction to the style of the restaurant, the hot antipasto plate is hard to beat: grilled vegetables, a taste of the seafood of the day, grilled Italian sausage, spinach gnocchi, and red-pepper toast with Georgia goat cheese all make sense next to one another.

In an extraordinarily good appetizer, portobello mushrooms bigger than most saucers are propped satellite dish style on a plate with a grilled duck sausage and two golden cakes of Georgia goat cheese fried in cornmeal. At lunch, the same mushrooms are meaty enough to be featured in a mock cheeseburger with bacon, roasted onions, and "the works."

Big kernels of milky raw corn dot the plate where chef Chris Sedgwick's fresh lump crab cakes luxuriate on a red-pepper beurre blanc. Wonderfully fresh corn is also used in a summer chowder with chicken. Sweet potatoes are puréed in an interesting twist on the traditional Vichyssoise.

Smoked double-cut pork chop with pork tasso gravy, seared grits cakes, and vegetables have an excellent regional identity. Other dishes go a little farther in search of interesting flavors: French vinegar chicken with leeks and tarragon cream sauce; scallops and salmon with whole roasted shallots and slivered jalapeño pepper; white-fleshed kobia salmon in parchment with bok choy, red-pepper butter, and sesame oil.

Pastas and stir-fries bring the taste of home-cooked meals

into the dining room. It's all a little thick and a little innocent, but the honesty wins you over. The sweet end of the meal is given a lot of drama: a switch to wildly colorful plates, a chilled fork, and beautiful garnishing with fresh fruit put you on red-hot alert. This is going to be special. And it is. White-chocolate banana-cream pie, warm berry tart with a crumb topping, and pound cake with chocolate ganache share the same knack for wholesome goodness. The style, Michelle Sedgwick's, is individual, the flavor fresh and rich.

The wine list is in keeping with the menu: friendly rather than intimidating, fair priced, with about fifteen selections by the glass.

★ The Varsity $ ✗

61 North Ave. (at Spring St.). Map C. (404) 881-1706.
Daily 9 A.M. to midnight (Friday and Saturday till 1 A.M.).
No reservations or credit cards. Large parking deck.

You will never *belong* in Atlanta if you don't know the taste of The Varsity's chili dogs with onion, or if you haven't had the juice of a "glorified hamburger" run down your sleeve. How can you call yourself an Atlantan if you don't even understand the lingo? "One naked dog walking and a bag o' rags," for example, will get you a plain hot dog to go and some French fries.

Since the 1930s, this Atlanta landmark has served a staggering number of people daily in its honeycomb of small, harshly lit rooms furnished with vintage Formica. Big color TVs are permanently on, tuned to a variety of stations unless a major sports event focuses the town's attention on one channel. All sections of the city gravitate toward this magnet, reputedly the world's largest drive-in under one roof. The parking lot sprawls on several levels. A platoon of nimble and frequently eccentric carhops runs along the curb with red cardboard boxes of goodies. The smell of chili dogs wafts blocks away.

Inside is pandemonium. Picture Grand Central Terminal at rush hour with every commuter balancing food and drink on a tray. A counter runs the full length of the building. Figuring out where to line up is not easy for the first-time visitor. While some stations take orders across the board, others are reserved exclusively for onion rings and fries, or orange slush, malts, and peach ice cream. Some serve large parties only, and one used to be for ladies only. Be prepared to talk fast when it's your turn. Any hesitation is rewarded by blistering looks from a crew that relays orders with the seasoned speed of cattle auctioneers.

One of the prime tourist attractions is the glass-walled onion rings room, where a tearless crew wearing plastic caps slices thousands upon thousands of fat yellow onions into massive rings. Thinly battered, sumptuously greasy, the rings have no equal in town. The famous chili dogs are soft in their cottony buns, but the flavor of chili and the crunch of raw onion block these unpleasant sensations. Beer is no longer served to cut the grease, but orange slushes and Cokes will help you swallow.

A much smaller operation on Lindbergh Drive at Cheshire Bridge serves the same food in a considerably less interesting environment.

★★★ Veni Vidi Vici $$$ ⊗⊗⊗

41 14th St. (in the IBM Tower Parking Deck). Map C. (404) 875-VICI.

Monday to Thursday 11:30 A.M. to 11 P.M. Friday 11:30 A.M. to midnight. Saturday 5 P.M. to midnight. Sunday 5 to 10 P.M. Reservations and all major credit cards accepted. Valet parking.

They came, they saw, they didn't conquer. Neither the original team nor the subsequent owner were able to operate Veni Vidi Vici as a viable economic proposition. Not so much flying to the rescue as raiding, the Buckhead Life Group has assumed control of this exquisite dining room, one that Pano Karatassos had always fancied. We should all breathe a sigh of relief for it would have been a pity to see something as beautiful as Veni Vidi Vici go to waste or have to watch while its design became trivialized by a new scheme.

Describing the location as the parking garage attached to

the IBM Tower doesn't begin to convey the glamor of the space in the low, postmodern building across West Peachtree from Atlanta's most stunning new construction. A terrace overlooking two long bocce courts stretches in front of Veni Vidi Vici. Inside, it's soaring ceilings, columns that twist like modern dancers, miles of parquet. This is a very public space, in which you will feel on display.

Custom-made features speak of big budget. Large opalescent globes with Vici's *V* logo illuminate the brilliant scene; a delicate frieze runs high on the walls; elegantly proportioned cabinets act as room dividers or wine storage bins. The kitchen is open behind a tall counter that serves as a readying station for antipasti.

The new food concept isn't outrageously different from the previous one (a taste of Italy's regions) but the restaurant has moved closer to Pricci. The dishes are busier, more likely to show off than before. If you want to read the menu of antipasti piccoli from Soft Polenta with Gorgonzola and Small Veal Sausages to Octopus Salad with Potatoes and Crushed Red Pepper, you'd better tune up your speed reading. As soon as a table is seated, the kitchen readies a sampler tray of antipasti. All look too wonderful for words, but they are in your face before you have settled down.

Braised artichokes Roman style are pure before-the-fall Vici. The vitello tonnato is identical to the one at Pricci in a smaller size. The appetizer section can be recommended 100 percent. Among the pastas, one recognizes the wonderful orrechiette from Pricci and welcomes with enthusiasm the thin, supple fettuccine with white beans, pancetta, onions, and tomatoes. Seafood ravioli in sage brown butter can be unevenly cooked but the flavor is delicious.

Recommended entrées include the suckling pig fresh from the new rotisserie, sliced over garlic-chive mashed potatoes, lima beans, and braised red cabbage, the braised red snapper in light tomato sauce, and the ossobucco alla Milanese. If there is a better dessert than the hazelnut chocolate bars (like a sublime KitKat), where is it? Instead of the phases of the moon done in hard caramel, you will find the *V* logo planted like a flag on top of the desserts.

The bar is drop-dead gorgeous. The dining room has a

★★ Vickery's $ ⊗

1106 Crescent Ave. (near 13th St.). Map C. (404) 881-1106.
Monday to Thursday 11:30 A.M. to 1 A.M. Friday 11:30 A.M. to 2 A.M. Saturday 11 A.M. to 2 A.M. Sunday 11 A.M. to midnight. Brunch Saturday and Sunday 11 A.M. to 3:30 P.M. No reservations. All major credit cards. Difficult street parking only.

People flock to Vickery's from Midtown and beyond because of its copious, inexpensive food and understated chic and because it's fun. Located in an old house restored with considerable humor and an odd brand of taste, it is as much a bar as a restaurant.

Come for the bar scene; stay for the food! If you haven't sat at the bar and eaten French fries with pepper gravy while watching bartender Scotty Clarke acknowledge every request with the same delightfully polite "certainly," you haven't lived. The menu is an ideal bar/bistro menu—not the usual list of greasy convenience food served to drunks all over town, but a gathering of strong, original dishes the like of which you are unlikely to come across anywhere else, especially not late at night.

Shrimp hash with creamy grits and (perfectly) poached eggs belongs in the hall of fame in the comfort food category. The Cuban roasted chicken with black beans and rice has a crackling skin rubbed with hot spices, juice-squirting flesh, and good fixings. Sliced flank steak with green salsa and hashbrowns is another excellent late-night encounter.

Every entrée comes with a crisp salad. From Cuban sandwich (classic or Reuben) to burgers, fried calamari in a dark, pepper-flecked batter, or black bean cakes served on fresh spinach leaves, there is nothing you wouldn't gladly eat again. Hot and spicy mustard greens are close to weird as a side dish but grilled Cuban bread is a treat, especially if there is a bowl of pepper gravy nearby. Top dessert is a chocolate cookie pie, wonderfully rich and messy like the eruption of a sweet volcano.

Dave the Dog, Vickery's celebrity pooch, is memorialized on the wall near the entrance. The various pics and photographs are always worth checking on the dark, dark mocha walls and there is hardly a hipper patio in town or a funkier (meant as a positive) transformation of a small residence into a den of energy.

★★ Villa Christina $$$ ⊗⊗⊗

45 Perimeter Summit Blvd. (off I-285 and Ashford Dunwoody Rd., Dunwoody). Map H. (404) 303-0133.

Monday to Thursday 11:30 A.M. to 10:30 P.M. Friday 11:30 A.M. to 11:30 P.M. Saturday 5:30 to 11:30 P.M. Reservations and all major credit cards accepted. Valet parking.

Even the most casual observer will be able to tell that this brand-new lavish restaurant and special-event facility in a hard to locate Dunwoody office park has a serious credibility problem. Billed as an Italian villa and a Tuscan grill with a mix of Italian and American influences, Villa Christina has created a romantic fiction to justify its not so unlikely concept.

First there is the hostess who tells you that yes, reservations are absolutely necessary but who can seat any number of people with only a few minutes' notice and welcomes you to a half-occupied gigantic dining room.

The back of the menu will tell you the story of Garth the WWII bomber plowing into the hills of Tuscany and the "ravishing" Countess Christina, who nursed him back to health and ended up (after a few absurd twists) resettling in Atlanta, where she and her new American hubby became "the darlings of high society."

Villa Christina looks a lot more like the Ballard's design catalogue than any Tuscan residence you can imagine: glitter in the paint on the walls; Miami-pink neon under a sky-and-clouds ceiling with crystals and minilights; more combed finishes, zigzags, metalwork, gauzy curtains, and custom upholstery than in a Buckhead hair salon. The design bill, including a wealth of tabletop accessories from knife rests to clever little coiled metal holders for the breadsticks, must have been staggering for national restaurateur and consultant Walter Staib.

Many dishes look suspiciously like the kind of fancy productions appropriate for an important corporate affair. Presentation often counts more than taste. Take the case of the opal shrimp. Fresh and firm, but also stuffed with opal basil, wrapped in applewood bacon, swirled with an acidic sauce, and paired with sausage-mushroom polenta and wilted dandelion, the poor crustaceans don't have a chance. Much more tasty but still design driven, the halibut special sandwiches snow-white, beautiful fish between disks of pasta dough with a julienne of summer vegetables and rests on an incredibly bright saffron beurre blanc.

The pasta course sometimes misses by a mile, and even in the best of cases (a delicious farfalle with almond-crusted scallops and tomato-basil cream), there is a sort of gourmet posturing at the opposite end of Tuscan earthiness. The peppered smoked salmon on crisp pasta cakes with herbed crème fraîche is good but affected. Ditto the clammy galantine of chicken passed as a terrine.

Garth and his inamorata could have a lovely, sexy dinner with an appetizer of sweetbreads piccata on sage demiglace and a rustic ragout of rabbit thigh in brunello sauce served over soft polenta. The Tuscan Hills bean soup is exceptional as well, a mixture of pretty beans and stubby pasta with a chiffonade of Swiss chard. You may want to avoid the gourmet extremes and opt for a simple steak or even prime rib. Lunch is more sensible than dinner and far less costly.

The pastry chef earns his salary with exquisite compositions such as a cage of chocolate cradling a tiramisù garnished with candied coffee beans and gold glitter, a cappuccino torta made with thin oat cookies and topped with a cloud of whipped cream, and a charming meringue ring with fresh berries and a tart lime sauce.

The service is less than uniform. The wine list includes prestige selections and dessert wines but no printed list of wines by the glass.

★★ Violette $$ ⊗

3098 Briarcliff Rd. (at Clairmont Rd.). Map E. (404) 633-3323.
2948 Clairmont Rd. (at I-85). Map E. (404) 633-3363.
   Lunch Monday to Friday 11 A.M. to 2 P.M. Dinner nightly 5:30 to 10 (Friday and Saturday till 11). Reservations recommended. V, MC, AE. Ample parking.

Say "French" and almost everyone thinks fancy. While more obsessive about food than the Americans, the French don't always gorge on cuisine. The thing to love about Violette is the total absence of hoopla. Named after a woman once dear to the owner's heart, this small neighborhood restaurant has none of the phony romance associated with Gallic clichés.

Owner Guy Luck has kept things basic, running the kind of establishment one would be happy to stumble upon in one of Paris's least touristy streets. He has learned to accommodate the American taste for large portions, but that's it for concessions. No one makes as delicious an assiette de crudités, meaning an assortment of incredibly distinctive salads, each with its own taste and level of vinaigrette. Add a slice of pâté to the assiette and you are in French heaven.

The list of dishes has grown at a snail's pace over the years. French-style meatballs over garlicky spaghetti are an example of the everyday (as opposed to fancy) cooking style of Violette. Garlicky snails, pork sautés with cream and green peppercorns, and beef Bourguignon are not only genuine but inexpensive as well.

The Chicken Tarragon is still tops, the new nage de poisson (with easily available seafood instead of the typical rockfish from the south of France, a fragrant golden stock, and a pungent rouille) a fabulous idea. The steaks are very French as well, relatively thin by American standards but juicy and assertively seasoned. An impromptu cake with pears and chocolate icing and a bittersweet chocolate mousse are exactly in step with the preceding part of the menu.

Tables aren't nearly as easy to come by as before, but the restaurant may be moving to a larger location on Clairmont Road. Violette #2 operates at the moment as a separate entity. The decor, far more romantic and opulent, and the more eclectic menu from various regions of France have been a delicious surprise.

★★ Virginia's $ ⓧ

1243 Virginia Ave. (at Briarcliff Rd.). Map C. (404) 875-4453.
Daily 10 A.M. to 11 P.M. No reservations or credit cards.
Street parking.

Atmosphere, one of the many factors by which to judge a restaurant, is the most crucial aspect of a coffeehouse. Yes, the mouth feel of the coffee and the quality of the edibles matter, but the main function of a coffeehouse is to offer a congenial place for such activities as talking, reading, and plain old-fashioned hanging out. On account of atmosphere alone, Virginia's holds a special magic. At night especially, the colors are so improbably beautiful that you may hesitate at the edge of Technicolor. An eerie green light hovers around the facade like a mysterious vapor. Inside, the most extraordinary shade of ripe tangerine has been lavished on the ceiling. Large patches of painted plaster cling to partially exposed brick, creating a background for changing, always dramatic artwork.

The tables are beautiful: each a multimedia construction rimmed in studded metal, each sturdily and gracefully resting on three colorful arches. Real candles drip in one-of-a-kind iron candelabra. Fringed Art-Deco glass shades descend from the ceiling. A sunburst of mirrored mosaic explodes on the back wall. A purple banquette trimmed with gold looks as if it belongs in the Egyptian Ballroom of the Fox Theatre. A tablecloth dipped in plaster transforms the occasional round table into a work of art. A huge, softly polished country table holds all the hip magazines you could ever wish to read. The patio is a magic spot.

What does one do at Virginia's? Drink coffee (good, strong) and tea (dozens of exotic varieties); eat sandwiches (try the Brie melt with Dijon mustard and thinly sliced tomatoes); sip tomato or onion soup from a small spoon; share Gado Gado (a famous Indonesian salad of cucumbers, carrots, boiled potatoes, and hard-boiled eggs served on a bed of spinach and topped with spicy peanut sauce and shrimp chips); order breakfast late at night; nibble on cookies, scones, or biscotti from reliable suppliers.

Unless you know the neighborhood by heart, Virginia's is as devilishly hard to find as Stone Soup or Savage Pizza directly across the street. The best strategy is to turn onto Virginia Avenue from Briarcliff Avenue as opposed to meandering in from Virginia-Highland.

★★ The Vortex $ ⊗

1031 W. Peachtree St. (at 11th St.). Map C. (404) 875-1667.
Monday to Thursday 11:30 A.M. to 1 A.M. Friday 11:30 A.M. to 2 A.M. Saturday 6 P.M. to 2 A.M. Sunday 6 P.M. to 1 A.M. No reservations. All major credit cards. Street parking or neighboring lots.

A name implying velocity, centrifugal force, and the likelihood that one will be sucked into a different world isn't a bad thing to call a neighborhood bar—especially something as eccentric as The Vortex, the best possible stop on West Peachtree if you are looking for a spot of relaxation. Let's say you are a connoisseur of beers and hamburgers. You also like jukeboxes with funky selections. You'll love The Vortex!

This isn't Pee Wee Herman's playhouse nor is it a motorcycle bar. But the owners (a sister and two brothers, young, good-looking) are interested in bikes and playful junk. They have created a unique atmosphere as well as a culture, reaping success where failure has been the norm.

The clientele isn't age specific. Bizarre and sometimes poetic things hang everywhere without anything feeling contrived. A pink Hoover flies overhead. A spotted sailfish wears a cowbell. A barrel of TNT swings at the end of a rope. A mounted squirrel scampers up the wall. A live waiter sports the biggest handlebar mustache you've seen in a long time.

Beer signs and signs of beer are everywhere. The cooler behind the bar calls itself The Hall of Foam. On tap and in bottles, the selections are diverse and interesting.

The food is bar food, most of it good to very good, with a few exceptions. The hamburgers (real sirloin or veggie burger) are terrific: big juicy patty, tasty bun spread with mayonnaise, a big slice of red onion, just enough lettuce and tomato, and a plateful of real fries. In its own crunchy, healthy way, the health burger is equal to the real stuff. If you want a classic BLT on wheat or an enormous club sandwich impaled on toothpicks, look no further. Half-sandwich half-salad options are worth pursuing. But when it comes to nachos, skip the goodies topped with a chili that is full of kidney beans.

The Vortex is as pleasant by day as it is by night. A tiny upstairs room may be a good place for you to hide. Parking is no sweat, either on the street or in a neighboring lot.

★ Winfield's $$ ✗✗

100 Galleria Pkwy. (in the Galleria). Map G. (770) 955-5300.
Lunch Monday to Saturday 11:30 A.M. to 3 P.M., Sunday 11 A.M. to 3 P.M. Dinner nightly 5:30 to 10 (Friday and Saturday till midnight). No reservations. All major credit cards. Mall parking, sometimes difficult.

Creating a product with mass appeal rather than a superior one to be enjoyed and paid for by the fickle few has been the Peasant's modus operandi since 1973. The formula has yet to be proven wrong. When people go to a restaurant such as Winfield's, they get a good run for their money. Live music, sophisticated decor, professional service, and a constantly updated bill of fare are usually not available *all together* in the price range of this handsome establishment.

Among Peasant restaurants, Winfield's has a unique, sweeping feel of elegance. Bar and dining room are astonishingly spacious. The open floor plan resembles that of a turn-of-the-century dining hall or one of those glorious Montparnasse brasseries where the lost generation used to drink the night away. Soaring French windows are repeated in tall mirrors. Hunter green trimmed with white makes for a noble color combination. Waiting for a table can scarcely be avoided. But, with a large glass of wine to sip from and a pianist bent over appropriately sappy, swingy, and delicate selections, one surrenders easily to the charm of this comfortable cocktail hour.

Sometimes stimulating and sometimes not, the preparations lack the true finesse of a distinguished kitchen. A trip to the dessert bar may frighten you into asking for the check without accepting the challenge of pastries created for a race of giants. The chocolate velvet mousse, encased in soft panels of dewy chocolate, is bigger than your kid's model railroad tunnel. Winfield's should also be remembered as a very useful bar: elegant enough for guests and sufficiently private for conversational duties and artful loafing.

★★★ Yakitori Den Chan $$ ⊗

3099 Peachtree Rd. (at W. Paces Ferry Rd.). Map B. (404) 842-0270. Dinner only, Tuesday to Thursday 5 P.M. to midnight, Friday and Saturday 5 P.M. to 3 A.M., Sunday 5 to 10 P.M. Reservations recommended for large parties. All major credit cards. A few parking spaces in back or difficult street parking.

Call him Dennis and the superenergetic young man working the grill as much as the crowd may be too identified with his Japanese persona to respond to his Christian name. What causes a Dennis Lange to become a Den Chan able to not only keep up with but earn the respect of a Japanese clientele that includes many restaurateurs? Two years in southern Japan, teaching and learning, and jobbing in restaurants as well.

Yakitori Den Chan is tons of fun. A red lantern by the door announces the style of cooking to the Japanese culture buffs who are attracted to this new operation like iron filings to a magnet. Every customer's entrance is acknowledged with a sort of barked joyful noise echoed by the staff. Orders completed are another opportunity for loud hand claps and more explosion of language.

The restaurant poured itself into a long, narrow space framed in brick. There are tables and chairs, a small tatami space in a window, and a short noodle counter on the way to the back door, but most of the energy happens around the long bar, a hollow rectangle with a gas grill at one end. Where some of the other yakitori chefs in town tediously paint the skewers with sauce and turn them forever (or until you stop feeling hungry), hyperkinetic Dennis Lange does it all in a few well-timed motions.

The skewers are visible in refrigerated compartments flush with the bar top. There are specials every night such as buffalo, blue marlin, chicken skin, and little pregnant sardines full of minuscule caviar. Unadventurous eaters can have hot dogs threaded on skewers, corn on the cob with delicious char marks, plainly delicious chicken wings sprinkled with salts, asparagus rolled in turkey bacon, and much more.

Whether you choose the serendipity of daily offerings (squid legs, eel, deer, chicken hearts, fermented soybean in tofu) or evolve your own list of favorites from the menu (tongue, enoki wrap, deep-fried tofu, shiitake mushrooms, meatballs), you can count on delicious treats. Crisp, coarse cabbage topped with a soy dressing is constantly replenished on your plate. You may order rice from the kitchen but the rice balls sprinkled with sesame and turned slowly on the grill are infinitely more stimulating. If there are more than three of you, table seating becomes an attractive option and combination platters will be fun and easy for everybody.

You will willingly trade in all the boiled peanuts you have ever tasted for an order of delicious boiled and salted soybeans. Tiny little cream-cheese crisps, good dumplings, and a few other items including comforting stews, wonderful noodle dishes, and occasional tasty oddities such as pig feet can also serve as snacks. The quest for the perfect noodle became an obsession with Den Chan. You can taste the fruit of his labor in wonderful brimming bowls of udon and soba noodles with items ranging from tempura to kimchee and fish cakes.

Yakitori is a great bar as well. Beer flows freely either on tap or in oversize bottles. Sake dispensed from tiny jars or (in the case of draft) clean, square wooden boxes fuels many impromptu conversations, some of them bilingual.

★★ Yin Yang $ ⓧ

64 3rd St. (at Spring St.). Map A. (404) 607-0682.
Monday to Thursday 11 A.M. to 2 A.M. Friday 11 A.M. to 4 A.M. Saturday 6 P.M. to 4 A.M. Sunday 6 P.M. to 2 A.M. No reservations. All major credit cards. Street parking or rutted back lot.

A cool café for Generation X, Yin Yang is further off the mainstream than most of its competitors. If you come late on a weekend, you may be spooked by the location (the parking lot is an urban nightmare, there are strange shadows waiting to get into the clubs nearby), but at any other time, especially during the day, have no misgivings.

Yin Yang looks a bit like an avant-garde gallery, a bit like a bar, and a great deal like a European-style artists' café. The old walls have been scraped of most of their plaster, leaving only a few patches here and there painted in incandescent green for interesting effect. Art is everywhere: oils, small drawings on boards suspended by metal clips, metalwork, sculptures, multimedia boxes. Odd surfaces have been painted as well in the most enchanting way. There is even a small room entitled "Les Rêves de Miró" and entirely painted in the style of the famous Spanish-born surrealist. The rest rooms are art installations too. Everything is challenging but comfortable and a bit eerie. There is terrific music on the sound system. The furniture, all recycled stuff, is cozy and generously proportioned.

Yin Yang doesn't lack ambition. The proprietors want to have live music, wine tastings—all sorts of happenings. In the meantime, you can enjoy a light menu including several great salads. The fresh and abundant Greek salad and the spicy jerk-chicken salad with fresh oranges both use a pretty mix of young lettuces.

Yin Yang offers a daily choice of tapas. A sampler of these may include a scallop ceviche, black beans with roasted jalapeños, marinated cucumbers and carrots dressed with curry, ripe tomatoes with mozzarella, small feta and spinach empanadas, and a god-awful Thai chicken salad, the only exception in an otherwise great selection. The restaurant bakes its own cookies and buys a few desserts.

★★ Zab-E-Lee $

4835 Old National Hwy. (west of I-85, College Park). Map F. (404) 768-2705.

Lunch Monday to Friday 11 A.M. to 3 P.M. Dinner Monday to Friday 5 to 10 P.M. Saturday 11 A.M. to 10 P.M. Sunday 4 to 9 P.M. No reservations. All major credit cards. Ample parking.

The name of this unusual, authentic Thai restaurant means "very wonderful." And so it is. The location is obscure at best, the space without a great deal of character. On the other hand, if you live south of the city or if you are going to some cultural event at Spivey Hall, you could hardly pick a better restaurant for the money.

Zab-E-Lee is in a mainstream shopping strip anchored by Service Merchandise. The staff, part of the cook's family, is thoroughly pleasant and helpful. The food, characteristic of eastern Thailand, is spicy and distinctive. Larb (a salad of chopped chicken, beef, or pork seasoned with toasted brown rice, chile, and lime juice) comes with a small basket of excellent sticky rice. For a heavenly treat, you roll the rice into a little ball and press it onto the meat.

Other highly delicious choices include squid salad (*yum ba munk* on the menu), papaya salad (som tum) with chile and fish sauce, and stuffed chicken wings. The soups are fiery hot and tart. Some of the curries aren't too great but the noodle dishes can be extraordinary. If you are offered fried bananas for dessert, jump at the opportunity.

★★ Zocalo $ ⊗

187 10th St. (between Piedmont and Juniper). Map C. (404) 249-7576.

Tuesday to Sunday 11 A.M. to 10 P.M. No reservations. All major credit cards. Small parking lot.

The difference between this authentic Mexican taqueria and all the other authentic Mexican taquerias sprinkled throughout the city is in the atmosphere as well as the regional characteristics. Zocalo is hip and happening. One of the owners is Lucero Obregon, formerly Paul Luna's right hand at Bice and Luna Si.

A tiny structure with a sprawling covered patio, Zocalo leans against a McFrugal Auto Rental like a vibrant young neighbor sporting the colorful clothes of another country. With rough stucco and buckets of marigold-yellow paint, with fans and canvas, flowerpots and hand-shaped, hand-colored details—including a fountain by the door—Zocalo brings the joyous flavors of Mexico to its little corner of the world.

The patio, partially encased and covered by a red canvas awning, is set up for dining with brightly painted tables and chairs. Fans churn the air overhead. Latin music races through the speakers. You ought to at least look inside even though you can't sit there. The serious grill, tortilla press, great jars of frescas (homemade soft drinks based on fruit extracts), flurry of family activity, and youthfulness of everybody involved will tell you a lot about the restaurant.

Don't expect a chip-and-salsa kind of place. Zocalo is scrupulously authentic: the delicious little tacos made with griddle-roasted fresh masa-dough tortillas, the grilled spring onions served with fresh lime, the typical antojitos (snacks) and tortas (hot sandwiches). The tiny soft tacos are served open faced with incredibly distinctive fillings. Don't choose between the rajas con queso (fresh corn, strips of poblano peppers, onion, and cheese), the papas con chorizo (potatoes and sausage), the cochinita pilbil (roasted pork with marinated onion), the grilled steak con queso, and the chicken mole. Have them all!

What else is good? The flautas with shredded chicken and queso fresco; the crisp tostadas topped with beans, chicken, lettuce, sour cream, pico de gallo, and crumbled queso fresco; and the wonderful gorditas de frijol, bean cakes with sour cream, salsa, and queso fresco. The chiles campesinos, grilled poblanos oozing cheese and served with three tortillas, are as delicious as the more familiar chile rellenos.

Make sure that you try some of the house drinks, which are a little bit like homemade Snapple. If you need something stronger, brownbag it.

Beyond Atlanta

The following restaurants may be reached from Atlanta by automobile in less than two hours.

★ Fresh Air Barbeque $ ⊗

On U.S. 23, just under three miles south of the Butts County courthouse in Jackson. (404) 775-3182.
Daily during daylight hours. No reservations or credit cards. Adequate parking.

Since 1929, hunters in Middle Georgia have been stoking up at this picturesque log structure by the side of the highway. If the varyingly accommodating staff are in a pleasant mood, they may show you their ingenious system for smoking meat in the *L*-shaped tunnel connected to a wide stone chimney. Placing the hams in front of or beyond the elbow of this tunnel controls the intensity of heat reaching the meat.

Seating is at long plank tables on the sawdust-covered porch or inside a plain room with varnished plank walls and no decorations. Chopped pork is the only meat available, served with a vinegar sauce already added. The stale-tasting brunswick stew is not recommended. Packaged white bread, soft drinks, and potato chips complete the bill of fare.

★★★ Hogan's Heros $$ ⊗

235 Hwy. 29 South in Hogansville. (706) 637-4953.
Lunch Monday to Friday 11 A.M. to 2 P.M. Dinner Monday to Thursday 5 to 9:30 P.M., Friday 5 to 10 P.M. Saturday noon to 10 P.M. Reservations accepted. No credit cards. Adequate parking.

Life's not fair! At least not if you live in Atlanta. Why did the Italian restaurant you are always looking for (casual, huge portions, fantastic food, nice folks, pleasant waiters) have to open halfway to Columbus? When the owners of this sensational trattoria decided to up and leave New Jersey and bring their brand of good food to the South, they looked for a location that would pull people in from Alabama as well as Georgia and settled in an old bus station in a mill town. The low-ceilinged dining rooms are brightly lit and most of the atmosphere comes from people sitting elbow to elbow and having a great time.

If you unexpectedly find yourself in this neck of the woods, you may not be able to get into Hogan's Heros. (You might need to reserve three weeks in advance for a Saturday night.) What is the attraction? A platterful of ossobucco topped with gremolata over saffron risotto, a gigantic stuffed veal chop over green and yellow linguine in a spectacular mushroom sauce, and a divine salmon with a crust of angel-hair pasta and a cornucopia of radicchio brimming with spicy black-eyed peas answer this question.

There is more: a tender Chicken Wallet with a pocket of zucchini and cheese in a delicious lemon butter sauce, majestic veal parmigiana, mussels in Verdicchio, tournedos Rossini, delicious Italian mixed grill. The abundant salad that accompanies your meal comes with four cruets of homemade dressings (our favorite: the unusual blue cheese and red wine vinaigrette). There are also quite hearty appetizers, but who needs them after devouring a loaf or two of the warm homemade bread?

The desserts shown on a groaning tray are homemade, too: white-chocolate banana pie, banana surprise, crème brûlée, tiramisu cake, three kinds of parfaits, and many more. You can find a decent Italian wine. The staff are famously entertaining but serious about their jobs. Everyone assumes that you have a working knowledge of gourmet terms.

★★ Major McGill's Fish House $$ ⊗⊗

Main St., Flowery Branch. Take Exit 3 off the Lanier Pkwy. (Georgia 365), and follow signs to "The Best Little Fish House in Georgia." (770) 967-6001.

Dinner only, Tuesday to Saturday 5 to 10 P.M. Reservations accepted. V, MC. Adequate parking.

This cheerfully decorated, airy cottage is an especially convenient destination for fish-loving frolickers at nearby Lake Lanier, and it's a short, pleasant ride from the city. The dining rooms occupy the former front porch and several interior rooms of the cottage. Walls are hung with local paintings, photographs of sports personalities, and fish paraphernalia. Flanking the entrance from the porch are posters illustrating freshwater and saltwater fish. The atmosphere is casually comfortable, most of the staff warmly amiable.

The menu, which at one time focused narrowly on a few smoked and fried fish, has been significantly expanded to include such ambitious seafood offerings as soft-shell crabs, as well as some big beef items like prime rib. For once, such a major move away from a kitchen's area of expertise shows no sign of diminishing quality. The soft-shells are very delicately breaded and simply sautéed, leaving their nutty, buttery substance intact.

The smoked trout remains a stellar achievement, as good as any available in town—meaty, assertively smoked, yet not so as to camouflage the trout's natural flavor and texture. The restaurant prepares fish in its own smokehouse instead of buying smoked products from a wholesaler as most places do. Owner Steve Major (who used to be in partnership with a Mr. McGill, hence the restaurant's name) is from Yugoslavia, where he learned the secret recipe for the marinade he says the fish are bathed in before being smoked over Texas mesquite wood. As an appetizer, you can share the substantial serving of smoked trout salad.

Keep an eye out for deep-fried smelts, when available. Entrée platters come with good, crunchy coleslaw and greasy fried potatoes. You'll forgive this last indignity when you bite into the hushpuppies—large round, dark balls crisp on the outside and elegantly fluffy, oniony, and corny inside. The Cheesecake is a marvel.

Indexes

TYPE OF CUISINE

AMERICAN

Atkins Park, 52
Atlanta Fish Market, 53
Azalea, 56
Bacchanalia, 62
Baker's Café, 63
Blue Ridge Grill, 71
Bone's, 73
Break Away Café, 76
Brickery, The, 77
Brooklyn Café, The, 79
Buckhead Diner, 80
Cabin, The, 83
Café at The Ritz-Carlton Atlanta, The, 84
Café at The Ritz-Carlton Buckhead, The, 85
California Café, 94
Canoe, 97
Charthouse, The, 103
Cheesecake Factory, The, 104
Chefs' Café, 105
Chops, 108
Chow, 110
City Grill, 113
Coach and Six, The, 115
Colonnade, The, 117
Cowtipper's, 122
Dailey's, 123
East Village Grille, 131
1848 House, The, 134
Embers, 138
Flying Biscuit Café, The, 146
French Quarter Food Shoppe, 148
Georgia Grille, 151
Gorin's Diner, 153
Greenwood's on Green Street, 154
Hal's, 155
Hard Rock Café, 157
Heaping Bowl and Brew, The, 162
Highland Tap, 166
Horseradish Grill, 169
Houston's, 172
Indigo Coastal Grill, 175
Joey D's Oak Room, 182
Kudzu Café, 188
Lickskillet Farm, 199
Longhorn Steaks, 203
Magnolia Tea Room, 205
Major McGill's Fish House, 333
Marra's, 212
Mary Mac's, 213
McKinnon's Louisiane, 215
Mick's, 218
Morton's of Chicago, 223

Murphy's, 225
Nava, 226
Nickiemoto's, 228
OK Café, 234
Old Vinings Inn, 236
Otto's, 241
Our Way Café, 272
Palm Restaurant, 244
Pano's & Paul's, 246
Partners, 247
Paschal's, 248
Peachtree Café, 251
Peasant, The, 252
Peasant Uptown, The, 253
Pilgreen's, 255
Pittypat's Porch, 256
Pleasant Peasant, The, 257
Public House, The, 259
Ray's on the River, 264
RJ's Café, 270
R. Thomas Deluxe Grill, 272
Ruth's Chris Steak House, 274
Savannah Fish Company, 279
Showcase Eatery, The, 283
Silver Skillet, The, 284
Slocum's Tavern, 285
South City Kitchen, 290
Steamhouse, The, 291
Stringers, 292
Taste of New Orleans, A, 298
Tavern at Phipps, The, 299
Terra Cotta, 300
Tiburon Grille, 305
Tom Tom, 306
Top of the Plaza, 307
Van Gogh's, 315
Winfield's, 326

CHINESE

Buford Tea House, 81
Canton House, 99
Chin Chin, 107
Chopstix, 109
First China, 144
Ho Ho, 167
Hong Kong Harbor, 167
Honto, 168
House of Chan, 171
Hsu's, 172
Little Szechuan, 201
Oriental Pearl Restaurant, 239
Orient at Vinings, The, 240
Pung Mie, 260
Uncle Tai's, 313

CONTINENTAL

Abbey, The, 39
Amusé, 43
Anthonys, 47
Babette's Café, 61
Bistango, 68
Café Nirvana, 88
Café Renaissance, 89
Café Tu Tu Tango, 92
Capo's Café, 100
Carbo's Café, 101
Ciboulette, 111
Country Place, The, 121
Dailey's, 123
Dante's Down the Hatch, 124
Dining Room at The Ritz-Carlton Buckhead, The, 128
Florencia, 145
Hal's, 155
Hedgerose Heights Inn, The, 164
Joey D's Oak Room, 182
Kurt's River Manor, 190
Lickskillet Farm, 199
Lindy's, 200
Luna Si, 204
Mansion, The, 210
Nikolai's Roof, 230

Old Vinings Inn, 236
103 West, 237
Otto's, 241
Palisades, 243
Pano's & Paul's, 246
Partners, 247
Peachtree Café, 251
Peasant, The, 252
Peasant Uptown, The, 253
Pleasant Peasant, The, 257
Public House, The, 259
Ray's on the River, 264
Restaurant at The Ritz-Carlton Atlanta, The, 265
Resto Nax, 266
Tavern at Phipps, The, 299
Toulouse, 311
Villa Christina, 321
Winfield's, 326

FRENCH

Anis, 45
Babette's Café, 61
Bistango, 68
Bistro at Andrews Square, The, 70
Brasserie Le Coze, 74
Café Diem, 85
Café Nirvana, 88
Ciboulette, 111
Claudette's, 114
Colette, 116
Le Giverny, 198
Riviera, 269
Toulouse, 311

INDIAN

Calcutta, 93
Haveli, 161
Heera of India, 165
Indian Delights, 174
Maharaja, 206

Raja, 263
Touch of India, 310

ITALIAN

Abruzzi Ristorante, 40
Arturo's, 48
Azio, 57
Bertolini's, 66
Brooklyn Café, The, 79
Camille's, 96
Dominick's, 130
Fratelli di Napoli, 147
Ippolito's, 177
La Grotta, 192
La Strada, 195
Lindy's, 200
Lombardi's, 202
Luna Si, 204
Mi Spia, 221
Nino's, 231
Pasta da Pulcinella, 249
Pasta Vino, 250
Pricci, 258
Sfuzzi, 281
Veni Vidi Vici, 318

JAPANESE

Asuka, 51
August Moon, 54
Hama, 156
Harry & Sons, 158
Hashiguchi, 159
Joli Kobe, 184
Kamogawa, 185
Kobe Steaks, 187
Nakato, 226
Nickiemoto's, 228
Ru San's, 273
Sakana-Ya, 276
Shiki, 282
Soto, 287
Suntory, 294

Sushi Huku, 296
Toyo Ta Ya, 312
Yakitori Den Chan, 327

KOREAN

Asiana Garden, 49
Garam, 150
Mirror of Korea, 220
Seoul Garden, 280

MEXICAN

Azteca Grill, 58
Azuni Grill, 60
El Charro, 136
El Taco Veloz, 137
La Paz, 194
Mexico City Gourmet, 217
Nuevo Laredo Cantina, 232
Sundown Café, 293
Zocalo, 330

MIDDLE EASTERN

Basil's, 65
Lawrence's, 196
Nicola's, 229
Oasis Café, 233

PIZZA

Arturo's, 48
Azio, 57
Bertolini's, 66
California Pizza Kitchen, 95
Camille's, 96
Everybody's, 140
Fellini's Pizza, 143
Ippolito's, 177
Jagger's, 178
Pasta Vino, 250
Rocky's Brick Oven Pizzeria, 271

SANDWICHES AND LIGHT FOOD

Alon's, 42
Atkins Park, 52
Aurora, 55
Baker's Café, 63
Breakaway Café, 75
Café Diem, 85
Café Intermezzo, 87
Café Tu Tu Tango, 92
Carey's Place, 102
Cheesecake Factory, The, 104
Corner Café/Buckhead Bread Co., 120
Delectables, 125
Dessert Place, The, 126
French Quarter Food Shoppe, 148
Galletto Espress-oh, 149
Good Old Days, 152
Gorin's Diner, 153
Hard Rock Café, 157
Havana Sandwich Shop, 160
Heaping Bowl and Brew, The, 162
Houston's, 172
Jake's, 179
Java Jive, 180
Jersey, 181
Johnny Rockets, 183
Joli Kobe, 184
La Fonda Latina, 191
Landmark Diner, 193
Majestic Food Shop, 207
Manuel's Tavern, 211
Mel's Steaks and Hoagies, 216
Mick's, 218
MOCHA, 222
Murphy's, 225
OK Café, 234

Rainbow Natural Foods, 262
R. Thomas Deluxe Grill, 272
St. Louis Bread Co., 275
Snack 'n Shop, 286
Taco Mac, 297
Tortillas, 309
Urban Coffee Bungalow, 314
Varsity, The, 316
Vickery's, 320
Virginia's, 324
Vortex, The, 325
Yin Yang, 329

SEAFOOD

Atlanta Fish Market, 53
Charthouse, The, 103
Embers, 138
Indigo Coastal Grill, 175
Major McGill's Fish House, 333
Rio Vista, 268
Savannah Fish Company, 279
Stringers, 292

SOUL FOOD

Aleck's Barbecue Heaven, 41
Beautiful, 66
Burton's Grill, 82
Paschal's, 248
Soul Vegetarian, 288
Thelma's Kitchen, 304

SOUTHERN

Anthonys, 47
Blue Ridge Grill, 71
Cabin, The, 83
Colonnade, The, 117
Corky's, 119
1848 House, The, 134
Fat Matt's Rib Shack, 141
Fresh Air Barbeque, 332
Greenwood's on Green Street, 154
Harold's Barbecue, 157
Horseradish Grill, 169
Kudzu Café, 188
Lickskillet Farm, 199
Lindy's, 200
Magnolia Tea Room, 205
Major McGill's Fish House, 333
Mary Mac's, 213
Melear's Pit Cooked Barbecue, 216
Old South Barbecue, 235
Our Way Café, 272
Pilgreen's, 255
Pittypat's Porch, 256
Rio Vista, 268
Showcase Eatery, The, 283
Silver Skillet, The, 284
South City Kitchen, 290
Stringers, 292
Top of the Plaza, 307

SOUTHWESTERN

Azteca Grill, 58
Azuni Grill, 60
Georgia Grille, 151
La Paz, 194
Nava, 226
Rio Bravo Cantina, 267
Sundown Café, 293
Tortillas, 309

STEAKS

Bone's, 73
Charthouse, The, 103
Chops, 108
Coach and Six, The, 115

Cowtipper's, 122
Highland Tap, 166
Joey D's Oak Room, 182
Kobe Steaks, 187
Longhorn Steaks, 203
Morton's of Chicago, 223
Palm Restaurant, 244
Ruth's Chris Steak House, 274
Tavern at Phipps, The, 299

THAI

Annie's Thai Castle, 46
Harry & Sons, 158
King and I, The, 186
Surin of Thailand, 295
Thai Chilli, 302
Thai Restaurant of Norcross, 303
Zab-E-Lee, 330

VEGETARIAN

Café Sunflower, 90
Eats, 132
Eat Your Vegetables, 133
Flying Biscuit Café, The, 146
Heaping Bowl and Brew, The, 162
Indian Delights, 174
Pasta da Pulcinella, 249
Rainbow Natural Foods, 262
R. Thomas Deluxe Grill, 272
Soul Vegetarian, 288
Tortillas, 309
Zocalo, 330

MISCELLANEOUS ETHNIC

Bien Thuy (Vietnamese), 67
Bridgetown Grill (Caribbean), 78
Evelyn's Café (Greek), 139
Havana Sandwich Shop (Cuban), 160
Imperial Fez, The (Moroccan), 173
La Fonda Latina (Spanish/Cuban), 191
Malaysia House (Malaysian), 208
Mambo (Cuban), 209
Moscow (Russian), 224
Pho Hoa (Vietnamese), 254
Salar (Persian), 277

TOP-RATED RESTAURANTS

★ ★ ★ ★

Dining Room at The Ritz-Carlton Buckhead, The, 128
Soto, 287

★ ★ ★

Annie's Thai Castle, 46
Arturo's, 48
Asuka, 51
Atlanta Fish Market, 53
Bacchanalia, 62
Bien Thuy, 67
Bistro at Andrews Square, The, 70
Blue Ridge Grill, 71
Bone's, 73
Brasserie Le Coze, 74
Buckhead Diner, 80

Canoe, 97
Chefs' Café, 105
Chops, 108
Chopstix, 109
City Grill, 113
Corner Café/Buckhead Bread Co., 120
Delectables, 125
1848 House, The, 134
El Taco Veloz, 137
Flying Biscuit Café, The, 146
Fratelli di Napoli, 147
Georgia Grille, 151
Greenwood's on Green Street, 154
Hedgerose Heights Inn, The, 164
Horseradish Grill, 169
Indian Delights, 174
Indigo Coastal Grill, 175
La Grotta, 192
La Strada, 195
Little Szechuan, 201
Luna Si, 204
Malaysia House, 208
Mambo, 209
Nava, 226
Nickiemoto's, 228
103 West, 237
Palm Restaurant, 244
Pano's & Paul's, 246
Partners, 247
Pricci, 258
Pung Mie, 260
Riviera, 269
Shiki, 282
Sundown Café, 293
Sushi Huku, 296
Terra Cotta, 300
Thai Chilli, 302
Tom Tom, 306
Veni Vidi Vici, 318
Yakitori Den Chan, 327

FULL MEALS UNDER $15

Aleck's Barbecue Heaven, 41
Alon's, 42
Atkins Park, 52
Azteca Grill, 58
Beautiful, 66
Bien Thuy, 67
Breakaway Café, 75
Bridgetown Grill, 78
Buford Tea House, 81
Burton's Grill, 82
Café Diem, 85
Calcutta, 93
Canton House, 99
Colonnade, The, 117
Corky's, 119
Delectables, 125
Eats, 132
Eat Your Vegetables, 133
El Charro, 136
El Taco Veloz, 137
Evelyn's Café, 139
Everybody's, 140
Fat Matt's Rib Shack, 141
Feeders, 142
Fellini's Pizza, 143
First China, 144
Flying Biscuit Café, The, 146
French Quarter Food Shoppe, 148
Fresh Air Barbeque, 332
Hama, 156
Harold's Barbecue, 157

Havana Sandwich Shop, 160
Heaping Bowl and Brew, The, 162
Ho Ho, 167
Indian Delights, 174
Java Jive, 180
Jersey, 181
Johnny Rockets, 183
Joli Kobe, 184
King and I, The, 186
La Fonda Latina, 191
Little Szechuan, 201
Maharaja, 206
Majestic Food Shop, 207
Malaysia House, 208
Manuel's Tavern, 211
Mary Mac's, 213
Melear's Pit Cooked Barbecue, 216
Mel's Steaks and Hoagies, 216
Mirror of Korea, 220
Nuevo Laredo Cantina, 232
Oasis Café, 233
OK Café, 234

Old South Barbecue, 235
Our Way Café, 72
Pasta da Pulcinella, 249
Pho Hoa, 254
Pung Mie, 260
Rainbow Natural Foods, 262
Raja, 263
Rio Vista, 268
R. Thomas Deluxe Grill, 272
St. Louis Bread Co., 275
Seoul Garden, 280
Silver Skillet, The, 284
Snack 'n Shop, 286
Soul Vegetarian, 288
Taco Mac, 297
Thelma's Kitchen, 304
Tortillas, 309
Varsity, The, 316
Virginia's, 324
Vortex, The, 325
Yin Yang, 329
Zab-E-Lee, 330
Zocalo, 330

OPEN ON SUNDAY

Abbey, The, 39
Aleck's Barbecue Heaven, 41
Alon's, 42
Amusé, 43
Anis, 45
Annie's Thai Castle, 46
Arturo's, 48
Asiana Garden, 49
Asuka, 51
Atkins Park, 52
Atlanta Fish Market, 53
Aurora, 55
Azalea, 56

Azio, 57
Azuni Grill, 60
Babette's Café, 61
Beautiful, 66
Bertolini's, 66
Bien Thuy, 67
Blue Ridge Grill, 71
Bone's, 73
Brickery, The, 77
Bridgetown Grill, 78
Brooklyn Café, The, 79
Buckhead Diner, 80
Buford Tea House, 81

Indexes 343

Café at The Ritz-Carlton Atlanta, The, 84
Café at The Ritz-Carlton Buckhead, The, 85
Café Diem, 85
Café Intermezzo, 87
Café Renaissance, 89
Café Sunflower, 90
Café Tu Tu Tango, 92
Calcutta, 93
California Café, 94
California Pizza Kitchen, 95
Camille's, 96
Canoe, 97
Canton House, 99
Capo's Café, 100
Carbo's Café, 101
Carey's Place, 102
Charthouse, The, 103
Cheesecake Factory, The, 104
Chefs' Café, 105
Chin Chin, 107
Chops, 108
Chopstix, 109
Chow, 110
Colonnade, The, 117
Corky's, 119
Corner Café/Buckhead Bread Co., 120
Country Place, The, 121
Cowtipper's, 122
Dailey's, 123
Dante's Down the Hatch, 124
Dessert Place, The, 126
Dominick's, 130
East Village Grille, 131
Eats, 132
1848 House, The, 134
El Charro, 136
El Taco Veloz, 137
Embers, 138
Everybody's, 140

Fat Matt's Rib Shack, 141
Feeders, 142
Fellini's Pizza, 143
First China, 144
Flying Biscuit Café, The, 146
Fratelli di Napoli, 147
French Quarter Food Shoppe, 148
Fresh Air Barbeque, 332
Galletto Espress-oh, 149
Garam, 150
Georgia Grille, 151
Good Old Days, 152
Gorin's Diner, 153
Greenwood's on Green Street, 154
Hama, 156
Hard Rock Café, 157
Harry & Sons, 158
Heera of India, 165
Highland Tap, 166
Ho Ho, 167
Hong Kong Harbor, 167
Honto, 168
Horseradish Grill, 169
House of Chan, 171
Houston's, 172
Hsu's, 172
Imperial Fez, The, 173
Indian Delights, 174
Indigo Coastal Grill, 175
Ippolito's, 177
Jagger's, 178
Jake's, 179
Java Jive, 180
Jersey, 181
Joey D's Oak Room, 182
Johnny Rockets, 183
Joli Kobe, 184
Kamogawa, 185
King and I, The, 186
Kobe Steaks, 187

Kudzu Café, 188
La Fonda Latina, 191
Landmark Diner, 193
La Paz, 194
La Strada, 195
Lickskillet Farm, 199
Lindy's, 200
Little Szechuan, 201
Lombardi's, 202
Longhorn Steaks, 203
Maharaja, 206
Majestic Food Shop, 207
Malaysia House, 208
Mambo, 209
Mansion, The, 210
Manuel's Tavern, 211
Marra's, 212
Melear's Pit Cooked Barbecue, 216
Mexico City Gourmet, 217
Mick's, 218
Mi Spia, 221
MOCHA, 222
Morton's of Chicago, 223
Moscow, 224
Murphy's, 225
Nakato, 226
Nava, 226
Nickiemoto's, 228
Nicola's, 229
Nikolai's Roof, 230
Nino's, 231
Nuevo Laredo Cantina, 232
OK Café, 234
Old South Barbecue, 235
Old Vinings Inn, 236
Oriental Pearl Restaurant, 239
Orient at Vinings, The, 240
Otto's, 241
Palm Restaurant, 244
Partners, 247
Paschal's, 248

Pasta Vino, 250
Peachtree Café, 251
Peasant, The, 252
Peasant Uptown, The, 253
Pho Hoa, 254
Pittypat's Porch, 256
Pleasant Peasant, The, 257
Pricci, 258
Pung Mie, 260
Raja, 263
Ray's on the River, 264
Resto Nax, 266
Rio Bravo Cantina, 267
Rio Vista, 268
RJ's Café, 270
Rocky's Brick Oven Pizzeria, 271
R. Thomas Deluxe Grill, 272
Ru San's, 273
Ruth's Chris Steak House, 274
St. Louis Bread Co., 275
Sakana-Ya, 276
Salar, 277
Savannah Fish Company, 279
Seoul Garden, 280
Sfuzzi, 281
Slocum's Tavern, 285
Snack 'n Shop, 286
Soul Vegetarian, 288
South City Kitchen, 290
Steamhouse, The, 291
Stringers, 292
Suntory, 294
Surin of Thailand, 295
Sushi Huku, 296
Taco Mac, 297
Tavern at Phipps, The, 299
Terra Cotta, 300
Thai Chilli, 302
Thai Restaurant of Norcross, 303
Tiburon Grille, 305

Tom Tom, 306
Tortillas, 309
Touch of India, 310
Toyo Ta Ya, 312
Uncle Tai's, 313
Urban Coffee Bungalow, 314
Van Gogh's, 315
Varsity, The, 316
Veni Vidi Vici, 318

Vickery's, 320
Violette, 323
Virginia's, 324
Vortex, The, 325
Winfield's, 326
Yakitori Den Chan, 327
Yin Yang, 329
Zab-E-Lee, 330
Zocalo, 330

OPEN LATE AT NIGHT

Asiana Garden, 49
Atkins Park, 52
Aurora, 55
Azio, 57
Buckhead Diner, 80
Café at The Ritz-Carlton Atlanta, The, 84
Café at The Ritz-Carlton Buckhead, The, 85
Café Diem, 85
Café Intermezzo, 87
California Café, 94
Carey's Place, 102
Cheesecake Factory, The, 104
Corky's, 119
Dante's Down the Hatch, 124
Dessert Place, The, 126
East Village Grille, 131
Everybody's, 140
Fat Matt's Rib Shack, 141
Fellini's Pizza, 143
First China, 144
Garam, 150
Good Old Days, 152
Gorin's Diner, 153
Hard Rock Café, 157
Highland Tap, 166
Hong Kong Harbor, 167
Jagger's, 178

Java Jive, 180
La Fonda Latina, 191
Landmark Diner, 193
Little Szechuan, 201
Majestic Food Shop, 207
Manuel's Tavern, 211
Mick's, 218
MOCHA, 222
Nickiemoto's, 228
Nuevo Laredo Cantina, 232
OK Café, 234
Otto's, 241
Pho Hoa, 254
Pung Mie, 260
Rio Bravo Cantina, 267
R. Thomas Deluxe Grill, 272
Seoul Garden, 280
Soto, 287
Steamhouse, The, 291
Sushi Huku, 296
Urban Coffee Bungalow, 314
Taco Mac, 297
Varsity, The, 316
Vickery's, 320
Virginia's, 324
Vortex, The, 325
Yakitori Den Chan, 327
Yin Yang, 329

BREAKFAST

- Alon's, 42
- Aurora, 55
- Beautiful, 66
- Break Aaway Café, 75
- Burton's Grill, 82
- Café at The Ritz-Carlton Atlanta, The, 84
- Café at The Ritz-Carlton Buckhead, The, 85
- Corner Café/Buckhead Bread Co., 120
- Dessert Place, The, 126
- Flying Biscuit Café, The, 146
- Galletto Espress-oh, 149
- Good Old Days, 152
- Gorin's Diner, 153
- Heaping Bowl and Brew, The, 162
- Java Jive, 180
- Kamogawa, 185
- Landmark Diner, 193
- Majestic Food shop, 207
- Mary Mac's, 213
- MOCHA, 222
- Murphy's, 225
- OK Café, 234
- Paschal's, 248
- R. Thomas Deluxe Grill, 272
- St. Louis Bread Co., 275
- Silver Skillet, The, 284
- Snack 'n Shop, 286
- Thelma's Kitchen, 304
- Urban Coffee Bungalow, 314
- Varsity, The, 316
- Virginia's, 324

BRUNCH

- Anis, 45
- Atkins Park, 52
- Atlanta Fish Market, 53
- Azio, 57
- Babette's Café, 61
- Baker's Café, 63
- Blue Ridge Grill, 71
- Brooklyn Café, The, 79
- Buckhead Diner, 80
- Café at The Ritz-Carlton Atlanta, The, 84
- Café at The Ritz-Carlton Buckhead, The, 85
- Café Diem, 85
- Café Intermezzo, 87
- Café Tu Tu Tango, 92
- California Café, 94
- Canoe, 97
- Canton House, 99
- Capo's Café, 100
- Cheesecake Factory, The, 104
- Chefs' Café, 105
- Chow, 110
- Corner Café/Buckhead Bread Co., 120
- Country Place, The, 121
- 1848 House, The, 134
- First China, 144
- Flying Biscuit Café, The, 146
- Good Old Days, 152
- Gorin's Diner, 153
- Hard Rock Café, 157

Harry & Sons, 158
Heaping Bowl and Brew, The, 162
Highland Tap, 166
Hong Kong Harbor, 167
Honto, 168
Horseradish Grill, 169
Indigo Coastal Grill, 175
Java Jive, 180
Kudzu Café, 188
Landmark Diner, 193
Le Giverny, 198
Lickskillet Farm, 199
Lindy's, 200
Magnolia Tea Room, 205
Maharaja, 206
Mansion, The, 210
Mick's, 218
Murphy's, 225
Nava, 226
OK Café, 234
Old Vinings Inn, 236
Oriental Pearl Restaurant, 239
Palm Restaurant, 244
Peachtree Café, 251
Peasant, The, 252
Ray's on the River, 264
Rio Bravo Cantina, 267
RJ's Café, 270
Rocky's Brick Oven Pizzeria, 271
R. Thomas Deluxe Grill, 272
Sfuzzi, 281
Slocum's Tavern, 285
Snack 'n Shop, 286
South City Kitchen, 290
Tavern at Phipps, The, 299
Tom Tom, 306
Vickery's, 320
Villa Christina, 321
Virginia's, 324
Winfield's, 326
Zocalo, 330

OUTDOOR SEATING

Anis, 45
Annie's Thai Castle, 46
Atkins Park, 52
Azalea, 56
Azuni Grill, 60
Basil's, 65
Bistango, 68
Brasserie Le Coze, 74
Bridgetown Grill, 78
Brooklyn Café, The, 79
Café Diem, 85
Café Intermezzo, 87
Café Nirvana, 88
Café Tu Tu Tango, 92
Camille's, 96
Canoe, 97
Charthouse, The, 103
Chow, 110
Corner Café/Buckhead Bread Co., 120
Cowtipper's, 122
Delectables, 125
Dessert Place, The, 126
East Village Grille, 131
Eats, 132
Everybody's, 140
Fat Matt's Rib Shack, 141
Feeders, 142
Fellini's Pizza, 143
French Quarter Food Shoppe, 148
Georgia Grille, 151

Good Old Days, 152
Highland Tap, 166
Horseradish Grill, 169
Houston's, 172
Indigo Coastal Grill, 175
Jake's, 179
Johnny Rockets, 183
Kurt's River Manor, 190
La Fonda Latina, 191
La Grotta, 192
Lickskillet Farm, 199
Lindy's, 200
Mambo, 209
Mansion, The, 210
Marra's, 212
Mi Spia, 221
MOCHA, 222
Nava, 226
Palm Restaurant, 244
Pasta da Pulcinella, 249
Pasta Vino, 250
Peachtree Café, 251

Ray's on the River, 264
Rio Bravo Cantina, 267
RJ's Café, 270
Rocky's Brick Oven Pizzeria, 271
R. Thomas Deluxe Grill, 272
Sfuzzi, 281
South City Kitchen, 290
Steamhouse, The, 291
Sundown Café, 293
Taco Mac, 297
Tavern at Phipps, The, 299
Tiburon Grille, 305
Tom Tom, 306
Tortillas, 309
Urban Coffee Bungalow, 314
Veni Vidi Vici, 318
Vickery's, 320
Villa Christina, 321
Virginia's, 324
Zocalo, 330

RECOMMENDED FOR CHILDREN

Arturo's, 48
California Pizza Kitchen, 95
Cheesecake Factory, The, 104
Chin Chin, 107
Everybody's, 140
Fellini's Pizza, 143
Gorin's Diner, 153
Hard Rock Café, 157
Honto, 168
Ippolito's, 177
Jake's, 179

Johnny Rockets, 183
Landmark Diner, 193
Mary Mac's, 213
Mick's, 218
OK Café, 234
Oriental Pearl Restaurant, 239
Rocky's Brick Oven Pizzeria, 271
Stringers, 292
Varsity, The, 316

PROXIMITY TO MARTA STATION

Aleck's Barbecue Heaven (Ashby Street), 41
Alon's (North Avenue), 42
Azio (Peachtree Center), 57
Beautiful (MLK), 66
Bertolini's (Lenox Square), 66
Bistango (Midtown), 68
Brasserie Le Coze (Lenox Square), 74
Bridgetown Grill (North Avenue), 78
Burton's Grill (Inman Park), 82
Café at The Ritz-Carlton Atlanta, The (Peachtree Center), 84
Café at The Ritz-Carlton Buckhead, The (Lenox Square), 85
California Pizza Kitchen (Lenox Square), 95
Chow (Peachtree Center), 110
City Grill (Five Points), 113
Claudette's (Decatur), 114
Country Place, The (Arts Center), 121
Dailey's (Peachtree Center), 123
Dante's Down the Hatch (Five Points), 124
Delectables (Peachtree Center), 125
Dining Room at The Ritz-Carlton Buckhead, The (Lenox Square), 128
Florencia (Arts Center), 145
French Quarter Food Shoppe (Midtown), 148
Gorin's Diner (Arts Center), 153
Hard Rock Café (Peachtree Center), 154
Houston's (Lenox Square), 172
Hsu's (Peachtree Center), 172
Johnny Rockets (Lenox, Five Points), 183
King and I, The (Brookhaven), 186
Lombardi's (Five Points), 202
Mansion, The (North Avenue), 210
Mick's (Lenox, Five Points, Decatur), 218
Morton's of Chicago (Peachtree Center, Lenox), 223
Nikolai's Roof (Peachtree Center), 230
Palm Restaurant (Lenox Square), 244
Paschal's (Ashby Street), 248
Pasta da Pulcinella (Midtown), 249
Peasant Uptown, The (Lenox Square), 253
Pilgreen's (Oakland City), 255
Pittypat's Porch (Peachtree Center), 256
Pleasant Peasant, The (North Avenue), 257
Restaurant at The Ritz-Carlton Atlanta, The (Peachtree Center), 265

Ruth's Chris Steak House (Lenox Square), 274
Savannah Fish Company (Peachtree Center), 279
Soul Vegetarian (West End), 288
South City Kitchen (Midtown), 290
Taste of New Orleans, A (Midtown), 298
Tavern at Phipps, The (Lenox Square), 299
Thelma's Kitchen (Omni), 304
Tom Tom (Lenox Square), 306
Top of the Plaza (Decatur), 307
Touch of India (Midtown), 310
Uncle Tai's (Lenox Square), 313
Varsity, The (Civic Center), 316
Veni Vidi Vici (Arts Center), 318
Vickery's (Midtown), 320

Keep current with the ever-changing Atlanta restaurant scene by subscribing to *Knife & Fork: The Insider's Guide to Atlanta Restaurants*. Each issue of the monthly eight-page newsletter contains reviews of new restaurants, updates of old ones, and such features as Top Ten lists, reports on where to hold private parties, and important news about restaurant openings and closings. A year's subscription costs $24. Fill out the form below, and mail to *Knife & Fork*, **Box 15464, Atlanta, GA 30333.**

Name_____
Street Address_____
City_____
State_____ **Zip** _____

_____ **My check for $24 is enclosed**
_____ **Bill me**